TEXTS IN GERMAN PHILOSOPHY

ON LANGUAGE

THE DIVERSITY OF
HUMAN LANGUAGE-STRUCTURE
AND ITS INFLUENCE ON
THE MENTAL DEVELOPMENT
OF MANKIND

TEXTS IN GERMAN PHILOSOPHY

General Editor: CHARLES TAYLOR

Advisory Board: RÜDIGER BUBNER, RAYMOND GEUSS,
PETER HEATH, GARBIS KORTIAN,
WILHELM VOSSENKUHL, MARX WARTOFSKY

The purpose of this series is to make available, in English, central works of German philosophy from Kant to the present. Although there is rapidly growing interest in the English-speaking world in different aspects of the German philosophical tradition as an extremely fertile source of study and inspiration, many of its crucial texts are not available in English or exist only in inadequate or dated translations. The series is intended to remedy that situation, and the translations where appropriate will be accompanied by historical and philosophical introductions and notes. Single works, selections from a single author and anthologies will all be represented.

WILHELM VON HUMBOLDT

ON LANGUAGE

(1836)

THE DIVERSITY OF
HUMAN LANGUAGE-STRUCTURE
AND ITS INFLUENCE ON
THE MENTAL DEVELOPMENT
OF MANKIND

*

TRANSLATED BY
PETER HEATH

WITH AN INTRODUCTION BY
HANS AARSLEFF

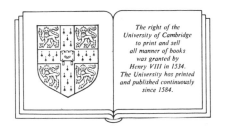

The right of the
University of Cambridge
to print and sell
all manner of books
was granted by
Henry VIII in 1534.
The University has printed
and published continuously
since 1584.

CAMBRIDGE UNIVERSITY PRESS

CAMBRIDGE
NEW YORK   NEW ROCHELLE
MELBOURNE   SYDNEY

Published by the Press Syndicate of the University of Cambridge
The Pitt Building, Trumpington Street, Cambridge CB2 2RP
32 East 57th Street, New York, NY 10022, USA
10 Stamford Road, Oakleigh, Melbourne 3166, Australia

First published 1988
Reprinted 1989

Printed in Great Britain by
the University Press, Cambridge

British Library cataloguing in publication data

Humboldt, Wilhelm von
On language. –
(Texts in German philosophy).
1. Languages – Philosophy
I. Title II. Series
401 P106

Library of Congress cataloguing in publication data

Humboldt, Wilhelm, Freiherr von, 1767–1835.
On language: the diversity of human language-structure
and its influence on the mental development of mankind.
(Texts in German philosophy)
Originally published as the introduction to the author's
Über die Kavi-Sprache auf der Insel Java (1836–1840) and
also issued separately (1836) with title: Über die Verschiedenheit
des menschlichen Sprachbaues und ihren Einfluss
auf die geistige Entwickelung des Menschengeschlechts.
Bibliography.
Includes index.
1. Language and languages. 2. Intellect.
I. Heath, Peter Lauchlan, 1922– . II. Title. III. Series.
P103.H813 1985 410 84–28561

ISBN 0 521 25747 6 hard covers
ISBN 0 521 31513 1 paperback

Contents

Introduction by Hans Aarsleff   vii
Translator's note   lxvi
Glossary   lxviii
Preface by Alexander von Humboldt   3
Note on transliteration of foreign alphabets   7

 1 Distribution and cultural connections of the Malayan
   races. Plan of the present work   15
 2 General consideration of the course of man's development   20
 3 The same, continued   23
 4 Effects of exceptional mental power. Civilization, culture
   and education   29
 5 Conjoint action of individuals and nations   37
 6 The same, continued   41
 7 Transition to closer consideration of language   46
 8 Form of languages   48
 9 Nature and constitution of languages as such   54
10 Sound-system of languages. Nature of the articulated
   sound   65
      Sound-changes 69; Allocation of sounds to concepts
      71; Designation of general relations 74; The sense of
      articulation 77
      Sound-system of languages   79
      Technique of this   80
11 Inner linguistic form   81
12 Combination of sound with inner linguistic form   88
13 The procedure of language more fully explained   90
      Verbal affinity and verbal form   93
14 Isolation, inflection and agglutination of words   100
15 Verbal unity more closely examined. Incorporative system
   of languages   109
      Means of designating verbal unity. The pause 111;
      Letter-change 113
16 Accent   125
17 Incorporative system of languages. Framing of the
   sentence   128
18 Congruence of sound-forms in languages with grammatical requirements   140

19 Main division of languages, according to the purity of
their formative principle 143
20 Character of languages 148
Poetry and prose 168
21 Power of languages, to evolve felicitously from one to
another 182
Act of spontaneous positing in languages 184; The Verb
186; The Conjunction 200; The Relative Pronoun 201;
Inflected languages, considered in their progressive
development 202; Languages evolved from Latin 207
22 Retrospect on the course of the inquiry so far 214
Languages that deviate from purely regular form 216
23 Nature and origin of less perfect language-structure 220
The Semitic languages 223; The Delaware language 226
24 The Chinese language 230
The same, continued 233
The Burmese language 237
25 Whether the polysyllabic language-structure has evolved
from the monosyllabic 262

Index 289

Introduction

HANS AARSLEFF

I

The man and the writing

In the long history of western reflection on language and its relation to ourselves and the world we live in, few works have the stature of Wilhelm von Humboldt's great essay on the philosophy of language which is here offered in Peter Heath's excellent translation from the original German. It was first published posthumously in 1836, within a year of the author's death, under a title that proclaims the central theme that had inspired his study of language and languages since he first turned his attention to the subject around 1800: *The Diversity of Human Language-Structure and its Influence on the Mental Development of Mankind*. It appeared as the general introduction to a very large work with the simple title *On the Kawi Language on the Island of Java*, a work of nearly two thousand pages in three volumes that were published in the transactions of the Berlin Academy during the years 1836–9. Obviously, the publication of so large a work in the transactions must be seen as a tribute and memorial to the academy's most illustrious member over the preceding decades, for it meant setting aside the rule that only papers actually read in the sessions could appear in the transactions, a rule that in this case was met only by the fact that a few small parts had been delivered before the academy in earlier years. Humboldt was a public figure, both as statesman and diplomat and as scholar. It is the aim of this introduction to do three things: first, to tell who Humboldt was and what he did; secondly, to set forth the prominent features of his argument and philosophy; and thirdly, to explore the intellectual background and context of his thought. Since our text is known as the Kawi Introduction, I shall for convenience use the abbreviation KI.

Humboldt was born in Berlin in 1767 as the son of a court-official and of a woman who was much younger than the father and a wealthy widow when he married her. His brother Alexander, the famous scientist and traveller, was born barely two years later, and the two boys were educated together at home by carefully chosen private tutors, from whom they, in addition to thorough instruction in the classical languages, received the kind of general education that would prepare them for the public careers they were expected to

vii

follow. After the father's death in 1779, their education was guided by the ambitious and rather cold-hearted mother, who sent them, still under supervision, to the minor but safely traditional university at Frankfurt an der Oder before they were allowed to proceed to the modern and liberal University of Göttingen, where they benefited from the lively intellectual atmosphere and studied under famous scholars. Wilhelm completed his legal studies and for a short while held a government post in Berlin, but gave it up in 1791 when he married a wealthy woman, who already knew Schiller and Goethe. Humboldt never had to work for a living, and for the next dozen years he did what he prized most: he cultivated his mind and explored his individuality in all the ways that were open to him. He resided in different places: on his father-in-law's estate near Erfurt, in Weimar and Jena to be close to Goethe and Schiller, in Dresden, and on the family estate near Berlin, Tegel, which he later rebuilt with great deliberation in the classical style and made his preferred residence. He also began to make himself a minor literary figure in the company of the great. He studied much, wrote a great deal, and published little – a pattern that persisted for the rest of his life. He preferred study, found writing hard and disagreeable, and left many more writings unfinished than he completed and put into print.

In 1796 the mother's death left both sons with very large inheritances. In spite of the vast expense and a growing family, Wilhelm decided to live in Italy for a while, but when war blocked the way, they all instead journeyed to Paris. Here they spent four years between November of 1797 and late summer of 1801, interrupted by a seven-month journey through southern France and Spain, where the wife, it seems to Humboldt's surprise, gave birth to a child, and a shorter journey through the Basque regions by Humboldt alone during the spring of 1801. It was in these years, when the world was made new, that Paris was becoming the capital of the nineteenth century. From all parts of Europe poets, scholars, writers, and scientists streamed to Paris to be part of the action, which was both politically and intellectually exciting. Among them was Wordsworth. The Paris experience had a profound impact on Humboldt's thought, and he made it emphatically clear in letters he wrote at the time. A year after his arrival he wrote to a friend in Germany that in spite of much he found disagreeable, 'nevertheless I cannot deny...that my residence here opens a new epoch in my thinking'. In the same year he wrote to another friend, who was planning to leave Paris, that he did not approve of the decision, 'whatever you say, Paris is always interesting, and you wish to return to Berlin, to a place that is less important by a wide margin'. In the fall of 1801, soon after the return to Berlin, he wrote to a correspondent that an outbreak of scarlet fever in the region of Tegel had forced the family to reside in the town house in Berlin. This forced removal did not make Humboldt happy, 'for if one must choose a town to live in, all others except Paris are and remain simply unattractive'. Some four months later, he wrote to his good friend, Mme de Staël, that he was planning to return to Paris, though there were little problems about 'this favored plan, but which I hope to overcome'. Since it was during these years that his decisive turn to language occurred, we shall later return to this subject.

But his favored plan did not work out. After barely a year in Berlin, the growing family now travelled to Rome, where Humboldt remained until 1808 as Prussian resident accredited to the Vatican. These were years of moderate leisure that left time for greatly intensified study of languages in the newly conceived spirit. At this time he was first introduced to American Indian languages when his brother, now back from his widely acclaimed travels in equatorial America, brought him a large number of grammars from the many Jesuit mission stations he had visited. But in 1808 he was recalled to Germany, and now followed a dozen busy years in public service that left little time for his treasured study, though he never had to give it up entirely. During 1809–10 he was director of the education section in the Ministry of the Interior, and in his role he had a profound and long-lasting effect, that eventually reached beyond the borders of Germany, on the aims and organization of education on all levels. He was the effective creator of the new university of Berlin and thus of the academic institutionalization of knowledge and education that, for better or worse, the world has lived with since that time. This is undoubtedly the single most important achievement in Humboldt's public life. During the following years he took part in the complicated negotiations, including the Congress of Vienna, that followed the collapse of Napoleon's empire. During 1817–18 he spent a year in London as ambassador to the Court of Saint James, then for a year returned to government service in Berlin until he was released at the very end of 1819 owing to conflicts over policy. Except for minor official duties, he now entered private life for good, living mostly at Tegel, where he died in early April of 1835. For the first time in years, he could again devote all his energies to languages in the private pursuit of his treasured cult of self-education.

First of all, he expanded his linguistic cosmos until it included virtually all recorded language of the globe. With the exception of Basque and the living languages he knew and heard spoken, his study was based entirely on the written materials he could collect in his study. He studied each language in meticulous detail, often working out entire grammars on his own, for he always insisted that a comprehensive philosophy of languages and their diversity must be based on sound empirical knowledge. Having started out in life with a thorough command of Greek and Latin, he first studied Basque around 1800 and soon added the languages of Central America with the help of the grammars Alexander had brought him, but after 1820 things moved much faster. He now intensively studied the following groups of languages, roughly in this order and citing only the most important: The Sanscrit, North-American Indian, Chinese, Polynesian, and Malayan languages until he finally around 1830 made the Kawi language the center both of his cosmos and of the large work that was designed to display the ultimate synthesis of his philosophy of language.

All of these languages are used in the KI, where they fall into two distinct categories. In one category are what Humboldt called the Sanscritic languages (our term is normally the Indo-European), with Sanscrit and Greek being by far the most prominent, though some others – among them Latin, German, and English – are also mentioned; in the other category are all the distant non-European languages. The reader will soon become aware of this division, though it has in fact received little attention in the literature on Humboldt. He makes the grounds of the division perfectly clear. He was convinced that there is an ideal of the 'most perfect linguistic' form and that 'the Sanscritic languages come closest to this form, and are likewise those in which the mental cultivation of mankind has evolved most happily in the longest sequence of advances. We can therefore regard them as a fixed point of comparison for all the rest' (216). These are plain words about the Europo-centrism of Humboldt's entire enterprise; taken together the non-European category of languages is inferior to the other. This is not linguistic relativism but linguistic absolutism. One might also call it incipient racism, and that is precisely what Humboldt's well-informed North-American correspondents noted in his arguments. We shall later return to this subject.

Before 1820 Humboldt had published very little on his favorite subject, though he had written a great deal, but he now began to give papers in the regular sessions of the Berlin Academy. Since they were published in its transactions, they gained much attention in the larger world at a time when they were virtually ignored in Berlin. They were read with interest and engagement in Paris and in North America by scholars who shared Humboldt's focus on non-European languages and the philosophical orientation that made it the primary aim of language study to relate languages to the mentalities of their speakers, thus going beyond the mere description and historical affiliation of languages to larger issues of cultural diversity and anthropology. For Humboldt these contacts became a steady inspiration for the work of his later years. He eagerly entered into dialogue with these scholars; with the people in North America he had already by 1821 begun an exchange of letters that became the most fruitful linguistic correspondence of his life.

In Paris Humboldt's writings were reviewed in the *Journal des Savants* and in the *Journal Asiatique* by two prominent scholars who were both associated with the École des langues orientales vivantes, which ever since its creation by the National Convention in 1795 has made Paris the center for the study of non-European languages. One of these scholars was Silvestre de Sacy, who was the teacher of both Franz Bopp (now in the post Humboldt had secured for him at the new University of Berlin) and Champollion, whose work on hieroglyphic decipherment Humboldt helped introduce and defend in Berlin. Another was the student of Chinese, Abel Rémusat, who was also the editor of the *Journal Asiatique* in which Humboldt published several pieces. Humboldt was in fact so eager to have readers in Paris that he during the 1820s had Alexander, then living in Paris, circulate a French translation of an as yet unpublished essay. One significant result of this dialogue was the book-form publication of Humboldt's *Lettre à M. Abel Rémusat sur la nature des formes grammaticales en général, et sur le génie de la langue chinoise en particulier* (1827). It is clearly written and, like other writings of these years, it anticipates much that he later put into the KI. Rémusat wrote both an introduction and a series of long notes in which he took up the dialogue with Humboldt. In North America Humboldt's contacts were John Pickering and Peter S. Duponceau, who were engaged in the study and collection of Indian languages then being promoted by the American Philosophical Society in Philadelphia, of which Humboldt became a foreign member. From Pickering came a flow of materials that gave Humboldt access to those languages.

But in spite of fairly busy publication, Humboldt also during these years wrote and left unfinished much more than he completed and put into print. Three of these writings were long, and all pointed toward the synthesis of the KI, one of them, at more than half the length of the KI, even under the similar title 'About the Diversities of Human Language-Structure'. Quite extensive passages from these and other writings, also from earlier years, went *verbatim* in the KI, which in this sense became a sort of collage. This was an old practice with Humboldt; he always had difficulty with disposition, expression, and completion. Already in the 1790s he had admitted that if something did not come out right the first time he put it down, he did not find it possible to improve it in revision but had to start over again, a need that became more urgent in the later years because he felt he had to begin afresh every time he had mastered a new language. The last one he added was the language that appears in the title.

The Kawi was the old literary and sacred language of Java, and it first became known in the West from materials that Thomas Stamford Raffles published in his *History of Java* (1817). In our text it is mentioned only twice (20, 53) in brief passages that suggest why Humboldt became interested in it. Its vocabulary was largely Sanscrit, while its form was Malayan, thus being a mixed language or 'linguistic union' that revealed 'the most intimate intertwining of Indian and indigenous culture' on the island of Java. In fact, the word Kawi is Sanscrit for 'poet' or 'maker'. In a more technical sense, Humboldt wished to show that, since grammatical structure is the criterion of linguistic affinity, the Kawi language was Malayan in spite of its Indian vocabulary. It did not, therefore, as was maintained by some, stand in the same intimate relationship to Sanscrit as the Pali language. But seen in larger perspective, it was important by virtue of its geographical location, which linked it to practically all the known languages of the globe, from the African shores of the Indian Ocean to the west across the great archipelago in the middle to the Americas in the east and to China and India on the Asian mainland. In the Kawi he had late in life found the global vantage point that would enable him to achieve the synthesis he had always aimed for.

We have some independent evidence about this search for global unity. In 1832 the young French linguist E. Jacquet, who at the time was in touch with Humboldt, made an illuminating observation. Humboldt's researches, wrote Jacquet, had made him 'regard the tendency toward unity as the most eminently philosophical method in ethnography', and for this reason 'he could not fail to examine what support comparative philology offered in treating the immense question of the existence of relations between the old world and the new: he had understood that Polynesia was the only possible transition between the two continents, and this idea led him directly to the study of all Polynesian languages'. This is a plausible explanation, for Humboldt's comparison of Basque with Central-American languages had long ago convinced him that no linguistic affinity could be established across the Atlantic, so now he was, so to speak, going around the other way in order to secure the unity of his linguistic cosmos. He could with confidence place the KI at the head of the large three-volume work that bore the title *About the Kawi Language on the Island of Java.* The KI was the theoretical and philosophical prolegomenon, devoted as he wrote 'to more general considerations, whose development will make better preparation for the transition to the facts and historical inquiries' that followed (20–1). The entire work was conceived in the late summer of 1828 when Humboldt and his wife returned to Germany after long visits to Paris and London.

Humboldt always felt invigorated by travel, and, coming after ten years of living in Berlin, the tour revived his spirits and gave fresh impulses to his thought. The couple spent a month in Paris before proceeding to London for two months until the middle of July. In Paris he gave a paper at the Institute (121) and in London another before the Royal Asiatic Society, of which he was a foreign member. He was excited to see both cities again, and he noted the contrast to the provincial atmosphere of German cities. When on the way back they spent a week in Paris, he felt so much at home that he thought of returning for an entire year with his wife, who shared his enthusiasm. Seeing old acquaintances again and making new ones, he recalled with fondness his residence there in earlier years, thinking of the nearly four years he had lived there around 1800 when he first encountered the philosophy and study of language that became his nearly obsessive avocation.

But the optimism was soon dashed. Within a year his wife's death left him isolated and disconsolate on the estate near Berlin, and soon his own health also began to break down. By 1830 his right hand was beginning to give trouble so that he had to use a secretary for most of his writing, and over the next years his hearing and eyesight weakened. Even the long annual vacations at Nordeney on the North Sea failed to have the expected restorative effect. Moments of confidence alternated with depression over the magnitude of the task and apprehension that he would not live to complete it. In the end he did not. The published volumes were put together by his amanuensis, who also wrote substantial parts of them. Alexander remarks on these problems in his Preface. All the same, Humboldt pushed on heroically.

On their way back to Berlin the couple rested for a month in late summer at a resort near Salzburg, and it was here that Humboldt suddenly felt he had gained a clear view of the work he now had in mind. Late in the year he described his plans to an old friend, the classicist F. G. Welcker. His researches had taken a new direction, he wrote, and having once entered that path, he would now continue on it. He did not think the task would be endless, for he was not concerned with the external aspects of languages, not, in other words, with the time-devouring study of details which he often blamed for stealing his time.

My aim is much simpler and also more esoteric, namely a study that treats the faculty of speech in its inward aspect, as a human faculty, and which uses its effects, languages, only as sources of knowledge and examples in developing the argument. I wish to show that what makes any particular language what it is, is its grammatical structure and to explain how the grammatical structure in all its diversities still can only follow certain methods that will be listed one by one, so that, by the study of each language, it can be shown which methods are dominant or mixed in it. Now, in these methods themselves I consider of course the influence of each on the mind and feeling, and their explanation in terms of the causes of the origins of the languages, in so far as this is possible. Thus I connect the study of language with the philosophical survey of humanity's capacity for formation [Bildung] and with history. I have for some years been engaged in a work on this subject and made good progress. But only the stay at Gastein this year has brought my ideas on these matters to a certain maturity.

This exciting passage outlines the entire program for the Kawi work, and it shows at the same time that Humboldt's central interest, now as before, was the philosophy of language he expounded in the KI. The rest of the work presented the supporting evidence, and in the event this part stole the time that was needed to write the philosophical introduction. Part of the trouble was that he could not after all stay away from the detailed study. From London he brought 'excellent and very rare materials' that would have to be mastered, and he was also waiting for a better text of the Kawi poem than the one Raffles had published, promised and ultimately sent by John Crawfurd whose *History of the Indian Archipelago* (1820) Humboldt had admired and relied on. The introduction was pushed aside until it became the last part he worked on.

Early in 1830 Humboldt wrote to Welcker that he now planned to place the Malayan languages in relation to Chinese on the one side and to Sanscrit on the other, for here he felt he had found the point of view from which he could survey the diversities of linguistic procedures both in regard to word formation and to grammar. If he could complete this project according to his plan, then he believed that it would 'all at once throw light on and more clearly explain all the ideas I have hitherto conceived about language'. This remark about the continuity of his linguistic studies supports the widely credited assessment that the late work relates closely to the ideas we find in the earliest writings around 1800, when he first outlined his plans for what he called an 'encyclopedia of language study and languages', a project he mentioned often over the years.

The first explicit mention of the KI occurs as late as the summer of 1834 in a letter (in French) to John Pickering, in which, after a remark about his 'ever more uncertain health', he wrote that he was soon bringing out a work 'on the ancient poetic language of the island of Java' to be preceded by 'an introduction on the diversity of the languages of the world and on its influence on the development and progress of the mind' – or in the original which more clearly calls to mind the French way of talking about this subject, 'sur la marche et les progrès de l'esprit humain'. We next hear about the KI three months later when he wrote to Bopp that the 'introduction is indeed moving forward every day, but always more slowly than I could wish', but not till February of 1835 did he send a clean copy of the early parts, though he now hoped he would be able to continue without interruption. Finally, on 12 March – a month before he was buried – he sent over two hundred pages. As Alexander explains in the Preface, there was not enough time to complete the KI. It became another of Humboldt's unfinished writings.

We need to bear in mind that the KI was written in very difficult circumstances, but they merely exacerbated Humboldt's lifelong problems with form and style. They were noticed as early as the 1790s by his best friends, who found that his writings lacked form, got stuck in too many details, lapsed into excursions, and moved on a level that was too high and abstract to hold the reader's attention. In 1794 Schiller suspected that Humboldt did not have 'the right talent to become a writer', and their mutal friend Körner was impatient with lack of clear disposition; he could make out the sense of sentences, 'but I am now too old to be satisfied with such intimations. I must know what I am engaged in. What for me seems to stand in the air collapses when I cannot find its foundations. And here these foundations – when they actually exist – lie in the inner depths of metaphysics'. Körner even wrote that, 'speaking in general, I have not found any sign of genius in Humboldt, but a feeling for all sorts of excellent things and receptivity to great and all-embracing ideas'. Some of these remarks were made about the *Aesthetic Essays on Goethe's Hermann and Dorothea* (1799), which during his lifetime was Humboldt's largest publication and a work hc had hoped would especially appeal to the very friends, including Schiller, who gave it such a cool reception. A projected second part was never written. It is understandable that Humboldt would become beset by anxieties over writing.

Peter Heath's deft translation has solved these problems for us as well as was possible, but he has of course respected the terminology of the original. Humboldt's writings abound in terms and phrases that have gained currency and become cited as if we know what they mean, though in their contexts they are neither made clear nor consistently used. A good example is the term 'inner form,' which in the KI occurs twice in section headings (81, 88) and occasionally elsewhere in the same or slightly different formulations, but what it means is never revealed either by way of explanation or example, let alone definition which is a device he seems to have spurned. It is generally believed that 'inner form' is a central concept in Humboldt's thought, but for a hundred years all discussion has failed to converge on any accepted meaning. This is typical of Humboldt interpretation – which may suggest that it has not addressed the right problems. It is as if conceptual perplexities have gone begging in a terminological cloudscape that is often made still hazier by frequent pronouncements that something 'deep', 'mysterious', 'inscrutable', 'incomprehensible', or 'unfathomable' is at work. It has in fact been observed that if Humboldt had really been a Kantian and not merely at times used Kantian-looking terms, then the terminology would have become settled. Humboldt never had to lecture or write for a living. He prized his individuality and privacy above all, and this attitude had an effect on the esoteric quality and obscurity of his writing. Even his greatest admirers have been unsparing with observations on Humboldt's failure to master form and expression.

Humboldt himself was well aware of these problems. When a friend in the 1790s pointed out to him that, though he could write individual passages that made an impression, he failed to give shape to the discourse at large, Humboldt agreed and even admitted that he did not feel he was destined to become a writer. His working habits were too personal, his writing too impressionistic; his best thoughts and observations were rarely the fruit of disciplined meditation but rather of luck, even of a certain 'tact'; his enthusiasm for the subject matter left no room for attention to form; and having his mind set on what was subjectively true for himself, he neglected to make it objectively clear to the reader. In writing the first draft, he admitted, he was totally preoccupied with the matter, even possessed by it, and he could never succeed in a second revision. As already suggested this insight may explain why he always started over again instead of revising and completing earlier drafts. In the fall of 1803 he wrote from Rome that he was immersing himself in language study, that he would need to work endlessly, and 'that perhaps it will never come to writing. One of them always does harm to the other, and I always prefer the former because it more easily succeeds for me and gives me greater satisfaction'. For the self-educating individual, the reader was a barely tolerated presence.

Nearly a decade later Humboldt gave a revealing reason why he was so attached to his 'dry and laborious' linguistic studies. In the few years that were left to him, he wished 'to accomplish something that I can call Something. When one is not, as is my case, born to produce a work of art, then the best satisfaction, if it succeeds, is to give a definite direction to a particular kind of study'. For the writer or even artist *manqué* that he felt himself to be, the next best thing was immersion in the languages of all humanity. About the time when he was making these admissions in a letter, he was writing an 'Essay on the Languages of the New Continent' (in French), in which he made one of his very frequent remarks on the similarities between languages and physiognomies. Their particular qualities and the differences among them are evident at first glance, but we get lost as soon as we try to analyze and identify them. All the rules of beauty, even when based on the best models, are indeterminate and nearly useless. In the end, therefore, in our efforts to determine what constitutes perfection of features in a face, we find that none of them can be described, 'but merely divined by the creative genius of the artist'. In the study of languages and their philosophy Humboldt became an artist, thus assuming the character that was otherwise denied him. If divination is a creative act, we also understand why so much remains 'deep' and 'inscrutable', and why neither rules nor arguments are quite sufficient to get to the heart of the matter. The fundamental nature of language was an aesthetic problem, accessible only to the artist. Speaking and writing are creative activities that must be reciprocated by the hearer's or reader's creative response. One imagination triggers another. It is on both sides a question of *energeia*. Reading Humboldt it is as if we are made to share the writer's private trance in meditation upon something so profound that it cannot be grasped except by an imaginative effort that transcends mere understanding and argument.

II

The philosophy of language

Humboldt's Kawi Introduction is a rich and rewarding text, but the reader will soon find that it is not an easy one to follow. It thwarts

[handwritten margin note: & I points toward a center that is never reached]

our usual expectation of moving in measured stages from argument to argument toward a conclusion that has steadily unfolded before us along the way. Instead, the text is rather like a long and private meditation that in a series of *aperçus* points toward a center that is never reached. The core of the matter is inscrutable. We see consequences but cannot know their ultimate source. Axioms and theories swirl around the center, but they are rarely either clearly articulated or conveniently ordered. To come to terms with the text, the best one can do is therefore to read through the entire thing to the end without fussing unduly over details and momentary failures of understanding, for the circle must be closed before the haze will begin to rise. One should also be careful not to pour too much premature interpretation into particular and well-known phrases, such as that language is the organ of thought or that it is not *ergon* but *energeia*. Much Humboldt interpretation is puffy verbalizing over phrases that are invested with profound meanings when they are in fact both banal and unoriginal. It is the overall conception and coherence of argument that matter, that is, the nearly hidden argument that lies scattered throughout the text. In the following I shall try to bring out the main features of that conception with the aim of showing both how Humboldt explained the diversity of language-structure and how he related it to the mental development of mankind. I use the terms of the text, but I have deliberately – I hope for the reader's benefit – abstained from making references to it.

Humboldt's entire view of the nature of language is founded on the conviction that thinking and speaking, thought and language form so close a union that we must think of them as being identical, in spite of the fact that we can separate them artificially. Owing to this identity, access to one of the two will open nearly equal access to the other. All Humboldt's work on language is devoted to exploration of the possibilities that lie in this identity. They are obvious and have momentous consequences, for the identity promises that the study of languages in all their diversity will provide both the best and the most plentiful kinds of evidence for understanding and knowledge of the processes of mind, which by their nature, whether pertaining to feeling or reason, remain hidden beyond hope of direct inspection. In their relationship, the mind is always the active party, though language will, as we shall see, work back on thinking in a manner that may become harmful if the mind does not retain its mastery. There are of course other modes of human expression, but none rival the dominant status of language, which in addition rules virtually alone in the sphere of intellectual activity. Humboldt held that the form of all languages is essentially the same and that their differences lie in the means they employ to express the common structure. He accepted the doctrine that the traditionally known parts of speech belong to the ideal universal grammar of all languages. Their diversity, even the inferiority of some, will therefore be determined not least by the degree to which they respect and express these categories.

The relation between language and thinking is intimate because only the former makes the latter possible. The words of language segment or cut up, so to speak, the undifferentiated synthesis that the mind draws from experience, thus securing both the existence and the stability of our concepts and in turn making possible the fruitful extension of thought. It is in this sense that language is the organ of thought; it is not the mere adventitious or epiphenomenal outward manifestation or garb of thought for the utilitarian purpose of communication, for if that were the case we would be making the false assumption that words merely constituted a nomenclature of tags for concepts that had been offered ready-made to the mind by the self-sufficiency and autonomy of perception. Language is not like a tool-box with discrete instruments and parts designed for particular tasks that are known in advance. It is not already given work, like the contents of the tool-box, but a creative power – or in Humboldt's famous words, it is not *ergon* but *energeia*, a conception he stated again and again in other terms before he gave it this formulation in our text. Only by virtue of language do we gain self-awareness, knowledge, and mastery of reality. It is like a second world in which we know both our own selves and the outward face of things, like a middle ground between subjective being and objective existence. This philosophy does not have room for the copy-theory of knowledge; language is not merely designative; it is not representation but expression. Language is constituent of thought and for that reason it must stand at the center of any viable epistemology.

Now, at this point we face the crucial question: how does all this begin? The answer is simple, we do not know. We must fall back on the axiom that language is an involuntary emanation of the spirit or mind, of a mental power or, as he called it in French, an 'esprit créateur' that suddenly flashes forth in sound with the miraculous unexpectedness of a spark, lightning, or a thunderbolt. With this crucial act of sound-formation language and thus also thinking begin, and for that reason this act also manifests the humanity that sets us apart from the animal world – 'der Mensch ist nur Mensch durch Sprache' as Humboldt had said some years earlier to express a banality that has been the subject of much verbalizing. This act of sound-formation is called articulation, and it must encompass two separate components of language, namely on the one hand the words or roots that stand for concepts and on the other the forms that express the grammatical relations, which whether fully expressed or not are assumed, as in universal grammar, to be the same for all mankind, even at the most primitive stage. These forms that indicate the grammatical categories (or parts of speech) are created by what Humboldt calls an intellectual instinct of reason, thus pointing to their source in our common rationality. This articulation or minting into sounds determines the form in which all of language is moulded; form is more than what is conventionally understood by grammar.

The form or structure of each language is determined in the moment of articulation, which is itself an act of imagination, inexplicable like the work of an artist. Therefore the formation of language cannot be understood as an act of reason, for this would imply purposiveness and intentionality that cannot be assumed to operate in the flash of creativity. In articulation a synthesis is created that will differ from one language to another according to the liveliness and energy of the imagination that gives it expression. Languages are like works of art; indeed they are art, and not all artists are equally good. Thus it is in the moment of articulation that the diversity arises. Each language has an individuality which, as with a person, is the expression of its genius. This fundamentally aesthetic view of the nature of language is the central conception in Humboldt's philosophy, but before we explore the implications we must consider what he says about a topic that has now been raised, namely the origin of language.

By taking the position that language is not *ergon* but *energeia*, not a product but a process of making, Humboldt can stress the continuing creativity that operates in language. Its right understanding must therefore be genetic; from the point of origin that determines its potential follows an evolution that constantly shapes and more clearly defines the particular individuality and ultimately the character of each language. But despite the importance of what happens in the first moment, Humboldt does not wish to start from it because it would have occurred in a state of nature which lies so far back in time that we can have no evidence for worthwhile conjecture on it; all the languages we know already have a long history. His theory is therefore about formation and not about origin in the radical sense. Thus he avoids facing the question whether the origin of language was monogenetic or polygenetic.

If it were monogenetic, then the argument would have to show how the evolution occurred from a single type, which then itself could not be made the source of diversity, and in that case diversity would instead have to be explained by the later action of such factors as climate, geography, and physical as well as mental aspects of race. Monogenesis would also tend to support the view that all languages move through the same stages of progress, and if so the diversity we observe might be merely a function of time. Polygenesis avoids both consequences. Here the universal capacity for language is shared among mankind, but not its actualization, which can then in its diverse forms be attributed to the inherent genius and individuality of nations, that is, to their varied creative energies of mind. This means, among other things, that if one language is considered more perfect than another, as for Humboldt Sanscrit was in relation to Chinese, then the more perfect need not be taken as the later evolution of an earlier and simpler type. Individual languages may show progress, but that concept does not apply to the totality of languages. It would seem that Humboldt never openly addressed the problem of monogenesis versus polygenesis, but since it was well known – his brother, for instance, argued for polygenesis – it is safe to assume that he was familiar with it. His avoidance of it is therefore significant.

The essential nature of language cannot be conceived as something of which there gets to be more and more in the course of time. Quantity does not apply to it; it is a quality or form – still remembering that form embraces all of language, both its internal form in thinking and its complement in the outward form of sounds. In this sense language is like a seed that contains the entire form. Its first flashing forth in articulation is like conception, like the mysterious creation of an individual. We do not construct it and cannot make it on purpose. It emerges by the simultaneous self-activity of a collective being or group – a family, a tribe, a nation – whose members as yet have no separate individualities, but speak with a single voice, as it were, from the totality of the original design they share. Animals act by instinct and need, while we are driven into language by a radically different instinct that gives proof of our humanity. Language is the spontaneous expression of thought and feeling, with freedom and autonomy that set us apart from the animals; no response to or even awareness of need is involved. The beginning is communal, involving both speakers and hearers, but since it does not depend on social interaction it happens without agreement or convention.

In short, the beginning is the moment of articulation. What takes shape in it determines the future evolution of that language, for it cannot overcome the limits and restraints that have now been set.

"moment — one"
"stage — two"

Humboldt stresses again and again that the mental energies of nations are not the same, and that these differences show in the initial articulation. Each nation is like an individual artist, and some artists have more genius and imagination than others. The diversity begins at this moment. Since we shall mention it again, let us call it moment-one or m-one, by contrast to stage-two or s-two, to which we can now turn. I have deliberately chosen disparate but sequentially linked terms.

M-one vs. S-two

M-one is the mere expression of feeling; being collective and natural, it is independent of social life. Sociality is not a function of the desire for assistance or the relief of helplessness, not even in animals – the elephant is both the most powerful and the most social of creatures. This, incidentally, is a curious argument, for in so far as language is involved here, it would seem to have little force unless we could know that the elephant was so comfortable with its social flair that it had decided not to bother with language. And the small helpless bees, which are endearingly social, do have a language. In any event, m-one has nothing to do with need, purpose, communication, and convention, but in s-two all of these play decisive roles.

In actuality language develops only socially as we keep testing the rightness of our words by adjusting them, so to speak, by trial upon others – a process known as rectification. The trial is made necessary by the radical impossibility that others can have direct access to what goes on in our minds. Wordsworth called it 'the sad incompetence of human speech', and it involves what had long been recognized as the privacy of language. This familiar conception underscores the nature of Humboldt's philosophy of language. Privacy has its source in the fact that language and words are not mere representations of already secured concepts, that words are not designative and do not constitute a fixed nomenclature, which of course would not need rectification. Hence, as he says, every understanding is also a not-understanding. Rectification obviously works by tacit consent, which is all the convention doctrine needs to make sense. Communication can be compared to an effective ecological culture in which each individual benefits from the presence of all. Communication is interaction that gives the individual awareness of others who feel and think likewise, and for this reason it is also the condition for individual self-consciousness or awareness of being a person, something that could not arise, except possibly in its barest rudiments, in the collective individuality of m-one.

Now, if m-one was all there ever was, we would never have what we normally call language; we would merely have undifferentiated, unintentioned expression, much like a never-ending swarming of bees that produces an even-toned buzzing hum without getting to the purposeful task of sustaining life by social interaction for the benefit of each and all. But the buzzing would have the crucial effect of making each bee aware, as it were, that there are other bees like itself, endowed with the same needs and potentialities. Similarly, beyond the instinctive buzzing hum, a nation's welfare demands the exercise of its innate sociality to meet the physical needs of life, and this use occurs when the individual realizes that its need for assistance must be satisfied by combining with others in shared action that at the same time calls for understanding through language. Owing to the already achieved communal expression in m-one and the innate capacity for language, this situation triggers the continued language-making that now begins in s-two, all along being guided in the process of communication both by need and purpose as well as by the give-and-take of rectification that ensures sufficient agreement or convention for the maintenance of adequate understanding. Thus what happens in s-two is largely determined by function. M-one is the condition for s-two, but they are radically different.

Sparked by feeling and instinct, m-one is the instantaneous, multi-faceted articulation of a state-of-mind while s-two becomes an evolving process that must be guided by the understanding in order to maintain the purposefulness that life and reality demand. Put briefly, m-one is energetic and creative like poetry; s-two produces prose and the daily use of language, and it is here that a nation's individuality becomes displayed in a world-view that is its own. Languages are the richest, most accessible evidence we have for the diverse mentalities of nations. Humboldt's entire view of language is not contained in either m-one or s-two, but in both taken together, and the distinction that is typified by the contrast between poetry and prose was not his invention, a fact that is clearly brought out by Wordsworth's penetrating discussion of this problem. As we shall see, it is a fateful error to identify Humboldt's view of the essential nature of language only with m-one and that of his non-German predecessors and contemporaries only with s-two.

The questions now are: how does m-one determine s-two, what are the consequences, and how can we know? We can never know the original seed in the mind nor even the first sprout in articulation – hence the impossibility of working forward from the point of origin. But we can know what grew from that sprout because it is placed before us in s-two in the variety of forms that confronts us in the languages we can study. All languages must perform two tasks: on the one hand they must in roots or words give expression to concepts that relate both to the external world and to the mind's own creations; on the other they must, by whatever means, be capable of fusing the parts of an utterance together into a single entity. We may call these the lexicon and the grammar of a language, but the division is artificial since either one alone accomplishes nothing. Both taken together constitute the form of the language and express the world-view of its speakers. Humboldt insists that speech consists of total utterances or sentences from which words emerge in our artificial analysis; each sentence is a synthesis and it cannot be conceived in terms the mechanical addition of word to word until it is completed. Language is like an immense fabric or web that displays the design of its world-view; it is a structure in which all parts are so intimately interdependent that the whole forms an organism or, as Humboldt said when he wrote in French, languages are essentially characterized by '*organisation*'. Both tasks may be performed more or less successfully, depending upon the mental energy, creative power, imagination, and intellectual force of the speakers. The result is apparent in the lexicon, but it is the second task that most clearly reveals the diversities of language-structures and mentalities. The performance of the second task has produced distinct types of languages.

No type is so pure that it does not use means that also appear in one or several of the other types, but we can all the same distinguish four dominant types. Agglutinating languages perform the grammatical task by sticking or gluing together forms that already exist as separate words; their method is compounding, as when in English we form such adjectives as 'businesslike' and 'tablelike.' Here the adjectivity is created by mechanically joining words to form a new compound. This process is different from what we observe in 'painterly,' where the adjective is created by the ending -ly, which has no independent existence as a word, that is, no meaning in the ordinary sense. Therefore Humboldt would say that 'painterly' is a more genuine form than 'tablelike,' but he would still object to the fact that -ly can also create adverbs, as in 'harshly,' for this dual use of the same ending introduces confusion in the form system, which in turn implies failure on the part of the speakers who have let it happen. Next there are the incorporating languages (sometimes also called polysynthetic) in which words appear only as total utterances that are fusions of forms that cannot exist separately. The American-Indian and Inuit languages are examples of this type. Radically different from these two types are the isolating languages, represented by Chinese. Since it has only monosyllabic words, neither compounding nor affixing can occur in it, which in turn means that the words cannot be marked as belonging to particular grammatical

[handwritten top margin: (4) inflective Sanscrit (but also Semitic?]

categories and that the grammatical relations among words are *[handwritten: pace]* shown by word order alone – or at least that is the way Humboldt *[handwritten: said)]* understood it. Finally, there are the languages that create their grammar by inflection. In these all grammatical features are marked *[handwritten: see p 107 –]* either by internal modification (as in the tenses of the verb sing- *[handwritten: where]* sang-sung) or, more often, by particular sets of endings which are *[handwritten: Semitic]* added to roots in such a way that the entire sentence achieves the *[handwritten: languages]* maximum of synthesis and fixity by the greatest economy and clarity *[handwritten: don't differ]* of forms. This type is found only in the Indo-European languages; *[handwritten: in type from]* Latin is a good illustration, but for Humboldt the most perfect *[handwritten: inflected ones]* example is Sanscrit, followed closely by Greek, which in fact in some *[handwritten: only in]* respects is superior to Sanscrit. *[handwritten: relative success]*

Humboldt constantly describes the non-inflecting types as being *[handwritten: in attaining]* faulty, defective, imperfect, and full of misapprehensions and mis- *[handwritten: inflection]* conceptions when compared with the truly fruitful life-principle that is at work in Sanscrit. The agglutinating and inflecting languages can indeed be said to belong to the same type in so far as both types create grammatical forms by accretions to the ends of words, but even though the former type is in this sense striving for inflection, it still falsifies the essence of it because the compounding leaves the accretions recognizable as separate words instead of abolishing the recognizability. For this reason these languages cannot create but rather ruin word-unity, which is achieved only when endings are joined to a root to form an organic whole. The incorporating languages, by contrast, do even worse by jamming all the parts together in a single word that equals a sentence, with a corresponding loss of clear intellectual distinctions among the parts. Concepts that should stand out in single words are lost in the mass, but these languages also fail in other ways. Thus the Mexican languages leave the nouns unmarked, and the American-Indian languages neglect gender and make the mistake of putting constellations in the same grammatical class as men and animals. In general, the incorporating languages fail adequately to respect the categories of universal grammar; with some of these categories being overdetermined and others not at all, the result is both redundancy and paucity which together violate the principles of clarity and economy. For Humboldt *[handwritten: but]* the incorporating type is sharply opposed to the Sanscrit model, and *[handwritten: see]* for this reason he took it to be the most primitive in the pejorative *[handwritten: p 217]* sense of the word. Both this and the agglutinating type made efforts in the direction of inflection but failed. Chinese tells a very different story.

Humboldt had respect for the perfect consistency of the Chinese language, but in spite of his fascination by it he also found it the most

imperfect of all. It is monosyllabic, even at best makes only the
feeblest efforts at expressing grammatical features, and depends on
word order to create the coherence of a sentence. It lacks imagination,
is like mathematics in being purely designative and lexical, leaves the
listener to figure out the structure of an utterance, and for all these
as well as other reasons it is an inferior organ of thought and is
consequently also blocked from progress. All these opinions belong
to a tradition of European lore about the static nature of Chinese
culture and its language, and the same can be said about his
judgments on the American-Indian languages. His evaluations were
familiar ones long before he found them confirmed by his study of
the influence of language-structure on the diverse mentalities of
mankind. It is of course least surprising of all that he should find the
most perfect form in Sanscrit. The deficiencies of Chinese will become
apparent if we look at the perfections of Sanscrit.

Since Humboldt believed that the principles of universal grammar
represent the laws of thinking that are common to all humanity, it
follows that the highest achievement in language-making will be
found in the language that most fully gives expression to all of these
principles. Sanscrit meets this demand more than any other
language, and for that reason it is the most perfect linguistic form.
In Sanscrit each word is made a constitutive part of the sentence;
the markings or endings attached to each root to form a word weave
into the word its relations to every other part of the sentence. The
result is true inner fixity, which he calls a principle of genius born
of a correct intuition of language.

This outward fixity expresses the inner synthesis that only the
imagination can create; it cannot be brought about by forethought
but comes like an electric spark or stroke of lightning, like creating
order out of chaos. It is formed by an intellectual instinct that has
a presentiment of the entire structure of the language. The fortunate
beginnings of a language are therefore determined in the initial
moments of articulation when thought becomes embodied in sound-
forms that stand objectively before the speaker as they become heard
by the ear. These sound-forms constitute the effective agent for the
more or less successful development of the language, both in self-
hearing and in exchange with other speakers. The right path is
entered in the formative period, in the epoch of language-making.
On this point, let us make an exception and quote Humboldt's
words: 'The intellectual merits of language therefore rest exclusively
upon the well-ordered, firm and clear mental organization of peoples
in the epoch of making and remaking language, and are the image,
indeed the direct copy, of this' (81). Hearing is as much an act of

imagination as speaking; the greater the fixity of the sentence, the better the synthesis that the hearer can achieve by the imaginative re-creation of the synthesis that was in the speaker's mind. M-one determines the evolution that occurs in s-two, but before we look at the development we must consider two other factors in early formation.

Just as the elements of language must express the laws of thinking, they must also perform the task of relating language to reality in forms that express concepts. This formal conceptualization is also the work of the imagination, and it can be done more or less successfully. Like the grammar, the lexicon is a record of the mental energy of the speakers, hence the world-view embraces both the grammar and the lexicon. The intellectual sophistication of a nation appears also in the lexicon. Another factor emerges in Humboldt's discussion of the Semitic languages. He praises them above any other group of non-Indo-European languages for their organic rigour and artistic simplicity, yet finds them faulty because they allow only consonants in the roots that convey meaning and only vowels in the grammatical indicators. This practice puts a constraint on the word-form by limiting the freedom of choice that is apparent in Sanscrit. More serious is the fact that the consonantal roots that carry the meanings of concepts cannot actually appear without the interpolated vowels that indicate grammatical relations; thus the root cannot be perceived apart from the grammar that is, so to speak, poured into it. The Semitic languages therefore fail to show the necessary sharp and clear distinctions between meaning and grammar, and for that reason they deviate from the right path of mental development. In light of the basic demands that Humboldt places upon language, this is, for several reasons, a curious argument, but it serves to show that he would accept only what he found in the model of Sanscrit, true inflection. In the spirit of universal grammar, his system was preconceived to fit only the Indo-European languages.

We are now prepared to understand the final stages of Humboldt's argument, the process that we can call feedback and the evolution of language toward prose and discursivity. The epoch of language-making that begins in s-two grows from m-one like the sprout from the seed. The initial articulation is perfectly free, but its quality depends on the degree of mental power and imagination that produce it, and this in turn means that the created material determines the potential of language-making in s-two, for this reason: in the ongoing work of making the mind will be restrained by the forms that now stand before it like objects. The sound-form becomes the effective agent. Language itself becomes an alien object that exerts dominion over the mind, which is now no longer free to exercise its unhindered creativity. There is a constant process of reaction or feedback as the mind on the one hand seeks to make the best use of the new linguistic objects, while on the other it strives to maintain its own freedom. The greatest spurt of creative energy occurs in the freedom of m-one, while the success of continued creativity will depend both on the mind's use of the new objects and on their quality. Language can have more or less fortunate beginnings. In s-two it becomes a question of both *energeia* and *ergon*; if the *ergon*, the already produced work, is good, then the *energeia* will be free to continue its creative work at the highest level, but if the *ergon* is poor it will lack the life-principle that ensures continued success. In the latter case the initial seed will grow a feeble sprout.

The process of feedback has a central position in Humboldt's thought, but it was not new. Wordsworth also said that 'language and the human mind act and react on each other', and it was precisely for this reason that the right choice of diction became the poet's first problem. Good diction is a remedy against the alienation that wrong diction will invariably confirm and intensify. The alternative is degenerate poetry just as for Humboldt there were degenerate languages. For Wordsworth our expressions 'are not what the garb is to the body but what the body is to the soul, themselves a constituent part and power or function of the thought', but if words are not 'an incarnation of the thought but only the clothing for it, then surely will they prove an ill gift. Language, if it do not uphold, and feed, and leave in quiet, like the power of gravitation or the air we breathe, is a counter-spirit, unremittingly and noiselessly at work to derange, to subvert, to lay waste, to vitiate, and to dissolve'. For Humboldt and his great English contemporary the structure of the argument is the same: language is constitutive of thought and to remain healthy and creative the mind must retain its dominion and freedom against the counter-spirit of linguistic degeneracy.

The non-inflective language types have assumed their individualities and diversities because they began with inferior material and thus could not pursue the right path from the beginning. Their speakers would invariably seek to remedy the initial imperfections, for instance by trying to express fully the categories of universal grammar that are shared by all humanity, but whatever their success, it was never possible for them to attain the perfection of a language that, like Sanscrit, had the good fortune to be endowed with a superior life-principle from the start. The agglutinating and incorporating languages offer evidence of this impossibility, while Chinese barely even tried for a remedy. The nobility of the Sanscrit is lost in the inferior Kawi language because it cannot survive the transplantation, but the Romance languages triumph with renewed vigour and creative energy, like a phoenix, on the ashes of Latin. By contrast, the nations of Eastern Europe have never been able to remedy the collapse of ancient Greek, but the 'staunch and sturdy races' of Western Europe have languages of such energetic maturity that they can cast away inflections without losing their capacity for continued creativity. Thus, what would by Humboldt's own criteria seem to constitute decline, is in fact not so – or is not admitted to be so.

Humboldt's conception of language-making follows from his aesthetic view of language. The artist, a painter for instance, does not imitate or copy something that perception presents to the mind but seeks to express the ideal model which the free imagination has created in the mind. As soon, however, as the first design for the painting has been put down, the sketch becomes, like the first articulation, an objective form that will determine the ultimate artistic quality of the painting. The expression of the ideal model corresponds to the inner form of language. A poor sketch can never be corrected into one that truly embodies the ideal model; future success is in the first sprout. The painter can of course hope for better results by starting over again, but language has only one beginning. It will, so to speak, have to keep working on the initial sketch by struggling to remedy a poor start. Poor painters cannot do any better even if they begin afresh, for they lack the genius of the artist whose execution is so assured that it spontaneously embodies the imagination's ideal model in the design of the first sketch. In this sense the good artist can also be said – indeed was said – to work by a kind of instinct; the presentiment of the whole is present from the start. Spectators will know the difference in proportion to the degree of imagination they themselves can bring to the viewing of the painting, for the viewing is itself a creative act, like hearing in language. The painting is of course completed in the course of time, but with genius the result will be a synthesis that immediately, as in a flash, stands before the spectator in its naked simultaneity, like a 'tableau'. 'Tableau' was, as we shall see, the word Diderot used in this sense; Humboldt called it 'Bild' in German and 'tableau' when he wrote in French. Both painter and spectator can forget the successivity of the labor that went into the making of it. We are now at the last stage of Humboldt's argument.

The initial articulation is the spontaneous expression of a state of mind; it is a synthesis that has no extension in time, and for that reason it also does not have discursivity – it cannot be true or false. It is not designative. But once the mind and language in s-two begin to respond to the demands of life and reality, concepts are minted into sound-forms that constitute an analysis of any given state of mind. This will become a never-ending process that continues to add to the lexicon by stocking it with the ideas and concepts we need for the conduct of life. Thus at any given moment in history, a nation's speakers will inherit a mass of forms that contain the work already done, the *ergon*, and since these forms record the analysis already performed they also express the nation's world-view. In response to the purposefulness it must serve, the analysis is performed by reason, it produces designative forms, and the utterance becomes strung out in the dimension of time. Instead of the simultaneity of the first articulation, we now have the successivity of prose and the daily uses of language, which becomes intellectualized as feeling and imagination are left behind. As prose, language becomes a method of thinking; becoming discursive, it also grows more and more analytic as it seeks to meet the increasing demands of science and philosophy. Thinking is made possible only by concept-formation, but cannot occur unless the concepts are objectified in sound-forms that return to the subject's ear. Even solitary thinking needs these forms, which can develop only in the social exchange of communication. The evolution of language is like a stream that keeps flowing past us toward greater degrees of conceptual analyticity and prose.

We are the beneficiaries of this flow, for by bringing to us the work already done, we receive an organ of thought that puts us in a better position to undertake a continuation of the work, which will be the more fruitful in proportion to the quality of what we receive. But this *ergon* will also pose a threat to the creativity or *energeia* that is the condition for further discovery, for expansion, that is, of our mastery of reality. There is a danger that the creative linguistic sense will relax and become static.

For this not to happen two conditions must be met in both of which reason and imagination play a role together: the lexical forms must have clarity and richness that mesh with reality to the highest possible degree, and the grammar must make it possible to join these forms into an unbreakable synthesis. This imperative demand follows from the fact that the basic unit of language is not the word but the sentence, which alone constitutes a closed thought. Thought and language meet in the sentence. Now, since all thought consists in separating and combining, in reciprocating analysis and synthesis, thinking cannot occur unless all the materials of a thought are simultaneously present to the mind. To ensure the most effective and creative thinking, the language must be capable of recreating the simultaneity of thought in the grammatical fixity and mental synthesis of the sentence. When this happens the unit of articulation, the sentence, will again, as in m-one, express a state of mind, though now with the crucial inclusion of discursivity. The grammar is therefore a remedy for the successivity that analysis has produced in the movement from poetry to prose.

This true expression of synthesis is possible only in the inflected languages, and it is most beautifully and successfully illustrated in the grammatical fixity of Sanscrit. Its procedures allow the roots that signify concepts to stand out, in relief as it were, while the 'meaningless' endings at the same time both create perfect word-unity and weld the words together in the simultaneity of synthesis. True synthesis is the product of superior mental power in language-formation. The agglutinating languages could not achieve this synthesis because their grammatical accretions retained recognizable meanings, thus not allowing the concept-words to stand out in relief. The incorporating languages, on the other hand, failed to give clarity to the concept-forms by losing them in the mass of the single-word sentence. For effective simultaneity of thought, word-unity is as important as sentence-unity. Chinese is capable of concept clarity in its monosyllabic words, but since it has no grammatical markings it can neither distribute its words among the parts of speech nor create fixity and synthesis. Therefore Chinese is an inferior organ of thought, and by that token it is blocked from progress. Only the polysyllabic inflected languages are truly organic, and their organization (or their being organisms) is the response of high mental power to the need for recreating simultaneity of thought from the discrete lexical forms that analysis keeps making in the flow of time.

Sanscrit is the most perfect linguistic form because its structure is best adapted to the mind. Since it has the best fit, its *ergon* does not hinder but rather advances continued creativity. Its fortunate organism makes it an inspiring instrument for the imaginative creation of new forms in the ongoing work of giving the subject greater mastery of life and reality. It allows the mind to remain the prime mover in the language, and for this reason Sanscrit confers the greatest freedom on the mind. Its inner form best honors both reason and imagination – light and warmth, '*Licht und Wärme*', or with the more familiar associations of the French words: *lumière et chaleur*.

If we ask what Humboldt has said about the diversity of language-structure and its influence on the mental development of mankind, then the most obvious answer is that he has argued why Sanscrit is the best form and shown why, by his criteria, other types are inferior.

He has also shown that there are distinct types of structure and, on that basis, he contended that a structure once formed either limits or aids mental development. This is a considerable accomplishment. The diversity itself, however, is drawn from the postulated varieties of mental energies among the language-making nations, and their languages are not considered merely in light of their abilities to serve the needs of their cultures, but measured on the absolute scale of Sanscrit. The result is not linguistic relativism but absolutism. Furthermore, it seems inescapable that the merits of the languages themselves are prejudged by already formed opinion about the level of culture and civilization of the nations that speak them; in that perspective the argument merely confirms what was already postulated: inferior nations have inferior languages and their inferiority is prior to their languages. As already mentioned and as we shall later see in more detail, this result caused, for obvious reasons, great discomfort to some very knowledgeable readers. The outcome of Humboldt's argument was chiefly the consequence of combining determined insistence on the unforgiving demands of universal grammar with the aesthetic view of the nature of language.

III
The context

Readers who remember Wordsworth's Prefaces to *Lyrical Ballads* will easily see that his and Humboldt's thought share conceptions that come together in the very texture of their arguments. Since we can safely assume both that the two writers did not read each other and that the agreement cannot be accidental, it would seem an inescapable inference that they shared a background that had already articulated and discussed the philosophy of language in terms that included the constituent presence of language in thinking, the interaction between language and thought, the problem of prose versus poetry, the role of imagination in language and artistic creation, and the trajectory of the rise, maturity, and decadence of language with all its implications for speaking and the nature of poetry. The short and sufficient answer is that both had been to France, literally as well as spiritually. About Wordsworth not much is known, but about Humboldt there is much material that has barely been used. In this final section I wish to examine Humboldt's relation to French writings on the subject he made his own, concentrating on Condillac, Diderot, and on the idéologues Marie-Joseph Degérando and Joseph-Dominique Garat. I shall close with the reaction of Humboldt's American correspondents to his work. But before proceeding, it will be necessary to make some observations on how what amounts to the official and trusted study of Humboldt has treated this problem.

The still very active official version has it that Humboldt owes nothing to the French, except at most by way of innovative reaction to their views, and that his forbears, in so far as he is allowed to have had any, are such German figures as Hamann and especially Herder and the German movement (or 'Deutsche Bewegung') they are said to represent. Only a dozen years ago the Nestor of German Humboldtians proclaimed that from 'Rudolf Haym (1856) we have the thorough, still unsurpassed biography that also treats the linguistic work in detail', at the same time conferring upon it the encomium that it could be cited 'above and in place of all other studies'. Since Haym did not have access to the unpublished writings on language that now make up more than half the total that has been put into print since about 1900, and since very little of the extensive and revealing correspondence had been published by 1856, the praise of Haym in these terms is so incredible that one would dismiss its very possibility if it was not an evident fact. Haym is the source of, among other things, the claim that Humboldt was chiefly indebted to Herder, a claim that was empty even then since no alternatives were considered; yet, every time that claim is repeated, as it has been often, the repetition is taken to constitute renewed proof – which is like claiming a great and well-merited victory for a candidate whose name is the only one on the ballot. The quoted statement shows what can rightly be called the official mothballing of the nineteenth-century version of Humboldt; now more than 125 years old, the mothball (in the sense of a protective cocoon that preserves old naval ships for future contingencies) has even up to the present been jealously kept in good repair – from the inside, of course. The mothball has proved effective because it is in turn sheltered in the larger envelope of trusted accounts of the late eighteenth-century philosophy of language which Herder and Humboldt are said to have reacted against.

The classic and often-cited exponent of these views is Ernst Cassirer. In the first volume of the *Philosophy of Symbolic Forms* (1923) he gave this version of the basic features of the philosophy of language before Herder and Humboldt: the French philosophers treated language exclusively as an instrument of cognition; found its origin in need and agreement for the single purpose of communication; saw the workings of ordinary language in terms of the ideal model of a perfect philosophical language; relied on a doctrine that made perception a passive and autonomous supplier of ready-made and unproblematic ideas to which words merely needed to be added to produce a safe nomenclature for communication; left no room for diversities of languages except in the trivial outward forms of the sounds we call words; based their thought on the rationalist principles of universal grammar; and banished feeling, imagination, and creativity from all processes of language. All the items in this catalogue were well known when Cassirer wrote them up again, and every one of them is false. As he saw the matter, however, the leaven that exploded them was the concept of the genius of languages, with its implication of both creativity and diversity. He also offered a bit of history in support. The concept came, he said, from James Harris's *Hermes* (1751) – that most severe of universal grammars – from which it wandered into the thought of Hamann, Herder, and ultimately Humboldt. Thanks to this concept, said Cassirer, language came to be seen as *energeia* and not as the mere *ergon* of the French philosophers. Cassirer suffers a brief moment of dismay when he admits that Diderot in the *Letter on the Deaf-Mutes* (1751) said something important on this very issue, but quickly recovers by tracing Diderot's view back to the Cambridge Platonists via Shaftesbury, who then is said to stand behind Harris. Conveniently, Diderot can be ignored.

For Cassirer the chief representative of the French philosophy was Condillac's *Essay on the Origin of Human Knowledge* (1746), in which he totally ignored the crucial chapter 'On the Genius of Languages,' thus preserving the integrity of his tinpot history. In this chapter Condillac wrote that 'everything confirms that each language expresses the character of the people who speak it'; 'that of all the writers, it is with the poets that the genius of languages gains the most lively expression'; that 'it is to the poets that we owe the first and perhaps also the greatest obligations'; and that, 'for anyone who understands them well, languages would be a painting of the character and genius of each people. He would see how the imagination has combined ideas according to the given outlook and the passions'. In that chapter Condillac also wrote that 'analysis and imagination are such different operations that one of them usually places obstacles in the way of the other' – imagination creates synthesis, analysis is the work of reason.

For Condillac the very beginning of language in m-one was an involuntary, inexplicable emanation of the mind, an expression of pure feeling without any thought of need; at the same time, it was, again as in Humboldt, the condition for the evolution of language in s-two. For Condillac the genius of each language is controlled by the analogy that determines its individuality and organization. It is by virtue of its analogy that a language can be said to be an organism, and for Condillac as well as Humboldt this analogy and thus also the organism are impaired when a language becomes mixed with elements taken from a language that obeys another analogy – this, we may recall, was precisely the problem that for Humboldt made it so interesting to observe the mixing of Sanscrit into the inferior Kawi language. For Condillac language is constituent of thought and the condition for self-awareness and knowledge; we think in and with our language, which influences our mode of thinking – there is feedback. Condillac makes language the crucial factor in the making of discursive thought and knowledge; the problem of the origin of knowledge becomes the question of the origin of language. Obviously, if Condillac had accepted the mere copytheory-representation-nomenclature-communication doctrine that Cassirer attributes to him, language itself would have been a passive, adventitious something that would have been irrelevant for the solution of his problem – indeed the problem would have vanished.

Condillac's chapter 'On the Genius of Languages' was not, of course, an aberration in the *Essay*. Like other chapters, e.g., 'On the Origin of Poetry' and 'On Music,' it formed an integral part of his argument, which he developed at greater length in many other and later writings. But it has been possible to misconceive his argument especially for two reasons. Owing to reactionary hostility to French eighteenth-century thought, it very early became typed as being wholly dominated by a mechanical, soulless, rationalist philosophy that accepted the sign-doctrine of universal grammar: since words were unproblematic signs for independently given ideas, language played no constituent role in thought. This view is the foundation of the belief that our philosophers located their model of language in a perfect, universal, and philosophical language. This is a surprising and very ignorant error, for when the philosophers talked about this language at all they dismissed it, calling it the equivalent of such chimeras as perpetual movement or the philosopher's stone. It is an impossibility since the ideas in the mind of each individual are radically private, with the consequence that, even if one could imagine that such a language were for a moment successfully instituted, it would immediately begin to go the way of all languages as individuals would again apply their own private meanings, for which even rectification is no sure remedy. When Humboldt dismissed the thought of such a language, he was merely joining a long tradition he is himself said to have rejected. It is, incidentally, curious that Leibniz, who more than anyone certainly did believe both in the possibility and the desirability of a philosophical language, is not ruled out of the canon, while those who did not believe in it are blamed for having done so. But that is the sort of thing that can happen inside the mothball.

The other reason – also a bad one – why Condillac's argument has been misrepresented is that he was in the *Essay* concerned with the possibility of knowledge and its growth, that is, with the cognitive role of language. He was therefore chiefly interested in the continuing analysis that occurs in and thanks to language as its speakers respond to the demands of life and reality, guided by reason and understanding. In the process language moves from its non-cognitive beginning across the spectrum toward meeting the needs of philosophy and science; language becomes increasingly prosy and by the same token seemingly less creative because there is now, so to speak, more *ergon* in it. It becomes, as both Condillac and Humboldt said, a method of thinking. In so far as it performs this role well, it demands less creative effort – that's the advantage – while at the same time giving greater thrust to continuing discovery and creativity. *Energeia* remains the crucial quality of language; its use, if successful, remains creative. The aim is not to cancel its natural energy, but to preserve and protect it against the slackness that the ready-made *ergon* may invite. When Condillac said that a good science is a well-made language, he was saying both that language is constituent of thought and that the well-made language best ensures the energy for continued discovery; but he certainly was not saying that a language that was not well made in that sense, such as poetry, was not worth talking about. For Condillac and Diderot poetry emerges from the heat of the imagination, from enthusiasm and passion, and for that reason it cannot be submitted to plan or manipulation. Better science and new discovery are helped along though certainly not guaranteed by a well-made language, but there is no prescription for poetry; it takes genius, and genius is not subject to rules.

The distinction between poetry and prose is not a matter of style and technique, but a consequence of the development of language. Poetry and prose are fundamentally different modes of grasping reality, and for that reason the proper contrast to poetry is, as Wordsworth made beautifully clear, not prose but philosophy. Condillac and Diderot often treated this contrast and its rationale, and for that reason it was also discussed in the same terms by Herder and Humboldt. It is especially likely to come up in discussion of the ages of language. Both in France and in Germany the problem of language is inherently an aesthetic one, but Cassirer's radical misconception locates it only in German writings. His misconception is the fateful error I mentioned in the previous section: that of believing that the French conception of the nature of language is entirely contained in the processes of s-two and that in s-two everything is reduced to non-constituent, nomenclatural signs.

Like Humboldt accepting human sociality as an axiom, Condillac had in the *Essay* argued that once the initial, involuntary articulation had occurred in m-one, reflection, which is an innate human capacity, realized the possibility of making further signs, thus starting the process of responding to need through communication. In the *Essay* he called these signs arbitrary in the precise sense that there is no natural connection between sound and concept. In French and English the words 'horse' and 'cheval' both refer to the same animal; to believe otherwise would entail the absurdity that horsiness was naturally different in the two countries, and that the difference of the sounds expressed this difference of horsiness. The arbitrariness of the relation is the condition for the creativity and freedom of the language-makers, for if it were not arbitrary they would be bound by nature, as in the concept of the Adamic language. It also implied that ideas or concepts are not innate, for if they were they would, as Condillac cogently argued, also be submitted to passivity. We segment and analyze reality as we respond, more or less effectively, to the needs of life and reality; the analysis is our creative making, and we can make it fit, so to speak, owing to the benevolent congruency that exists between nature and the mind's potential. This is an idea that is very prominent in Condillac; we are perverse if we do not learn from nature.

The ideas and concepts we have are of course not arbitrary in relation to us, for they are determined by our needs; if we have horses, we will also have a word for horse. Thus both the cultural need and the process of segmentation will contribute to the genius of a language, and for this reason the language will express the world-view of its speakers. The concept of the linguistic world-view was not Humboldt's invention. But in the *Essay* Condillac also said that once we are inside our native language, so to speak, our articulations and forms are not arbitrary, both because we are socially bound to respect the tacit consent we have given to the meanings of our shared words and, more importantly, because each language is ruled by an overall analogy that differs from one language to another according to the collective mentality of its speakers. Thus in relation to the world our signs are arbitrary, but in relation to ourselves they are not. Condillac therefore later argued that in the latter relation they are artificial in the sense that we have made them, by contrast to the involuntary articulation in m-one that is the synthetic expression of an emotive state of mind; it is non-discursive and thus cannot be either true or false. This first articulation forms part of the natural language of action, which involves all sorts of other bodily gestures. Hence early language in s-two for a long time remained a mixture of gestures, like sounds, song, music, dance, and miming; but in the movement toward prose all but the sounds tend to be lost under the pressure of analysis and the deceptive sufficiency of words. Elements of this expressive gestural language can, however, be reinvoked, as is the case with rhythm and accent or intonation, which for this reason are noted by Diderot and Humboldt. The constant linking of language and music is especially prominent in Diderot and thus also in Humboldt, though there to a lesser extent.

There is especially one conception that brings all the basic aspects of language into single focus: the privacy of language. Since the ideas in anyone's mind are radically private and since words are about those ideas, there can never be any assurance that one person's meaning is the same as another's. Rectification may help, but can never guarantee agreement. This fact of privacy is so full of consequences that Locke, Condillac, Destutt de Tracy (one of the prominent idéologues), Herder, Humboldt, and many others often noted it, but none so often and emphatically as Diderot. If we can share our signs, said Diderot, it is owing to their insufficiency. If God suddenly gave each individual a language that truly expressed its sentiments, we would no longer understand each other. It may even happen that we think we have understood someone else perfectly well when we have not at all gotten the same meaning; indeed, we may, without knowing it, have gotten the opposite meaning.

For Diderot 'all understanding is also a non-understanding', as Humboldt said. This fact explains both Diderot's preference for the dialogue form and the uses he made of it. The generating force in all the famous dialogues is the effort to clear up misunderstanding. In *Le Neveu de Rameau*, the two interlocutors, *moi* and *lui* (pronouns are enough, they don't even need names), are constantly groping for a common ground of understanding as they struggle to overcome the privacy of language by giving scope to the reciprocating creative acts of hearing and speaking. For these reasons Diderot often lapses into dialogue even in works that are not cast in that form, for instance, in the *Salons*. The most striking example is the long passage on the paintings of Vernet in the *Salon de 1767*, where the dialogue becomes a meditation both on painting and on language at the same time. Diderot's basic view of language was a sort of semantic agnosticism.

The same problem arises among languages as between individuals; each language has its own genius and world-view. Like each person, a language also has a distinct individuality. Therefore Locke,

Condillac, Humboldt and others often discussed the problem of translation, but again Diderot more often than anyone; in fact, when Humboldt in 1799 read Diderot in Paris, he noted one of those passages. Speaking and hearing demand reciprocating imaginations, and so does translation. For Diderot the translation of poetry is most demanding and hardly possible, but as we move toward prose it becomes easier; it is a mark of its functional adequacy that scientific discourse is translatable – thus here we again encounter the contrast between poetry and prose. In m-one and the early period of s-two language was less insufficient than it has later become in the process of analysis. Creative energy is therefore constantly needed to overcome this insufficiency. The privacy of language makes the philosophy of language an aesthetic problem; like all art language is not imitation but expression. Wordsworth argued against the neoclassical imitation doctrine in terms that are already evident in Condillac.

Now, if the French philosophy of language was everything that our typical exponent, Cassirer, said it was, then the problem of privacy would never have arisen – that is one way of realizing how false his account is. With the representationist, nomenclatural, passive copy-theory of language, the problem would never become an aesthetic one; the ideal of a perfect philosophical language would appear possible, though that is precisely what Cassirer's Frenchmen, unbeknownst to him, denied. For them the ideal was the energy, concentration, and imaginative power of poetry that had existed at the beginning of languages, and they sought the retention and recreation of those qualities with the materials we now have in the linear discourse that analysis has perforce left us with. The chief task is to lose as little *energeia* as possible, to overcome the alienation that slackness will cause. That was Wordsworth's problem, and that is why he offers such a wonderful refutation of Cassirer. These were also the ideas that Humboldt encountered when he came to Paris.

A little over a dozen years ago a book, which relied heavily on Cassirer, was published on what the author called the Copernican revolution of language in Humboldt. Inside the mothball it was not realized that the revolution had already taken place. By stark contrast, in a series of brilliant books – one of them entitled *Diderot: Poète de l'énergie* (1984) – Jacques Chouillet has increased our understanding of Diderot and demonstrated the centrality of aesthetics in his thought. About a dozen years ago he wrote that until the last twenty years our view of the French *Encyclopédie* had been falsified by the academic criticism of the nineteenth century, which wished to see in that work only a 'scientism' that was radically opposed to their academic 'humanism'. But from the issue of Diderot's Prospectus to the *Encyclopédie* in 1750 to the last volume of plates in 1772, wrote Chouillet, the *Encyclopédie* 'is an inexhaustible source of information' about the aesthetic – and that means not least linguistic – philosophy of those years. Anyone who seeks dramatic proof of that statement should take a look at the three volumes (1782–6) of the *Encyclopédie méthodique* that are devoted to grammar and literature. They contain most of the relevant material from the larger work and much that is new. Though people rarely bother to credit reference works, it is certain that those volumes were widely distributed and used. They would have been a goldmine for Humboldt, but however that may be, he was also in Paris.

It was during the Paris years that Humboldt entered the path of language study he followed for the rest of his life. We have already seen that he, within a year of his arrival, wrote to a friend that his residence there was epoch-making for his thought. In the first month after his arrival in November of 1797 he had written to the same friend that 'for the culture of a nation, there is simply nothing that is more important than its language'. Toward the end of 1799 he wrote from Madrid: 'In the future I feel that I shall devote myself more exclusively to language study, and that a thorough and philosophically oriented comparison of several languages is a task that I can shoulder after some years of serious study.' During these and the next few years, he often reiterated his new commitment, for instance in the summer of 1804 when he wrote from Rome: 'Basically everything I work at, also my Pindar, is language study. I believe I have discovered the art of using language as a vehicle to range over the highest and the lowest levels of the world and its multiplicity, and I am steadily becoming more engrossed in this view.' These statements reveal his own awareness of the intensity of the change that had come over his mind. We already clearly discern the outlines of what he aimed to do in the Kawi Introduction. What had happened?

In Paris he absorbed as much as he could with great determination and energy. He attended meetings of the National Institute, especially in the section devoted to 'the analysis of sensations and ideas', which was the focus for the idéologues' work on Condillac's philosophy. He often met with the idéologues both in groups and individually, and he systematically read through the first collected editions of the works of Condillac and Diderot, both published in 1798. Humboldt noted that the Condillac edition was published on the initiative of his friend Garat. He also knew about the official efforts during the early 1790s to ensure that French – 'the language of liberty' – was understood and spoken by all the twenty-five million citizens of the land.

At the time some five million had no French at all and another five could barely conduct a simple conversation in it. At first these efforts were directed against foreign languages spoken within the borders, such as Breton, Basque, Italian, and German; later, at the urging of Henri Grégoire, it was proposed also to replace dialects with French, but his proposal did not pass. For these efforts the idéologues have been said to lack linguistic insight, so that whatever they thought about language could have no relevance for Humboldt or anyone else – for don't all academics know that dialects are indispensable for serious linguistic study, if not right at the moment at least later (say, toward the end of the nineteenth century)? This is typical of mothball thinking. It takes little knowledge of France's political situation during those years, both internally and externally, to see the absurdity of this view, for it assumes that intangible scholarly concerns should have been given priority over evident political necessity – one wonders if anyone knows of a single example in which this priority was accepted, even in less grave circumstances. The chief support for these efforts came in fact from the non-French speakers who wished to be part of the events they did not understand. Since the republic was one and indivisible under a single law and the equality of patriots, it must also have one language and do away with the distinction between the French-speaking élite and the rest of the population. The aim was liberation, not repression.

Furthermore, the policy was advocated precisely because it was understood that culture and language are constituent of each other; it was based on the very principle Humboldt was now adopting. It was also made an integral part of the policy to preserve the dialect records that were collected in connection with it, precisely because it was realized that they were valuable for cultural and historical study, in the spirit of the distinguished earlier work of La Curne de Sainte-Palaye, which is mentioned as an example in this very context. Grégoire's position on this question must be seen in the same light as his advocacy of the emancipation of the Jews, the abolition of slavery, the importance of black literature, the prevention of revolutionary vandalism, and the reunion of the divided churches. Humboldt in fact knew Grégoire, visited him several times, and noted in his diary that Grégoire had collections of dialect records. One result of all this was that Basque was much discussed in Paris, as Humboldt knew very well before he began his own study of that language. Thus the efforts for which the idéologues have been so ignorantly blamed both expressed and promoted the very kinds of language study they are said to have been indifferent to. Similarly, later in the nineteenth century the threatened loss of American-Indian languages also caused intensified collection and study, with equally significant consequences. We may also recall that the École des langues orientales vivantes was established by the National Convention in the spring of 1795.

When during the late spring of 1798 Humboldt took notes on Condillac's chief works he was very critical, from a Kantian point of view, both of the general tenor of the philosophy and of what he saw as its nomenclatural conception of signs, which he traced to the sign-doctrine of universal grammar. Since he later often made statements to the effect that this doctrine was the chief obstacle to a true understanding of language and its nature, it has, in the spirit of Cassirer, been believed both that Condillac accepted that sign-doctrine and that Humboldt was opposing his own philosophy to Condillac's. But quite apart from the fact that Humboldt misread Condillac, this is an unfounded inference. In none of those statements does Humboldt mention Condillac (or anyone else), and on at least one occasion, around 1810, he made it clear that this old sign-doctrine had long since been overcome: 'Language is an autonomous being, both our guide and our creation; and the error has long ago disappeared that language is the embodiment of signs outside it for independently existing things and mere concepts.' His critical statements about the universal-grammar sign-doctrine must be seen in this light as simply reiterating the fact that that doctrine was not compatible with his own, that is, with the constituent conception of signs that is central to Condillac's argument. When Humboldt in our text pays little attention to this matter, it may be because he realized that it was a dead issue. Two other details reveal Humboldt's relation to Condillac.

In his notes Humboldt made the puzzling statement that Condillac had 'entirely overlooked that language is of no use at all for philosophy, but at most for reasoning'. It is presumably made in the spirit of Kant's notorious and, it seems, deliberate indifference to the philosophy of language that was going on all around him and for which Hamann and Herder took him so severely to task. The statement is puzzling for two reasons: because Condillac neither said nor meant that, and because Humboldt himself surely abandoned that view; to think otherwise makes nonsense of all Humboldt interpretation. We cannot step outside language. The other detail is this: in the formation of language Condillac assigned the crucial role to reflection, but when he took his notes Humboldt did not seem to have understood that. Condillac said that 'it is thanks to reflection that we begin to have a glimpse of everything the soul is capable of', and this means that reflection is the condition for self-awareness which is denied to animals, to Condillac's speechless statue (in the *Treatise of Sensations*), and, he surmised, to deaf-mutes. Thanks to reflection we can, said Condillac, render account to ourselves of our experience. In the notes Humboldt said that Condillac had no conception of self-awareness, but a few years later, in a text we are coming to soon, he wrote a sentence that faithfully recapitulates Condillac's (and thus also Herder's) understanding of the role of reflection for language and awareness of self: 'He who spoke the first word, first raised himself to the condition of being human; he was struck by the sudden realization that he could reflect, that he could suddenly stand still in the midst of the flow of his dream-like brooding, could confront and behold an object, and in that moment he began to speak.' Perhaps as little as a year later, he wrote that 'owing to reflection we have made a double being of ourselves'. He had then already in Condillac read the statement that 'there are somehow two selves in each human being, the self of habit and the self of reflection'. It is the self of reflection that makes us double, for the other self is all the animals have, thus being denied self-awareness.

Both of Humboldt's statements have been cited to point to the core of his philosophy, but since they are in fact repetitions of Condillac it is clear that he changed his mind, whatever he first thought of Condillac when he read him in the light of the opinions he carried to that reading. Since it is a mark of lively minds to be open for change, it is rather discreditable to Humboldt to think that he could not have changed his. There is a good lesson in an anecdote about John Maynard Keynes. Someone once said to Keynes in a reproachful tone of voice, 'I see that you have changed your mind'; to which Keynes, looking him straight in the eye, said, 'when I have new information, I change my mind. What do you do?' Humboldt did not lack impulses to change his mind.

Among the idéologues Humboldt met was Garat, who, he said, had an 'exceptionally good mind'. He knew that Garat was a native speaker of Basque, born at Ustaritz near Bayonne, and that he had written for the *Mercure de France*. In one of several unidentified notes, Humboldt took down this passage in French:

Monsieur Rivarol pretends that in Latin the sense is suspended until the end of the sentence. But I do not know any language in which the sense can be completed before the sentence; that's just one more of those things that everyone repeats without at least once trying to examine what he says.

In all the languages of the world, it is only with the phrase that the sense can be complete and the sense is suspended until the last word.

To this passage Humboldt added his German translation of the next sentence that 'languages with inversions favour clarity because they offer more means of expression'. Inversion, of course, means transposition of words away from any sentence order that one may consider normal or natural. We shall soon see that the matter of inversion is important in the formation of Humboldt's philosophy of language, just as it was for both Condillac and Diderot. It is, for instance, not least the problem of inversion that makes the sentence, not the word, the effective linguistic unit. For the moment, let us stick with Garat, who in fact wrote the quoted passages in a review (published in 1785 in the very journal to which Humboldt knew Garat had been a contributor) of Antoine de Rivarol's famous *Discours sur l'Universalité de la Langue française*, which in 1784 with another submission shared the prize for its answer to a topic that had been set by the Berlin Academy.

The best part of Rivarol's *Discours*, wrote Garat, was the passage explaining the principle that Rivarol had stated in these words: 'If speech is a thought that manifests itself, it must also be true that thought is interior and hidden speech.' This principle was profound, added Garat, because nothing serves better to reveal the nature of the human mind: 'It links the arts of imagination and taste to the arts of analysis and the philosophical mind. It shows that the art of good style and the art of perfecting reason are not merely two intimately related arts that we can join together, but that they are in fact one and the same art; that speech is as necessary to thought as thought to speech.' This principle was one of the most beautiful discoveries of the century, and for that reason it was important to credit it, as Rivarol had failed to do, to its author, Condillac, 'who has discerned this great truth right from his first work, the *Essay*'. Language is constituent of thought, and this truth embraces both the arts and the sciences, both the words of imagination and of reason. Condillac, Garat, Diderot, Herder, and Humboldt were all committed to this principle.

In the review of Rivarol Garat also stated the consequence of this principle:

There is no need to be surprised that it should be in the study of grammar and the principles of languages that the most important discoveries have been made on the nature of the human mind. It is there, and there only, that we are obliged to make them because it is in language alone that we have been able to observe all the manners of conceiving and rendering ideas.

That's where we find the human mind in its entirety, and it does not exist anywhere else.

Garat proceeded to dismiss the over-hasty generalization and sub-mission to doctrine that had hitherto obscured this truth. This pas-sage by Garat states what was for Humboldt and many others the rationale and benefit of language study, among them Silvestre de Sacy, who in 1811 spoke these words in a lecture:

It is today a truth acknowledged by all good minds that the comparative study of languages is truly the study of the human mind...By taking as our guide this interesting and difficult part of philosophy, language – this living and animated 'tableau' in which the human mind reflects itself, so to speak, and paints itself as the maker of the universe portrays himself in the works of his omnipotence – we no longer risk losing ourselves by following the illusions and phantoms created by the spirit of system and the caprices of the imagination.

Like Garat and Humboldt, de Sacy saw the need to explore the human mind not merely in the grammar but also in the lexicon.

Since we shall soon come to the problem of inversion, we need not examine what Garat said about it, except to mention that right around 1785 he wrote an entry on the Basque language for the *Encyclopédie méthodique*, in which he said that, though his native language showed even greater boldness of inversions than Latin and Greek, he always understood it no matter how fast it was spoken; it was false, therefore, to say that 'in languages with inversions the mind remains suspended and entangled until the last word', by contrast to languages that are said to follow an order that is presumed to be natural. Garat had in fact more briefly made the same point in the review, but it surely seems likely that Humboldt also knew this signed entry – indeed that he was familiar with all the three volumes devoted to grammar and literature – and in that case the linking of Basque and the problem of inversion is significant. Before getting to Diderot, we must consider Humboldt's close relation to another idéologue, Degérando.

During Humboldt's years in Paris, Degérando was one of the most active idéologues. He was a protégé of Humboldt's friend, Mme de Staël, and a member of the National Institute's section on 'analysis of sensations and ideas'. Humboldt saw him regularly and later had a warm correspondence with him. During the summer of 1800 Degérando wrote a set of directions for an expedition to the South Pacific, an expedition Alexander von Humboldt had planned to join, but in the event fortunately did not, for it was ill-fated. The directions were prepared under the auspices of La Société des Observateurs de l'Homme and were first delivered as one or several papers before being published in September under the title *Considerations on the diverse Methods to follow in the Observation of savage Peoples*. The report was thoroughly within the idéologue tradition, and it has in recent years gained high commendation from anthropologists as an important and prescient document in the history of their subject. It caused much excitement at the time, and it is not plausible that Wilhelm did not see it. He was in Paris at the time, and both he and Degérando had a general interest in these matters that also involved many of their mutual philosophical friends. Furthermore, as we shall soon see, we have some fragments of a Humboldt text (written soon after in Berlin, between the fall of 1801 and the late spring of 1802), and in these fragments a number of details and conceptions occur that were also in the *Considerations*. Degérando did not forget Humboldt and his interests. In May of 1828 when Humboldt was in Paris, Degérando sent him a copy of his recent two-volume work on *L'Éducation des sourds-et-muets de naissance* (1827), for which he received thanks in a letter of 11 May: 'I shall study it with care as soon as I return to my literary work, and I am confident that I shall find it a source of instruction. A work on languages that I am presently engaged in had guided me to this subject and I had in vain sought a work to enlighten me on it.'

In the report Degérando urged the travellers to abandon 'those unjust prejudices that in our eyes put a stigma on savage nations'. Accepting that language is the central fact of culture, he placed primary emphasis on the imperative need to know the language of the observed nations in order to understand their cultures and mentalities. 'It is a delusion to suppose', he wrote, 'that one can properly observe a people whom one cannot understand and with whom one cannot converse. The first means to the proper knowledge of savages is to become, after a fashion, like one of them; and it is by learning their language that we become their fellow citizens.' Knowing their language we share their conceptions and enter, as it were, their minds.

In this context Degérando revealed a new conception of history, for by the study he outlined we shall, he said, 'in a way be taken back to the first period of our own history; we shall be able to gain certain empirical knowledge of the origin and generation of their ideas, on the formation and development of language, and on the relations between these two processes'. When the traveller encounters some 'general or reflective ideas, he will do his utmost to find out in what circumstances it was formed; he will try to wrest from the savage the secret of his intellectual history'. Our own human history is not like the mere natural history of animals; thanks to our insight into language, history becomes the understanding of the inner formation of cultures; it becomes the history of thought. This momentous reorientation and innovation in western culture was, as Garat also understood well, the consequence of the philosophy of language that Condillac had expounded in the *Essay*. It was not Herder's invention. It was this radical innovation that more than any other factor inspired the nature of historical language study during the nineteenth century.

Like Condillac, Diderot, and Humboldt, Degérando gave priority to the imagination; it is 'the first faculty to be studied, since it nourishes all the others. Imagination is always the first faculty to develop in the individual'. But in a passage that repeats Condillac's statement that reflection is the source of self-awareness, Degérando also called for paying special attention to reflection, which is 'the faculty by which we turn back on ourselves to render account to ourselves of our feelings, our thoughts, and to penetrate into the innermost secrets of our manner of being'. These insights are revealed not in single words but in sentences; travellers have been wrong to limit their observation to 'taking at random names of various objects with scarcely any relation between them...It was not enough to be content with some detached words, but would have been proper to record whole sentences to give some ideas of the construction of their discourse'.

To this end Degérando gave detailed lists of questions about syntax and word-formation, for instance, whether 'words were simple or composite, as their length would often lead us to suppose; whether they were qualified by any articles or remained in the absolute; and whether they were subject to any kind of grammatical laws'. This is a matter of the analogy of each language. Degérando outlined a program of empirical study of language to replace the over-hasty generalization and speculation that had hitherto falsified language study. 'The spirit of systems is past', he said, echoing a commitment we have already met in Garat and in Silvestre de Sacy's later statement. It goes without saying that the report also mentioned wild children, for it was in 1799 that the Aveyron Boy was brought to Paris so that it for the first time became possible, as it was thought, to study such a child rather than merely reading about reported cases, of which Condillac had discussed several in the *Essay*. Degérando made it clear that his program aimed for the better understanding of mankind at large through the study of linguistic diversity, and that his method was comparison, as in the natural sciences. 'If it could be reduced to a program', he wrote, 'the art of properly studying these languages would be one of the masterpieces of philosophy.'

It is now almost an insult to the reader's intelligence to point out that Degérando's program for the study of distant languages outlined the project Humboldt pursued all his life, right down to the end in our text. It is not a matter of speculation but evidence. Late in 1800 Humboldt wrote to Goethe that he had 'for some time been thinking of an essay on national character and the diversity of speaking and their influence'. In May of 1802 he wrote to Schiller that he had been deeply engaged in language study and was now planning to go to work on 'a general encyclopedia of everything that pertains to language and hence of all languages', in which he would combine philosophy and the study of nations. For the next twenty years or more he kept mentioning this encyclopedia (by that word), which he repeatedly began afresh. All he ever wrote on language are large or small fragments of this enterprise.

Humboldt was writing to Schiller from Tegel during the months he was spending there between his return from Paris and the departure for Rome. At this time he was working on a monograph on the Basque nation and its language, and of that work we have some short fragments that were first published in 1907, one of which has the title 'About the study of language, or plan for a systematic encyclopedia of all languages'. In these pieces, which, it may be plausibly assumed, were preserved because he found them important, Humboldt repeated all the salient points of Degérando's *Considerations*: imagination, reflection (the Humboldt passage quoted earlier about language beginning in the moment of reflective self-awareness and articulation occurs in one of these pieces), analogy, wild children, the prejudice of deprecating savage languages, the need for empirical study, and the rejection of over-hasty speculation. Such a 'systematic survey of the entire process of language in man' would sharpen our sense of penetrating into 'the genius of language' – 'systematic', of course, means according to plan and method, and has nothing to do with the spirit of system.

Such a study Humboldt wrote, would abandon the false value placed on languages according to the excellence of their literatures and the unjustified deprecation of those that had none. 'The study of the languages of the earth', he wrote, 'is also the world history of the thoughts and feelings of mankind.' Beginning with the philosophical analysis of the capacity for language, Humboldt said about his program that if, at the same time,

it had, based on reason and experience, detailed the different ways in which different nations of the earth have, each in its own way, solved the diverse tasks that fall to language and thus completed the picture of the possible language diversity, then it would further describe the character of each in particular and indeed all along, by grouping them together according to the degree of their affinity, go from the more similar to the more divergent.

Humboldt says several times that his program was new, but that of course is true only in the sense that it was recent, not in the sense that it was his own. Degérando had presented his program as a way of overcoming the errors of the past, of which he gave a detailed critique.

When Humboldt wrote with excitement to his friends about his recent commitment to language study and its promise, he had already read and misunderstood Condillac from his own Kantian point of view, but this reading had been followed by close knowledge of the long review in which Garat had both credited Condillac with the great insight of the century – that language is not a mere nomenclatural means of communication, but constituent of thought and thus a record of it – and also stressed that this insight had momentous consequences for our understanding of the human mind and the diversity of mentalities. This reading had been followed by Degérando's detailed program for putting Condillac's philosophy to use in a systematic and empirical study of distant languages that would produce a comprehensive anthropology, with the stirring promise that it would become one of the masterpieces of philosophy. In Degérando Humboldt had also met the idea that the form of language is more than what was conventionally called grammar, for it also included the principles of word-formation. Degérando's question whether words were composite or simple is a question about whether a language is what we would call synthetic or analytic, that is, whether it does or does not rely heavily on inflections and compounding. This distinction had been discussed for more than a generation as an aspect of the very problem of inversion that Garat had drawn attention to in his review. The fragments Humboldt wrote at Tegel soon after his return from Paris show his estimation and appropriation of these problems, and by that token they also make it plain that he had overcome his misreading of Condillac, who was both Garat's and Degérando's source. But one more piece had fallen into place in the fragments, for they show that he remembered his recent reading of Diderot and saw its relation to the other problems.

In the fragments Humboldt observed that a language is not the copy of a people's ideas, but the 'total energy of the people, embodied, as if by a miracle, in certain sounds'. Different languages are not so many nomenclatures for the same thing, but present

[margin handwritten note: Humboldt – language the total energy of a people's ideas]

[handwritten: Humboldt: languages are hieroglyphs, imprintings of imagination and world]

[handwritten in left margin: origin of Humboldt's hieroglyph concept in Diderot]

different views of it. 'They are hieroglyphs in which each individual [whether a person or a people] imprints its imagination and the world.' And since 'the world and the imagination remain on the whole the same, and since the imagination links one formation to another by analogy, these hieroglyphs interact in further creation, multiply, and undergo continued formation'. Thus the diversity of languages follows upon the development of the imaginative hieroglyphs that existed at the beginning, and in this lies for us the great promise of the study of savage languages: 'Our dry intellectual culture will be invigorated by the youthful imagination of these peoples, who fixed each impression that the still young world presented to their as yet unweakened senses in the form of a lively and moving 'tableau' [Bild].' Humboldt repeated this argument about the hieroglyphs in closely similar formulations in 1812 and 1821, and he often made the same point even when he did not use the word hieroglyph. The concept of the hieroglyph has these qualities: it sums up the energetic and creative beginning of languages; it prefigures and explains the individuality of each language; and it tells us that this first poetic synthesis unfolds in the course of time toward the language of our less energetic and less imaginative prose culture. Both the concept of the hieroglyph and its qualities are Diderot's creations; furthermore, for Diderot the hieroglyph was the key to the problem of inversion.

Toward the end of his life Goethe wrote that 'Diderot is Diderot, a unique individual; whoever carps at him and his oeuvre is a Philistine, and they are legion.' Even during his lifetime, Diderot was widely read and translated in Germany. Kant recommended the article 'On the Beautiful' (in the *Encyclopédie*) to Hamann; Herder cited him both with and without acknowledgement and counted him among the great philosophers of the world along with Plato, Spinoza, and Shaftesbury; Lessing admired and translated him; so did Schiller who in the 1780s published a translation of a famous episode in *Jacques le Fataliste;* Goethe translated parts of *Essais sur la Peinture* and, of course, *Le Neveu de Rameau*, of which Schiller had gotten a copy, on the sly so to speak, from the manuscripts kept at St Petersburg; and Humboldt's tutor, J. J. Engel, was perhaps Diderot's closest follower in Germany. We now consider Diderot's aesthetic writings the central and greatest among his manifold distinguished achievements, and to these German readers in fact had better access than the French, for several of them – including the signally important *Salons* – appeared in Melchior Grimm's *Correspondance littéraire* (after 1773 continued by J. H. Meister), which on subscription was sent to a number of European courts outside France, including several ducal houses in Germany. One copy went to Weimar where Herder, Schiller, and Goethe are known to have had access to it.

When Humboldt arrived in Paris he had just spent two years at Jena in frequent contact with Schiller and Goethe; it is therefore not surprising that from Meister he had secured an introduction to Diderot's daughter, Angélique Vandeul, for as Meister wrote to her, since Humboldt could not hope to meet Diderot himself, 'he would at least be able to converse about the great man with the person most worthy of cherishing and honoring his memory'. Humboldt saw Mme Vandeul often while he was in Paris. On his way to Paris he had with great excitement read *Discours de la Poésie dramatique*, and soon after his arrival he even thought of writing a book on Diderot. His passion for Diderot was satisfied when he read through all fifteen volumes of Naigeon's recent edition, which contained a number of works that had not before appeared in print, including the book-length *Salon de 1767*. Unfortunately, we do not have the reading notes he took in the fall of 1798, but we do have some from January of 1799. They contain such exclamations as 'an exceptionally interesting piece', 'magnificent passage on friendship, to be compared only with Montaigne', 'a masterpiece in the art of philosophical reasoning by way of narrative', 'masterly and extremely characteristic and important', and again 'an exceptional piece'. Humboldt saw the importance of these pieces at once, and he took the notes with great care, for he often referred back to 'my earlier papers', presumably meaning the lost notes from the fall of 1798 or even earlier.

Humboldt's reading of Diderot first showed in a new introduction he wrote in the latter part of 1798 to his essays on Goethe's *Hermann und Dorothea*, in time for publication early in 1799. Here Humboldt explained that it was his aim to gain insight into the nature of the artist by direct observation of his work, thus also learning about art itself. 'It is this', he wrote, 'that is so valuable in Diderot's aesthetic writings, the wealth of observations and experiences that, for example, makes his *Essai sur la Peinture* and *De la Poésie dramatique* so fruitful for the artist and the theoretician.' But since he was eager to reach a French audience, he wrote a shorter French version of his work, prepared after the reading of Diderot's works and published in the fall of 1799, dedicated to Mme de Staël, under the title 'Essais aesthétiques'. This piece has been called Humboldt's essay on the imagination. It very obviously shows his reading of Diderot, and for this we have a peculiar sort of support.

It was republished some twenty years ago in a German book

entitled *Poetry and Imagination. On Humboldt's poetic Theory*, with facing translation, an introduction, and notes. The editor, Kurt Müller-Vollmer, claims that today's reader is struck by the radicality of Humboldt's poetic theory because it finds its match 'only much later in the poetics of Baudelaire and the symbolists'. Humboldt presents 'a doctrine of the autonomy and dominion of the imagination as the highest principle in poetry. He argues the absolute character of the work of art as a self-contained world which in its pure ideality is opposed to reality. He says that it is the function of poetry to create an "état d'âme"...When Humboldt's essay begins "the domain of poetry is the imagination", who doesn't think of similar formulations in Baudelaire, e.g., "l'imagination seule contient la poésie"'. Humboldt is made a prescient anticipator of Baudelaire, though the editor does not suggest the improbability that the latter read the former. This is a puzzle, though not for the editor.

The editor is aware that Humboldt had recently read Diderot, but pays no attention whatsoever to Diderot's writings or any possible relation between the two figures. But there lies the answer to the puzzle, for it is hardly a secret (though it is to the editor) that Baudelaire was among the first nineteenth-century readers and admirers of Diderot; Baudelaire's great creative geniuses were Shakespeare, Diderot, and Goethe. The editor ignores the readily available literature on the subject, e.g., Gita May's *Diderot et Baudelaire, critiques d'art* (1957) and even such an obvious source as the first volume of Arthur M. Wilson's Diderot biography (1957), which has this statement in a passage on the *Letter on the Deaf-Mutes*: 'Thus the reader, who has almost forgotten that he started out by reading a brief essay on the deaf-mutes, finds he has arrived at an aesthetic theory which leads directly to Baudelaire and the Symbolists.' The reason for this startling academic incident is no doubt that it long ago came to be thought inconceivable that Diderot could have had anything to do with poetry, the imagination, and aesthetics. Diderot had been typed as a materialist.

Materialist he was, much like Humboldt who said that the spiritual is the finest bloom of the physical. But more than anyone else in the eighteenth century Diderot was also interested in the process of artistic creation. Genius is rare, it is the mark of a strong individuality, creates by a sort of inexplicable instinct, makes its own rules, and is fired by imagination, enthusiam, and passion. The genius is preeminently the language-maker. Already in the Prospectus (1750) to the *Encyclopédie*, Diderot had made poetry the archetype of all the arts, 'we [i.e., the editors] relate architecture, music, painting, sculpture, engraving, etc., to poetry, for it is no less true to say of a painter that he is a poet, than to say of a poet that he is a painter, and of a sculptor or an engraver that he is a painter in relief or in depth, than of a musician that he is a painter through his sounds'. Thus Diderot's aesthetic becomes concentrated in the language-maker, the poet, whom he constantly compares and contrasts with the painter. Language is the archetypical aesthetic problem. The painter's 'palette is the image of chaos and from it he draws the work of creation', and like the painter the poet also has a palette: 'It is pure instinct of nature that inspires the poet without his being aware of it; the poet's palette is language. Just consider how often it happens that this palette is poorly supplied without it being in the power even of genius to enrich it.'

Seen together poetry and painting pose a problem to which Diderot returns again and again. A finished painting, a 'tableau,' is all simultaneity and synthesis; it can be neither narrative nor discursive. Poetry, however, cannot escape the successivity that is now in the nature of the language it must use, but is must all the same strive for simultaneity and synthesis. When the poet is successful, the creation is like a hieroglyph or like the painter's instantaneous 'tableau'. This creation is so difficult that Diderot believed good poets were much rarer than good painters. These conceptions also formed the core of Humboldt's conception of language; when he wrote in German he used the world 'Bild' for what he in French called 'tableau'. The central text is the *Letter on the Deaf-Mutes*, which, it is agreed, builds on and develops ideas that Condillac argued in the *Essay*, especially in the chapter 'On Inversions,' a subject on which he had more to say in later writings. In a number of brilliant writings, Ulrich Ricken has in recent decades demonstrated the centrality of the problem of inversion in the linguistic thought of the eighteenth century.

Inversion was the issue that separated the rationalist universal grammarians from the followers of Locke. Since for the former the model of language was governed by reason, the proper sentence order was subject-verb-object, as in logic. This order was taken to be natural and thus, as in modern French and English, without inversion by contrast to, e.g., Latin which most often showed inversion. Thus when inversion occurred in French, it was for purely rhetorical and stylistic reasons that had no bearing on the nature of language. It was to this view of natural order that Garat objected when he said that it was not only in Latin but in all languages that the sense of an utterance was not complete until the last word. The tradition of universal grammar, however, made it possible to believe that a sentence was a mere addition of one word to another, because the prior expectation of the completion of a fixed order gave the impression that the sentence was complete at any stage along the way. It is consistent with this view that the typical universal grammarian considered language a divine gift, which its passive recipients sought to use so as best to recapture the original and rational form. For the same reason words were considered unproblematic signs for given ideas; language was not constituent of thought but a mere instrument of communication. Since the creation of language had occurred elsewhere, our speaking had nothing to do with creation and imagination, but only with rhetoric and style when feeling was allowed to produce minor variations of the given form.

All this changed completely when the followers of Locke began to argue that language was not a premeditated invention but a human creation. Now neither the natural order nor the unproblematicness of signs could be taken for granted any longer. In the chapter on inversions in the *Essay*, Condillac had concluded that the notion of natural order was merely a result of the habit we had contracted owing to the form of our own language, French. There was, in other words, no absolute criterion of inversion. He also found that with the habitual order, the imagination played a small role, while it was exercised more energetically with inversions, which of course demanded inflections as in Latin. In terms of imagination, which Condillac prized very highly as a creative agent, Latin therefore had a number of advantages over French. It would recapture the concentration and synthesis of the original language of action, 'in which a single sign often was the equivalent of an entire phrase'. From this ability followed a still greater virtue of inversions, namely that they 'make a 'tableau', that is, they unite in a single word all the circumstances of an action, much like the way the painter joins them on his canvas; if those circumstances were presented one after the other, it would merely be a simple sequential narrative'. Concentration, synthesis, and the 'tableau' effect of simultaneity are among the virtues that inflection makes possible.

Both the making and the reception of this effect Condillac called vivacity; Diderot called it energy, a word that recurs with great frequency in all of his writings. It also occurs often in other French aesthetic and linguistic writings of the time. In the *Encyclopédie méthodique* it even had an entry which said that 'energy is the quality that, in a single word or in a small number of ideas, makes us perceive or feel a large number of ideas; or which, by means of a small number of ideas expressed in words, excites in the mind sentiments of admiration, respect, horror, love, hate, etc., which the words themselves do not signify'. Energy, then, is a creative means of overcoming the inadequacy of words. Energy belongs with geniuses, with poets and artists and speakers. Neither the conception of linguistic energy nor the emphasis on it was Humboldt's invention. It had since Condillac's *Essay* been an integral part of the philosophy of language. Its prominence in Diderot explains why Jacques Chouillet called Diderot the 'poet of energy'.

The *Letter on the Deaf-Mutes* is the central text in Diderot's aesthetics, it is about language, and it focuses on the problem of inversion. By considering the natural language of action that is the congenital deaf-mute's only means of expression, Diderot concludes that 'there are no inversions in the mind'. A thought is instantaneous but in our artificial and now habitual language it must be strung out successively in the dimension of time. But by comparison with the original, energetic language – the language of action and gesture as in m-one – this forced successivity is a loss in terms of creativity. In English we must say 'I am hungry', but in Latin the single word 'esurio' does as much and the speaker of it no doubt takes it to express a single idea. This leads Diderot to conclude that sensation has no time dimension in the mind, so that 'if the mind could command twenty mouths, each mouth saying its word, then all the ideas felt will be expressed all at once'. Of course, this is an impossibility, but 'esurio' suggests something important:

We have attached several ideas to a single expression. If these energetic expressions were more common instead of language constantly trailing after the mind, then the number of ideas that are rendered all at once would become such that the mind, with language running ahead of it, would be forced to run after it. What then would become of the inversion which implies decomposition of simultaneous movements in the soul and a multitude of expressions? Though we have few such terms that equal a long discourse, do not the facts that we have some, that Greek and Latin teem with them, and that they are used and understood on the spot, suffice to convince you that the soul feels a mass of perceptions, if not at once, at least with such tumultuous rapidity that it is barely possible to make out their order.

This passage shows that Diderot, like Condillac, Garat, and Humboldt, believed that languages with inflections greatly favour expressions that truly reveal what goes on in the momentary state of mind or *état de l'âme*.

On the suggestion of what Diderot has said in the passage above, a series of remarkable passages now follow in quick succession, all with conceptions and terms that Humboldt made his own, as we have met them in passages already quoted. First on the state of mind, on simultaneity and the 'tableau' by contrast to sucessivity:

The state of mind in an indivisible moment was represented by a multitude of terms which the precision of language demanded and which divided the integral impression into parts; and since these terms were spoken in succession and were understood only in the course of being spoken, it came to be believed that the affections of the soul they represented had the same succession. But that's not true. The state of mind is one thing, the account of it that we render to ourselves or someone else is another; the total and instantaneous sensation of this state is one thing, another the successive and detailed attention that we are forced to give it in order to analyze it, state it, and make ourselves understood. Our mind is a 'tableau' in motion after which we incessantly paint: we use lots of time to render it faithfully; but it exists as an integral whole and all at once; the mind does not go step by numbered step like the expression. The brush completes only in the course of time what the eye of the painter grasps in an instant. The formation of languages demanded decomposition; but to *see* an object, to *consider* it beautiful, to *feel* an agreeable sensation, to *desire* having it, that's the state of mind of an instant, and Greek and Latin render it in a single word. Ah! Monsieur, how much our understanding is modified by signs; how much even the liveliest diction is a cold copy of what goes on in it.

Here the word state of mind occurs no less than three times to link the indivisible suddenness of a thought with the synthesis of the painter's finished 'tableau', and it is again recalled that we encounter this synthesis in the inflected Latin and Greek. Diderot also used the term *état de l'âme* in *Essais sur la Peinture* and in *Salon de 1767*. It was this concept and term that the editor of Humboldt's 'Essais aesthétiques' took to be Humboldt's especially prescient anticipation of Baudelaire and the symbolists.

Furthermore, in this passage we also meet the idea of the mind as a 'tableau' in motion which as we have seen, Humboldt used in the fragments he wrote within a few years of having read Diderot. In those fragments, he also used the closely related concept of the hieroglyph, and to this Diderot comes a few pages later, still on the same subject but now writing about poetry:

There is in the discourse of the poet a spirit that gives motion and life to every syllable. What is this spirit? I have sometimes felt its presence; but all that I know about it is, that it is it that causes things to be said all at once; that in the very moment they are grasped by the understanding, the soul is moved by them, the imagination sees them, and the ear hears them; and that the discourse is not merely an enchainment of energetic terms that

art as mensonge, fable
in Diderot

reveal the thought with force and elevation, but is even more a web of
hieroglyphs accumulated one after the other and painting the thought.

From then on in the *Letter* Diderot often discusses the nature and
effect of this poetic hieroglyph, with the use of that word. Since it
is made possible by inflectional endings in the languages we know,
it is especially prominent in Latin and Greek (though he also finds
it in Italian and English by contrast to French), and it serves best
to express imagination and passion. They are therefore the languages
'of fiction and of the untruth' – 'de la fable et du mensonge'. This
notion of the lie or untruth occurs elsewhere in Diderot to underscore
that art is not imitation but expression of the 'ideal model' in the
artist's mind, which creates something that never was or is, something
that is not real in any normal sense – we shall soon return to that.
French, on the other hand, has become a language of instruction, an
analytical language that is best for science and philosophy because
it has moved toward the prose end of the spectrum. For this reason
it has lost warmth, eloquence, and energy ('de la chaleur, de
l'éloquence, et de l'énergie'). There are more thousands of people
who understand a geometer than a poet.

Hieroglyphs are products of the first ages of language, like the
eager stuttering of a child in the first exuberant moments of
language. Later they are created only by poets of genius, and that
is why Virgil says, according to Diderot, that it is as difficult to steal
a verse from Homer as to tear out a spike from Hercules' club, for
'the more a poet is charged with hieroglyphs, the more difficult he
is to render in translation; and Homer's verse abounds in them'.
Since the Greeks had no tradition, their language was fresh, without
dissimulation and alienation. They had not the baggage of the *ergon*
that hinders the free exercise of *energeia*. With no art to imitate, he
wrote in the *Salon de 1767*, it was easier for them to conceive 'the ideal
model of beauty, the true line, which degenerates and is lost so that
a nation can perhaps never recover it except by a return to the state
of barbarousness'. For the ancients, language 'was an instrument
with a thousand strings under the fingers of genius'. Both Diderot
and Humboldt naturally gravitated toward admiration for Greek,
with the climax in Homer, and toward musical analogues for
language, though Diderot much more often than Humboldt.

I hope I have shown that Diderot's conception of the nature of
language and its formation was aesthetic; language is the archetypical form of artistic creation. This conception is brought out by the
concepts of the hieroglyph; of the 'tableau'; of poetry as the original
and still, at its best, most truthful language; and in the admiration

for Homer. Each genius has a distinct individuality, a particular energy that produces the character of the creation of each genius, hence the diversity of their productions. Diderot wrote in the *Essais sur la Peinture* that 'in every part of the world, each country; in the same country, each province; in a province, each town; in a town, each family; in a family, each individual; in an individual, each moment has its physiognomy, its expression'. A few pages later he wrote, that 'in society, every order of citizens has its character and its expression: the artisan, the noble, the common citizen, the man of letters, the ecclesiastics, the magistrate, the military man'. These ideas are, of course, also prominent in Humboldt, who commented 'an exceptional piece', when he first read Diderot's *Satire première sur les caractères et les mots de caractère, de profession, etc.*, which, as the title tells, is precisely about this kind of diversity and individuality. It is no wonder that Humboldt quickly absorbed Diderot's aesthetics, first in the French essay on imagination, then in a letter he wrote to Schiller in September of 1800, and soon after in the fragments. His use of the terms *état de l'âme*, 'tableau', 'Bild', and hieroglyph as well as the conceptual schemes in which these terms occur, testify to that absorption. The debt is also evident in his adoption of the concept of the ideal model.

Diderot's conception of the expressive, non-imitative nature of art is summed up in the term 'ideal model', which he first used toward the end of the *Discours de la Poésie dramatique* and later developed in the magnificent letter to Grimm that opens the *Salon de 1767*. In this letter Diderot refutes the notion that the artist imitates or copies a norm of nature, 'la belle nature', for it nowhere exists for the artist merely to see. Nature is raw, sometimes beautiful but at other times ugly, imperfect, and without evident beauty. It is absurd, therefore, to think that the artist can from such particulars compose the form and beauty of the work of art, which thus cannot be an imitation. Art is expression and the artist works from the ideal model that exists nowhere but in the artist's mind; it is the synthetic, unpremeditated creation of the imagination. The artist does not make something that is nor even something that might be in what we call reality. True genius transcends tradition, but its work is all the same an expression of the culture and nation to which it belongs. The Greeks were fortunate because they had no tradition, no models, but were forced to seek inspiration directly in nature. As with language, our inheritance can be an obstacle to true creation. Like true genius today, the ancients were endowed 'with an exquisite tact, a taste, an instinct, a sort of inspiration given to exceptional geniuses'.

Diderot says that what he has argued is true of 'the human mind in all its researches', or, in other words, that without the mind's and imagination's original synthesis, nothing will ever happen. In a wonderful passage in the article 'Encyclopédie' (in the *Encyclopédie*), Diderot says that if man or the thinking, self-aware, and contemplative being were banished from the earth, the universe would fall silent and mute, for it is only our presence that makes the existence of beings interesting. The same idea occurs in another form in the *Letter on the Deaf-Mutes*, where he says that a person looking at a painting is like a deaf person observing mutes who are conversing on the same subjects as the spectator. This means that nature like art is our creation; understanding occurs thanks to the reciprocating imaginations of maker and spectator. For this reason, says Diderot in that article, the editors had decided to place man at the center of the *Encyclopédie*. Thus, since for Diderot language is the archetypical human creation, it occupies the same position between subjective being and objective existence as it came to occupy in Humboldt.

Humboldt quickly absorbed these ideas after reading Diderot, and this absorption occurred at the very time when language for him became a problem in aesthetics. In the fragments he wrote that after studying a language for a while, one gains 'a tact [his word] not so much for ferreting out what one has not yet actually learned, but for having a sure presentiment of it'. This use of the word 'tact', sometimes combined with 'instinct', occurs often in Diderot as well as in Humboldt. In a work published in 1816, but probably written earlier, Humboldt wrote that if one were to speculate on the human formation of a word, 'then it would appear like the formation of an ideal form ['einer idealen Gestalt'] in the imagination of the artist. This form also cannot be drawn from anything in reality; it arises from a pure energy of the mind, and in the true sense from nothing.' Here Humboldt is repeating Diderot's insistence on the unreality of art. In 1812 Humboldt wrote that the 'organization of languages is not purely mechanical... In this respect they resemble works of art and are open to an ideal beauty... All ideal beauty rests firmly on a strongly expressed individuality', that is, on genius. What Diderot's ideal model is for the artist, the inner form of language is for the speaker and hearer. The painter's ideal model finds expression in the design of the first sketch, which by fixing the form, like articulation in language, determines the success of the work of art. In the *Critique of Judgment* (par. 14), Kant made the same point as Diderot about the priority of design and form.

In Diderot's aesthetic of art and language and of language as art, Humboldt found ready made the conceptions he made his own. The problem of inversion dissolved the sign-doctrine of universal grammar, and by putting the creativity of language into particularly sharp focus it revealed not only the insufficiency and even inability of the prose language we now have to express the energy of the mind, but also the privacy of language. This realization explains Diderot's ever-present sense of the radical insufficiency of our words, which corresponds to what has been called the anti-semiotic quality in Humboldt's thought. This sense is also found in Condillac's *Essay* and still more evidently in his later writings; Diderot was not correcting Condillac but extending his thought. Condillac was not locating the essence of language at the far prose-end of the spectrum, even though this was the end that was most relevant to his interest in the cognitive aspects of language; also for him the basic nature of language was best revealed in m-one and the early stages of s-two. That Cassirer got all this wrong is no reason why we should not try to get it right.

Diderot brought these problems to the foreground by projecting his 'tableau', hieroglyph, and state of mind onto the contrast between simultaneity and successivity, which recapitulates the opposition between poetry and prose as well as between m-one and s-two. In both art and language synthesis is the work of genius and imagination. The energetic imagination speaks more fruitfully than our pedestrian everyday language and the dry, intellectual discourse of science and philosophy. This is the thought that inspired Humboldt when he read Diderot. Not even by the wildest stretch of speculation can Humboldt's linguistic thought be derived from Kant or be claimed to constitute a reversal of what he read in Condillac, Garat, Degérando, and Diderot.

It is by now obvious why the heavily inflected Sanscrit must be Humboldt's most perfect linguistic form. It gives the best expression in roots to the concepts and ideas that relate to life and reality, and by means of its rich inflections it ensures the word-unity and sentence-fixity that create a maximum of imaginative synthesis. The perfection of language lies in 'the combination of the sound-form with the inner laws of language', and the greatest perfection rests,

on the fact that this combination, proceeding always in simultaneous acts of the language-making spirit, becomes a true and pure permeation. From the first elements onward, the production of language is a synthetic procedure, and that in the truest sense of the word, where synthesis creates something that does not lie, *per se*, in any of the conjoined parts. The goal is therefore reached only when the total structure of sound-form and inner shaping are fused together with equal firmness and simultaneity' (88).

In the *Lettre à Abel-Rémusat*, Humboldt explained that this is the effect that Chinese cannot produce; it cannot create what he in that French text called the 'tableau'. Soon after the passage just quoted from our text, Humboldt continued: 'Language in general is often reminiscent of art...The true synthesis springs from the inspiration known only to high and energetic power. In the imperfect one, this inspiration has been lacking; and a language so engendered likewise exerts a less inspiring power in its use.' Just as there are inferior artists, there are also inferior languages. It was to this unabashedly deprecatory evaluation of all the non-Indo-European languages that Humboldt's American correspondents, John Pickering and Peter Duponceau, objected so strenuously when they met it in an academy lecture Humboldt gave in 1822 'On the Formation of grammatical Forms and their Influence on the Development of Ideas'.

[margin handwriting: P. 217 / he is / abashed, / Though']

In this lecture Humboldt had advanced the same argument as in our text about the superiority of inflected languages with their 'genuine grammatical forms' by contrast to languages, including American-Indian languages, that did not have such forms. By the time the lecture was published he was in correspondence with John Pickering and Peter Duponceau, who both were already deeply engaged in the study of the Indian languages of the eastern United States. This study was promoted by the American Philosophical Society in Philadelphia, of which Destutt de Tracy and later also Humboldt were foreign members. From Philadelphia Humboldt received publications that were important to him on those languages, and he in turn sent his own publications, e.g., the *Lettre à Abel-Rémusat*. Both in their letters and in publications that Humboldt saw, the two Americans took him severely to task for his evaluation of languages by the yardstick of the inflected Latin, Greek, and Sanscrit. It is against this criticism that Humboldt tried to defend himself in our text (217–19) with the claim that 'any impartial scholar' could hardly dispute that the structure 'is more excellent in the Sanscrit than in Chinese, and in Greek than in Arabic', for 'however we might try to weigh off their respective virtues, we should always have to admit that one of these languages is animated by a more fruitful principle of mental development than the other'. He felt that his approach to these problems was perfectly justified. It is a curious defence, and it is hard to find it convincing. Since the argument of his entire philosophy claimed that the linguistic diversity and quality of each language flowed from the mental energy poured into its formation at the beginning, it is evident that the evaluation of languages by the yardstick of the most perfect form he found in the inflected Sanscrit was also an evaluation of the unequal mental

"languages are objects of nature"

See p. 265 where Humboldt admits this

capacities of the nations who had had the misfortune not to be Indo-European.

Pickering and Duponceau were not persuaded by his answers. They found that Humboldt displayed the 'pride of civilization' which found justification in principles of universal grammar that were based on a few European and Oriental languages. He was putting *a priori* theory before the facts. Humboldt assured Duponceau that he regarded 'languages as objects of nature, and I strive to judge them with perfect impartiality'. All the same, in that letter he also wrote that 'the grammatical forms [of American-Indian languages] do not carry the free imprint of every material idea, the absolute fixity [la fixité absolue], and the character that immediately indicates to the ear that the thing presents itself with several relations, such as we find in the Greek and Sancrit languages.'* Does that carry conviction?

The two Americans were not wrong when they found the source of Humboldt's linguistic absolutism in his attachment to universal grammar. Already before the controversy began, Humboldt had told Pickering that each language must of necessity have something that corresponds more or less precisely to the forms of universal grammar, such as 'substantives, adjectives, verbs, etc.', in order to form the phrases of discourse. When Pickering later objected that saying that a language is imperfect, is the same as saying that 'the nation that speaks it has not attained a certain degree of civilization', Humboldt answered that on that very point he felt he had made important observations that had not been seen in their true light, for he believed both that the intellectual faculties that contribute to the invention and perfecting of language are very different in different nations and that no matter how great the influence of culture and civilization later were on such a language, it would never be able to change its original quality. That surely is discouraging news for the nation that is told it has an inferior language, and it does not help when Humboldt explains that 'whether a nation is or is not endowed with the fine and delicate tact [ce tact fin et délicat], with the intellectual instinct (if the expression may be permitted), with the fortunate collaboration of mind, imagination and ear..., that is something that depends entirely on its particular organization, almost as some nations evidently have greater genius than others for painting, music, etc.' His justification was the application of the aesthetics of language.

---

* I am grateful for permission to quote from the Duponceau Papers, American Philosophical Society Library, Philadelphia, Pennsylvania.

The most surprising effort to meet their objections came in a letter to Pickering in 1831 and is directed to something Duponceau had said in print to the effect that, judging by the 'genuine grammatical forms' of the inflected Latin and Greek, Humboldt had assigned the Indian languages to 'an inferior rank in the scale of languages considered in the point of view of their capacity to aid the development of ideas'. Humboldt answered that he had never either thought or wished to say that languages of savage nations were inferior to those of civilized nations, but that he had spoken of the structure that is imposed on languages at their very beginning. Then came this murky argument:

This structure dates necessarily from the beginning of the social state which cannot be a state of civilization, because civilization is acquired only successively and slowly. The Greek and Sanscrit languages, whose grammatical form I admire, have consequently and with the same forms been languages of savage nations (if one can use that term), just like Basque and the American languages, and it is not at all from civilization that I derive their advantages. What I have tried to say and still believe to be true is that the grammatical form of Sanscrit, from which all the European languages derive, is preferable for giving the mind the habit of methodical reasoning and for the development of all the intellectual forms of man. Civilization adds very little to that.

Surely, this is worse than no answer at all. Since he had argued at length in his writings that s-two depends on m-one, it will not get him off the hook to say that since he placed the crucial source of diversity in m-one, he has offered no disparaging implications about civilization in s-two. His words also flatly contradict an argument that was important to him, namely that what he considered a more advanced form of language was not necessarily a later formation from a simpler one; the form of Sanscrit might be as old as that of Chinese.

Pickering and Duponceau never gave in; in plain terms their objection was that Humboldt's linguistic thought was racist, an idea that must surely also occur to today's readers. His argument was not merely excessively Indo-European and Europo-centric; it was determined by his inflexible demand that the forms of thought found in universal grammar must be the criterion of linguistic merit. A recent German collection of Humboldt texts that includes the lecture in question has an editorial note that, without mention of the two Americans and their criticism, says there is no foundation for attributing crypto-racism to Humboldt. But, surely, one does not need to have read Pickering and Duponceau to find that statement hard to understand and accept.

There is another aspect of Humboldt's relationship with the two Americans that is instructive. They disagreed with Humboldt's linguistic evaluations precisely because they shared the same conceptions and expectations of language study and, like him, were engaged in the study of non-European languages. Both were well informed about the background of their linguistic thought, especially Duponceau who in his youth had been secretary to Court de Gébelin before coming to America when he was not yet twenty years old. He was one of the important linguists of the nineteenth century, and like Humboldt, he had close contacts with Abel-Rémusat in Paris. In 1835 he was awarded the Volney prize of the Institut de France for a work on the grammatical system of Indian languages in North America.

Duponceau saw his work in the French tradition of language study: Condillac, Maupertuis, de Brosses, and Destutt de Tracy. He cited Maupertuis because he (around 1750 and after reading Condillac's *Essay*) had called for innovation in language study beyond the familiar European languages by showing 'the necessity of studying the languages even of the most distant and barbarous nations, "because," he said, "we may chance to find some that are formed on *new plans of ideas*"'. In the passage in question, Maupertuis had said that some distant languages seem to be formed on 'plans of ideas so different from ours that one can hardly translate into ours what has once been expressed in those languages'. More recently it has, with good reason, been suggested that Maupertuis' plan of ideas corresponds to Humboldt's inner form. Duponceau cited Destutt de Tracy's *Éléments d'idéologie* as a significant work in language study, and he divided language study in the three branches of 'phonology', 'etymology', and 'ideology'. By ideology Duponceau meant 'the comparative study of the grammatical forms and idiomatic construction of languages, by which we are taught to analyze and distinguish the different shapes in which ideas combine themselves in order to fix perceptions in our minds, and transmit them to others; while we observe with wonder the effects of that tendency to order and method and that natural logic which God has implanted in the mind of every man'. Those words describe what was also Humboldt's enterprise. Both Pickering and Duponceau said that what in particular characterized a language was its 'organisation', the word then used both in French and English for what is also called the 'organism' of language. As we have already seen, when Humboldt wrote in French he used the word 'organisation'. This conception is not a German invention.

In connection with Degérando we have noted the new historical orientation that was a consequence of Condillac's thought. We find it also in Duponceau, who wrote that the 'study of the forms of language initiates us into the most hidden mysteries of the human understanding. It is the foundation of all philosophy'. To make sure we did not miss it, he wrote on the same page, that 'the science of languages is the history of the progress and evolution of the human mind; in each epoch the trained eye sees in it, as in a mirror, the arts, the sciences, the knowledge and even, to a certain degree, the customs, usages and manners that existed in the earliest epochs'. As with the concept of organisation, this is revealing, for though neither Pickering nor Duponceau were the beneficiaries of German philosophy and linguistic thought, they shared the fundamental conceptions which in Humboldt have been credited to an exclusively German movement or 'Deutsche Bewegung'. This philosophy was French.

Once Humboldt had overcome his initial misreading of Condillac, he found this philosophy confirmed in Garat, Degérando, and not least in Diderot, who in his discussion of inversion had advanced the aesthetic conception of language that Humboldt made his own. The nomenclatural sign-doctrine of the universal-grammar tradition had already been exploded when Humboldt turned his attention to language. Language is a human creation and for that reason it is constituent of thought; it is the organ of thought. We can call to mind the basic conceptions and their interrelations by contemplating these two strings of terms: Simultaneity, poetry, expression, passion and feeling, imagination, synthesis, warmth, and energy; and by contrast this string: successivity, prose, imitation, reason and understanding, science and philosophy, analysis, discursivity, and light. These two strings define the contrast between m-one and the early stages of s-two on the one hand and on the other the late stages of s-two. Since the movement toward prose is irreversible, the slackness it may cause can now be overcome only by art and energy. Good poetry recaptures the early state of language. Humboldt found this ideal in the Indo-European Sanscrit, which thanks to its battery of inflections was naturally capable of producing the fixity and synthesis that create an instantaneous 'tableau'. Sanscrit of course was not our language, but it was a warming thought that the modern languages of western Europe belonged to the same staunch and sturdy race. The rest of the world was less fortunate.

Translator's note

The aim of this translation is to provide a plain unvarnished text of the 'Introduction' prefixed to von Humboldt's posthumous treatise, *Über die Kawi-Sprache auf der Insel Java*, which was published in three volumes, from 1836 to 1839. The *Introduction* also appeared separately in 1836. A facsimile of the latter volume was reissued in 1960 by Dümmler, the original publishers, to mark the 125th anniversary of the author's death, and it is this reprint which has been followed, with virtually no modification, in preparing the present text. Since the modern reader is presumably more interested in von Humboldt's speculative arguments than in the evidential detail he offers in their support, there has seemed no point in meddling with that evidence, or in trying to improve on it by amendment or annotation. However antiquated or questionable the author's premises, they are still premises on which his arguments have to rely. For much the same reasons, no attempt has been made to up-date von Humboldt's archaic technical vocabulary, or to bring it into line with more modern usage. His improvized terms are therefore reproduced much as they stand, in the belief that this is still probably the best way of preserving the style and substance of his reasoning, for both linguist and layman alike.

In this respect the present translation differs on principle from its only predecessor in English, the version published in 1971 by a pair of American philologists, George C. Buck and Frithjof A. Raven, under the title *Linguistic Variability and Intellectual Development*. As professional linguists, they saw fit to employ a modernized terminology, to provide annotations, and even to make minor changes in the arrangement of the text. Warranted or no, such refinements do not suffice, unfortunately, to save a translation which fails in so many places to decipher the author's syntax, and comes so regularly to grief in the endeavour to extract a meaning from his admittedly Delphic prose. By their own confession, Messrs Buck and Raven, like other lost explorers, were frequently a prey to despair. Nevertheless, and for all its imperfections, the present translator is very much indebted to their work. Without it, he would undoubtedly have gone astray more often than he has, and even its errors have at times been helpful, in directing him unwittingly to a better rendering than he could easily have found for himself. In his choice of terminology he has sought throughout for solutions appropriate to their context, rather than aiming at a consistency that could only lead to awkward and artificial results. But since not every reader may be willing to accept such decisions on trust, a selection of the vaguer terms, with their various English equivalents, is given in the Glossary that follows.

It remains only to thank Eusebia Shifflett, Anne Cox and Christopher Propert, for their diligence and skill in typing the manuscript; and Professor Hans Aarsleff, not only for his Introduction, but also for timely and profitable advice.

University of Virginia   P.H.

Glossary

Abwechslung: variation
Anbildung: accretion
Andeutung: indication, reference
Anfügung: addition
Anschauung: intuition
Bedeutung: meaning, significance
Begriff: concept, notion
Beschaffenheit: nature, constitution, make-up
Bestimmung: determination, definition
Bezeichnung: designation
Beziehung: relation
Bildung: formation, creation, cultivation
Eigenheit, Eigenthümlichkeit: individuality, peculiarity, particularity, characteristic, idiosyncrasy
Einbildungskraft: imagination
Einverleibung: incorporation, embedding
Einzel-, Einzelheit: detail, particular
Empfänglichkeit: receptivity, sensibility
Empfindung: feeling
Entwicklung: development, evolution
Erzeugung: production, generation
Formbildung: form-creation
Gattung: class, kind, species
Geist: mind, spirit
Geisteskraft, -thätigkeit: mental power, activity
Gemüth, Gemüthsbestimmung: mind, soul, disposition, frame of mind, temper
Gesetzmässigkeit: regularity, order
Gestaltung: shaping, conformation
Innere Sprachform: inner speech-form, linguistic form
Lautform, -neigung, -umformung, veränderung: sound-form, -tendency, modification, -change
Redefügung: word-order, construction
Satz: sentence, period, clause
Schaffen: creation, fashioning
Selbstthätigkeit: spontaneity
Setzung: positing
Sprachbau, -bildung: language-structure, -making
Sprachsinn: sense of language, linguistic sense

lxviii

Stamm: family, tribe, race, stem
Stimmung: mood, modulation, temper
Übereinstimmung: agreement, conformity, congruence, concordance
Unterscheidung: distinction, difference
Verbindung: combination, bonding
Verknüpfung: connection, coupling, linkage
Verschiedenheit: diversity, difference
Verwandlung: transformation, conversion
Verwandtschaft: affinity, kinship, relationship
Vorstellung: idea
Wirksamkeit: efficacy
Zergliederung: analysis, division
Zusammenfassung: synthesis, conjunction
Zusammenhang: connection, coherence
Zusammensetzung: compound, compounding
Zusatz: addition, appendage, supplement
Zuwachs: increment

THE DIVERSITY OF
HUMAN LANGUAGE-STRUCTURE
AND ITS INFLUENCE ON
THE MENTAL DEVELOPMENT
OF MANKIND

Preface

ALEXANDER VON HUMBOLDT

I have a sad and serious duty to perform. With the publication of this work from my brother's literary remains, scarcely a year after his passing, I must say a few words about its preparation and plan. Given the direction of my own studies, it would betray a blithe self-assurance, were I to do more here than touch upon its outward form, and ventured to follow the deceased on the road he has travelled, into the uncharted realm of language.

The work appears, indeed, in a self-contained form; but in certain portions it would assuredly still have undergone much change and greater elaboration at the author's own hand. For the *Introduction*, which traces the influence of language on the mental evolution of mankind, he envisaged many additions, that were referred to in enlivening conversations, but not written down. Only the printing of the whole *first* book was seen to by my brother himself; the most searching revision of the manuscript, and the publication of the whole work in its present form, are due, however, to the diligence and learning of a young scholar, who for many years has repaid an honorable trust with the most loyal devotion. Dr Buschmann, Curator at the Royal Library, was recommended to the deceased by a dear friend, Professor Bopp; his versatility of knowledge, and enthusiasm for the languages of South-East Asia, have especially equipped him to provide such aid.

The *second* book, to be preceded by the part that follows, depicts the grammatical structure of the Kawi language, evolved from the *Brata Yuddha* epic, in continuous comparison with all other known Malayan and South Sea languages. In the *third* book, the character of each of these idioms is set forth in detail, especially that of the Madecassian, Tagalic, Tongan, Tahitian and New Zealand languages. The ties among the peoples of that great world of islands, and their diffusion from a common centre, proclaimed by such various analogies, lead the investigation back in a remarkable fashion, though only in a few details, to the solid ground of Sanscrit. Since, shortly before his death, my brother had received new and important materials from Mr Crawfurd in London, he has incorporated supplements to some passages on language in the first book into the volumes that follow.

Among the foreign scholars whose communications have particularly enriched this work, pride of place must go to the talented author

3

of the *History of the Indian Archipelago,* and the *Embassy to the Court of Ava,* Mr John Crawfurd, who, from the great store of his collection of writings in Malayan languages, made freely available to my late brother three manuscript Javanese dictionaries and a handwritten Javanese grammar, as well as a copy of the aforementioned Kawi epic. In view of the inadequacy of all published guidance, it would have been impossible, without this information, to gain a full mastery of Javanese and the Kawi language in all their peculiarities. Mr Crawfurd, whose personal acquaintance I first came to enjoy in Paris, will assuredly accept this expression of gratitude from both brothers with the same goodwill which led him to provide such important materials, collected entirely by his own industry, for profitable use.

In everything to do with the philosophy of language-study, or the organism of Sanscrit in particular, my brother continued until his death to rely on the counsel of one who was bound to him by ties of long-standing friendship and mutual respect, and who by acumen and tireless activity has come to exert an ever-increasing influence on the course of comparative general linguistics. Professor Bopp received from the departed every completed sheet of the first volume, with a request for severe criticism. A public expression of thanks is due here to the intellectual stimulus afforded by such a friend.

If it was granted to my lamented brother, by the power of his intelligence no less than by the strength of his will, by the favour of outward circumstances, and by studies which his frequent changes of residence and public mode of life were unable to interrupt, to penetrate deeper into the structure of a larger number of languages than have probably yet been encompassed by any *single* mind, we may doubly rejoice at finding the last, I might well say the highest, results of these researches, which cover the whole domain of language, unfolded in the *Introduction* to the present work. I would need almost to traverse the entire circle of my brother's scientific connections, forged on his travels in Germany, England, France, Italy and Spain, were I to name all those persons who have helped him in these general inquiries, and in founding the great linguistic collection which has been deposited, by his bequest, in the Royal Library. Many of his general views, as they gradually came to him, were submitted to the scrutiny of able and learned linguists with whom he kept in correspondence: A. W. von Schlegel, Gottfried Hermann, brought close to him by his translation (amid the turmoils of war) of Aeschylus' *Agamemnon,* Silvestre de Sacy, Gesenius, Burnouf, Thiersch, Lassen, Du Ponceau in Philadelphia, John Pickering in Salem, Rosen in London, P. von Bohlen in Königsberg, Stenzler in Breslau, Pott in Halle, Lepsius in Rome, Neumann in Munich,

Kosegarten, the Egyptian traveller G. Parthey, Champollion, Abel-Rémusat, Klaproth and Friedrich Eduard Schulz, who met his death in the East, in an enterprise of renown. The pages that follow bear witness to my brother's indebtedness to that profound scholar of the whole of classical antiquity, our friend August Böckh, and especially to his profitable researches into general metrics and the many-sided influence of tribal differences among the Hellenes.

Confining myself to the narrower cycle of the languages that are analysed individually in the work itself, I list in gratitude, for Javanese, Baron van der Capellen, former Governor-General of the Dutch possessions in India; the Earl of Minto, from whom my brother obtained his cast of the great Javanese inscription, made famous by Raffles: Roorda van Eysinga, an expert linguist; and Herr Gericke in Batavia. For Malayan, the instructive correspondence with Sir Alexander Johnston; Dr William Marsden; and the learned M. Jacquet of Paris. For Madecassian, and the languages of the South Sea Islands, Mr Freeman, missionary at Antananarivo in Madagascar; Professor Meyen of Berlin; Dr Meinicke of Prenzlow; Lesson in Paris; and Adalbert von Chamisso, who with rejuvenated zeal is investigating the language of the Sandwich Islands, which he has himself, in earlier days, had the good fortune to visit.

Just as the languages of the Asiatic island world are dealt with in the work now presented, so the deceased, on the same principles, and in even greater detail, had made a study of the American languages, which occupied him most seriously for many years. A large amount of this preparatory work is suitable for publication; and I hope that Dr Buschmann, who himself has lived in a little-known part of New Spain, and with whom my brother had intended to publish in collaboration a series of studies on the languages of this part of the world, will soon find leisure, with the help of the materials already assembled, to execute this wide-ranging plan. The allusions in the present South Asiatic work to the linguistic wealth of America arouse the liveliest desire to see such important aids to a knowledge of the idioms of the new continent put to use by the friends of a general philosophical linguistics. According to my late brother's plan, a Mexican-Latin dictionary, together with a Grammar, will begin the new undertaking.

I cannot think of the Royal Library, so enriched of late by our sovereign's graciousness, in which the above-mentioned manuscripts are deposited for public use, without at the same time expressing – as if paying a legacy – my sincerest thanks to the Chief Librarian, Privy Councillor Wilken, esteemed alike as both linguist and historian, for the obliging kindness with which he has provided everything that could be needed for the preparation and publication of this work on language. The easy and constant use of a public collection was favoured by its close proximity to the charming country estate where the deceased, alone, with death approaching, amid the aroma of ancient art, lived only for his earnest studies, his grand recollections of a turbulent era, and a family to whom he clung with a gentle, loving heart until the hour of his death.

As has been said by one of the noblest of our age[1], 'It is a common prejudice to estimate a man's worth by the *matter* he deals with, not the *manner* in which he treats it.' But where, so to speak, the matter dominates and evokes the form, where grace of language emerges from the thought, as from the tenderest blossoms of the mind, it is easy to annul the separation which that prejudice implies. If all my hopes do not deceive me, the present work, in enlarging so mightily the circuit of ideas, and in teaching us to descry, as it were, in the organism of language the spiritual destiny of peoples, must fill the reader with an edifying faith that does honour to mankind. It must instil the conviction that a certain grandeur in the treatment of a subject arises, not from intellectual talents alone, but primarily from grandeur of character, from a free mind, forever unconfined by present concerns, and from unfathomed depths of the heart.

Berlin, March 1836.   ALEXANDER VON HUMBOLDT.

---

[1] Schiller, in the *Philosophische Briefen* (*Works*, XI, 336).

Note on transliteration of foreign alphabets

Method

whereby foreign alphabets are transliterated
in this work

After numerous attempts in this connection, I consider it impracticable to employ the same method of transcription everywhere, and believe it will serve the reader's convenience if, while following on the whole the best of what has already become accepted in these matters, I nevertheless forego systematic consistency in allowing myself such deviations as are appropriate to the material and purpose actually in hand. Thus in the present work I have always kept in mind that my main concern – and often in so many words – is with Javanese and Sanscrit writing, and with a topic predominantly dealt with by English authors. My object has therefore been to present the foreign alphabets in such a way that, with the adoption of a few rules created from the spelling of these languages, the reader should most unmistakably and definitely recognize therein the original foreign orthography, in the simplest and most uniform fashion, at every point where he encounters a word. For from this requirement, not the slightest relaxation can ever be permitted.

Words such as *Java, Sanscrit, pandit* and so on, which have already passed entirely into our own literary usage, I have neither changed in their spelling nor burdened with signs. I normally cite Sanscrit names and words in their basic form, and only by exception in the nominative, where there is particular reason to do so.

I

Sanscrit alphabet

The long vowels, and the diphthongs *e* and *o*, I designate with a circumflex;

the *r*-vowel (ऋ) by a dot under the *r* and an added *i* (*ṛi*);
the mute palatal consonant (च) by *ch*;
the sounded palatal consonant (ज) by *j*;
all lingual consonants by the corresponding dentals with a dot beneath;

the first semivowel (य) by *y*, the final semivowel (व) by *w*;

the palatal sibilant (श) by *s* with a *spiritus lenis* placed above it (ś);

the lingual sibilant (ष) by *sh*;

all aspirated consonants by the unaspirated ones with an added *h*;

the *anusvâra* and all nasal consonants, except dental *n* and *m*, by an *n* with a dot beneath (ṇ). A further distinction of these sounds is not needed, since according to the letter directly following, the reader knows which Sanscrit signs are to be put in place of the ṇ.

the *visarga* I designate by *h* with a dot beneath (ḥ). But it scarcely occurs, since where it appears in the nominative of Sanscrit words, this nominative is more correctly indicated by *s*.

2
Javanese alphabet

[Since there is virtually no reference to Javanese in von Humboldt's introductory volume, this section is omitted. -Tr.]

3
Malayan proper

Here I quite simply follow the orthography adopted by Marsden, and also retain his customary length-sign, such as the hyphenation over *ng* (*n͠g*), wherever he employs it.

4
Burmese

Of the vowels, I write the first six, the long and short *a*, *i* and *u*, as in Sanscrit;

the seventh as *e*;
the eighth as *ai*;
the ninth as *au*;
the tenth as *aû*;
and the triphthongs made up of *a*, *i* and *u* as *ô*.

The mute and sounded unaspirated letters of the five classes of consonants, I write exactly as in Sanscrit.

In the mute and sounded aspirates, I merely make the following change, that I do not write the *h* after the consonants, as in transcribing Sanscrit, but in front of them, i.e. *hk*, *hch*, *ht*, etc. This reversal, which is not in itself unnatural, by the way, since the consonant does not merely accept the aspiration, but is forced out along with it, has no other purpose here but to distinguish these letters from the thirtieth Burmese consonant. For the latter has just the sound of English *th*, and I would not therefore care to designate it in any other way.

The nasals of the first three classes, in addition to the *anusvâra*, could be indicated in Sanscrit by the same sign, since their usage is founded on specific rules. In Burmese, this is not the case. I therefore designate the guttural by a Spanish *n con tilde* (*ñ*), the palatal by *ng*, the nasals of the other three classes as in Sanscrit, and the *anusvâra* by *n* with a dot above it (*ṅ*).

The four semivowels are written as in Sanscrit, and the consonant following them with a *th*. In Burmese, this sound is one of the sibilants. The Burmese script has adopted no sibilants from the Sanscrit alphabet. But in the spoken language we find the lingual, the English *sh*. This is indicated in the script by an *h* appended to the first three semivowels and the *th*. This *h* I therefore prefix to these letters, so that *hy*, *hr*, *hl* and *hth* express the English *sh* of pronunciation. But with the *l* this pronunciation does not appear constant. For Hough writes the pronunciation of *hlyâ*, tongue, as *shyâ*, where for *hlê·*, to fly, he gives the pronunciation *hle·*.

For the thirty-first Burmese consonant I write *h*, as in Sanscrit.

The heavy accent I designate, as is the case in Burmese itself, by a double dot placed at the end of the words(:); the single dot indicating the light accent I put, not under the last letter, as is done in Burmese, but after it, about halfway up (*a·*).

5

In the other languages, which I cannot discuss here in detail, I employ the orthography adopted by the main writers on each of them, which normally follows that of their mother-tongue; so that in the North American, some Asiatic, and most South Sea languages, we must have regard to the English sound-system; in Chinese and Madecassian, to that of French; while in Tagalic and the languages of New Spain and South America, it is that of Spanish.

§1

If we consider their dwelling-places, their mode of government, their history, and above all their language, the peoples of *Malayan race*[1] stand in a stranger connection with races of different culture than perhaps any other people on earth. They inhabit merely islands and archipelagoes, which are spread so far and wide, however, as to furnish irrefutable testimony of their early skill as navigators. Their continental settlement on the Malacca peninsula is scarcely deserving of special mention here, since it occurred later and originates from Sumatra; and still less are we concerned here with the even more recent colonies on the coasts of the China Sea and the Gulf of Siam, in Champa.[2] But nowhere else, even in earliest antiquity, can we point with any certainty to Malayans on the mainland. If we now take together the members of these races who deserve to be called Malayan in the narrower sense, since by assured grammatical investigation they speak closely related and mutually explicable languages, we find these people, to name only points where the linguist encounters adequately studied material, on the Philippines, and there in the most richly developed and individual state of language, on Java, Sumatra, Malacca and Madagascar. But a large number of incontestable verbal affinities, and even the names of a significant number of islands, give evidence that the isles lying close to these points have the same population too, and that the *more strictly Malayan speech-community* extends over that whole area of the South Asiatic Ocean which runs southwards from the Philippines down to the western coasts of New Guinea, and then west about the island chains adjoining the eastern tip of Java, into the waters of Java and Sumatra, up to the strait of Malacca. It is regrettable only that the languages of the great islands of Borneo and Celebes, of which the foregoing is probably no less true, do not yet permit of proper grammatical assessment.

East of the narrower Malayan community here delineated, from New Zealand to Easter Island, from there northwards to the

---

[1] I include under this name, along with the population of Malacca, the inhabitants of all the islands of the great southern ocean, whose languages belong to one and the same stock with that called Malayan in the narrower sense, on Malacca. On the pronunciation of the name, see Bk I, p. 12, n. 2.

[2] The name of this district, which is very variously written, is found in the above spelling in the Burmese language. See Judson's *Lexicon*, s.v.

Sandwich Islands, and again west to the Philippines, there dwells an island population betraying the most unmistakeable marks of ancient blood-relationship with the Malayan races. The languages, of which we also have an exact grammatical knowledge of those spoken in New Zealand, Tahiti, the Sandwich Islands and Tonga, prove the same thing, by a large number of similar words and essential agreements in organic structure. The same likeness occurs in customs and usages, especially insofar as the Malayan element can be detected pure and unaffected by Indian ways. How far the races living to the northwest in this part of the ocean are mainly or wholly affiliated to the rest of this section, or to the Malayan in the narrower sense, or form a connecting link between the two, can not yet be decided on the materials presently available, since even the investigations made on the language of the Mariana Islands have still not been given to the public. Now all these peoples possess such social arrangements that it would be wrong to exclude them entirely from the comity of civilized nations. They have a firmly-based, and by no means entirely simple, political system, religious precepts and practices, in part even a sort of spiritual government, show skill in a variety of handicrafts and are bold and handy seafarers. In many places we find among them fragments of a sacred language now unintelligible even to themselves, and the custom, on certain occasions, of ceremonially reviving antiquated expressions is evidence, not only of the wealth, age and depth of the language, but also of attention to the changing designation of objects over time. But with this they tolerated among themselves, and in part still tolerate, barbaric customs incompatible with human civilized behaviour, seem never to have attained to the possession of writing, and thus forego all the cultivation dependent on this, though they are equally not lacking in pregnant sagas, penetrating eloquence, and poetry in markedly different styles. Their languages have in no wise arisen from a corruption and transformation of Malayan of the narrower order – it is far easier to believe that we see in them a more formless and original state thereof.

Besides the peoples here mentioned, in the two divisions aforesaid of the great southern archipelago, we meet on some islands of it with men who, to all appearance, must be assigned to a wholly different race. Both the Malayans in the narrower sense, and the more easterly inhabitants of the South Sea, belong undoubtedly to the same race of men, and constitute, if we enter more accurately into colour-differences, the more or less light-brown among whites in general. The tribes we now speak of approximate, on the other hand, by blackness of skin, a partly woolly curliness of hair, and quite individual facial features and body shape, to the African Negroes, although by the most credible evidences they are still in turn utterly and essentially different from the latter and can by no means be accounted a single race with them[3] In distinction from the African Negroes, they are sometimes called Negritos, by writers on these parts, and sometimes Austral Negroes, and are few in numbers. On islands, such as the Philippines, that are simultaneously inhabited by Malayan peoples, they commonly keep to the centre of the islands, upon inaccessible highlands, to which they seem to have been gradually driven back by the more numerous and predominantly white population. But in this respect they must be carefully distinguished from the Haraforas[4] or Alfuris, and the Turajas[5] in Celebes, who are to be found in Borneo, Celebes, the Moluccas, Mindanao and some other islands. These seem equally to have been driven back by their neighbours, but belong to the light-brown races, and Marsden actually attributes their eviction from the coasts to Mohammedan persecution. In savagery they approximate to the black race, and are always a population standing on a different level of culture. Other islands, some large, such as New Guinea, New Britain and New Ireland, and some of the New Hebrides, are peopled solely by these negroid stocks, and the inhabitants of the great continent of New Holland and Van Diemen's Land, so far as there has hitherto been opportunity to gain acquaintance with them, belong to the same race. But although this race, in its three habitations here described, bears general indications of resemblance and affinity, it is still far from having been adequately established, as to what extent essential racial differences may also exist within it. Their languages, that is, have as yet by no means been examined in a manner that could satisfy a thorough linguistic research. For the assessment of the organic and grammatical structure we have merely the materials collected, by the missionary Threlkeld, from a tribe in New South Wales. This race is everywhere marked off from those of lighter colour by a greater savagery and lack of culture, and the variations in this respect are doubtless due solely to closer or remoter contacts with strains of the latter. The inhabitants of New Holland and Van Diemen's Land appear to stand at the lowest level of culture which man has yet reached anywhere on earth. It is a strange phenomenon to encounter the light and dark races side by side again,

[3] On the shades of colour, cf. Klaproth: *Nouv. Journ. Asiat,* XII, 240.
[4] *Marsden's Miscell. Works* pp. 47–50.
[5] This name has such a Sanscrit form and ring that one cannot refrain from considering it a designation given by people left uncultivated by educated Malayan stocks. This very fact may well point to a much earlier separation of this two-fold population.

even on the Malacca peninsula. For the Semang, who inhabit a part of the mountains there, are, on quite irrefutable evidence, a woolly-haired negrito people. Since these latter are to be found on this one point of the Asiatic mainland[6] they have incontestably migrated thither only in recent times. Of the lighter race also, as the obviously Malayan *oran benūa, peoples of the country*, seems to prove,[7] there has doubtless been more than one migration. Both occurrences therefore demonstrate only that the same local conditions at different times produce the same historical effects, and have to that extent nothing striking about them. But in regard to the cultural state of the various peoples of this island sea, the explanation via migration thither becomes precarious. For enterprising nations, the sea, indeed, has the power of easily connecting, rather than cleaving asunder, and the ubiquity of the active, seamanlike Malayans can in this way be explained by voyages from island to island, sometimes deliberately with support, sometimes swept along by the power of the prevailing winds. For this activity, adroitness and seamanship are characteristic, not merely of the Malayans proper, but of more or less all the light-brown population. I need only refer here to the Bugis on Celebes, and to the South Sea islanders. But if the same explanation is to hold of the negritos and their dispersal from New Holland to the Philippines, and from New Guinea to the Andaman islands, these peoples must have sunk further than can be accepted in declining from a civilized state and reverting to savagery. Their condition today is far more favourable to the intrinsically not improbable hypothesis, that by natural revolutions, to which age-old sagas on Java still allude, a populated continent was split up into the present mass of islands. So far as human nature is able to survive such changes, these men could then have remained behind, like debris, on the splintered island-fragments. Only in combination, perhaps, can these two types of explanation do some sort of justice to the distribution of these two races, which now seem so different to us, even if the fragmentation by natural forces and the bonding by human migrations should have been thousands of years apart.

Tanna, one of the Hebrides, whose name, however, is of Malayan origin,[8] New Caledonia, Timor, Endeh (Flores) and some other

---

[6] Klaproth has proved with thoroughness and learning the wrongness of the claim that there are black races on the Kuen-lun mountains below the 35th parallel N., dividing Tibet from Little Bokhara, and on the hills between Annam and Cambodia. *Nouv. Journ. Asiat.* XII, 232–43.

[7] *Marsden's Miscell. Works* p. 75. Raffles *On the Malayu Nation* in the *Asiat. Rev.*, XII, 108–10.

[8] *Tānah* means, in the Malaysian language proper, land, earth, soil.

islands have a population of which research leaves it doubtful whether they should be regarded, with Crawfurd,[9] as a third race, or with Marsden,[10] as a mixture of the other two. For in bodily configuration, curliness of hair and colour of skin, their inhabitants stand midway between the light-brown race and the black. But if a similar claim should also prove true of their language, then this very fact tells decidedly in favour of mixing. It remains, in general, an important question, though on information so far available it can scarcely admit of a satisfactory solution, as to how far older and deeper minglings of the white and black races may have occurred in these regions, and how far they may have occasioned gradual transitions in language, and even in colour and growth of hair, whose curliness, moreover, is also artificially assisted in some places by love of adornment.[11] For a correct assessment of the negroid race in its pure form, we shall always have to start from the inhabitants of the great southern mainland, since no direct contact is conceivable between them and the brown races, and in their present state even the nature of an indirect one is hard to imagine. It remains, however, all the more striking – since in general we possess only a small number of them – that in some words even the language of this stock shows visible affinities with words of the South Sea islands.

Now in these geographical and more-or-less neighbourly circumstances, some Malayan peoples have assimilated *Indian* culture so abundantly, that nowhere else, perhaps, do we find a second example of a nation that, without surrendering its independence, has been permeated to this degree by the mental cultivation of another. The phenomenon as a whole is intrinsically very intelligible. A large part of the archipelago, and one, indeed, that was exceptionally attractive by reason of climate and fertility, lay at a modest distance from the Indian mainland; there could thus be no lack of opportunities and points of contact. But where one occurred, the predominance of a civilization so ancient and so cultivated in every branch of human activity as that of India was bound to attract to it nations of an alert and lively sensitivity. This was more a moral change, however, than a political one. We recognize it from its consequences, from the

---

[9] *Foreign Quarterly Review*, 1834, no. 28, Art. 6, p. 11.

[10] *Miscell. Works*, p. 62.

[11] Dr. Meinicke of Prenzlow, from whose thorough research, and studies devoted for many years to this field of ethnology, we may justly expect something significant, directs his inquiries primarily to the point as to whether the negrito race may not possibly constitute the whole basis of all the present island population, albeit gradually changed by mingling with foreign immigrants and by adventitious culture, so that the question of another origin for the Malayan group of peoples would automatically come to nothing.

Indian elements which forcibly intrude upon our notice in a certain range of the Malayan peoples; but how did this mingling come about? Among the Malayans themselves, as we shall see, only dubious and obscure tales are current on this subject. If mighty movements of population and great conquests had brought this situation about, clearer traces of these political events would have been preserved. Intellectual and moral forces work unnoticed, like nature itself, and spring up suddenly from a seeding that eludes observation. Even the whole way in which Hinduism struck roots among the Malayan peoples shows that as a spiritual force it again excited the mind, set the imagination to work, and became powerful through the impression wrought upon the admiration of peoples capable of development. In India itself, in what we know of Indian history and literature, we find, so far as I am aware, no mention of the south-eastern archipelago. Even though Lankâ, perhaps, was taken to run further south than Ceylon extends, this was doubtless only dim and uncertain knowledge or mere poetic speculation. From the archipelago itself, as is also easy to understand, nothing came forth that could have any significant influence on the mainland. India exerted the powerful effect, and probably did so through settlements, which had no idea of regarding the mother country as their home any longer, or of maintaining ties with it. The causes of this could have been manifold. How far the Buddhist connections may have been operative thereunder, I shall discuss in what follows.

But in order to arrive at a just assessment of the mingling of Indian and Malayan elements, and the influence of India on the whole south-eastern archipelago, we must distinguish the various modes of its operation, and start, indeed, precisely from that which, however early it may have begun, has been prolonged into most recent times, because it has also, of course, left the clearest and most unmistakeable traces behind it. Here the influence is exerted, not only – as in all mingling of peoples – by the alien tongue spoken, but also by the whole culture that has blossomed in and with it. Now such influence is undeniably visible in the transference of Indian languages, literature, myths and religious philosophy to Java. This, though with closer reference to language, is the topic of all that follows in this work, and I can therefore be content merely to mention it here. This type of influence affected only the Indian archipelago proper, the Malayan circle in the narrower sense, and even that not entirely perhaps, and certainly not to the same degree. The focus of it was so concentrated in Java, that one may well remain doubtful whether the influence on the remainder of the archipelago was not largely a mere mediate one, emanating from this island. Apart from it, we find clear and complete evidence of Indian literary culture only among the Malayans proper, and the Bugis on Celebes. A true literature can arise, and this for internal reasons of linguistic culture itself, only with a script that is simultaneously given and comes into use. It therefore represents an important factor in the cultural relations of the south-easern archipelago, that it is precisely the ring of islands described as Malayan in the narrower sense, not everywhere, indeed, but exclusively in comparison with other parts, which possesses an alphabetic script. But there is a difference, in this connection, that should not be overlooked. The alphabetic script in this part of the world is the *Indian* one. This is inherent in the natural cultural relations of these regions, and in the majority of these alphabets, if we except somewhat from that of the Bugis, is visible also in the similarity of the letters; not to mention the inner arrangement of the sound-notation, although this, since it could also be fitted later only to the alien alphabet, yields no decisive proof. But full similarity, by mere adaptation to the simpler sound-system of the native tongue, prevails only in Java and somewhat in Sumatra. The Tagalog and Bugis scripts depart so significantly that they can be viewed as a stage in the invention of an alphabetic script. On Madagascar the *Arabic* script has established itself, just as the Indian has at the mid-point of the archipelago. But when this may have happened is unknown. Nor is there any trace of a native script that was suppressed by it. As an obviously later introduction, the use of Arabic writing among the Malayans proper settles nothing about the cultural relations we are speaking of here. The want of all writing on the South Sea islands, and among the negroid races, I have already referred to above (p. 12). The traces of Hinduism that we here have in view are such as to be everywhere clearly discernible, and thus at once distinguishable as alien elements. There is here no true interweaving, still less a merging together, but merely a mosaic-like combination of alien and native. In matters of custom and usage in Indian antiquity one may clearly recognize the foreign words, not wholly divested, even, of their grammatical form, in the Sanscrit that has come down to us; we can even discover the laws that have regulated this transplanting of alien speech-elements to the native soil. It is this that forms the basis of the refined and poetic speech on Java, and is connected most precisely with the transmission of literature and religion. By no means everything of this kind has also made its mark on the popular speech, and there is equally little ground for claiming that, where the latter possesses Indian words, it has acquired them solely in this way. Hence, if we pursue the various types of Indian influence, there arise two deep-lying questions, evoked by factual circumstances, but difficult to answer with certainty: whether, that is, the whole civilization of the archipelago is entirely of Indian origin? and whether, too, from a period preceding all literature and the latest and most refined development of speech, there have existed connections between Sanscrit and the Malayan languages in the widest sense, that can still be demonstrated in the common elements of speech? To the first of these two questions I would be inclined to return a negative answer. It seems to me established that there was a true and indigenous civilization among the brown race of the archipelago. It is still to be found in the eastern part, and even in Java has not succumbed beyond recognition. It could be said, nevertheless, that the population of the archipelago became gradually dispersed from the centre, which India initially had influenced, and expanded thence towards the east, so that the specifically Indian character became more diluted at the end-points. But such an assumption, however, becomes the less supported by specific resemblances, when, precisely in that which does not proclaim itself to be primarily Indian at all, striking coincidences have been noted in the customs of the peoples of the more central and easterly archipelago. Nor is it at all evident why a people such as the Malayans should be denied a social civilization of their own creation, seeing that the process of population and gradual acculturation may in any case have taken this direction or that. The very capacity of its constituent peoples to assimilate the Hinduism transmitted to them is a proof of this, and still more so the manner in which they nevertheless interwove it with native elements, and almost never allowed the Indian contribution to retain its quite alien shape. Both would necessarily have had to be otherwise, if the Indian incursions had encountered these races as raw uncultivated savages. When I speak here of *Indians*, I mean of course only the Sanscrit-speaking branch, not inhabitants of the Indian mainland as such. To what extent the latter were encountered by this branch, and perhaps driven out by it, is another question, which I do not enter into here, where my concern is only to show by what diverse cultural circumstances the Malayan races were encompassed.

The second question, referring only to language, must, however, in my opinion, be answered in the affirmative. In this respect the boundaries of Indian influence are more extensive. Without yet mentioning Tagalic, which incorporates a fair number of Sanscrit words for quite different classes of objects, we also find in the language of Madagascar, and in that of the South Sea islands, right down to the pronoun, sounds and words belonging directly to Sanscrit; and even the stages of sound-change, which can be viewed as a comparative index of the antiquity of mingling, are themselves different in such languages from the narrower Malayan circle, in which, as in Javanese, there is also visible an influence from Indian language and literature that was exerted at a much later date. Now how we are to explain this, and what mutual relationship we should assign to the two great speech-communities that adjoin in this respect, remains, of course, extremely doubtful. But I shall come back to the subject in more detail at the end of this work, since here it is enough for me to have drawn attention to an influence of Sanscrit upon the languages of the Malayan race, which differs essentially from that of the mental cultivation and literature transplanted to them, and seems to belong to a much earlier period and to different relationships among the peoples concerned. I shall then also deal with the languages of the negroid races, but must here observe in advance that if resemblances to Sanscrit words should be found in some of them, e.g. in the Papua language of New Guinea, this still in no way provides proof of any direct connections between India and those islands, since such common words may also have been conveyed there indirectly by Malayan seafaring, as has manifestly been the case with Arabic (see Book I [of *Über die Kawisprache*], pp. 246, 251).

If we survey the sketch here attempted of the cultural state of the great archipelago, we find then, the Malayan peoples squeezed, as it were, between such contrasting affinities and influences. On the same islands and island-groups which even to this day still harbour, in part, a population that stands on the lowest human level, or where such a population existed in earlier antiquity, there has simultaneously taken root an age-old and most prosperously flourishing culture from India. The Malayan races have made it their own, in part, in all its fullness. Yet they are obviously kin to those inhabitants of the South Sea islands who, in comparison with this culture, must be regarded as savages, and it is still doubtful whether their language, at least, is quite alien to the negroid race. They have kept themselves apart from these rude peoples in a manner peculiar to themselves, and in a speech-form which belongs, in its perfection, to them alone, and can be depicted in definite outline. That population of the great archipelago which, from what we know at present, cannot be attested on the continent of Asia, is to be found more or less, if we discount foreign influences, either in an entirely rude and savage state, or at the stage of civilization of an incipient society. This is most precisely true if we confine our attention simply to the negroid race and the South Sea islanders, and separate from them those who may be called Malayan in the narrower sense, although there is no very sufficient reason to attribute to the latter, prior to all Indian influence, a very much higher degree of culture. For even today, among the Battas of Sumatra, in whose myths and religion an Indian influence is quite unmistakeable, we encounter the barbaric custom of eating human flesh on certain occasions. But the great archipelago extends out under the whole length of Asia, and, bounded to west and east by Africa and America, outflanks it on both sides. Its mid-point is located at what is still a moderate distance for navigation even from the outermost extremities of the Asiatic mainland. Hence, too, the three great foci of the earliest cultivation of mankind, China, India, and the seat of the Semitic language-group, have operated on it at different times. In relatively later periods it has undergone influence from all of them. But India alone had a truly profound effect on its earlier shaping; Arabia, if we leave out Madagascar, which itself remains doubtful in point of chronology, had no influence at all; and China, apart from its early migrations, was of equally little importance. Even an affinity of the Chinese language with the South Sea dialects, to which a certain use of particle-type words might lead us, has not as yet been demonstrated.

Such a situation and inter-relationship of peoples and languages confronts ethnographic and linguistic research with problems of the utmost importance, but also of the greatest difficulty. It is not my intention to enter into discussion of them here. So far as anything adequate can be ascertained on the subject, it can only be the topic of concluding remarks, after due presentation of the facts. But in order to begin this from the point at which the historical data are clearest and most certain, I shall take up the inquiry in the first two books of this work at the period when the Indian influence was most deeply and penetratingly at work upon Malayan culture. This culminating point is obviously the flowering of the Kawi language, as the most intimate intertwining of Indian and indigenous culture on the island that possessed the earliest and most numerous Indian settlements. Here I shall always be looking primarily to the indigenous element in this linguistic union, but will take an extended view of it in its entire kinship, and will pursue its development up to the point where I believe I find its character most fully and purely evolved in the Tagalic tongue. In the third book, so far as the available means permit, I shall spread myself over the whole archipelago, return to the problems just indicated, and so try to see whether this way, together with that discussed hitherto, may lead to a more correct judgement of the relations among peoples and languages throughout the entire mass of islands.

The present introduction I think should be devoted to more general considerations, whose development will make better preparation for the transition to the facts and historical inquiries. The division of mankind into peoples and races, and the diversity of their languages and dialects, are indeed directly linked with each other, but are also connected with, and dependent upon, a third and higher phenomenon, the *growth of man's mental powers* into ever new and often more elevated forms. They find here their valuation, but also their explanation, so far as research is able to penetrate into them and grasp their connection. This revelation of man's mental powers, diverse in its degree and nature, over the course of millennia and throughout the world, is the highest aim of all spiritual endeavour, the ultimate idea which world history must strive to bring forth clearly from itself. For this uplifting or extension of inner being is the only thing that the individual, so far as he participates in it, can regard as unshakeably his own, and from which, in a nation, great individualities unfailingly continue to develop. The *comparative study of languages*, the exact establishment of the manifold ways in which innumerable peoples resolve the same task of language formation that is laid upon them as men, loses all higher interest if it does not cleave to the point at which language is connected with the shaping of the *nation's mental power*. But insight into the true essence of a nation, and into the internal connection of a single tongue, as also into the latter's relation to the demands of language as such, itself depends wholly on consideration of the overall individuality of mind. For only through this, as nature has furnished it and circumstances have worked upon it, is the character of the nation bonded together, on which alone depend the deeds, arrangements and thoughts which that nation produces, and in which lie the power and virtue that are again handed down to individuals. *Language*, on the other hand, is the organ of inner being, this being itself, as it successively attains to inner knowledge and outward expression. It therefore strikes with all the most delicate fibres of its roots into the national mentality; and the more aptly the latter reacts upon it, the more rich and regular its development. And since, in its integrated webwork, it is only an effect of the national feeling for language, there can be no basic answer to those very questions which refer to the formation of languages in their inmost life, and from which at the same time their most important differences arise, if we do not ascend to this point of view. We cannot, indeed, seek there the material for a comparative linguistics, which by nature must be dealt with in merely historical fashion; but we can only obtain there that insight into the original connection of the facts, and that apprehension of language as an internally connected organism, which then promotes in its turn the correct evaluation of the individual.

Consideration of the connection that links linguistic diversity and the distribution of peoples with the growth of man's mental power, as a process that gradually develops in varying degrees and novel forms, is the topic – so far as these two phenomena can throw mutual light on each other – that will occupy me in these introductory discussions. It has seemed to me necessary in a work that enters into the formal differences of two great branches of language and numerous individual tongues, and projects us into the linguistic and cultural state of an area which, itself comprehending a multitude of languages and dialects, is subject to the influence of that very part of the world from whence proceed the greatest and most remarkable linguistic phenomena, from the unisyllabic nature of Chinese to the wealth of forms in India, and on top of that again the uniformly fixed pattern of the Semitic language-structure.

§2

A closer examination of the present state of political, artistic and scientific *culture* leads to a long chain, running through many centuries, of mutually conditioning *causes* and *effects*. But in pursuing it we soon realize that two distinct elements prevail therein, with which the inquiry is not in equal measure successful. For while a portion of the continuing causes and effects can be adequately explained from one another, we run from time to time – as is shown by every attempt at a cultural history of mankind – into knots, so to speak, which resist further resolution. The trouble lies in that mental power, which can neither be wholly penetrated in its nature, nor calculated beforehand in its effect. It accompanies the product created by and around it, but treats and forms it according to the individuality with which it is invested. From every *great individual* of a period we could begin the world-historical development, whatever the basis he may have emerged on, and however the work of the preceding centuries may have gradually established this. It is possible only to demonstrate how he has made his activity, thus conditioned and supported, into that which bears his individual stamp, and not so much to state as to feel it, nor can we derive it in turn from another. This is the natural and everywhere recurring phenomenon of *human action*. Everything in it was at first *internal* – feeling, desire, thought, decision, speech and act. But as the internal makes contact with the world, it goes on working, and by means of the pattern peculiar to it determines other action, within or without. With the progress of time there arise *means of preserving* what at first was fleetingly effected, and increasingly less of the work of past centuries is lost to those that follow. Now this is the field in which research can follow, stage by stage. But it is constantly balked at the same time by the operation of new and incalculable *inner forces*, and without a proper separation and assessment of these two elements, of which the matter of the one can become so powerful that it threatens to suppress the force of the other, there can be no true estimation of the best that the history of all ages has to show.

The deeper we descend into the *past*, the more, of course, the mass of material handed on by succeeding generations merges together. But we then encounter another phenomenon, which to some extent diverts inquiry into a new field. The assured *individuals*, known through their outer circumstances of life, come more rarely and

language spun
out of mental
individuality
of peoples

uncertainly before us; their destinies, their very names, are in doubt,
and it even becomes uncertain whether what is attributed to them
is solely their own doing, or their name a mere blanket-term for the
work of many; they become lost, as it were, in a class of shadow-figures.
This is the case in Greece with Orpheus and Homer, in India with
Manu, Wyàsa and Wàlmiki, and with other celebrated names of
antiquity. But specific individuality vanishes still more if we move
still further back. A language so rounded as the Homeric must
already have long journeyed to and fro in the waves of song,
throughout ages of which no record now remains to us. This is still
more clearly evident in the original *form of languages* themselves.
Language is deeply entangled in the spiritual evolution of mankind,
it accompanies the latter at every stage of its local advance or retreat,
and the state of culture at any time is also recognizable in it. But there
is an epoch at which it is all we see, where it not only accompanies
spiritual evolution, but entirely takes the latter's place. Language,
indeed, arises from a depth of human nature which everywhere
forbids us to regard it as a true product and creation of peoples. It

language
an involuntary
emanation of
the spirit

possesses an autonomy that visibly declares itself to us, though
inexplicable in its nature, and, seen from this aspect, is no production
of activity, but an involuntary emanation of the spirit, no work of
nations, but a gift fallen to them by their inner destiny. They make
use of it without knowing how they have fashioned it. Yet languages,
for all that, must always have evolved with and by way of the
burgeoning of peoples, must have been spun out of their mental
individuality, which has imposed many restrictions on them. It is no

language
arising
in autonomy
solely from
itself and
divinely
free

empty play upon words if we speak of language as arising in
autonomy solely from itself and divinely free, but of languages as
bound and dependent on the nations to which they belong. For they
have then entered into specific restraints.[1] When speech and song at
first flowed freely, language took form according to the measure of
inspiration, and of the freedom and strength of the cooperating
mental forces. But this could only proceed from everybody at once;
each individual would have had to be carried therein by the others,
for inspiration gains new uplift only through the assurance of being
felt and understood. Thus there opens here a glimpse, however dim
and weak, into a period when individuals are lost, for us, in the mass
of the population, and when language itself is the work of the
intellectually creative power.

[1] Cf. further below, §6, 7, 22.

§3

In every survey of *world-history* there is a *progress*, also alluded to here. But it is by no means my intention to set up a system of purposes, or process of perfection extending *ad infinitum*; on the contrary, I am to be found here on an entirely different path. Peoples and individuals proliferate vegetatively, as it were, like plants, spreading across the earth, and enjoy their existence in happiness and activity. This life that dies away in every individual goes on undisturbedly, without regard to effects for the centuries that follow; nature's determination that everything which breathes shall complete its course to the last gasp, the purpose of beneficent ordering goodness, that every creature shall attain to enjoyment of its life, is carried out, and each new generation runs through the same circuit of joyous or painful existence, of successful or frustrated activity, but where *man* appears, he acts in a human way, combines gregariously, creates organizations, gives himself laws; and where this has occurred in a more imperfect fashion, supervening individuals or dynasties transplant thither what has succeeded better in other places. With the rise of man, therefore, the seed of *civilization* is also planted, and grows as his existence evolves. This humanization we can perceive in advancing stages, indeed it lies partly in its own nature, partly in the extent to which it has already prospered, that its further perfecting can hardly, in essence, be disturbed.

In the two points here specified there lies an unmistakeable *purposiveness*; it will also be present in others, where we do not encounter it in this fashion. But it should not be presupposed, lest the search for it should lead us astray in unravelling the facts. What we are here in fact discussing can least of all be subjected to it. The appearance of *man's spiritual power* in its various forms is not connected with the progress of time and the accumulation of data. Its origin can no more be explained than its effect can be calculated, and the highest in this kind is not just the latest to appear. If we wish, therefore, to peer here into the products of *creative nature*, we must not foist ideas upon her, but take her as she presents herself. In all her creations she brings forth a certain number of forms expressing what has been brought to reality by each species, and suffices to complete its idea. We cannot ask why there are not more or different forms; there are just no others about – would be the only appropriate answer. But from this viewpoint we can regard that which lives in

25

spiritual and corporeal nature as the effect of an underlying force, developing according to conditions unknown to us. If we are not to forego all discovery of a connection between phenomena in the human race, we still have to come back to some independent and original *cause*, not itself in turn conditioned and transitory in appearance. But we are thereby most naturally led to an inner life-principle, freely developing in its fullness, whose particular manifestations are not intrinsically unlinked because their outer appearances are presented in isolation. This viewpoint is totally different from that of the purposive theory, since it does not proceed towards a set goal, but from an admittedly unfathomable cause. Now it is this which, to me, seems solely applicable to the diverse shapings of human mental power, since – if it is allowable to divide in this fashion – the customary requirements of mankind are satisfactorily fulfilled through the powers of nature and the quasi-mechanical advancement of human activity, whereas the emergence of major *individuality* in persons and populations, which no really adequate derivation is able to explain, then makes a sudden and unforeseen intrusion into this obviously cause-and-effect-governed path.

Now the same view, of course, is equally applicable to the major manifestations of *human mental power*, and in particular to *language*, on which we here intend to dwell. Its diversity can be regarded as the striving with which the power of speech that man is universally endowed with, favoured or hampered by the mental power inherent in peoples, breaks forth with greater or lesser success.

For if we look at languages genetically, as a *work of the spirit* directed to a specific purpose, it is automatically evident that this purpose can be attained in a lower or higher degree; we can even perceive the various major points in which this inequality of goal-attainment will consist. For the better success may lie in the strength and abundance of the mental power as such that operates upon language, and beyond that again in the special aptitude of this to language-making, and thus, for example, in the particular clarity and perspicuity of ideas, in the depth of penetration into the nature of a concept, so as to wrest from it at once the most characteristic feature, in the activity and creative strength of imagination, in the justly-felt delight in the harmony and rhythm of sounds, with which, therefore, agility and suppleness of the vocal organs and acuteness and fineness of ear are also associated. But we must additionally take note of the quality of the transmitted material and the historical milieu in which a nation finds itself at the time of a significant reshaping of language, between a prehistory that works upon it, and the seeds of further development that lie within itself. There are also elements in languages that can

[handwritten margin note at top: more gifted nations possess languages superior to others who are not so gifted]

actually be judged only by the effort directed to them, and not equally well by its success. For languages do not always contrive to carry through completely an endeavour that may yet be all-too-clearly evinced in them. To this belongs, for example, the whole question of flexion and agglutination, on which a great deal of misunderstanding has prevailed, and still continues to do so. Now, that nations of happier gifts, and under more favourable circumstances, possess languages superior to others, lies in the very nature of the case. But we are also led to the more deep-lying cause just referred to. The *bringing-forth of language* is an *inner need* of man, not merely an external necessity for maintaining communal intercourse, but a thing lying in his own nature, indispensable for the development of his mental powers and the attainment of a world-view, to which man can attain only by bringing his thinking to clarity and precision through communal thinking with others. Now if, as we can hardly help doing, we regard every language as an attempt, and, taking the range of all languages together, as a contribution to the fulfilment of this need, it may well be assumed that the language-making power in man does not rest until, either in individuals or as a whole, it has brought forth that which answers the most and most completely to the demands to be made. In the light of this assumption, therefore, we may be able to discover, even among languages and linguistic families that betray no historical connection, an advancement in varying degrees of the principle of their formation. But if such be the case, this connection of outwardly unlinked phenomena must lie in a common inner cause, which can only be the evolution of the force at work. Language is one of the fields whence the general mental power of man emerges in constantly active operation. To put it otherwise, we see in it the *endeavour* to secure being in reality for the idea of *linguistic completeness*. To follow and depict this endeavour is the task of the linguist in its final, yet simplest, analysis.[1] Linguistics, to be sure, has no need at all of this possibly too hypothetical-seeming viewpoint as a foundation. But it can and must employ it as an incentive to testing whether such a gradually progressing approach may be discovered in languages, towards the completion of their formation. For there could be a series of languages of a simpler and more composite structure which, on comparison with each other, betrayed in the principles of their formation a progressive approach to the attainment of the most successful language-structure. The organism of these languages would then, even in involved forms, have

[handwritten margin note: bringing forth of language is an inner need of man]

---

[1] Compare my essay on the task of the historian in the *Abhandlungen der Akademie der Wissenschaften zu Berlin*, 1820–1, p. 322.

to bear within it the nature of their striving for linguistic completion more readily recognizable in its consistency and simplicity than is the case elsewhere. Progress on this line would primarily be found in such languages, first in the separation and completed articulation of their sounds, and hence in the formation of syllables that depends on this, the pure severance of the latter into their elements, and in the structure of the simplest words; next in the treatment of words, as vocal wholes, so as to obtain thereby real word-unity, corresponding to the unity of the concept; lastly, in the appropriate division of what should appear in language independently, and what should merely appear, as form, *from* the independent, for which a procedure is naturally required to distinguish mere mutual attachment in language from the symbolically fused. But in this consideration of languages I separate entirely the *changes* that can develop from one another in each, according to their destinies, and what is for us their first *original* form. The circle of these *primordial forms* seems to be closed, and in the state in which we now find the development of human powers, to be unable to return. For however internal language may altogether be, it yet has at the same time an independent outer existence that exerts dominion against man himself. The emergence of such primordial forms would thus presuppose a differentiation of peoples which now, and especially combined with more animated mental power, can no longer be thought of; unless, what is still more probable, a specific epoch in mankind, as in individual men, was dependent on the breaking forth of new languages as such.

§4

The *mental power* that intrudes, from its inner depth and fullness, into the course of world events, is the truly creative principle in the hidden and, as it were, secret evolution of mankind, of which I have spoken above, in contrast to the overt sequence obviously linked by cause and effect. It is the outstanding peculiarity of the spirit, enlarging the concept of human intellectuality, and emerging in a manner unexpected, and, in the ultimate depths of its appearance, inexplicable. It is especially marked out by the fact that its products are not mere foundations on which further construction can be effected, but carry within them at the same time the rekindling breath that engenders them. They propagate life, because it is from full life that they proceed. For the power that produces them works with the tension of its whole endeavour and in its full unity, yet at the same time truly creatively, regarding its own procreation as something inexplicable even to itself; it has not just seized upon novelty by chance, or merely latched on to the already known. Thus arose the *plastic art of Egypt*, which was able to build up the human form from out of the organic centre of its circumstances, and which thereby first impressed upon its works the stamp of true art. In this way, though otherwise more closely related, Indian poetry and philosophy and classical antiquity possess a character inherently distinct, and in the latter case also a Greek and Roman manner and cast of thought. So, later, from Romance poetry and the mental life which suddenly developed, with the downfall of Latin, in the now independent European West, there came the major part of modern culture. Where such phenomena have not occurred, or have been stifled by adverse circumstances, even the finest talent, once obstructed in its natural course, could no longer shape anything of great novelty, as we see from the Greek language, and so many relics of Greek art, during the centuries when Greece, through no fault of its own, was kept in barbarism. The old form of the language then becomes fragmented and mixed with the alien one, its true organism collapses, and the forces that press upon it are unable to reshape it for the start of a new path, or to breathe into it a newly inspiriting principle of life. In explanation of all such phenomena we can point to favourable and restrictive, preparing and retarding, circumstances. Man always clings to *what is there*. Of every idea whose discovery or implementation lends a new impetus to human endeavour, it can be shown by acute

29

kindling breath of genius sometimes missing in certain ethnic groups

man transcends the present moment does not remain sunk in sensuous enjoyment

"linguistic evolution is always the outcome of ergon - energeia" dialectic

and careful research how it was already there previously and gradually growing in the minds of men. But if the kindling breath of *genius* is lacking in individuals or peoples, the dimness of this glimmering coal never bursts into glowing flames. However little the nature of these creative forces may allow them to be properly understood, at least this much is evident, that there always prevails in them a capacity to master the given material from within outwards, to transform or subject it to ideas. Even in his earlier circumstances, man transcends the *present* moment, and does not remain sunk in mere sensuous enjoyment. Among the roughest tribes we find a love of adornment, dancing, music and song, and beyond that forebodings of a world to come, the hopes and anxieties founded on this, and traditions and tales which commonly go back to the origin of man and of his abode. The more strongly and brightly does the *spiritual power*, working independently by its own laws and forms of intuition, pour out its light into this world of the past and future, with which man surrounds his existence of the moment, the more purely and variously does the mass, simultaneously, take shape. Thus do *science* and *art* arise, and the goal, therefore, of mankind's developing progress is always the fusion of what is produced independently from within with what is given from without, each grasped in its purity and completeness, and bound into the subjection which the current endeavour by its nature demands.

But though we have depicted *spiritual individuality* as something primary and exceptional, we can and must equally regard it, even where it has reached the highest level, as in turn a *limitation* of nature in general, a path that the individual has been forced on to, since everything individual can be so only through a predominating and therefore exclusive principle. But precisely through confinement, power is enhanced and tautened, and exclusion can still be so guided by a principle of *totality*, that many such individualities are again joined into a whole. This is at bottom the foundation for that higher combination of men in friendship, love or grand collective endeavour devoted to the welfare of fatherland or mankind. Without pursuing further the consideration of how it is just the limitation of individuality which opens to man the only way of approaching ever nearer to unattainable totality, it is enough for me here to point out, merely, that the *power* which truly makes man into man, and is thus the simple definition of his nature, is disclosed in its contact with the *world*, in what we may call the vegetative life of mankind, proceeding somewhat mechanically on a given path, in particular phenomena revealing itself and its diversified endeavours in new shapes that enlarge its concept. Thus the discovery of *algebra* for example, was a new shaping of this sort in the mathematical bent of the human mind, and thus similar examples can be given in every science and art. We shall seek them out more fully in language later on.

Yet they are not confined merely to modes of thought and representation, but are also found quite especially in the *formation of character*. For what proceeds from the whole of man's power cannot rest until it again reverts into the whole; and the totality of inner appearance, feeling and disposition, coupled with the externality it suffuses, must let it be perceived that, permeated by the influences of these enlarged individual efforts, it also reveals the whole of human nature in an extended form. From this, indeed, arises the most general effect, and that which elevates mankind to its greatest worth. But it is *language*, the intermediary, uniting the most diverse individualities through communication of outer exertion and inner perceptions, which stands in the closest and most active interplay with character. The most energetic and readily susceptible temperaments, the most penetrating and fruitfully alive within, pour into it their strength and tenderness, their depth and inwardness, and it sends forth from their bosoms the kindred sounds to propagate the same sentiments. Character, the more it is enobled and refined, levels and unites the individual aspects of temperament and gives them, like plastic art, a shape to be grasped in its unity, yet one which bodies forth even more purely from within the outline at any moment. But language it is that is fitted to present and promote this shaping, through the delicate harmony, often invisible in detail, but woven together in its whole wonderful symbolic web. The effects of character-formation are simply far harder to calculate than those of merely intellectual advances, since they largely depend on the mysterious influences whereby one generation is connected with the rest.

In the evolution of mankind there are thus *advances*, achieved only because an uncommon power has unexpectedly taken its flight thither; cases where, in place of ordinary explanation of the effect produced, we must postulate the assumption of an *emission of force* corresponding to it. All spiritual progress can only proceed from an internal emission of force, and to that extent has always a hidden, and because it is autonomous, an inexplicable basis. But if this inner force suddenly creates so mightily of its own accord, that it could not in any way have been led to do so by what went before, then by that very fact, all possibility of explanation automatically ceases. I trust I have made these statements clear to the point of conviction, since in application they are important. For it now follows at once that where enhanced appearances of the same endeavour are perceivable, we cannot, unless the facts imperatively demand it, presuppose a

[handwritten marginal note: all spiritual progress proceeds from an internal emission of force]

gradual progress, since every significant enhancement appertains, rather, to a peculiar creative force. An example may be drawn from the structure of the Chinese and Sanscrit languages. One might certainly suppose here a gradual progression from the one to the other. But if we truly feel the nature of language as such, and of these two in particular, if we reach the point of fusion between thought and sound in both, we discover there the outgoing creative principle of their differing organization. At that stage, abandoning the possibility of a gradual development of one from the other, we shall accord to each its own basis in the spirit of the race, and only within the general trend of linguistic evolution, and thus ideally only, will regard them as stages in a successful construction of language. By neglecting the careful separation here proposed of the calculable stepwise progress and the unpredictable, immediately creative advance of human mental power, we banish outright from world-history the effects of *genius*, which is no less displayed at particular moments in peoples than it is in individuals.

But we also run the risk of wrongly evaluating the different states of human society. Thus *civilization* and *culture* are often credited with what cannot in any way proceed from them, but is effected by a power to which their own existence is due.

As to *languages*, it is a very common idea to attribute all their features and every enlargement of their territory to these factors, as if it were merely a question of the difference between *cultivated* and *uncultivated* tongues. If we call upon history to witness, such a power of civilization and culture over language is in no way confirmed. Java manifestly received higher civilization and culture from India, and both in a significant degree, but the indigenous language did not for that reason alter a form that was more imperfect and less adapted to the needs of thought; on the contrary, it robbed the incomparably nobler Sanscrit of its own form, to force it into the local one. And India itself, however early it was civilized, and not through foreign mediation, did not obtain its language from this; the principle thereof, profoundly created from the truest linguistic sense, flowed rather, like that civilization itself, from the gifted mentality of the people. Thus even language and civilization by no means always stand in a like relation to each other. Whatever branch of its arrangements may be considered, Peru under the Incas was easily the most civilized country in America; but assuredly no linguist will equally give preference over the other New World languages to the common Peruvian tongue, which was attemptedly spread by war and conquests. In my conviction, anyway, it is notably inferior to the Mexican. Moreover, admittedly crude and uncultivated languages may possess striking felicities of structure, and possess them genuinely, nor would it be impossible for them to surpass more cultured ones in this respect. Even a comparison of Burman, to which Pali has undeniably imparted a measure of Indian culture, with the Delaware language, let alone the Mexican, should leave judgement of the latter's superiority in little doubt.

But the matter is too important for us not to discuss it more fully, and to consider the inner reasons for it. So far as civilization and culture convey to the nations ideas from abroad that were previously unknown to them, or develop such ideas from within, this view is in one aspect undeniably correct. The need for a *concept,* and its resultant clarification, must always precede the *word,* which is merely the expression of its completed clarity. But if we one-sidedly remain at this standpoint, and think that in this way alone we shall discover the differences in the merits of languages, we fall into an error that is damaging to a true assessment of language. It is already in itself most precarious to seek to assess from its *dictionary* the range of concepts possessed by a people at a given time. Without touching here on the obvious pointlessness of attempting this from the incomplete and casually-assembled word-lists that we have for so many non-European nations, it must already strike us automatically that a large number, especially of non-sensuous concepts, on which these claims are predominantly founded, may be expressed through metaphors, to us unfamiliar and hence unknown, or else by circumlocutions. There resides, however, and this is by far the more crucial here, no less in the concepts than in the language of every people, however uncultivated, a *totality* corresponding to the range of the untrammelled human capacity for cultivation, from which everything particular that humanity encompasses can be created, without alien assistance; and we cannot call alien to language what attention directed to this point unfailingly encounters in its bosom. A factual proof of this is provided by the languages of uncultured nations which, like those of the Philippines and America, for example, have long been studied by missionaries. We find even highly abstract concepts designated in them, without any supervenience of alien terms. It would indeed be interesting to know how the natives understand these words. But since such words are formed from elements of their language, they must necessarily couple some analogous meaning with them.

But that in which the above-mentioned view leads us chiefly astray is, that it considers language far too much as a spatial territory, to be extended, as it were, by captures from without, and thereby misapprehends its true nature in its most essential individuality. It is not just a matter of how many concepts a language designates with

[margin note: need for a concept must precede the word]

its own words. This occurs automatically if it otherwise follows the true path marked out for it by nature, and is not the aspect from which it must first be judged. Its authentic and essential efficacy in man rests upon his thinking and thinkingly creative power itself, and is immanent and constitutive in a far deeper sense. Whether and to what extent it promotes clarity and correct order among concepts, or puts difficulties in the way of this? Whether it retains the inherent sensuous perspicuity of the ideas conveyed into the language from the world-view? Whether, though the euphony of its tones, it works harmoniously and soothingly, or again energetically and upliftingly, upon feeling and sentiment? In these and in many other such determinations of the whole mode of thought and way of feeling lies that which constitutes its true character and determines its influence on spiritual evolution. But this rests upon the totality of its original design, upon its organic structure, its individual form. Nor do civilization and culture, which themselves enter only at a later date, pass over it in vain. The clarity and precision of language gain through the habit of expressing enlarged and refined ideas, perspicuity is enhanced in a heightened level of imagination, and euphony profits from the judgement and superior requirements of a more practised ear. But this whole progress of improved language-making can only go on within the limits prescribed to it by the *original design of the language*. A nation can make a more imperfect language into a tool for the production of ideas to which it would not have given the original incentive, but cannot remove the inner restrictions which have once been deeply embedded therein. To that extent even the highest elaboration remains ineffective. Even what later ages have added from without is appropriated by the original language, and modified according to its laws.

From the standpoint of *inner spiritual evaluation*, it is also impossible to regard *civilization* and *culture* as the summit to which the human spirit is capable of raising itself. Both have in recent times flourished to the highest degree and in the greatest generality. But whether, on that account, the inner aspect of man's nature, as we see it, for example, in some periods of antiquity, has also simultaneously returned as abundantly and powerfully, or even in higher degree, we can hardly wish to affirm with equal assurance; and still less whether this has been the case in the nations to which the dissemination of civilization and a certain culture has been chiefly due.

Civilization is the humanization of peoples in their outward institutions and customs, and the inner attitude pertaining thereto. *Culture* adds science and art to this refinement of the social order. But when we speak in our language of *cultivation* [Bildung], we mean by this something at the same time higher and more inward, namely the disposition that, from the knowledge and feeling of the entire mental and moral endeavour, pours out harmoniously upon temperament and character.

Civilization can come forth from *within* a people, and testifies, in that case, to that uplifting of the spirit which cannot always be explained. If, on the other hand, it is implanted in a nation from *without*, it spreads more quickly, and also, perhaps, penetrates more into every branch of the social order, but does not react so energetically upon mind and character. It is a splendid privilege of *our own day*, to carry civilization into the remotest corners of the earth, to couple this endeavour with every undertaking, and to utilize power and means for the purpose, even apart from other ends. The operative principle here, of universal *humanity*, is an advance to which only our own age has truly ascended; and all the great discoveries of recent centuries are working together to bring it to reality. The colonies of the Greeks and Romans were far less effective in this respect. The reason, to be sure, lay in the want of so many outer means of linking countries, and of civilizing as such. But they also lacked the inner principle, from which alone this endeavour can take a true life. They had a clear concept, deeply rooted in their disposition and temperament, of a higher and nobler human individuality; but the notion of respecting a man simply because he is human had never gained influence among them, and still less the sense of rights and obligations arising from this. This important aspect of the general civilizing process had remained foreign to their course of national development. Even in their colonies they probably did less to mingle with the natives than simply to push the latter back from their frontiers; but their colonists themselves developed differently in the altered surroundings, and hence, as we see in Southern Italy, Sicily and Spain, there arose in distant countries new orientations of the people in character, political attitude and scientific development. The Indians were quite exceptionally good at kindling and making fruitful the native powers of the peoples they settled among. The Indian archipelago and Java itself give us notable evidence of this. For there, on encountering Indian elements, we also commonly see how the local population mastered and built upon them. Along with their more perfect outward institutions, their greater wealth of means for a heightened enjoyment of life, their art and science, the Indian immigrants also carried abroad the living breath, by whose power of inspiration these things had first been fashioned among themselves. All particular social endeavours among the ancients were not yet so fragmented as they are with us; they were far less able to convey what they possessed, without the spirit that had created it. Since things are quite different with us nowadays, and a power residing in our own civilization is driving us ever more definitely in this direction, the peoples are acquiring under our influence a far more uniform shape, and even where it may possibly have occurred, development of the original individuality of a people is often nipped in the bud.

we are, spreading lovely uniformity

§5

In surveying the *mental evolution of mankind*, we have hitherto viewed it in its sequence through the different *generations*, and have outlined four factors which chiefly determine it; the peaceable life of peoples, according to the natural circumstances of their existence on earth; their activity in migration, wars etc., sometimes guided by intention, or arising from passion and inner urges, sometimes forcibly necessitated of them; the series of mental advances mutually linked with each other as causes and effects; and finally the mental phenomena which find their explanation only in the power that is disclosed in them. We now have to consider a second aspect, namely how there is effected in each *particular generation* the development which contains the ground of its progress at any time.

The efficacy of the *individual* is always a truncated affair, but one which, to all appearance, and up to a certain point in truth as well, proceeds in the same direction alongside that of the *whole species,* since as conditioned and also conditioning it stands in unbroken connection with time past and time to come. In another respect, however, and on examining its nature more deeply, the direction of the individual, as against that of the whole species, is nevertheless a divergent one, so that the web of world history, so far as it concerns the inner side of man, consists of these two criss-crossing, yet at the same time closely-linked tendencies. The divergence is directly evident from the fact that the destinies of the species proceed unbroken independently of the vanishing of the generations, although tending on the whole, so far as we can tell, towards enhanced perfection; the individual, however, is not only severed from all participation in those destinies, and often unexpectedly in the midst of his most important work, but does not even think, in his inner consciousness, in his foresight and convictions, that he stands for that reason at the end of his career. He therefore sees the latter as separate from the course of those destinies, and there arises in him, even while living, an opposition between *self-cultivation* and that *shaping of the world* which everyone grapples with, in reality, within his own sphere. That this opposition becomes ruinous neither to the development of the species nor to individual cultivation, assures the ordering of human nature. Self-cultivation can only further the world's shaping, and thoughout life man is attached to the destinies he forsakes by emotional needs and imaginative pictures, by family tics, the struggle for fame, and the

inwardness
is the key to the holiest
and mightiest
feelings

happy prospect that seeds he has planted will develop in time to come. But by means of this opposition, and even originally underlying it, there is formed an *inwardness* of mind on which the mightiest and holiest feelings depend. It works the more comprehensively when man regards not only himself, but all his kind, as equally determined to a lone and life-long self-development, and when all the ties that bind one mind to another acquire by this a new and higher significance. From the varying degrees attained by this inwardness, which severs the self from reality, even in the coupling therewith, and from its more or less exclusive dominance, nuances arise that are important for all human development. India itself provides a notable example of the purity to which it can be refined, but also of the abrupt contrasts into which it may lapse, and Indian antiquity can be largely explained from this standpoint. Upon *language* this determining of the soul exerts a special influence. It takes a different form in a people that gladly pursues the solitary paths of withdrawn contemplation, and in nations which chiefly have need of the mediating understanding for external concerns. The symbolic is quite differently apprehended by the former, and whole tracts of linguistic territory remain by the latter untilled. For language must first be introduced, by a still obscure and undeveloped feeling, into the spheres upon which it is to pour forth its light. How this broken-off existence here of the individual is united with the advancing development of the species, into a region perhaps unknown to us, remains an impenetrable mystery. But the operation of the sense of this impenetrability is pre-eminently an important factor in the inner cultivation of the individual, in that it awakens the reverential awe towards a thing unknown, which still remains behind after everything knowable has vanished. It is comparable to the impression of night, in which everything normally visible is likewise replaced by merely the single scattered sparkles of bodies beyond our ken.

The advance of the destinies of the species, and the cutting-off of individual generations, also has a very significant effect through the differing weight that the *future* thereby acquires for each of the latter. Those who come later find themselves set, as it were – and primarily through the perfecting of means for preserving information about the past – before a stage on which a richer and more brightly-lit drama unfolds. The hurrying stream of events also throws generations, seemingly by chance, into darker and more fateful, or brighter and more easily liveable periods. To the actual, living, individual view, this difference is less great than it appears to the eye of history. Many points of comparison are lacking, we experience at each moment only a part of the development, we engage in it, with enjoyment and activity, and the virtues of the present carry us over its vicissitudes. Like clouds emerging from the mist, an age only takes on a circumscribed outline when seen from a distance. Only in the influence that each exerts on its successor do we clearly see what its own experience was of the time ahead. Our modern culture, for example, rests largely on the opposition in which we stand confronted by *classical antiquity*. It would be difficult and depressing to say what might remain of it, if we were to cut ourselves off from everything pertaining to this antiquity. If we examine the state of the peoples comprising it, in all their historical details, they do not really correspond, either, to the picture that we carry of them in our minds. What exerts a powerful impression on us is the conception we have, which proceeds from the centre of their greatest and purest endeavours, which emphasizes more the spirit than the reality of their institutions, which leaves the points of contrast unregarded, and which makes no demand of them that does not agree with the received idea of what they were. It is, however, no arbitrary choice that leads to such a conception of their individuality. The ancients entitle us to it; of no other age would it be possible. The deep sense of their nature first lends to us the very capacity to uplift ourselves towards it. Since in their case reality always passed over with happy agility into idea and fantasy, and they reacted to it with both, we legitimately transplant them exclusively into this domain. For by the spirit that resides in their writings, their works of art and their fruitful practical endeavours, they describe in complete purity, totality and harmony – though reality among them did not everywhere correspond to it – the sphere assigned to man in his freest developments, and in this way left behind them a picture that works ideally upon us, as a higher form of human nature. As between a sunny and a cloudy sky, their superiority to ourselves lies not so much in the patterns of life itself, as in the wonderful light that in their case streamed over them. The Greeks themselves, however much of an influence we assume upon them from earlier peoples, were obviously quite lacking in such a phenomenon, which might have enlightened them from afar. In itself they had something of the kind in the Homeric ballads and those that succeeded them. As to us they seem beyond explanation, by nature and in the roots of their shaping, and become for us a pattern to emulate, the source of a great mass of spiritual enrichments, so even for the Greeks was that age, obscure and yet radiating towards them in such unique exemplars. For the Romans, the Greeks were not so much a kindred people as they are to us. Their effect on the Romans was merely that of a contemporary nation, of higher cultivation, possessing a literature beginning from an earlier period. India, for us, recedes into too dark a distance for us to be capable of passing a judgement on its prehistory. In the earliest times at least, its effect upon the West, since such influence would not have been so utterly erasable, was not through the characteristic form of its literary productions, but at most through particular opinions, discoveries and myths that have come down to us. The importance, however, of this difference in the mental influence of peoples on one another, is something I shall have occasion to deal with in more detail later on (Bk 1, Secs 1.2). Their own antiquity will have appeared to the Indians in a form resembling that of Greek antiquity to the Greeks. But this is very much clearer in China, through the influence and contrast of works in the old style and the philosophical teaching contained in them.

Since *languages*, or at least their elements (a distinction not to be neglected) are transmitted from one age to another, and we can only speak of newly beginning languages by completely overstepping the bounds of our experience, the relation of the *past* to the *present* enters into the utmost depths of their formation. But the difference of state that an age is put into, through the place it occupies in the series of those that are known to us, is immensely powerful even in languages already quite fully formed, since the language is simultaneously a mode of apprehending the whole way of thought and feeling, and this, presenting itself from a remote epoch to a people, cannot operate upon the latter without also becoming influential for their own tongue. Thus our languages today would on many points have taken on a different shape if Indian rather than classical antiquity had worked so persistently and penetratingly upon us.

languages are whole ways of thought and feeling influential in precisely those ways for those who learn them (or foreign languages?)

§6

The *individual man* is always connected with a whole, with that of his nation, of the race to which the latter belongs, and of the entire species. From whatever aspect one may look at it, his life is necessarily tied to *sociality*, and here, too, as we have already seen earlier in a similar case, the outer subordinate viewpoint and the inner superior one lead to the same point. In the merely vegetative existence, as it were, of man on the soil, the individual's *need for assistance* drives him to combine with others, and calls for understanding through *language*, so that common undertakings may be possible. But *mental cultivation*, even in the loneliest seclusion of temperament, is equally possible only through language, and the latter requires to be directed to an external being that understands it. The articulate sound is torn from the breast, to awaken in another individual an echo returning to the ear. Man thereby at once discovers that around him there are beings having the same inner needs, and thus capable of meeting the manifold longing that resides in his feelings. For the intimation of a *totality*, and the endeavour towards it, are given immediately with the sense of *individuality*, and gather strength in the same degree as the latter is sharpened, since every individual bears within him the collective essence of man, though only on a single line of development. Nor do we even have the remotest inkling of another as an individual consciousness. But this endeavour, and the seed of indelible longing implanted in us by the concept of humanity itself, will not let the conviction perish, that separate individuality as such is merely an appearance of the conditioned existence of a spiritual being.

The connection of the individual with a whole that enhances power and initiative is too important a point in the spiritual economy of mankind (if I may be allowed that expression), to have no need of being specifically referred to here. The unity of *nations* and *races*, which invariably evokes a simultaneous separation, depends, in any case, primarily upon historical events, themselves largely due to the nature of the places men live in and travel to. But even if we wish to separate from this all influence of inner agreement or repulsion, even of a merely instinctive kind – not that I would care to justify this view forthwith – still, every nation, quite apart from its external situation, can and must be regarded as a human *individuality*, which pursues an inner spiritual path of its own. The more we realize that the efficacy of individuals, at whatever level they may have placed

41

even their genius, is still only incisive and enduring to the degree in which they have been simultaneously carried up by the spirit residing in their nation, and are able in turn to impart new impetus to it from their own point of view, the more evident is the necessity of seeking the explanatory ground of our present stage of cultivation in these national spiritual individualities. History also presents them to us in distinct outlines, wherever it provides us with the data for judging the inner cultivation of peoples. Civilization and culture gradually remove the glaring contrasts of peoples, and still more successful is the striving for the more universal moral form of a more deeply penetrating and nobler cultivation. In agreement with this also are the advances of science and art, which always strive towards more universal ideals, unshackled by national outlook. But if the equal is sought, it can be achieved only in the varieties of the spirit, and the manifold ways in which human individuality can assert itself, without erroneous one-sidedness, extends into the infinite. But upon this very *diversity* the achievement of what is universally striven for unconditionally depends. For this demands the whole undivided unity of that force which can never be explained in its completeness, but is necessarily operative in its sharpest individuality. To penetrate fruitfully and powerfully, therefore, into the general course of cultivation, the issue for a nation is not merely one of success in particular scientific endeavours, but primarily of the total exertion in that which constitutes the centre of man's nature, which finds its clearest and completest expression in philosophy, poetry and art, and which streams out from thence over the entire mode of thought and disposition of the people.

In virtue of the connection here in view, between the individual and the mass surrounding him, every significant activity of the former belongs, albeit mediately only, and in some degree, to the latter as well. But the existence of *languages* proves that there are also spiritual creations which in no way whatever pass out from a single individual to the remainder, but can only emanate from the simultaneous self-activity of all. In languages, therefore, since they always have a national form, *nations*, as such, are truly and immediately creative.

Yet we must certainly beware of framing this view without the restriction proper to it. Since languages have grown up in inseparable association with man's inmost nature, and emanate automatically therefrom, far more than they are deliberately produced by it, we might equally well call the intellectual individuality of peoples their effect. The truth is that both proceed simultaneously and in mutual agreement from inaccessible depths of the mind. We have no empirical acquaintance with such a *creation of language*, nor are we anywhere presented with an analogy to judge it by. If we speak of original languages, they are so merely for our lack of knowledge of their earlier components. A connected chain of languages has run on for centuries before reaching the point which our inadequate information designates as the oldest. But not only the primitive formation of the truly original language, but also the secondary formations of later ones, which we know quite well how to resolve into their components, are to us inexplicable, precisely in respect of their actual gestation. All *becoming* in nature, but especially of the organic and living, escapes our observation. However minutely we may examine the preparatory stages, between the latter and the phenomenon there is always the cleavage that divides the something from the nothing; and this is equally so with the moment of *cessation*. All comprehension of man lies only between the two. In languages, a period of origination, from perfectly accessible historical times, affords us a striking example. We can follow out a multiple series of changes that the *language of the Romans* underwent during its decline and fall, and can add to them the minglings due to invading tribesmen: we get no better explanation thereby of the origin of the living seed which again germinated in various forms into the organism of newly burgeoning languages. An inner principle, newly arisen, rebuilt the collapsing structure, for each in its own fashion, and we, since we always find ourselves situated among its effects only, become aware of its transformations only by the multitude thereof. It may therefore seem that this point would better have been left wholly untouched. But this is impossible if we wish to depict the evolution of the human mind even in broadest outline, since the forming of languages, even of particular ones, in every type of derivation or composition, is a most essentially characteristic fact about the mind, and displays therein the collective action of individuals in a shape that does not otherwise occur. So while acknowledging that we stand here at a boundary which can be crossed neither by historical research nor by free speculation, the fact and its immediate consequences must still be faithfully described.

The first and most natural of these consequences is that this connection of the individual with his nation lies right at the centre from whence the total mental power determines all thinking, feeling and willing. For *language* is related to everything therein, to the whole as to the individual, and nothing of this ever is, or remains, alien to it. At the same time it is not merely passive, receiving impressions, but follows from the infinite multiplicity of possible intellectual tendencies in a given individual, and modifies by inner self-activity every external influence exerted upon it. It can, however, by no means be regarded, in contrast to mental individuality, as something outwardly distinct from this, and hence – though it may seem otherwise at first sight – it cannot properly be taught, but only awakened in the mind; it can only be given the threads by which it develops on its own account. So although languages are thus the work of *nations*, in a sense of the term[1] liberated from all misunderstanding, they still remain the self-creations of *individuals*, in that they can be produced solely in each individual, but only in such fashion that each presupposes the understanding of all, and all fulfil this expectation. Though we may now consider language as a world-view, or as a linkage of thoughts, since both these tendencies are united within it, it still always necessarily rests upon the *collective power of man*; nothing can be excluded from it, since it embraces everything.

Now in nations, both generally and in different epochs, this power differs individually in degree, and in the actual path possible in the same general direction. But the *diversity* must become visible in the result, namely language, and becomes so, of course, primarily through the preponderance either of external influence or of inner self-activity. So here too it happens that if we pursue the sequence of languages comparatively, we make more or less easy headway in explaining the structure of one from another, though there are also languages which appear separated by a real chasm from the rest. As individuals, by the power of their particular nature, impart a new impulse to the human mind in a direction as yet unexplored, so nations can do this in language-making. But an undeniable connection exists between language-structure and the success of all other kinds of intellectual activity. It lies primarily – and we consider it here from this angle only – in the animating breath which the formative power of language instils, in the act of altering the world, into thought, so that it diffuses harmoniously through all parts of its domain. If we may think it possible for a language to arise in a nation precisely as a word evolves most meaningfully and evidently from the world-view, reflects it most purely, and itself takes form so as to enter most readily and concretely into every vicissitude of thought, then this language, if it does but retain its life-principle, must evoke the same power, in the same direction, with equal success in every individual. The entry of such a language, or even one that approaches it, into *world-history*, must therefore establish an important epoch in man's course of development, and this in its highest and most wonderful products. Certain paths of the spirit, and a certain impulse carrying it on to them, are not thinkable until such languages have

---

[1] Cf. above, pp. 24, 25 and §22 below.

arisen. They therefore constitute a true turning-point in the inner
history of mankind; if we are to see them as the summit of
language-making, they are also the starting-points for a more
mentally abundant and imaginative cultivation, and it is to that
extent quite correct to maintain that the work of nations must
precede that of individuals; although the very observations here
made are indisputable evidence of how in these creations the activity
of each is simultaneously swallowed up in that of the other.

*work of nations
must precede that
of individuals
(but both are mutually
interdependent)*

*undeniable connection
between language power
and the success of all
other intellectual activity*

language and mental power are The same Thing, inseparable

We have now reached the point at which we recognize *languages* as the first necessary stage in the primitive cultivation of mankind, from whence nations are first able to pursue this higher human tendency. They grew up in similarly conditioned fashion, along with *mental power*, and form at the same time the animating inspiring principle of the latter. But neither proceeds in succession to or apart from the other, for each is utterly and inseparably the same act of the intellectual faculty. In that a people effects, from its inner freedom, the development of its language, as the instrument of every human activity within it, it seeks and simultaneously attains to the thing itself, that is, to something different and higher; and in that it gets on to the road of poetic creation and speculative thought, it simultaneously works back, in turn, upon language. If the first even raw and uncultivated attempts of intellectual endeavour are assigned the name of *literature*, language always takes the same road with it, and so both are inseparately tied to one another.

The *mental individuality* of a people and the *shape of its language* are so intimately fused with one another, that if one were given, the other would have to be completely derivable from it. For *intellectuality* and *language* allow and further only forms that are mutually congenial to one another. Language is, as it were, the outer appearance of the spirit of a people; the language is their spirit and the spirit their language; we can never think of them sufficiently as identical. How they actually conjoin with each other in one and the same source, beyond reach of our conception, remains inexplicably hidden from us. But without wishing to decide as to the priority of one or the other, we must see the real principle of explanation and true determining ground in the mental power of nations, since this alone stands independently living before us, whereas language only attaches to it. For so far as even the latter is revealed to us in creative independence, it is lost beyond the realm of appearance in an ideal essentiality. Historically, our concern is always with actually speaking men, merely, but we should not on that account lose sight of the true situation. Though we may separate intellectuality and language, no such division in fact exists. If language appears to us, rightly, as too high a thing to be ranked as a human artefact, like other evidences of the spirit, the situation would be different if man's mental power did not confront us merely in particular instances, but the very essence of it streamed in its unfathomable profundity towards us, and we were able to see into the connection of man's individuality; for even language transcends the separateness of individuals. For practical purposes it is, however, specially important to rest content with no mere lower principle for explaining languages, but really to ascend to this last and highest one, and to see as the fixed point of the whole mental configuration the principle that the structure of languages differs among mankind, because and insofar as the mental individuality of nations is itself different.

If we enter, however, as we cannot refrain from doing, into the nature of this *diversity* in the particular form of language-structure, we can no longer seek to apply to the details of language an investigation of mental individuality, first undertaken separately for its own sake. In the early epochs to which the present considerations transport us, we know the nations, as such, only by their languages, nor do we ever know exactly which people, even, we are to think of, by descent and affinity, in connection with each language. Thus Zend, for us, is really the language of a nation that we can define more exactly only by way of conjecture. Among all manifestations whereby spirit and character can be recognized, language, however, is also the only one suited to exhibit both, even to their inmost windings and recesses. If we look upon *languages*, therefore, as a basis for explaining successive *mental development*, we must indeed regard them as having arisen through intellectual individuality, but must seek the nature of this individuality in every case in its *structure*; so that if the considerations here introduced are to be carried to completion, it is now incumbent on us to enter more closely into the nature of languages and the possibility of their retroactive differences, in order thereby to couple the comparative study of languages to its last and highest reference-point.

Key to linguistic individuality is the language's structure

A certain line of linguistic research is called for, however, if the way above indicated is to be followed with success. We must look upon *language,* not as a dead *product,* but far more as a *producing,* must abstract more from what it does as a designator of objects and instrument of understanding, and revert more carefully, on the other hand, to its origin, closely entwined as it is with inner mental activity, and to its reciprocal influence on the latter. The advances that linguistic inquiry owes to the successful efforts of recent decades make it easier to survey this in its full extent. We can now approach nearer to the goal of setting forth the individual ways in which the business of producing language is brought to completion among the variously divided, isolated and conjoined populations of mankind. But in this lies the very cause of the diversity of human language-structure, and likewise the influence of this upon the mind's evolution, and thus the whole topic of our present concern.

But the moment we embark on this course of inquiry, an important difficulty stands in our way. Language presents us with an infinity of *details*, in words, rules, analogies and exceptions of every kind, and we are not a little perplexed at how to bring this mass, which, apart from the order already brought into it, still seems to us a bewildering chaos, into judicious comparison with the unity of the image of man's *mental power*. Even if we possess all the necessary lexical and grammatical detail of two major branches of language, e.g. Sanscrit and Semitic, we have still made but little progress thereby in the endeavour to catch the character of either in such simple outline as to permit a fruitful comparison of them, or a determination of their allotted place, by reference to the mental power of nations, in the general enterprise of language-creation. This still demands a special search for the communal *sources* of individual peculiarities, the drawing together of the scattered features into the image of an *organic whole*. Only so do we gain a purchase by which to hold on to the details. So in order to compare different languages fruitfully with one another, in regard to their characteristic structure, we must carefully investigate the form of each, and in this way ascertain how each resolves the main questions with which all language-creation is confronted. But since this term 'form' is used in various connections in investigations of language, I believe I must spell out more fully the sense in which I would wish it to be taken

[handwritten top margin: language is always encountered as ergon but is never ergon but energeia (activity)]

here. This appears the more necessary in that here we are talking, not of language as such, but of the various different peoples, so that it is also a matter of defining what is meant by one *particular language*, in contrast, on the one hand, to the linguistic family, and on the other to a dialect, and what we are to understand by *one* language, where it undergoes essential changes during its career.

Language, regarded in its real nature, is an enduring thing, and at every moment a *transitory* one. Even its maintenance by writing is always just an incomplete, mummy-like preservation, only needed again in attempting thereby to picture the living utterance. In itself it is no product (*Ergon*), but an activity (*Energeia*). Its true definition can therefore only be a genetic one. For it is the ever-repeated *mental labour* of making the *articulated* sound capable of expressing *thought*. In a direct and strict sense, this is the definition of *speech* on any occasion; in its true and essential meaning, however, we can also regard, as it were, only the totality of this speaking as the language. For in the scattered chaos of words and rules that we are, indeed, accustomed to call a language, there is present only the *particular* brought forth by this speaking, and this never completely, and first calling for new work, so as to detect from it the nature of the living speech and to provide a true image of the living language. It is precisely the highest and most refined aspect that cannot be discerned from these disparate elements, and can only be perceived or divined in *connected discourse*; which is all the more proof that language proper lies in the act of its real production. It alone must in general always be thought of as the true and primary, in all investigations which are to penetrate into the living essentiality of language. The break-up into words and rules is only a dead makeshift of scientific analysis.

[handwritten right margin: language is transitory / maintenance by writing is mummy like preservation of living utterance]

To describe languages as a *work of the spirit* is a perfectly correct and adequate terminology, if only because the existence of spirit as such can be thought of only in and as activity. The dismemberment of their structure that is indispensable for studying them does indeed oblige us to consider them as a *procedure* advancing by specific means to specific goals, and to that extent really to view them as *fashioned* by nations. The misconception that may thus arise has already been sufficiently acknowledged above,[1] and hence these terms cannot be harmful to the truth.

[handwritten right margin: spirit is activity]

I have already pointed out earlier on (pp. 42–3) that in our study of language we find ourselves plunged throughout – if I may so put it – into a historical milieu, and that neither a nation nor a language, among those known to us, can be called *original*. Since each has

---

[1] *Cf.* pp. 24, 25, 44, 46–7 and §22 below.

[handwritten bottom right: we dont know an "original" language or nation]

already received from earlier generations material from a prehistory unknown to us, the mental activity which, as earlier explained, produces the expression of thought, is always directed at once upon something already *given*; it is not a purely creative, but a reshaping activity.

Now this *labour* operates in a *constant and uniform* way. For the mental power which exerts it is the same, differing only within certain modest limits. Its purpose is *understanding*. Thus nobody may speak differently to another from the way in which the latter, under similar circumstances, would have spoken to him. In the end the material transmitted is not only of this kind, but also closely allied throughout with the train of thought, having itself a similar origin. The constant and uniform element in this mental labour of elevating articulated sound to an expression of thought, when viewed in its fullest possible comprehension and systematically presented, constitutes the *form* of language.

In this definition, form appears as an *abstraction* fashioned by science. But it would be quite wrong to see it also in itself as a mere non-existent thought-entity of this kind. In actuality, rather, it is the quite individual *urge* whereby a nation gives validity to thought and feeling in language. Only because we are never allowed to view this urge in the undivided totality of its striving, but merely in its particular effects on each occasion, are we also left with no recourse but to summarize the uniformity of its action in a dead general concept. In itself this urge is single and alive.

The difficulty of precisely the most important and refined inquiries into language resides very often in this, that something emanating from the total impression of the language is perceived, indeed, by the clearest and most convincing feeling, yet we fail in the attempt to set it out with sufficient fullness, and to define it in specific concepts. We now have to struggle with this here as well. The characteristic form of languages depends on every *single* one of their smallest *elements*; however inexplicable it may be in detail, each is in some way determined by that form. It is scarcely possible, however, to find points of which it can be maintained that this form has decisively attached to them, taken individually. So if we work through a given language, we shall find much that we could also well imagine to be otherwise without harming the nature of its form, and in order to perceive the latter in pure isolation are driven back to the *total impression*. Now here the opposite at once occurs. The most distinct *individuality* plainly strikes the eye and is borne inexorably in upon our feeling. Languages, in this respect, can least inaccurately be compared with *human countenances*. The individuality is undeniably

there, resemblances are recognized, but no measurement or description of the parts in detail and in their interconnection can subsume
the particularity in a concept. It rests upon the whole, and in the
equally individual apprehension; and hence, too, no doubt, each
physiognomy seems different to everyone. Since language, in whatever shape we may receive it, is always the spiritual exhalation of a
nationally individual life, both factors must also enter there as well.
However much in it we may fix and embody, dismember and dissect,
there always remains something unknown left over in it, and precisely
this which escapes treatment is that wherein the unity and breath
of a living thing resides. Given this nature of languages, depiction
of the form of any one of them in the sense here stated can never thus
succeed quite completely, but always up to a certain degree only,
though one that is adequate to a survey of the whole. But by this
concept the linguist is nonetheless apprised of the path on which he
must track the secrets of language and seek to unveil its nature. In
neglecting this route he unfailingly overlooks a multitude of research
points, must leave unexplained a great deal that is actually explicable,
and takes to be subsisting in isolation what is bound together by living
ties.

From the foregoing remarks it is already self-evident that by the
form of language we are by no means alluding merely to the so-called
grammatical form. The distinction we are accustomed to draw between
grammar and vocabulary can serve only for the practical purpose
of learning a language; it can lay down neither limits nor rules for
true linguistic research. The concept of the form of languages extends
far beyond the rules of *word-order* and even beyond those of *word-
formation*, insofar as we mean by these the application of certain
general logical categories, of active and passive, substance, attribute,
etc. to the roots and basic words. It is quite peculiarly applicable to
the formation of the *basic words* themselves, and must in fact be
applied to them as much as possible, if the nature of the language
is to be truly recognizable.

The form is contrasted, indeed, to a *matter*; but to find the matter
of linguistic form, we must go beyond the bounds of language. Within
the latter, it is only relatively speaking that one thing can be regarded
as the matter of another, e.g. the basic words in contrast to
declension. But the matter here is again perceived in other connections
as form. A language can also borrow words from an alien source and
genuinely treat them as matter. But if so they are such again in
relation to it, not in themselves. In an absolute sense there can be
no *formless matter* within language, since everything in it is directed
to a specific goal, the expression of thought, and this work already

[margin note: matter of language is sound as such]

begins with its first element, the articulated sound, which of course becomes articulate precisely through being formed. The true matter of language is, on the one hand, the sound as such, and on the other the totality of sense-impressions and spontaneous mental activities which precede the creation of the concept with the aid of language.

It is therefore self-evident that, in order to obtain an idea of the form of a language, we must first of all attend to the real nature of the *sounds*. Investigation of the form of a language begins right away with the alphabet, and this is treated as its primary basis throughout every part of it. The concept of form does not, as such, exclude anything factual and individual; everything to be actually established on historical grounds only, together with the most individual features, is in fact comprehended and included in this concept. It is only, indeed, if we follow the path here indicated, that all the *details* will be safely brought under investigation, since otherwise they readily run the risk of being overlooked. This leads, admittedly, to a laborious examining of fundamentals, which often extends to minutiae; but there are also details, plainly quite paltry in themselves, on which the total effect of languages is dependent, and nothing is so inconsistent with their study as to wish to seek out in them only what is great, inspired and pre-eminent. Exact investigation of every grammatical subtlety, every division of words into their elements, is necessary throughout, if we are not to be exposed to errors in all our judgements about them. It is thus self-evident that in the concept of linguistic form no detail may ever be accepted as an *isolated fact*, but only insofar as a method of language-making can be discovered therein. Through exhibiting the form we must perceive the specific course which the language, and with it the nation it belongs to, has hit upon for the *expression of thought*. We must be able to see how it relates to *other languages*, not only in the particular goals prescribed to it, but also in its reverse effect upon the mental activity of the nation. In its own nature it is itself an apprehension of particular *linguistic elements in mental unity* – such elements to be regarded as matter in contrast to this form. For a form of this kind resides in every language, and by means of this comprehensive unity a nation makes the language bequeathed by its forebears into its own. The same unity must therefore be found again in the depiction; and only if we ascend from the scattered elements to this unity do we truly obtain a conception of the language, since without such a procedure we are manifestly in danger of not even understanding the said elements in their true individuality, and still less in their real connection.

[margin note: a nation's expression of thought & its effect on mental activity of the nation]

As may be noted here in advance, both the *identity* and the *affinity of languages* must rest on the identity and affinity of their *forms*, since

[handwritten margin notes: family ties between languages depends on form, not on the number of loan words]

the effect can only be equal to the cause. So the form alone decides what other tongues a language is affiliated to by family ties. We shall apply this in the sequel to the Kawi language, which, however many Sanscrit words it may have incorporated, does not cease on that account to be a Malayan tongue. The forms of *several languages* may unite into a yet *more general form*, and the forms of *all* actually do this, in that we everywhere set out simply from the *most general*: from the connections and relationships of the ideas required to designate concepts and order speech, from the similarity of vocal organs, whose scope and nature permit only a certain number of articulated sounds, and finally from the relations obtaining between particular consonant and vowel sounds and certain sensory impressions, which then give rise to similarity of designation, without family relationship. For in language the *individualization* within a *general conformity* is so wonderful, that we may say with equal correctness that the whole of mankind has but one language, and that every man has one of his own. But among the linguistic similarities connected by closer analogies, the most outstanding is that which arises from the *genetic relationship* of nations. This is not the place to inquire as to the degree and nature of such similarity that is needed to justify the assumption of genetic relationship, where historical facts do not immediately establish it. We are here concerned merely with applying the above-developed concept of linguistic form to genetically related languages. Now in these it follows naturally from the foregoing, that the form of the particular related languages must reappear in that of the whole family. Nothing can be contained in them which would not be in accord with the general form; in the latter, rather, we shall normally find the peculiarities of each to be in some way indicated. And in each family there will be one language or another which contains the original form with greater purity and completeness. For we are speaking here only of languages that have arisen from one another, where a genuinely given matter (this term being understood always in a relative sense, as above explained) is conveyed and transformed, therefore, from one people to another in determinate sequence, though the latter can but seldom be exactly demonstrated. But the transformation itself may nevertheless remain a closely related one, given a similar way of thinking and trend of ideas in the mental power that effects it, a likeness in the speech-organs and traditional habits of utterance, and finally, where many historically external influences coincide.

[handwritten margin notes: whole of mankind has but one language; genetically related languages]

Since the diversity of languages rests on their form, and the latter is most intimately connected with the mental attitudes of nations and the power that suffuses them at the moment of creation or new conception, it now becomes necessary to develop this notion in greater detail.

In pondering on language in general, and analysing the individual tongues that are clearly distinct from one another, two principles come to light: the *sound-form* and the *use* made of it to designate objects and connect thoughts. The latter is based on the requirements that *thinking* imposes on language, from which the *general laws* of language arise; and this part, in its original tendency, is therefore the same in all men, as such, until we come to the individuality of their mental endowments or subsequent developments. The sound-form, on the other hand, is the truly constitutive and guiding principle of the diversity of languages, both in itself, and in the assisting or obstructing power it presents to the inner tendency of the language. As an element of the whole human organism, closely related to the inner mental power, it is, of course, equally precisely connected with the collective outlook of the nation; but the nature and basis of this tie are veiled in a darkness that scarcely permits of any clarification. Now from these two principles, together with the inwardness of their mutual interpenetration, there proceeds the *individual form* of each language, and they constitute the points that linguistic analysis must examine and try to present in connection. The most indispensable thing here is for the undertaking to be based on a correct and proper view of language, the depth of its origin and the breadth of its scope; and hence we must first of all take time to examine these latter.

I take the *practice of language* here in its widest extent, not merely in its relation to speech and the stock of its verbal elements, which are its direct product, but also in its connection with the capacity for thought and feeling. We are to consider the whole route whereby, proceeding from the mind, it reacts back upon the mind.

Language is the formative organ of *thought*. *Intellectual activity*, entirely mental, entirely internal, and to some extent passing without trace, becomes, through *sound*, externalized in speech and perceptible to the senses. Thought and language are therefore one and inseparable from each other. But the former is also intrinsically bound to the necessity of entering into a *union* with the verbal sound; thought

54

cannot otherwise achieve clarity, nor the idea become a concept. The inseparable bonding of *thought, vocal apparatus* and *hearing* to language is unalterably rooted in the original constitution of human nature, which cannot be further explained. The concordance of sound and thought is nevertheless plain to see. Just as thought, like a lightning-flash or concussion, collects the whole power of ideation into a single point, and shuts out everything else, so sound rings out with abrupt sharpness and unity. Just as thought seizes the whole mind, so sound has predominantly a penetrating power that sets every nerve atingle. This power that distinguishes it from all other sense-impressions is evidently due to the fact (which is not always so with the other senses, or is so differently), that the ear receives the impression of a movement, and in the echoing sound of the voice the impression, even, of a veritable action; and this action proceeds here from within a living creature, a thinking creature if the sound is articulated, and a feeling one if it is not. Just as thought at its most human is a yearning from darkness into light, from confinement into the infinite, so sound streams outward from the heart's depths, and finds a medium wonderfully suited to it in the air, the most refined and easily moveable of all elements, whose seeming incorporeality is also a sensuous counterpart to the mind. The cutting sharpness of the vocal sound is indispensable to the understanding in apprehending objects. Both things in external nature, and the activity excited within, press in upon man all at once with a host of characteristics. But he strives to compare, separate and combine, and in his higher purposes to fashion an ever more embracing unity. So he also insists upon apprehending objects in a determinate unity, and demands the unity of sound to deputize in place of it. But sound suppresses none of the other impressions which objects are capable of producing upon outer or inner sense; instead, it becomes the bearer of them, and in its individual composition, connected with that of the object – and this precisely according to the way that the speaker's individual sensibility grasps the latter – it appends a new designating impression. At the same time the incisiveness of sound permits an incalculable number of modifications which are yet precisely distinctive when presented, and do not mingle in combination, a thing not found to the same degree in any other sensory effect. Since intellectual effort does not just occupy the understanding, but arouses the whole man, this too is chiefly promoted by the sound of the voice. For as living sound it comes forth from the breast like breathing life itself, is the accompaniment, even without language, to pain and joy, aversion and desire, and thus breathes the life it flows from into the mind that receives it, just as language itself always reproduces, along with the

[handwritten margin note: sound in incorporeal air the sensuous counterpart to the mind]

object presented, the feeling evoked by it, and within itself couples, in ever-repeated acts, the world and man, or, to put it otherwise, the spontaneously active and the receptive sides of his nature. And suited, finally, to vocalization is the upright posture of man, denied to animals; man is thereby summoned, as it were, to his feet. For speech does not aim at hollow extinction in the ground, but demands to pour freely from the lips towards the person addressed, to be accompanied by facial expression and demeanour and by gestures of the hand, and thereby to surround itself at once with everything that proclaims man human.

After this preliminary view of the aptitude of sound to the operations of the mind, we can now go more accurately into the connection of *thought* and language. Subjective activity fashions an *object* in thought. For no class of presentations can be regarded as a purely receptive contemplation of a thing already present. The activity of the senses must combine synthetically with the inner action of the mind, and from this combination the presentation is ejected, becomes an object *vis-à-vis* the subjective power, and, perceived anew as such, returns back into the latter. But *language* is indispensable for this. For in that the mental striving breaks out through the lips in language, the product of that striving returns back to the speaker's ear. Thus the presentation becomes transformed into real objectivity, without being deprived of subjectivity on that account. Only language can do this; and without this transformation, occurring constantly with the help of language even in silence, into an objectivity that returns to the subject, the act of concept-formation, and with it all true thinking, is impossible. So quite regardless of communication between man and man, speech is a necessary condition for the thinking of the individual in solitary seclusion. In appearance, however, language develops only *socially*, and man understands himself only once he has tested the intelligibility of his words by trial upon others. For objectivity is heightened if the self-coined word is echoed from a stranger's mouth. But nothing is robbed from subjectivity, for man always feels himself one with his fellow-man; indeed it is strengthened, since the presentation transformed into language is no longer the exclusive possession of a single subject. In passing over to others, it joins the common stock of the entire human race, of which each individual possesses a modification containing the requirement for completion by others. The greater and more active the social collaboration on a language, the more it gains, under otherwise similar circumstances. What language makes necessary in the simple act of thought-creation is also incessantly repeated in the mental life of man; social communication through language provides him with conviction and stimulus. The power of thinking needs something that is like it and yet different from it. By the like it is kindled, and by the different it obtains a touchstone of the essentiality of its inner creations. Although the cognitive basis of truth, of the unconditionally fixed, can lie for man only within himself, the struggle of his mental effort towards it is always surrounded by the risk of deception. With a clear and immediate sense only of his mutable limitedness, he is bound to regard truth as something lying outside him; and one of the most powerful means of approaching it, of measuring his distance away from it, is social communication with others. All speaking, from the simplest kind onwards, is an attachment of what is individually felt to the common nature of mankind.

Nor is it otherwise with *understanding*. There can be nothing present in the soul, save by one's own activity, and understanding and speaking are but different effects of this power of speech. Conversing together is never comparable with a transfer of material. In the understander, as in the speaker, the same thing must be evolved from the inner power of each; and what the former receives is merely the harmoniously attuning stimulus. Hence it is also very natural for man to re-utter at once what he has just understood. In this way language resides in every man in its whole range, which means, however, nothing else but that everyone possesses an urge governed by a specifically modified, limiting and confining power, to bring forth gradually the whole of language from within himself, or when brought forth to understand it, as outer or inner occasion may determine.

But understanding could not, as we have just found, be based upon inner spontaneity, and communal speech would have to be something other than mere mutual arousal of the hearer's speech-capacity, did not the diversity of individuals harbour the unity of human nature, fragmented only into separate individualities. The comprehension of *words* is a thing entirely different from the understanding of *unarticulated sounds*, and involves much more than the mere mutual evocation of the sound and the object indicated. The *word*, to be sure, can also be taken as an indivisible whole, just as even in writing we recognize the meaning of a word-group, without yet being certain of its alphabetic composition; and it may be possible that the child's mind proceeds thus in the first beginnings of understanding. But just as not merely the animal's sensory capacity, but the human power of speech is excited (and it is far more probable that even in the child there is no moment when this would not be the case, however feebly), so the *word*, too, is perceived as articulated. But now what *articulation* adds to the mere evocation of its meaning (which naturally also occurs more perfectly thereby), is that it presents the word directly through its form as part of an infinite whole, a language. For even in single words, it is by means of this that we are given the possibility of constructing, from the elements of the language, a really indeterminate number of other words according to specific feelings and rules, and thereby to establish among all words an affinity corresponding to the affinity of concepts. The soul, however, would get no intimation at all of this artificial mechanism, would no more apprehend articulation than the blind do colours, if it did not harbour a power of rendering this possibility actual. For language cannot indeed be regarded as a material that sits there, surveyable in its totality, or communicable little by little, but must be seen as something that eternally produces itself, where the laws of production are determined, but the scope and even to some extent the nature of the product remain totally unspecified. The *speech-learning* of children is not an assignment of words, to be deposited in memory and rebabbled by rote through the lips, but a growth in linguistic capacity with age and practice. What is heard does more than merely convey information to oneself; it readies the mind also to understand more easily what has not yet been heard; it makes clear what was long ago heard, but then half understood, or not at all, in that a similarity to the new perception suddenly brings light to the power that has since become sharpened; and it enhances the urge and capacity to absorb from what is heard ever more, and more swiftly, into the memory, and to let ever less of it rattle by as mere noise. The advances thus accelerate in a constantly increasing ratio, since the growth of power and the acquisition of material mutually strengthen and enlarge each other. That in children there is not a mechanical learning of language, but a development of linguistic power, is also proved by the fact that, since the major abilities of man are alloted a certain period of life for their development, all children, under the most diverse conditions, speak and understand at about the same age, varying only within a brief time-span. But how could the hearer gain mastery over the spoken word, solely through the growth of that power of his own, developing in isolation within him, if there were not in both speaker and hearer the same essence, merely segregated individually and appropriately to each, so that a signal so fine, yet created from the very deepest and most intrinsic nature of that essence, as is the articulate sound, is enough to stir both parties, by its transmission, in a matching way?

One might wish to object to the foregoing that the children of any people, when displaced to an alien community before learning to speak, develop their linguistic abilities in the latter's tongue. This undeniable fact, we might say, is a clear proof that language is merely an echoing of what is heard, and depends entirely on social circumstances, without regard for any unity or diversity of the essence. In cases of this kind, however, it has hardly been possible to observe with sufficient accuracy how laboriously the native pattern has had to be overcome, or how perhaps in the finest nuances it has still kept its ground unvanquished. But even without paying attention to this, the phenomenon in question is sufficiently explained by the fact that man is everywhere one with man, and development of the ability to use language can therefore go on with the aid of every given individual. It occurs no less, on that account, from within one's own self; only because it always needs an outer stimulus as well, must it prove analogous to what it actually experiences, and can do so in virtue of the congruence of all human tongues. But the power of descent upon these can be seen, nonetheless, with sufficient clarity, in their distribution by nations. It is also readily intelligible in itself, since descent has so predominantly powerful an effect on the whole individuality, and the particular language at any time is again most intimately connected with this. If language, by its origin from the depths of man's nature, did not also enter into true and authentic combination with physical descent, why otherwise, for both cultured and uncultured alike, would the native tongue possess a strength and intimacy so much greater than any foreign one, that after long abstention it greets the ear with a sort of sudden magic, and awakens longing when far from home? This obviously does not depend upon its mental content, the thought or emotion expressed, but rather on the very thing that is least explicable and most individual, its sound; it is as if we were perceiving, in the native tongue, a portion of ourselves.

The picture of language as designating merely *objects*, already perceived in themselves, is also disconfirmed by examination of what language engenders as its product. By means of such a picture we would never, in fact, exhaust the deep and full content of language. Just as no concept is possible without language, so also there can be no object for the mind, since it is only through the concept, of course, that anything external acquires full being for consciousness. But the whole mode of *perceiving* things *subjectively* necessarily passes over into cultivation and the use of language. For the *word* arises from this very perceiving; it is a copy, not of the object in itself, but of the image thereof produced in consciousness. Since all objective perception is inevitably tinged with *subjectivity*, we may consider every human individual, even apart from language, as a unique aspect of the world-view. But he becomes still more of one through language, since

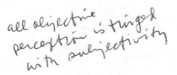

The fact that man is everywhere one with man

language enters into combination with physical descent

we see in the native tongue part of ourselves

every subjectivity is one

all objective perception is tinged with subjectivity

as we shall see later, by an added meaning of its own the word constitutes itself an object for the mind, and superimposes a new character. Via the latter, *qua* character of a speech-sound, a pervasive analogy necessarily prevails in the same language; and since a like subjectivity also affects language in the same nation, there resides in every language a characteristic *world-view*. As the individual sound stands between man and the object, so the entire language steps in between him and the nature that operates, both inwardly and outwardly, upon him. He surrounds himself with a world of sounds, so as to assimilate and process within himself the world of objects. These expressions in no way outstrip the measure of the simple truth. Man lives primarily with objects, indeed, since feeling and acting in him depend on his presentations, he actually does so exclusively, as language presents them to him. By the same act whereby he spins language out of himself, he spins himself into it, and every language draws about the people that possesses it a circle whence it is possible to exit only by stepping over at once into the circle of another one. To learn a *foreign language* should therefore be to acquire a new standpoint in the world-view hitherto possessed, and in fact to a certain extent is so, since every language contains the whole conceptual fabric and mode of presentation of a portion of mankind. But because we always carry over, more or less, our own world-view, and even our own language-view, this outcome is not purely and completely experienced.

Even the *beginnings of language* should not be thought restricted to so meagre a stock of words as is commonly supposed when, instead of seeking its inception in the original summons to free human *sociality*, we attribute it primarily to the need for mutual *assistance*, and project mankind into an imagined state of nature. Both are among the most erroneous views that can be taken about language. Man is not so needy, and to render assistance, unarticulated sounds would have sufficed. Even in its beginnings, language is human throughout, and is extended unthinkingly to all objects of casual sense perception and inner concern. Even the languages of so-called *savages*, who would have, after all, to come closer to such a state of nature, exhibit, in fact, a wealth and multiplicity of expressions that everywhere exceeds what is required. Words well up freely from the breast, without necessity or intent, and there may well have been no wandering horde in any desert that did not already have its own songs. For man, as a species, is a singing creature, though the notes, in his case, are also coupled with thought.

But language does not merely implant an indefinable multitude of *material elements* out of nature into the soul; it also supplies the latter

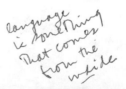

with that which confronts us from the totality as *form*. *Nature* unfolds before us a many-hued and, by all sensory impressions, a many-shaped diversity, suffused with a luminous clarity. Our subsequent reflection discovers therein a *regularity* congenial to our mental pattern. Aside from the bodily existence of things, their outlines are clothed, like a magic intended for man alone, with external beauty, in which regularity and sensory material enter an alliance that still remains inexplicable to us, in that we are seized and carried away by it. All this we find again in analogous harmonies within language, and language is able to depict it. For in passing, by means of it, into a world of sounds, we do not abandon the world that actually surrounds us. The regularity of language's own structure is akin to that of nature; and in thereby arousing man in the activity of his highest and most human powers, it also brings him closer, as such, to an understanding of the formal impress of nature, since, the latter, too, can after all be regarded simply as a development of mental powers. Through the rhythmical and musical form whose linkages are peculiar to sound, language enhances the impression of beauty in nature, transposing it into another sphere, but acts, even independently of this, through the mere cadence of speech upon the temper of the soul.

What is *uttered* at any time differs from *language*, as the body of its products; and before leaving the present section, we must take time to examine this difference more closely. A language, in its whole compass, contains everything that it has transformed into sounds. But just as the matter of thinking, and the infinity of its combinations, can never be exhausted, so it is equally impossible to do this with the mass of what calls for designation and connection in language. In addition to its already formed elements, language also consists, before all else, of methods for carrying forward the work of the mind, to which it prescribes the path and the form. The elements, once firmly fashioned, constitute, indeed, a relatively dead mass, but one which bears within itself the living seed of a never-ending determinability. At every single point and period, therefore, language, like nature itself, appears to man – in contrast to all else that he has already known and thought of – as an inexhaustible storehouse, in which the mind can always discover something new to it, and feeling perceive what it has not yet felt in this way. In every treatment of language by a genuinely new and great talent, this phenomenon is evinced in reality; and in order to encourage him in the constant labour of his intellectual struggle, and progressive unfolding of his mental life, man does in fact require that, beyond the field of past achievements, a vista should remain open to him into an infinite mass that still waits to be gradually unravelled. But language contains at the same time, in two directions, a dark unrevealed depth. For rearwards, even, it flows out from an unknown wealth that is still to a certain extent discernible, but then closes off, leaving only a sense of its unfathomability. For us, who receive light from a brief past only, language shares this *infinitude*, without beginning or end, with the whole existence of mankind. But in it we gain a clearer and more vivid sense of how even the distant past is still linked with the feeling of today; for language has traversed through the experience of earlier generations and preserved a breath of this; and these generations have a national and family kinship to us in these same sounds of the mother-tongue, which serve to express our own feelings as well.

This partly *fixed* and partly *fluid* content of language engenders a special relationship between it and the *speaking generation*. There is generated within it a stock of words and a system of rules whereby it grows, in the course of millennia, into an independent force. As we noted above, the thought once embodied in language becomes an object for the soul, and to that extent exerts thereon an effect that is alien to it. But we have primarily considered the object as having arisen from the subject, the effect as having proceeded from that upon which it reacts. We now encounter the opposite view, whereby language is truly an alien object, and its effect has in fact proceeded from something other than what it works on. For language must necessarily be a joint possession (pp. 56, 57), and is in truth the property of all mankind. Now since, in writing, it also keeps slumbering thoughts ready for arousal to the mind, it comes to enjoy a peculiar existence, which in every case, admittedly, can only hold good in the current act of thinking, but in its totality is independent of this. The two opposing views here stated, that language belongs to or is foreign to the soul, depends or does not depend upon it, are in actuality combined there and constitute the peculiarity of its nature. Nor must this conflict be resolved by making language in part something alien and independent, and in part neither one nor the other. Language is objectively active and independent, precisely in so far as it is subjectively passive and dependent. For nowhere, not even in writing, does it have a permanent abode; its 'dead' part must always be regenerated in thinking, come to life in speech and understanding, and hence must pass over entirely into the subject. But this act of regeneration consists, precisely, in likewise making an object of it; it thereby undergoes on each occasion the full impact of the individual, but this impact is already in itself governed by what language is doing and has done. The true solution of this opposition lies in the *unity of human nature.* In what stems from that, in what is truly one with myself, the concepts of subject and object, of dependence and independence, are each merged into the other. Language belongs to me, because I bring it forth as I do; and since the ground of this lies at once in the speaking and having-spoken of every generation of men, so far as speech-communication may have prevailed unbroken among them, it is language itself which restrains me when I speak. But that in it which limits and determines me has arrived there from a human nature intimately allied to my own, and its alien element is therefore alien only for my transitory individual nature, not for my original and true one.

When we think how the current *generation* of a people is governed by all that their *language* has undergone, through all the preceding centuries, and how only the power of the single generation impinges thereon – and this not even purely, since those coming up and those departing live mingled side by side – it then becomes evident how small, in fact, is the *power of the individual* compared to the might of language. Only through the latter's uncommon plasticity, the possibility of assimilating its forms in very different ways without damage to general understanding, and through the dominion exercised by every living mind over its dead heritage, is the balance somewhat restored. Yet it is always language in which every individual feels most vividly that he is nothing but an outflow of the whole of mankind. For while each reacts individually and incessantly upon it, every generation nevertheless produces a change in it, which only too often escapes notice. For the change does not always reside in the words and forms themselves, but at times only in their differently modified usage; and where writing and literature are lacking, the latter is harder to perceive. The reaction of the individual upon language becomes more apparent if we consider, as we must not omit to do if our concepts are to be sharply defined, that the *individuality* of a language (as the term is commonly understood) is only comparatively such, whereas true individuality resides only in the *speaker* at any given time. Only in the individual does language receive its ultimate determinacy. Nobody means by a word precisely and exactly what his neighbour does, and the difference, be it ever so small, vibrates, like a ripple in water, throughout the entire language. Thus all understanding is always at the same time a not-understanding, all concurrence in thought and feeling at the same time a divergence. The manner in which language is modified in every individual discloses, in contrast to its previously expounded *power*, a dominion of man over it. Its power may be regarded (if we wish to apply the term to mental forces) as a physiological efficacy; the dominion emanating from man is a purely dynamical one. In the influence exerted on him lies the *regularity* of language and its forms; in his own reaction, a principle of *freedom*. For a thing may spring up in man, for which no understanding can discover the reason in previous circumstances; and we should misconceive the nature of language, and violate, indeed, the historical truth of its emergence and change, if we sought to exclude from it the possibility of such inexplicable phenomena. But though freedom in itself may be indeterminable and inexplicable, its bounds can perhaps be discovered, within a certain sphere reserved to it alone; and linguistic research must recognize and respect the phenomenon of freedom, but also be equally careful in tracing its limits.

§10

The *articulated sound*, the foundation and essence of all speech, is extorted by man from his physical organs through an impulse of his soul; and the animal would be able to do likewise, if it were animated by the same urge. Already in its first and most indispensable elements, language is so utterly and exclusively rooted in man's spiritual nature, that its permeation is sufficient, though necessary, to transform the animal sound into the articulated one. For the *intent* and capacity to *signify*, and not just in general, but specifically by presentation of a *thought*, is the only thing that constitutes the articulated sound, and nothing else can be stated to describe its difference from the *animal cry*, on the one hand, and the *musical tone* on the other. It cannot be described by reference to its *constitution*, but only by the *way it is produced*, and this is not due to any incapacity on our part, but is typical of its very nature, since it is nothing else but the soul's *intention* to utter it, and contains only so much of the *physical* as external perception cannot do without.

This physical element, the *audible sound*, can even be in some degree separated from it, thereby bringing out the *articulation* more purely still. This can be observed in *deaf-mutes*. All access by ear is closed to them, but they learn to understand what is said from the movement of the speaker's vocal organs, and from writing, whose essence already consists wholly of articulation; and they speak themselves, when guided as to the position and motion of their vocal organs. This can only come about through the power of articulation that is present even in them, in that through the connection of *their* thought with *their* vocal organs they learn to divine in *another* from the one component, the movement of his vocal organs, the other component, his thought. The tone heard by us is disclosed to them through the position and motion of the organs and the accompanying script; by eye, and the strained endeavour to speak themselves, they grasp its articulation without the noise of it. A remarkable decomposition of the articulated sound therefore takes place in them. Since they read and write alphabetically, and themselves learn to speak, they really understand the language, and are not merely acquainted with ideas inspired by signs or pictures. They learn to speak not merely because they possess reason, as other men do, but quite especially because they also have the capacity for speech, a congruence of their thought with their vocal organs, and the urge

65

to have the two cooperate – both the one and the other being essentially rooted in human nature, though maimed in one respect. The difference between them and us is that their vocal organs are not roused to imitation by the example of a fully articulated sound, but must learn to express their activity by a circuitous, artificial, unnatural route. But it is also apparent in their cases, how deeply and narrowly writing is connected with language, even in the absence of mediation by ear.

Articulation rests upon the power of mind over the vocal organs, to compel them to deal with *sound* in accordance with the form of its own working. The point at which form and articulation meet, as in a binding medium, is that both divide their domains into *basic parts*, whose assembly does nothing but form such wholes as bear within them the striving to become parts of new wholes. *Thinking*, furthermore, demands collection of the *manifold into unity*. The necessary marks of the *articulated sound* are therefore a sharply apprehensible unity, and a character that can enter into specific relationship with any and every other articulated sound imaginable. The distinctness of the sound from all its contaminating *side-tones* is indispensable to its clarity and the possibility of harmonious euphony, but also flows directly from the intention of making it an element of *speech*. It stands there purely on its own, if the latter is truly vigorous; detaches itself from the confused and obscure animal cry; and emerges as the product of a purely human impulse and intent. The adaptation to a system, whereby every articulated sound bears something in itself, in relation to which other sounds may stand beside or over against it, is effected by the manner of production. For every individual sound is formed in relation to the others that are necessary, along with it, for the free completeness of speech. Though it cannot be said how this comes to pass, articulated sounds break forth from every people, and in that relation to each other which their language-system demands. The first major differences are due to the diversity of the *vocal organs* and the spatial *point* in each case where the articulated sound is produced. It is then allied to *secondary characteristics*, which may be peculiar to each system without regard for differences in the organs, such as aspiration, sibilance, nasal tone etc. But by these the pure *distinctness* of the sounds is endangered; and it is a doubly strong proof of the prevalence of a correct sense of language, if an alphabet contains these sounds so curbed by enunciation that they ring out completely, and yet pure and unmixed to the finest ear. These secondary characteristics must thereupon merge with the articulation underlying them, in a specific modification of the main sound, and be utterly proscribed in any other, irregular form.

The articulated sounds formed as *consonants* cannot be pronounced unless accompanied by a *gust of air* to provide resonance. Depending on *where* it is produced, and the *orifice* it flows through, this expiration furnishes sounds just as definitely different and rigidly contrasted to each other as those of the series of consonants. Through this simultaneous pair of sound-procedures the *syllable* is formed. But in this there are not two or more sounds, as our mode of writing might seem to suggest, but really only one sound expelled in a particular manner. The division of the simple syllable into a consonant and vowel, insofar as it is sought to think of them as independent, is merely an artificial one. In nature the consonant and vowel mutually determine each other in such a way as to constitute, for the ear, a quite inseparable unity. So if writing, too, is to designate this natural feature, it is more correct, as is done by some Asiatic alphabets, to treat the vowels, not as true letters at all, but merely as modifications of the consonants. Strictly speaking, even the vowels cannot be pronounced alone. The airstream that forms them requires a check to make it audible; and if no clearly sounding consonant provides this, an aspiration, be it ever so gentle, is needed for the purpose, which some languages prefix, even in writing, to every initial vowel. This aspiration can be gradually intensified into a true guttural consonant, and a language may indicate the different stages of this roughening by special letters. The vowel demands the same pure distinctness as the consonant, and the syllable must carry this double distinctness within it. But yet it is harder to preserve in the vowel-system, though more necessary for the perfection of language. The vowel combines not only with a sound that precedes it, but equally with a following one, which may be a pure consonant, but also a mere aspirate, like the Sanscrit *visarga* and in some cases the Arabic final *elif*. But precisely there, however, the purity of the sound is harder for the ear to catch than in initial position, especially if no true consonant, but only a secondary feature of the articulated sound is adjoined to the vowel; so that the writing of some peoples appears very deficient from this point of view. Through the two series of consonants and vowels, which constantly determine each other, though specifically differentiated as much by ear as in the abstract, there arises not only a new multiplicity of relationships in the alphabet, but also an opposition of these two series to one another, of which language makes manifold use.

In the total of articulated sounds, a two-fold feature can therefore be distinguished in every alphabet, whereby the latter operates more or less beneficially upon the language: namely, the absolute *abundance* of sounds in it, and the relative status of these sounds to each other,

and to the *completeness* and *regularity* of a *perfected sound-system*. For by
its schema, a system of this kind contains, as so many classes of letters,
the modes in which the articulated sounds are ordered in affinity to,
or contrasted in distinction from, one another – the contrast and
affinity being extracted from all the relations in which they can occur.
In analysing a particular language, we therefore begin by asking
whether the diversity of its sounds is complete or deficient in
occupying those points of the schema which indicate the affinity or
contrast; and hence whether the often unmistakeable abundance of
sounds is uniformly distributed according to a picture of the whole
sound-system conforming in all its parts to the people's linguistic
sense, or whether some classes are deficient while others have a
surplus. True regularity, to which Sanscrit actually comes very close,
would require that every articulated sound that differs in its point
of formation be carried through all the classes, and hence through
all the sound-modifications, that the ear is accustomed to distinguish
in languages. In all this part of any language, as is easily seen, it
primarily comes down to a fortunate organization of the *ear* and *vocal
organs*. It is also, however, by no means a matter of indifference, how
sonorous or sound-poor, how talkative or taciturn, the natural
disposition and sensibility of a people may be. For pleasure in the
articulate sound produced gives it a wealth and variety of connections.
Nor can we always deny even to the *unarticulated sound* a certain free
and therefore higher pleasure in producing it. It is often extorted,
indeed, by distress, as when sensations are unpleasant; in other cases
there is intention behind it, in that it entices, warns or summons help.
But it also flows out without need or intent from a sense of *joie-de-vivre*,
and not merely from crude enjoyment, but also from a gentler
pleasure in the more artistic clangour of the sounds themselves. The
latter is the poetic element, a glimmering spark amid the dullness of
the brute. These different kinds of sounds are very unequally
distributed among the more or less dumb and noisy species of
animals, and the higher and more joyful type has been granted to
relatively few. It would be instructive, even for language, to know
the source of this difference, but it will perhaps remain forever
unplumbed. That only the birds possess song might perhaps be
explicable in that they live more freely than any other creatures in
the element of sound, and in its purer regions, were not so many
species of them limited to a few monotones, like the beasts that
wander the earth.

In language, however, it is not just the wealth of sounds that
counts; on the contrary, it is a question, rather, of a chaste *restriction*
to the sounds necessary for speech, and to the proper balance between

them. The feeling for language must therefore include another thing that we cannot explain in detail, an instinctive presentiment of the entire system that language will have need of in this its individual form. What is actually recapitulated in the whole genesis of language, also occurs here. Language can be compared to an immense web, in which every part stands in a more or less clearly recognizable connection with the others, and all with the whole. Whatever his point of departure, man always makes contact in speaking with a merely isolated portion of this fabric, but invariably does so, instinctively, as if everything that this one portion must necessarily agree with were simultaneously present to him at the same moment.

The individual articulations constitute the basis of all sound-connections in language. But the bounds in which the latter are thereby enclosed receive at the same time a still narrower definition through the *sound-changes* peculiar to the majority of languages and attributable to particular laws and habits. They concern both the consonant-series and that of the vowels, and some languages are still further marked out by their employment, for choice, or for different purposes, of one or other of these series. The essential utility of such transformation consists in this, that while the absolute linguistic wealth and the multiplicity of sounds are thereby increased, it is still possible to recognize, in the transformed element, its original root. Language is thereby enabled to move more freely, without losing hold, in the process, of the threads required for comprehension and the pursuit of conceptual relationships. For the latter follow the change of sounds, or legislate for it in advance, and language thereby acquires a livelier clarity. A deficiency of sound-change impedes recognition, from the sounds, of the concepts designated, a difficulty that would be still more palpable in Chinese, if sound-analogy were not very often replaced there, in deriving and compounding, by analogy from the written character. But sound-transformation is subject to a pair of laws which often reinforce each other, though in other cases they also conflict. The one is a purely *organic* law, arising from the vocal organs and their cooperation, depending on ease or difficulty of utterance, and hence following the natural affinity of the sounds. The other is given by the *mental* principle of language, prevents the organs from succumbing to their mere inclination or inertia, and holds them to sound-combinations that in themselves would not be natural to them. Up to a certain point, both laws are mutually harmonious. In order to make for easier and more fluent utterance, the mental principle must so far as possible pay compliant homage to the other, and at times, even, to get from one sound to another, if such a linkage is deemed necessary by the designation, it must bring other, purely organic transitions into play. In a certain regard, however, the two laws are so opposed to each other that if the mental principle relaxes its influence, the organic gains the upper hand, just as chemical affinities take over in the animal body when the principle of life is extinct. The cooperation and conflict of these two laws bring forth, no less in what seems to us the original form of languages than in its sequel, a variety of phenomena which are discovered and enumerated by exact grammatical analysis.

The sound-changes here under discussion occur chiefly in two, or maybe three, stages of language-formation; in the *roots*, in the *words derived* from these, and in their further elaboration into the various general *forms* inherent in the nature of the language. The description of any language must begin with the characteristic system that it adopts in this respect. For it is, as it were, the bed in which the stream of the language flows from one era to the next; its general directions are governed thereby, and a persevering analysis is able to trace its most individual manifestations back to this foundation.

By *words* we understand the signs of particular concepts. The syllable represents a unity of sound; but it becomes a word only if it acquires significance on its own, which often involves a combination of several. In the word, therefore, a dual unity, of *sound* and *concept*, comes together. Words thereby become the true *elements* of *speech*, since syllables, with their lack of significance, cannot properly be so called. If we picture language as a second world, that man has objectified out of himself from the impressions he receives from the true one, then words are the sole objects therein for which the character of individuality must be retained, even in form. Speech flows on, indeed, with unbroken continuity, and until reflection on language supervenes, the speaker is contemplating therein the totality only of the thought to be designated. It is impossible to conceive the origin of language as beginning with the designation of objects by words, and then proceeding to put them together. In reality, speech is not compounded out of words that have preceded it; the words, on the contrary, emerge from the totality of speech. But they are also sensed already, without actual reflection, and even in the crudest and least cultivated speech, since word-formation is an essential requirement for speaking. The compass of the word is the limit to which language is spontaneously formative. The simple word is the perfect blossom that buds from it. It there possesses its finished product. To sentence and speech it prescribes only the regulating form, and leaves individual shaping to the speaker's choice. Words also often appear isolated in speech itself, though their true detection within its continuum can be achieved only by the

language as a second world (see p. 157)

acumen of an already more perfected linguistic sense; and this is very much a point at which the merits and defects of particular languages chiefly come to light.

Since *words* always parallel *concepts*, it is natural for *related concepts* to be designated by *related sounds*. If the pedigree of concepts is more or less clearly perceived in the mind, a pedigree in the sounds must correspond to it, so that conceptual and sound affinities coincide. The sound affinity, which should not, however, be identified with the sound, can only become apparent in that one part of the word undergoes a change subject to certain rules, while another part remains, on the contrary, quite unaltered, or changed only in a readily observable way. These *fixed parts* of words and word-forms are called the radical parts, and if presented in isolation are termed the *roots* of the language itself. In some languages these roots are seldom found naked in connected speech, and in others not at all. If the concepts are precisely separated, the latter, in fact, is always the case. For just as the roots enter into discourse, so they also take on in thought a category to match their combination, and hence no longer contain the naked and formless root-concept. On the other hand, however, they cannot be regarded in all languages as entirely a product of mere reflection, the final outcome of verbal analysis, and hence as no more than an artefact of the grammarian. In languages having specific laws of derivation for a great variety of sounds and expressions, the root-sounds must readily stand out in the speaker's memory and imagination as the truly original ones, but on their recurrence in so many conceptual shadings, as those that are generally designative. If deeply stamped, as such, upon the mind, they will readily have been interpolated, without alteration, into connected speech as well, and so also belong to the language in true verbal form. But even in primeval times they could have been useful in this way, during the period of formative development, so that they would really have preceded the derivations, and be fragments of a language that was later extended and transformed. It can thus be explained how, in Sanscrit, for example, if we consult the writings known to us, we find only certain roots commonly imported into speech. For in languages, too, there is naturally an element of chance in such matters; and if the Indian grammarians tell us that every one of their supposed roots can be used in this way, this may well be not a fact drawn from the language, but rather a law imposed on it by themselves. In forms, likewise, they seem in general to have not merely collected those in use, but to have carried every form through all the roots; and this system of generalization is plainly observable in other parts of the Sanscrit grammar as well. The enumeration of roots was the chief business of the grammarians, and the complete tabulation of these is undoubtedly their work.[1] But there are also languages which really have no roots, in the sense here employed, because they lack any laws of derivation or sound-change from simpler linkages of sound. In that case, as in Chinese, roots and words coincide, since the latter cannot be dismembered or expanded into any forms; the language possesses nothing but roots. It is conceivable that from such languages there might have arisen others, which added this sound-change to the words, so that the naked roots of those languages would consist of the word-stock of an older one, which in them had entirely or partially vanished from speech. But I cite this merely as a possibility; that such a thing has actually occurred in any language, could only be shown on historical grounds.

In reverting to the simple, we have here separated words from roots; but, ascending to the more complex, we can also distinguish them from truly *grammatical forms*. For in order to be fitted into speech, words must exhibit various states, and the designation of these can occur in the words themselves, so that a third sound-form arises from this, and usually an expanded one. If the separation here referred to is sharp and exact in a language, the words cannot fail to designate these states, and hence insofar as the latter are designated by sound-difference, such words cannot enter into speech unchanged, but can at best appear as parts of other words that carry these signs within them. Now where this happens in a language, these words are called *basic words*; the language then actually possesses a sound-form in three expanding stages; and this is the situation in which its sound-system is enlarged to the greatest extent.

Apart, however, from refinement of the ear and vocal organs, and the impulse to give maximum diversity and most perfect elaboration to the sound itself, the merits of a language, with regard to its *sound-system*, depend quite especially on the latter's relation to *meaning*. To represent outer objects, that speak to all senses at once, and the inner motions of the mind, entirely by impressions on the ear, is an operation largely inexplicable in detail. That connection exists between the *sound* and its *meaning*, seems certain; but the nature of this connection is seldom fully stateable, can often be divined merely, and far more often still is wholly beyond conjecture. If we

---

[1] Now this also explains why no regard is paid, in the form of the Sanscrit roots, to the laws of euphony. The tables of roots that have come down to us everywhere bear the mark of being a labour of the grammarians, and a whole number of roots may owe their existence solely to the grammarians' habit of abstraction. Pott's admirable researches (*Etymologische Forschungen*, 1833) have already assigned a great many to this region, and we may hope for many more from the continuance of his work.

fix our attention on simple words, since nothing can be said here of compounds, we perceive a three-fold reason for linking certain sounds to certain concepts, but feel at the same time that this does not remotely cover everything, especially in regard to the application. We can distinguish, accordingly, three ways of designating concepts: *imitative*

1. The *directly imitative*, where the noise emitted by a sounding object is portrayed in the word, to the extent that articulated sounds are capable of reproducing the unarticulated. This designation is, as it were, a pictorial one; just as a picture presents the way in which the object appears to the eye, so language depicts the way it is apprehended by the ear. Since the imitation here is always of unarticulated sounds, articulation is in conflict, so to speak, with such designation; and depending on whether it asserts its own nature too little or too much in this cleavage, there is either too much of the unarticulated left over, or it is blurred out of all recognition. For this reason such designation, where it appears at all strongly, can hardly be acquitted of a certain crudeness, makes less of an appearance in a pure and powerful feeling for language, and is gradually lost as the language progressively develops.

2. The designation that imitates, not directly, but by way of a third *symbol* factor common to both sound and object. We may call this the *symbolic*, though the concept of symbol in language is of very much wider extent. It selects, for the objects to be designated, sounds which, partly in themselves and partly by comparison with others, produce *st = fixity* for the ear an impression similar to that of the object upon the soul: *li = dissolution* as *stand*, *steady* and *stiff* give the impression of fixity; the Sanscrit *li*, *melt* and *dispersal*, that of dissolution; *not*, *nibble* and *nicety* that of the *n = sharply* finely and sharply separating. In this way objects that evoke similar *separating* impressions are assigned words with predominantly the same sounds, such as *waft*, *wind*, *wisp*, *wobble* and *wish*, wherein all the wavering, *w = wavering* uneasy motion, presenting an obscure flurry to the senses, is expressed *uneasy* by the *w*, hardened from the already inherently dull and hollow *u*. This type of designation, which relies upon a certain significance attaching to each individual letter, and to whole classes of them, has undoubtedly exerted a great and perhaps exclusive dominance on primitive word-designation. Its necessary consequence was bound to be a certain likeness of designation throughout all the languages of mankind, since the impressions of objects would have everywhere to come into more or less the same relationship to the same sounds. Much of this kind can still be observed in languages even today, and must in fairness prevent us from at once regarding all the likeness of meaning and sound to be encountered as an effect of communal descent. But if we wish to make a constitutive principle of this, and

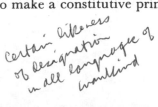
certain likeness of designation in all language of mankind

prove this type of designation to be pervasive in languages, instead of a mere constraint on historical derivation, or a check upon decision, due to an irrepressible doubt, we expose ourselves to great dangers, and pursue an altogether slippery path. Without considering other reasons, it is already much too uncertain what either the original sound was in languages, or the original meaning of the words; and yet everything comes down to this. It is very common for one letter to replace another through organic or quite accidental change, like *n* for *p*, or *d* for *r*; and it is now not always apparent where this has been the case. Since the same result, moreover, can be attributed to different causes, we cannot eliminate even a high degree of arbitrariness from explanation of this type.

3. Designation by sound-similarity, according to the relationship of the concepts to be designated. Words whose meanings lie close to one another, are likewise accorded similar sounds; but, in contrast to the type of designation just considered, there is no regard here to the character inherent in these sounds themselves. For its true emergence, this mode of designation presupposes verbal wholes of a certain scope in the system of sounds, or at least can be applied more extensively only in such a system. It is, however, the most fruitful of all, and the one which displays with most clarity and distinctness the whole concatenation of what the intellect has produced in a similar connectedness of language. This designation, in which the analogy of concepts and sounds, each in its own domain, is so pursued that each must keep step with the other, may be called the *analogical*.

In the whole field of what calls for designation in language, there are two radically different classes: the individual *objects* or *concepts*, and those *general relations* which can be combined with many of these, partly to designate new objects or concepts, and partly to link speech together. The general relations belong, in the main, to the *forms of thinking* itself, and in that they admit of derivation from an original principle, constitute closed *systems*. In these the individual item is determined by intellectual necessity, alike in its relationship to others, and to the thought-form encompassing the whole. If an extended sound-system, permitting multiplicity, is now appended to the language, the concepts of this class, and the sounds, can be carried through in a progressively concomitant analogy. Of the three types of designation enumerated above (p. 73), it is primarily the symbolic and the analogical which are applicable in these relations, and can actually be clearly recognized in a number of languages. If in Arabic, for example, a very common way of forming collective nouns is to insert a lengthened vowel, the assembled mass is symbolically represented by the length of the sound. But this can already be seen as a refinement due to a more highly developed sense of articulation. For some ruder tongues depict the same by a true pause between the syllables of the words, or in a manner that approximates to gesture, so that the allusion then becomes still more physically imitative.[2] Of like nature is the direct repetition of the same syllable for multiple reference, and also to indicate the majority, or time past. It is remarkable to see, in Sanscrit, and partly also in the Malayan family of languages, how superior tongues cope with the doubling of syllables by weaving it into their sound-system, altering it by laws of euphony, and thereby depriving it of the cruder, symbolically imitative jangle of syllables. The intransitive verb is most finely and significantly designated in Arabic by the weaker, yet incisively penetrating *i*, in contrast to the *a* of the active, and in some languages of the Malayan family by insertion of the hollow nasal tone, kept somewhat more internalized. The nasal must be preceded here by a vowel. But the choice of this vowel again follows the analogy of designation; apart from the few cases where this vowel assimilates to that of the syllable following, through a power exerted by sound over sense, the *m* is heralded by the hollow *u*, proceeding from the depths of the vocal organs, so that the intruded syllable *um* constitutes the mark of the intransitive.

But since language-making finds itself here in a wholly intellectual region, at this point also there develops, in a quite eminent way, yet another, higher principle, namely the pure and – if the term be allowed – quasi-naked *sense of articulation*. Just as the effort to lend meaning to sound engenders, as such, the nature of the articulated sound, whose essence consists exclusively in this purpose, so the same effort is working here towards a determinate *meaning*. This determinacy becomes the greater as the field of the designandum still hovers effectively before the mind; for this field is the soul's own product, though it does not always enter, as a whole, into the light of consciousness. The making of language can thus be more purely guided here by the endeavour to distinguish like and unlike among concepts, down to the finest degree, by choice and shading of sounds. The purer and clearer the intellectual view of the field to be designated, the more the making of language feels compelled to let itself be guided by this principle; and its final victory in this part of its business is that principle's complete and visible dominance. Thus if fineness of ear and vocal organs, and of the sense of euphony, be regarded as the first major advantage of the language-making

---

[2] Some particularly notable examples of this kind are to be found in my essay on the genesis of grammatical forms. *Abhandlungen der Akademie der Wissenschaften zu Berlin*, 1822, 1823. *Historisch-philologische Classe*, p. 413.

nations, the strength and purity of this sense of articulation constitutes the second. The crux of the matter is that significance should truly permeate the sound; that nothing in the sound but its meaning should appear, at once and unbroken, to the ear that receives it; and that, starting from this meaning, the sound should appear precisely and uniquely destined for it. This naturally presupposes great precision in the relations delimited, since it is these that we are chiefly discussing at this point, but also a similar precision in the sounds. The more specific and unphysical the latter, the more sharply they are set off from one another. Through the dominance of the sense of articulation, both the receptivity and spontaneity of the language-making power are not merely strengthened, but also kept on the one right track; and since this power, as I already said earlier (p. 69), invariably deals with every detail in language as if the entire fabric that the detail belongs to were simultaneously present to it by instinct, it follows that in this area, too, the same instinct is at work and discernible, in proportion to the strength and purity of the sense of articulation.

The *sound-form* is the expression which language creates for thought. But it can also be regarded as a receptacle that language fits itself into, so to speak. The *creation*, if it is to be a true and complete one, could hold good only of the original *invention of language*, and thus of a situation that we do not know about, but only presuppose as a necessary hypothesis. But the *application* of a sound-form already at hand to the inner purposes of language, can be deemed possible in intermediate periods of *language-making*. Through inner illumination and the favour of outer circumstances, a people might so utterly impart a different form to the language bequeathed to it, that this language would thereby become an entirely different and new one. The possibility of this in languages of altogether different form may reasonably be doubted. It is undeniable, however, that languages are guided by the clearer and more definite insight of the inner speech-form to create more varied and sharply delimited nuances, and now make use for this purpose, by *expansion* or *refinement*, of the sound-form they have available. In families of languages, a comparison of the individual related tongues then tells us which of them has preceded the others in this way. A number of such cases can be found in Arabic, if we compare it with Hebrew; and it will be an interesting inquiry, reserved for the sequel to this work, to discover whether and how the languages of the South Sea Islands can be regarded as the basic form, from which the Malayan tongues (in the narrower sense) of the Indian Archipelago and Madagascar have simply made further development.

The phenomenon as a whole can be completely accounted for by the natural course of *language-production*. Language, as is evident from its very nature, is present to the soul in its *totality*. Every detail in it, that is, behaves in such a way as to correspond to another that has yet to become clear, and to a whole given, or rather capable of creation, by the sum of the phenomena and the laws of the mind. The actual *development* goes on gradually, however, and the *new increment* is formed *by analogy* with what is already *present*. We not only require these principles as the starting-point for all explanation of language, but they also emerge so clearly from the historical analysis of languages, that we may do this with complete assurance. What has already been *shaped* in the sound-form pulls the *new act of forming* pretty forcibly towards it, and does not allow it to strike out an essentially different path. The various kinds of verb in the Malayan languages are indicated by syllables prefixed to the basic word. These syllables were obviously not always so numerous and finely differentiated as we find them in the Tagalic grammarians. But the successive additions always retain the same position unchanged. It is the same in those cases where Arabic attempts to mark distinctions left undesignated by the older Semitic tongue. The answer is to call upon auxiliary verbs for the formation of certain tenses, rather than, by adding of syllables, to give the word itself a shape unfitting to the spirit of the language-family in question.

It thus becomes readily explicable why it is chiefly the sound-form which accounts for the *difference of languages*. This is inherent in its nature, since the physical, actually formed sound is in truth alone in constituting language, and sound also permits a much greater variety of differences than can occur with the inner speech form, which necessarily brings with it more likeness. But its more powerful influence also arises, in part, from that which it exerts upon the *inner form* itself. For if, as we necessarily must, and as we shall bring out more fully below, we always consider the making of language as a collaboration between the mental effort to designate the material required by the inner linguistic purpose, and the production of the corresponding articulated sound, then the physical, with its shape already actual, and still more the law on which its multiplicity is based, must necessarily gain an easy ascendancy over the idea, which is first seeking to achieve clarity by taking on a new shape.

The *making of language* in general must be seen as a *producing*, in which the inner idea, to make itself manifest, has a *difficulty* to conquer. This difficulty is the sound, and the conquest does not always succeed to the same degree. In such a case it is often easier to give way on the idea side, and to employ the same sound or sound-form for what is actually different, as when languages form the future and subjunctive in the same way, owing to the uncertainty implicit in both (cf. below, §11). To be sure, there is then always a weakness operative in the sound-producing ideas as well, since the truly powerful sense of language always conquers the difficulty in triumph. But the sound-form uses its weakness, and makes itself master, as it were, of the new configuration. In all languages there are cases where it is clear that the *inner striving*, wherein, on another and sounder view, the true language should after all be sought, has been more or less diverted, in *taking on the sound*, from its original path. We have already spoken earlier (pp. 69–70) of those cases where the *vocal organs* one-sidedly assert their nature and repress the true base-sounds which carry the word's meaning. It is remarkable to see here and there how the *sense of language*, working outward from within, often submits to this for a long time, but then suddenly breaks through in a particular case, and, without yielding to the *sound-tendency*, actually clings inviolably to a single vowel. In other cases a new formation that it demands is indeed created, yet is also modified at that very moment by the sound-tendency, so that a mediating agreement, as it were, arises between the two. In general, however, essentially different sound-forms exert a decisive influence on the whole attainment of the inner linguistic objectives. In Chinese, for example, no inflection of words could arise to guide the bonding of speech, owing to the establishment of a sound-structure that held the syllables rigidly apart from each other, and resisted any transformation or compounding among them. The original causes of these obstacles can, however, be entirely opposite in character. In Chinese, it seems to lie more in a lack of inclination in that people, to endow the *sound* with imaginative *multiplicity* or the *variation* that fosters harmony; and where this is absent, and the mind does not see the possibility of also clothing the various relationships of thought in suitably graduated nuances of sound, it is less disposed to make fine distinctions among these relationships. For the impulse to produce a multitude of fine and sharply demarcated *articulations*, and the mind's effort to give language as many distinctive *forms* as are needed to fetter the infinite variety of fleeting *thoughts*, are always a stimulus to one another. Originally, in the invisible motions of the spirit, we should in no way think separately of that which relates to sound, and that which is demanded by the inner aim of language – the power of *designating*, and the power that produces the designandum. The general *capacity for language* unites and embraces them both. But as the thought, *qua* word, makes touch with the external world, as the power of an already-formed matter approaches, through the handing-down of an already existing language to man, who must yet always recreate it spontaneously in himself, it is possible for that division to arise, which entitles and obliges us to consider the *production of language* from these two different points of view. In the Semitic languages, on the other hand, the encounter between the organic differentiation of a rich multiplicity of sounds, and a fine sense of articulation, partly motivated by the nature of these sounds, is perhaps the reason why these languages possess a far more artistic and meaningful sound-form than they actually distinguish necessary and primary grammatical concepts with clarity and distinctness. The sense of language, by taking the one direction, has neglected the other. Since it was not pursuing the true, natural aim of language with proper decisiveness, it turned to the achievement of an advantage that lay in its way, namely meaningful and variously treated sound-form. But to this it was led by the natural tendency of the language. The root-words, normally formed in two syllables, got space to transform their sounds internally, and this formation primarily required vowels. Now since these are obviously finer and less physical than the consonants, they also awakened and determined the inner sense of articulation to greater refinement.[3]

There is yet another way in which we may conceive an ascendancy of the sound-form, quite specifically taken as such, to be determinant of the character of languages. The notion of all the means that language employs to reach its objectives may be called its *technique*, and this can again be divided into *phonetic* and *intellectual* technique. Under the former I include the *making of words and forms*, so far as this refers merely to the *sound*, or is motivated by the latter. It is richer if the individual forms possess a wider and more sonorous compass, and also if it provides, for the same concept or the same relation, forms that differ only by expression. Intellectual technique, on the other hand, comprises whatever needs to be *designated* and *distinguished* in language. Thus it includes, for example, the possession by a language of designations for gender, the dual, or for tenses, by all possible combinations of the concept of time with that of the course of action, and so forth.

In this aspect language appears as an *instrument* for a *purpose*. But

---

[3] The influence of the disyllabism of the Semitic root-words has not only been expressly noted by Ewald (in his *Hebräische Grammatik*, p. 144, §93; p. 165, §95), but also masterfully set forth, in its prevailing spirit, throughout the whole of linguistic studies. That the Semitic languages take on a special character, in that they create their word-forms, and in part also their inflections, almost entirely by changes within the words, has been fully worked out by Bopp, and applied in a new and ingenious way to the division of languages into classes (*Vergleichende Grammatik*, pp. 107–13).

since this instrument clearly inspires the purely mental, and likewise the noblest sensory powers, through the order of ideas, clarity and precision minted therein, as well as by euphony and rhythm, the organic language-structure – the language in itself and abstracted, as it were, from its purpose – is able to capture the enthusiasm of nations, and does in fact do this. Technique then exceeds the requirements for reaching the objective; and we may equally well suppose that languages in this respect *go beyond the need*, as that they *lag behind* it. If we compare the English, Persian and strictly Malayan languages with Sanscrit and Tagalic, we perceive such a difference, of the kind here referred to, in the range and wealth of linguistic technique, wherein the immediate aim of language, the reproduction of thought, does not suffer, however, since all these three languages not only achieve it as such, but do so in part by way of eloquent and poetic diversity. I shall reserve for the sequel a return to the *ascendancy of technique* as such and in general. I only wanted to mention here what the phonetic can claim over the intellectual. Thus whatever the advantages of the sound-system might be, a disparity of this sort always indicates a want of strength in the language-making power, since that which is intrinsically unitary and vital preserves undamaged, even in its operation, the harmony residing in its nature. Where moderation is not utterly overstepped, the wealth of sound in languages can be compared to coloration in painting. The impression of both evokes a similar feeling; and even thought reacts differently if, like a mere outline, it emerges in greater nakedness, or appears, if we may so put it, more coloured by language.

wealth of sound ~~images~~ in languages
is like coloration in painting such
Thought is richer if there is more coloration

(Hawaiian has few sounds –
maybe for that reason there is a
lot of repetition)

§11

All the merits of *sound-forms*, whatever their artistry and sonority, and even when coupled with the most active sense of articulation, remain, however, incapable of bringing forth languages worthily fitted to the mind, if the radiant clarity of the *ideas* relating to language does not suffuse them with its light and warmth. This wholly *internal* and purely *intellectual part* of language is what really constitutes its nature; it is the use for which language-making employs the sound-form, and this is why language is able, as ideas continue to take shape, to lend expression to everything that the greatest minds of the latest generations strive to entrust to it. This nature of language depends on the agreement and collaboration that the *laws* disclosed in it enjoy, both with one another, and with the laws of intuiting, thinking and feeling as such. But the mental capacity has its existence only in its *activity*; it is the successive outbursting of power in all its totality, but channelled in a single direction. Those laws, therefore, are nothing but the paths on which *mental activity* moves in producing language, or to use another metaphor, the *forms* in which it mints out the *sounds*. There is no power of the soul that would not be active in this; nothing within man is so deep, so rare or so wide-ranging that it may not pass over into language and be recognizable there. The intellectual merits of language therefore rest exclusively upon the well-ordered , firm and clear *mental organization* of peoples in the epoch of making or remaking language, and are the image, indeed the direct copy, of this.

It may seem as if all languages would have to be *like* each other in their *intellectual procedure*. For the sound-form, an infinite, uncountable multiplicity is conceivable, since the sensuous and bodily individual arises from such differing causes that the possibility of its gradations cannot be calculated. But that which rests solely on mental self-activity, as the intellectual part of language does, seems to have to be alike in all men, given the similarity of purpose and means; and this part of language does, indeed, preserve a large degree of uniformity. But from various causes, there also arises in it a significant diversity. On the one hand it is engendered by the numerous levels at which the *language-making power* is to any degree operative, both absolutely and in reciprocal relation to the activities occurring in it. But on the other, there are also powers at work here whose creations cannot be measured out by the understanding, and

81

according to mere concepts. *Imagination* and *feeling* engender individual shapings, in which the individual character of the nation again emerges, and where, as in everything individual, the variety of ways in which the thing in question can be represented in ever-differing guises, extends towards infinity.

But there are even differences in the purely ideal part

Yet even in the purely *ideal* part, which depends on the linkages of the understanding, there are *differences*, though in that case they are almost always due to wrong or defective combinations. To recognize this, we have only to dwell on the truly grammatical laws. The different forms, for example, which have to be separately designated, in accordance with the needs of discourse, in the structure of the *verb*, should be completely enumerated and correctly divided in the same manner in all languages, since they can be found by mere derivation from concepts. But if we compare Sanscrit with Greek on this point,

mood in Greek but not in Sanscrit

it is striking that in the former the concept of *mood* has not only remained obviously undeveloped, but even in the very production of the language has not been truly felt or clearly distinguished from that of tense. Hence it is not properly coupled with the concept of time and has in no way been carried through completely by means of this.[1] The same occurs with the *infinitive*, which has furthermore been drawn over to the noun, with a total misconception of its verbal nature. For all that one may justly prefer Sanscrit, it has to be admitted that in this respect it lags behind the later language. The nature of speech, moreover, is favourable to such inaccuracies, in that it knows how to render them harmless to the essential attainment of

---

[1] Bopp (*Jahrbücher für wissenschaftliche Kritik*, 1834, vol. II, p. 465) was the first to notice that the normal use of the *potential* mood consists in expressing general categorical claims, in separation and independence from any particular time-determination. The correctness of this observation is confirmed by a mass of examples, especially in the moral sayings of the *Hitôpadêśa*. But if we reflect more closely on the reason for this at first sight striking employment of this tense, we find it to be used in a quite peculiar sense in these cases as a subjunctive, except that the whole idiom must be explained elliptically. Instead of saying: 'The sage never acts otherwise', we say 'The sage would so act', the omitted words 'under all circumstances and at any time' being here understood. So in virtue of this usage I should not like to call the potential a mood of necessity. Here, rather, it seems to me to be the quite pure and simple subjunctive, abstracted from all material auxiliary concepts of can, may, should etc. The peculiarity of this usage lies in the mentally appended ellipsis, and only in the so-called potential insofar as this is motivated, precisely, by the ellipsis, primarily before the indicative. For there is no denying that the use of the subjunctive, as if by cutting off all other possibilities, has a stronger effect here than the simply assertive indicative. I mention this expressly, because it is not unimportant to preserve and cherish the pure and normal meaning of grammatical forms, so long as we are not unavoidably forced to do the opposite.

*speech compensates
well for certain absences
in language*

its purposes. It allows one form to take the place of another,[2] or is
content with circumlocutions, where the proper and short expression *still those*
is lacking to it. But such cases do not cease, on that account, to be *are
imperfections* any the less faulty imperfections, and that, precisely, in the purely
intellectual part of language. I have already remarked earlier (p. 77)
that the blame for this may sometimes fall upon the sound-form,
which, once accustomed to certain formations, leads the mind to pull
even concepts that require new kinds of formation into this its
formative path. But this is not always the case. What I have just said
about the treatment of mood and infinitive in Sanscrit may well be
in no way attributable to the sound-form. I, at least, am unable to
discover anything of the kind there. Its wealth of means is also enough
to lend adequate expression to the designation. The cause is obviously
a more intimate one. The ideal structure of the verb, its inner
organism completely divided into its various parts, did not unfold
clearly enough to the nation's formative mind. Yet this defect is all
the more wonderful, in that otherwise no language presents the true
nature of the verb, the pure synthesis of being and concept, in so true
or so idiomatic a fashion as Sanscrit, which knows simply no other
way of expressing it, save in a form that is never static and always
indicative of particular individual circumstances. For the root-words
cannot be regarded as verbs at all, nor even exclusively as verbal
concepts. Though the cause of such a defective development or
incorrect notion of a linguistic concept may have to be sought
externally, as it were, in the sound-form, or internally, in the ideal
conception, the fault always lies in a want of power in the capacity
for producing language. A projectile flung with the requisite force
cannot be thrown off its course by contrary impediments, and an
idea-content, seized and worked upon with suitable intensity,
develops with uniform perfection down to its subtlest refinements,
which only the finest analysis is able to dissect.

Just as *designation of concepts* and the *laws of syntax* appeared, in the
sound-form, as the two points chiefly to be noted, so the same holds
good in the inner, intellectual part of language. In *designation*, we also
have here, as we did there, the distinction as to whether we are
seeking to express quite *individual objects*, or whether *relations* are to
be represented, which if applicable to a whole number of instances,
collect them uniformly in a general concept – so that really there are
three cases to be distinguished. The designation of *concepts*, to which
the first two belong, was what constituted *word-making* in the case of

---

[2] This confusion of one grammatical form with another has been treated more at
length in my essay on the genesis of grammatical forms. *Abhandlungen der Akademie
der Wissenschaften zu Berlin*, 1822, 1823. *Historisch-philologische Classe*, pp. 404–7.

the sound-form, and is paralleled here by *concept-making*. For every concept must inwardly be held fast to markers peculiar to itself, or to relations with other concepts, while the sense of articulation discovers the designating sounds. This is even the case with external physical objects that are plainly perceivable by the senses. Even for them the word is not the equivalent of the object that hovers before the sense, but rather the conception thereof through language-production at the particular moment of finding the word. This is a notable source of the multiplicity of expressions for the same objects; and if in Sanscrit, for example, the *elephant* is now called the twice-drinking one, now the two-toothed one, and now the one equipped with a single hand, as many different concepts are thereby designated, though always the same object is meant. For language never represents the objects, but always the concepts that the mind has spontaneously formed from them in producing language; and this is the forming under discussion here, insofar as it must be seen as quite internal, preceding, as it were, the sense of articulation. But this division admittedly holds only for language analysis, and cannot be regarded as existing in nature.

From another point of view, the two latter of the three cases above distinguished stand closer to one another. The general *relations* for designating particular objects, and the grammatical *word-inflections*, are both based largely on the universal *forms of intuition* and on the *logical ordering* of concepts. There lies in them, therefore, a surveyable system, admitting of comparison with that which emerges from each particular language, and here again the two points strike the eye: the completeness and correct isolation of the *designandum*, and the *designation* itself that is ideally chosen for each such concept. For here comes in precisely what was already stated above. But since it is always a question here of designating *non-sensory* concepts, and often mere relationships, the concept must frequently, if not always, be taken, for language, in a *pictorial* way; and now here the real depths of the sense of language are apparent, in the combining of those *simplest concepts* that govern the whole language from the ground up. *Person*, plus pronoun, and *spatial relations* play the most important part in this; and it can often be shown how they are related to each other, and coupled in a perception that is simpler still. It here becomes evident what language as such, at its most characteristic, and quasi-instinctively, implants in the mind. Individual diversity should be given least scope here, and the difference among languages on this point should rely, rather, on the mere fact that in some it is partly that a more fruitful use is made of it, and partly that the designation drawn from this depth is indicated more clearly and more accessibly to consciousness.

natural individuality

The designation of particular inner and outer objects penetrates deeper into sensory intuition, imagination, feeling and, through the collaboration of these, into character as such, since here there is true combination of *nature* with *man*, of the partly actual material *substance* with the formative *mind*. In this area, therefore, it is chiefly the national *individuality* that shines forth. For man is approaching external nature in a comprehending way, and spontaneously develops his inner feelings according to the way that his mental powers are graded in different proportions against each other; and this is equally marked out in the production of language, insofar as it inwardly forms concepts over against the word. Here, too, the great borderline is whether a people puts more objective *reality* into its language, or more subjective *inwardness*. Although the clearer development of this always occurs gradually only, as culture advances, the seed of it already lies, nevertheless, in unmistakable connection in the *first beginnings*; and even the *sound-form* bears the stamp of it. For the more brightness and clarity the sense of language requires in depicting sensory objects, and the purer and less physically defined the determinacy it demands of mental concepts, the more sharply do the articulated sounds also make their appearance, and the more sonorously do the syllables range themselves alongside each other to form words; for within the soul, what we distinguish in reflection is undividedly one. This dichotomy of clearer and more fixed objectivity, and more deeply wrought subjectivity, strikes the eye on making careful comparison of Greek and German. But this influence of national individuality in language is apparent in two ways: in the *formation* of particular *concepts*, and in the relatively different *abundance* of the language *in concepts* of a certain kind. In one case imagination and feeling, guided by sensory intuition, are manifest ingredients of the particular designation; in another it is the finely-dissecting understanding; and in still another, the boldly-conjoining spirit. The same colour which thereby imbues the terms for all sorts of objects, also shows that of the nation's conception of nature. No less evident is the preponderance of terms attaching to a particular cast of mind. An example of this can be seen from Sanscrit, in the prevailing number of religious or philosophical words, unmatched, perhaps, in any other language. It must be added that these concepts are formed, for the most part, in the barest fashion possible, from their simple base-elements alone, so that the deeply abstractive temper of the nation is still more clearly reflected in this. Hence the language inherently bears the same stamp that we find again in the entire literature and mental activity of ancient India, and even in its outer life-style and morality. Language, literature and government unanimously attest that inwardly the quest for first causes and the

very intensely spiritual character of the
people who speak Sanskrit (their national character)

speculative often
threatening to
fall into nothing-
ness

final goal of human existence, and outwardly the condition exclusively
dedicated to this, namely meditation and endeavour towards divinity
and priesthood, were the dominant traits defining the national
character. An additional tint to all three was the habit of speculation,
often threatening to dissolve in nothingness, and even actually
working toward this goal, and the delusion of being able to transcend
the bounds of humanity by adventurous practices.

It would, however, be a one-sided notion to suppose that *national
uniqueness* of mind and character is solely revealed in forming
concepts; it exerts an equally large influence on the *ordering of speech*,
and is no less visible there. It can also be understood how the fire
that burns stronger or weaker, brighter or dimmer, quicker or slower
within, should predominantly so discharge into the expression of
complete thoughts, and the outflowing series of feelings, that its
individual nature is directly evinced from this. On this point also,
Sanscrit and Greek give rise to attractive and instructive comparisons.
But peculiarities in this part of language are set forth only to the
smallest extent in particular *forms* or specific *laws*, and the analysis
of language therefore finds here a more difficult and troublesome task.
The mode, on the other hand, of syntactically constructing whole
sequences of ideas is very closely connected with what we were
discussing earlier, namely the structuring of *grammatical forms*. For
poverty and indefiniteness of forms are a bar to letting the thought
roam in too broad a compass of speech, and necessitate a simple
sentence-structure, content with just a few pauses. Yet even where
a wealth of finely-distinguished and sharply-designated grammatical
forms is available, it must still be supplemented by an inner living
impulse towards the building of longer, more meaningfully tortuous,
more inspired sentences, if the ordering of speech is to grow towards
perfection. This impulse must have been working less energetically
during the period when Sanscrit took on the form of its currently
known products, since otherwise, as the genius of Greek did, it would
also have managed, with a certain prescience, to create the possibility
for what now, at least, is seldom disclosed to us by deed in its ordering
of speech.

But much in the sentence-structure and ordering of speech is not
reducible to *laws*, being dependent, rather, on the given speaker or
writer. Language then has the virtue of providing freedom and
abundance of means for the *multiplicity of idioms*, even though often
it merely furnishes the possibility of creating them oneself at any
given moment. Without changing the language in its sounds, and still
less in its forms and laws, time, through a growing evolution of ideas,
a heightened power of thought, and a more deeply penetrating

where does
this poverty
and indefiniteness
come from?
that limits
thought?
So it thought
that limits
thought or
language that
limits thought

you have to
leave longer
more
tortuous
more
meaningful,
inspired
sentences if
your language
is to grow
to perfection.
The inner
living impulse
that causes this

much is not reducible to laws
but to individual writers

capacity for feeling, will often bring into a language what it did not formerly possess. Another meaning is then installed in the same lodging, a different thing presented under the same guise, a differently ordered train of ideas suggested via the same laws of coupling. This is a continuing harvest from the *literature* of a people, though especially there from its *poetry* and *philosophy*. The extension of the other sciences does more to furnish language with a single material, or divides and defines the existing matter with greater fixity; but poetry and philosophy make contact, in a wholly different sense, with the innermost in man himself, and thus also have a stronger and more formative effect upon the language so intimately entwined with his nature. Those languages, therefore, in which, at least in one epoch, a poetic and philosophical spirit has been dominant, are also the most capable of *perfection* in their *progress*; and doubly so, if this dominance has sprung from a spontaneous impulse, and has not been aped from abroad. At times even in entire *families*, such as the Semitic and Sanscrit, the poetic spirit is so vital, that its occurrence in an earlier language of the family is resurrected, as it were, in a later one. Whether the wealth of *sensory intuition* is in this way capable of accretion in languages, might be difficult to decide. But that *intellectual concepts*, and the sounds formed from inner perception which designate them, convey, with progressive use, a deeper and more soul-stirring *content*, is shown by the experience of all languages which have undergone centuries of development. Talented writers give the words this enhanced content, and an eagerly receptive nation adopts and propagates it. Yet *metaphors*, on the other hand, which seem – and the languages themselves bear traces of it – to have wonderfully captured the youthful sensibility of earlier ages, become so worn out in daily use that they scarcely continue to be felt. In this simultaneous advance and retreat, languages exert that influence appropriate to progressive development, which is assigned to them in the larger spiritual economy of mankind.

§12

The *combination* of the *sound-form* with the *inner laws of language* constitutes the perfection of languages; and the highest point of this perfection of theirs reposes on the fact that this combination, proceeding always in simultaneous acts of the language-making spirit, becomes a true and pure *permeation*. From the first elements onward, the production of language is a *synthetic* procedure, and that in the truest sense of the word, where synthesis creates something that does not lie, *per se*, in any of the conjoined parts. The goal is therefore reached only when the total structure of sound-form and inner shaping are fused together with equal firmness and simultaneity. The beneficial consequence that results from this is then the absolute *appropriateness* of the one element to the other, so that neither, as it were, shoots beyond the other. If this goal is attained, then neither will the inner linguistic development pursue a one-sided path, on which it is abandoned by the phonetic production of forms, nor will the sound, in rampant exuberance, rush out beyond the precise requirements of thought. By those very inner stirrings of mind that prepare for language-production, it will be guided on the contrary, towards *euphony* and *rhythm*, will find in both a counterpoise to the mere tinkling of syllables, and discover by means of them a new path, upon which, if the thought do but breathe a soul into the sound, the latter, from its own nature will again return an inspiring principle to thought. The firm combination of the two main linguistic constituents is primarily expressed in the sensuous and imaginative life that thereby blossom in language, whereas a one-sided dominance of understanding, a dry and prosy quality, are the invariable consequences if language is intellectually extended and refined in a period when the constructive urge of sound no longer has the necessary strength, or where the powers have operated from the outset in a one-sided way. We see this in detail in those languages, such as Arabic, wherein certain tenses have been formed only by separate auxiliary verbs, and where the idea of such forms has thus no longer been effectively accompanied by the urge to frame sounds. In some temporal forms, Sanscrit has actually coupled the verb *to be* with the verbal concept, in a single word.

But neither this example, nor others like it, which could easily be enumerated, and especially from the field of word-formation, display the full significance of the requirement here stated. The *completed*

88

synthesis we are talking of does not proceed from details, but from the whole composition and form of the language. It is the product of power at the moment of language-production, and indicates exactly the degree of that power's strength. As a coarsely-minted coin reproduces, indeed, all the outlines and details of form, but lacks the brilliance that arises from definition and sharpness, so likewise is the situation here. Language in general is often reminiscent of *art*, but here most of all, in the deepest and least explicable part of its procedure. The sculptor and painter also limn the idea with matter, and in their works also it can be seen whether this combination, in its intimacy of permeation, radiates freely from true genius, or whether the separated idea has been laboriously and anxiously copied down, as it were, with chisel or brush. But here too, the latter is more apparent in the weakness of the total impression than in particular defects. Now I shall, in fact, be seeking to show later on, from some particular grammatical points, how the lesser success of the necessary synthesis of outer and inner speech-form is actually revealed in a language; but to pursue the traces of such a defect into the uttermost refinements of linguistic structure is not merely difficult, but even to some degree impossible. Still less can we everywhere succeed in depicting such defects in words. But feeling is not deceived on this point, and the fault is still more clearly and plainly evinced in the effects. The true synthesis springs from the inspiration known only to high and energetic power. In the imperfect one, this inspiration has been lacking; and a language so engendered likewise exerts a less inspiring power in its use. This can be seen in its literature, which, is less inclined to those genres which require such inspiration, or bears on its face a lesser degree of it. The smaller mental power of the nation, which carries the blame for this deficiency, then evokes the same again, through the influence of a more imperfect language, in subsequent generations; or rather the weakness is evinced throughout the whole life of such a nation, until a new transformation of spirit arises through some kind of shock.

[margin annotations:]

idea and matter

There are peoples of high energy and peoples of low ...

The smaller a nation's mental power the more apparent will be the weakness of the whole life of a nation

But there can be a transformation of spirit in a culture by some kind of shock (missionaries, invasions?)

§13

The aim of this introduction, to depict *languages*, in the *diversity* of their *structure*, as the necessary foundation for the *progress* of the *human mind*, and to discuss the reciprocal influence of the one upon the other, has obliged me to enter into the *nature of language* as such. In close adherence to that position, I must follow further along this path. In the foregoing sections I have set forth the *nature* of language only in its most general aspects, and done little more than to develop its *definition* in greater detail. If we seek the nature of language in the forms of *sound* and *idea*, and the correct and vigorous *interpenetration* of the two, it still remains for us to specify here a numberless multitude of *details* whereby application is confused. In order there-fore, as is here my intention, to blaze the trail for an individual, historical comparison of languages by means of preparatory con-siderations, it is necessary at the same time to set forth the *universal* more fully, while pulling together the *particular* which then emerges into a greater *unity*. The nature of language itself offers a hand to the attainment of such a median point. Since language, in direct conjunction with mental power, is a fully-fashioned *organism*, we can distinguish within it not only *parts*, but also *laws* of procedure, or rather (since I would sooner pick terms here throughout, which do not even seem to prejudge historical research), *directions* and *endeavours*. If we wish to contrast this organism with that of the body, we can compare such tendencies with *physiological* laws, whose scientific consideration also differs essentially from the analytical description of individual parts. We shall therefore not be talking here, as in our grammars, of sound-systems, nouns, pronouns and so on, each in succession, but rather of linguistic peculiarities which run through all those particular parts, and specify them in greater detail. This procedure will also appear more to the purpose here, from another point of view. If the above-mentioned goal is to be reached, it is precisely here that the inquiry must especially keep in view a diversity of language-structure which cannot be traced to the uniform character of one linguistic family. Now this diversity will primarily have to be sought where the practice of language is most closely tied to its finite endeavours. This leads us back, though in another connection, to the designation of *concepts* and the linkage of *thought* in a sentence. Both proceed from the aim of the inner completion of thought, and its outer comprehension. In partial independence of this, there simultaneously takes shape in language an *artistically* creative principle, which belongs quite specifically to it. For concepts are conveyed in language by tones, and the concord of all mental powers is therefore coupled with a *musical element*, which, on entering into language, does not abandon, but merely modifies, its nature. The *artistic beauty* of language is not therefore loaned to it as a casual adornment, but is, on the contrary, an essentially necessary consequence of the rest of its nature, an infallible touch-stone of its inner and universal perfection. For the inner work of the mind has only vaulted to its boldest summit when the latter is irradiated by the sense of beauty.

But the procedure of language is not simply one whereby a single phenomenon comes about; it must simultaneously open up the possibility of producing an indefinable host of such phenomena, and under all the conditions that thought prescribes. For language is quite peculiarly confronted by an unending and truly boundless domain, the essence of all that can be thought. It must therefore make infinite employment of finite means, and is able to do so through the power which produces identity of language and thought. But this also necessarily implies that language should exert its effect in two directions at once, in that it first proceeds outwards to the utterance, but then also back again to the powers that engender it. Both effects are modified in each particular language by the method observed therein, and so must be taken together in expounding and evaluating that method.

We have already seen earlier that the *invention of words* in general consists only of choosing analogous sounds for analogous concepts, according to the affinity perceived in the two domains, and of casting these sounds into a more or less definite form. So two things come into consideration here, the *word-form* and the *word-affinity*. The latter, further subdivided, is a three-fold relationship, namely the relation of the *sounds*, the logical relation of the *concepts*, and the relation arising from the *reverse effect* of words upon the mind. Since the affinity, insofar as it is a logical one, rests upon ideas, we are first reminded here of that part of the vocabulary in which words are reminted, according to concepts of *general relationship*, into other words – concrete into abstract, names of individual things into collective terms, and so on. But here I put it aside, since the characteristic modification of these words is quite closely allied to that which the same word undergoes in its various relationships to discourse. In these cases an always *unvarying part* of the word's meaning is coupled with another, *changing* one. But the same also happens elsewhere in language. In the concept common to the designation of different objects, we can very often recognize a stem-like *base-component* of the word, and the procedure of language can further or impede this recognition, can emphasize or obscure the stem-concept and how its *modifications* are related thereto. The designation of the *concept* by the *sound* is a coupling of things whose nature, in truth, can never be united. But the *concept* can no more detach itself from the *word* than a man can discard his countenance. The *word* is the individual shaping of the concept, and if the latter wants to leave this shape, it can only find itself again in other words. Yet the soul must continually try to make itself independent of the domain of language, for the word, after all, is a *constraint* upon its ever more capacious inner sensitivity, and often threatens to stifle the most individual nuances thereof by a nature that in sound is more material, and in meaning too general. The soul must treat the word more as a resting-place for its inner activity, rather than let itself be imprisoned within verbal limits. But whatever it protects and achieves in this fashion, it again attaches to the word; and hence, if the mental powers be lively enough, there issues from this constant striving and counterstriving of the soul an ever-greater *refinement* of language, a growing *enrichment* thereof in spiritual content, which enhances the demands made of language in precisely the same measure as they are better satisfied. As can be seen in all highly cultivated languages, the words contain a more comprehensive or deeply penetrating meaning to the extent that thought and feeling mount to a higher plane.

The coupling of the diverse natures of *concept* and *sound* requires, quite apart from the bodily ring of the latter, and simply on the face of it, the mediation of both by a third thing, in which they can meet. Now this intermediacy is always *sensuous* in character, as the idea of taking [*nehmen*] lies in the word *Vernunft* [reason], the idea of standing [*stehen*] in *Verstand* [understanding], the idea of flowing forth [*hervor-* quellen] in *Blüte* [flowering]; it pertains to outer or inner sensation or activity. If the derivation allows us to discover it correctly, we are able, by continually separating off the more concrete aspects, to trace it back either wholly, or apart from its individual character, to *extension* or *intension*, or change in both, so that we arrive in the universal spheres of space, time and sensory degree. If we now search in this manner through the words of a particular language, we may succeed, though with the exception of many individual points, in recognizing the threads of their connection, and depicting, at least in broad outline, the general procedure individualized therein. We then try to ascend from the *concrete words* to the quasi-radical *intuitions* and *sensations*, whereby every language, according to the genius that animates it, reconciles in its words the sound with the concept. But

Margin annotations:
Concept can't detach itself from the word

word is a constraint on mind's inner sensitivity
soul must try to be independent of language

in this strife the soul refines language

the sensuous intermediacy
"taking" in Vernunft
"standing" in Verstand
bleeding flowing forth flowering all united

trace words back to the sensory sphere

this comparison of language with the ideal domain, as that which it designates, seems conversely to demand that we descend from the *concepts* to the *words*, since only the concepts, as primal images, can contain what is necessary to appraise the verbal designation, according to its type and completeness. But the pursuit of this path will be hampered by an inner obstacle, since the concepts, once marked by individual words, can no longer represent something purely *general*, but only something well-nigh individualizing. Yet if we try to achieve the purpose by setting up *categories*, there remains between the narrowest category, and the concept individualized by the word, a gulf that can never be crossed. Hence the extent to which a language exhausts the number of concepts to be designated, and the fixity of method whereby it descends from the original concepts to the derived special ones, can never be depicted in detail with any completeness, since the path of conceptual ramification is impassable, and the path of words, though it shows what has been done, does not show what is going to be required.

The *vocabulary* of a language can in no way be regarded as an *inert completed mass*. So long as the language remains alive in the people's mouth, and even without considering exclusively the constant formation of new words and word-forms, the vocabulary is a continuous *generation* and regeneration of the *word-making capacity*, first in the stock to which the language owes its form, then in the learning of speech by children, and lastly in daily usage. The infallible presence in this usage of the word that is needed at any moment is certainly not simply the work of *memory*. No human memory would be equal to this, if the soul did not simultaneously carry by instinct within it the key to the formation of the words themselves. Even a foreign language is only learnt in that, bit by bit, and maybe only by practice, we master this key to it; and this only by virtue of the sameness of the speech-patterns as such, and the special affinity thereof that exists between particular peoples. With *dead languages*, matters are only slightly different. Their vocabulary, to be sure, is from our point of view a *closed totality*, in which fortunate research is alone in a position to make discoveries lying at a remote depth. Yet the study of them can likewise succeed only by appropriation of the principle that was formerly alive in them; they quite literally undergo a real, momentary revival. For under no circumstances can a language be examined like a dead plant. *Language* and *life* are inseparable concepts, and to *learn* in this area is always merely to regenerate.

From the standpoint here adopted, the *unity* of the *vocabulary* of every language is now displayed at its clearest. It is a whole, because

unity rests on
The connection between
intuitions and sounds

one force has produced it, and this production has been carried forward in an unbreakable chain. Its unity rests on the *connection*, guided by the affinity of concepts, between the mediating *intuitions* and the *sounds*. It is this connection, therefore, that we must begin by considering here.

The *Indian grammarians* built their system, certainly too artificial, but testifying as a whole to wonderful intelligence, on the assumption that the vocabulary of their language, as it lay before them, could be explained entirely from itself. They therefore saw their language as an original one, and also ruled out any possibility of foreign words having been adopted as time went on. Both views were indubitably false. For regardless of any historical reasons, or others to be elicited from the language itself, it is in no way probable that any truly original language should have survived to our own day in its *primal form*. Perhaps in their procedure the Indian grammarians were also looking more to the purpose of bringing the language into systematic order for convenience of learning, without actually troubling themselves about the historical correctness of this scheme. But it may also have fared with the Indians on this point, as with the majority of nations during the blossoming of their spiritual development. Man always begins by seeking the connection, even of external phenomena, in the domain of *thought*; the *historical* art is always the latest, and pure *observation*, to say nothing of *experiment*, only follow a long way after idealized or fanciful systems. Man first attempts to dominate nature by way of the Idea. This point conceded, the assumption that Sanscrit could be explained entirely from itself bears witness, nonetheless, to a correct and profound insight into the nature of language as such. For a truly original language, kept pure from foreign admixture, would really have to preserve within itself such a factually demonstrable connection of its entire vocabulary. It was, moreover, an enterprise worthy of respect for its very boldness, to plunge so assiduously into word-formation, as the deepest and most mysterious aspect of all languages.

The essential basis of *sound-connection* among words is that a moderate number of *root-sounds*, underlying the whole vocabulary, is applied, by *additions* and *changes*, to concepts increasingly definite and compounded. The recurrence of the same ancestral sound, or even the possibility of recognizing it by specific rules, and the regular significance of the modifying affixes or inner changes, thereupon determine that explicability of the language from itself which may be termed a mechanical or technical one.

In respect of their production, there is, however, an important difference among words, which also relates to the root-terms, but has

no primal form of language surviving to-day

root-postulate systems

explicability of language from itself you get only in an inflected language

hitherto been much neglected. The great majority of such terms are, as it were, narrative or descriptive in nature, and designate motions, properties and objects as such, without reference to a presumable or felt *personality*; in others, however, it is precisely the expression of this, or a straightforward relation to it, which constitutes the exclusive nature of their meaning. In an earlier essay,[1] I believe I have shown correctly that *person-words* must have been primary in every language, and that it is an altogether wrong notion to consider the pronoun as the latest of linguistic parts of speech. A narrowly grammatical mode of conceiving the replacement of the noun by the pronoun has here supplanted the insight more deeply drawn from language. The first thing is naturally the personality of the speaker himself, who stands in continuous and direct contact with nature, and cannot possibly fail, even in language, to set over against the latter the expression of his self. But in the I, the Thou is also given automatically, and by a new opposition there arises the third person, though since the field of the sentient and speaking has now been left behind, this is also extended to the inanimate. If concrete properties are disregarded, the person, viz., the I, is situated in the outer context of *space*, and the inner one of *sentience*. *Prepositions* and *interjections* are therefore annexed to the words for persons. For the former are relations of space, or of *time* (considered as extension), to a certain point, inseparable from their concept; while the latter are mere effusions of the sense of life. It is even probable that the truly simple person-words have their very origin in a spatial or sentient context.

The distinction here drawn is a fine one, however, and must be taken to divide exactly as specified. For on one side of it, descriptively and with universal objectivity, are formed all the words that designate inner sensations, along with those for outer objects. The above distinction rests solely on the fact that the essence of designation consists in the actual sensory response of a specific *individuality*. On the other side there can be, and really are, pronouns and prepositions in languages, that are taken from quite concrete adjectives. The person can be designated by something connected with its concept, the preposition likewise by a conceptually related noun, as *behind* by *back*, *before* by *breast*, etc. Words that have actually arisen in this way can in time become so unrecognizable, that it is hard to decide whether they possess such a derivation, or are original words. Though the point may be disputed in particular cases, it cannot, however, be denied on that account, that every language must initially have

---

[1] 'On the Relation of *Adverbs of Place* to the *Pronoun* in Some Languages', in *Abhandlungen der Akademie der Wissenschaften zu Berlin*, 1829, pp. 1–6. Cf. also the essay on the *Dual*, ibid., 1827, pp. 182–5.

had words of this kind, originating from the immediate sense of
personality. It is Bopp's important service to have first distinguished
this two-fold category of root-words, and introduced into the structure
of words and forms what had hitherto remained unnoticed. But we
shall see very shortly in what an ingenious way, first discovered by
him as well in the forms of Sanscrit, language couples the two for its
purposes, each in a different role.

What I have here distinguished as the *objective* and *subjective* roots
of language (if for brevity I may utilize this by no means exhaustive
description of them), do not therefore share quite the same nature
with each other, and so equally cannot, in strictness, be regarded in
the same way as basic sounds. The *objective* roots bear the appearance
of having arisen through *analysis*; the auxiliary sounds have been
detached, the significance expanded to a varying extent so as to
include all the words falling under them, and forms have been
thereby created, which in this shape can only be called spurious
words. The *subjective* have been visibly coined by language itself.
Their concept allows no latitude, and is everywhere, indeed, the
expression of sharp individuality; it was indispensable to the speaker,
and could suffice, up to a point, for the achievement of a gradual
enlargement of the language. As we shall be seeing more clearly in
a moment, it therefore points to a *primitive state* of languages, which,
without definite historical proofs, can be supposed only with great
caution of the objective roots.

The name of *roots* can be given only to those basic sounds which
attach directly to the concept under designation, without the
intervention of other sounds that already have meaning of their own.
In this strict sense of the term, the roots do not need to belong to
the language proper; and in languages whose form entails clothing
the roots with auxiliary sounds, this may, indeed, be hardly the case
at all, or at any rate only under certain conditions. For the true
language is merely that disclosed in discourse, and we cannot think
of *linguistic invention* as stepping downward on the same path that
analysis follows upward. If a root appears as a word in such a
language, like the Sanscrit युध्, *yudh*, fight, or as part of a compound,
as in धर्मविद्, *dharmavid*, judicious, these are exceptions which still
in no way entitle us to presuppose a state where even the naked roots
were coupled with speech, as they are in Chinese. It is, indeed, far
more probable that, the more the root-sounds gained currency in the
speaker's ear and consciousness, such individual cases acquired
thereby their naked employment. But in working back by analysis
to the root-sound, the question arises, whether we have everywhere
attained to the truly *simple*. In Sanscrit it has already been shown

with happy insight by Bopp, and by Pott in an important work already mentioned above, which will certainly serve as the basis for further research, that numerous alleged roots are composite, or have been derived by reduplication. But doubt can be extended even to those that really appear simple. I am thinking here especially of those which deviate from the structure of the simple surrounding syllables or clothe the vowel only with such consonantal sounds as merge with it to the point where it is hard to separate them. Such so-called roots may also harbour composites that have become unrecognizable and phonetically altered by contraction, dropping of vowels, and the like. I say this, not to put empty conjectures in place of facts, but rather to avoid the arbitrary inhibition of historical research from penetrating further into linguistic circumstances that are still not adequately understood, and because the problem which here concerns us, as to how languages are connected with the capacity for cultivation, makes it necessary to investigate all the ways that the evolution of linguistic structure may have pursued.

Insofar as the root-sounds announce themselves by their constant recurrence in very varying forms, they are bound to achieve a greater clarity to the extent that a language has fashioned the concept of the *verb* in closer conformity to its nature. For in view of the fugitive and mobile character of this part of speech, which is never, so to speak, at rest, the same root-syllable necessarily appears with ever-changing added sounds. The Indian grammarians were therefore proceeding with a perfectly correct sense of their language, when they treated all roots as verb-roots, and assigned each of them to specific conjugations. But it also lies in the very nature of linguistic development that – even historically – the concepts for motion and quality will be the first to be designated; for they alone can naturally, at once, and often in the same act, be the designators of objects, insofar as they consist of simple words. But *motion* and *quality* are intrinsically close to each other, and a lively sense of language assimilates the latter to the former more frequently still. That the Indian grammarians were also aware of this essential difference separating motion and quality from words referring to independent things, is shown by their distinction between the *krit-* and *unâdi-*suffixes. Words are directly derived from the root-sounds by both. But the former consist only of words in which the root-concept is itself equipped merely with general modifications, simultaneously applicable to a number of others. Actual substances are more rarely found among them, and only insofar as their designation is of this particular type. The *unâdi-*suffixes, on the contrary, comprise only terms for concrete objects, and in the words formed by means of them the obscurest part is precisely the suffix itself, which ought to contain the more general concept modifying the root-sound. There is no denying that a good many of these formations are forced and plainly unhistorical. We see too clearly their deliberate extraction from the principle of reducing all words in the language, without exception, to the roots once postulated. Among these terms for concrete objects there may lie, on the one hand, foreign compounds adopted into the language, and on the other, compounds that have become unrecognizable, of which latter there are already, in fact, detectable examples among the *unâdi*-words. This is naturally the most obscure part of all languages, and it has therefore been justly found preferable, of late, to form from a large proportion of the *unâdi*-words a special class, of those whose origin is uncertain and obscure.

The nature of the sound-connection rests upon the conspicuousness of the stem-syllable, which languages in general preserve with more or less care, depending on the degree to which they are properly organized. But in those with a very perfect structure, *auxiliary sounds* are appended as general modifiers to the *stem-sound*, which individualizes the concept. Now since, in the pronunciation of words, each has customarily but one main accent, and the unstressed syllables lapse in contrast to the accented ones (see §16 below), in properly organized languages the auxiliary sounds also occupy a smaller, though very important, place in the simple derived words. They are, as it were, the short sharp indicators for the understanding, as to where it must locate the concept of the stem-syllable, with its greater and more evident sensuousness. This law of sensory subordination, which is also connected with the rhythmic structure of words, seems to be generally prevalent throughout very purely organized languages, even as a formal feature, without the occasion for it proceeding from the words themselves; and the efforts of the Indian grammarians to treat all words of their language in accordance with it, testifies, at least, to a correct insight into the spirit of their own tongue. But since the *unâdi*-suffixes are said not to have been found among the earlier grammarians, they would seem to have been arrived at only later. The majority of Sanscrit words for concrete objects in fact exhibit this structure of a short, falling ending, joined to a dominant stem-syllable, and this can be very readily combined with our earlier remark about the possibility of compounds that have become unrecognizable. The same impulse has operated upon compounding as upon derivation, and compared with the more individual or otherwise definitely designating part, has allowed the other to decline gradually, in concept and sound alike. For if we encounter, cheek by jowl in languages, effacements and displacements of sound over time which seem almost unbelievable, and again an obstinate adherence, traceable through centuries, to quite simple and individual ones, this is doubtless largely due to the *striving* or *yielding*, for one reason or another, of the inner linguistic sense. Time does not erase on its own, but only insofar as the sense of language first allows a sound to drop, whether by inadvertence or design.

§14

Before we now turn to the mutual relations of words in connected speech, I must mention a property of languages, which extends, not only to these relations, but also to a part of word-making itself. I have already alluded in the foregoing (pp. 91, 98) to the likeness of the cases where a word is derived from the root by addition of a general concept, applicable to a whole class of words, and where it is designated in this way by its position in speech. The operative or restrictive property of languages here is actually that which we are accustomed to lump together under the terms: *isolation* of words, *flexion* and *agglutination*. It is the pivot about which the perfection of the language-organism revolves; and we must accordingly consider it by successively inquiring, from what inner demand it arises in the soul, how it is expressed in the treatment of sound, and how these inner demands are fulfilled, or remain unsatisfied, by this expression, following always the above-established division of the activities that are together operative in language.

In all the cases here assembled, there lies, in the *inner designation* of the words, a duality of functions whose utterly different natures must be carefully distinguished. For to the act of designating the *concept* itself there is allied also a special operation of the mind which transposes that concept into a particular *category* of thought or speech; and the word's full meaning is the simultaneous outcome of that conceptual expression and this modifying hint. But these two elements lie in quite different spheres. The designation of the concept belongs to the ever more objective practice of the linguistic sense. The transposing of it into a particular category of thought is a new act of the linguistic self-consciousness, whereby the single case, the individual word, is related to the totality of possible cases in language or speech. Only through this operation, performed in the utmost purity and depth, and firmly embedded in language itself, is there a coupling therein, in appropriate fusion and subordination, of the independent activity of language, springing from thought, and that other activity which responds, rather, in pure sensibility, to outer impressions.

There are therefore naturally *degrees* to which the different languages meet this requirement, for none can wholly disregard it in the inner process of linguistic shaping. Yet even in those where it attains to external designation, it is a question of the depth and vigour

100

The two-fold principle (1) objective one of designation
(2) subjective one of logical
classification

§14 *Isolation, inflection and agglutination* 101

with which they actually ascend to the original categories of thought,
and accord them validity in their interconnection. For these categories
again form a connected whole among themselves, whose systematic
completeness shines through the languages to a greater or lesser
extent. But the tendency to classify concepts, to define the individual
by the species it belongs to, can also arise from a need to distinguish
and designate, in that the species-concept is attached to the individual
one. In itself, therefore, such a tendency admits of various *stages*, and
either from this origin, or from the purer one arising out of the mind's
need for lucid logical order. There are languages which regularly add
the species-concept to the names of living creatures, and some among
them where the designation of this species-concept has become a true
suffix, recognizable only by analysis. These cases, indeed, are still
always connected with our earlier statement, in that a two-fold
principle, an objective one of designation, and a subjective of logical
classification, is also visible in them. But on the other side they are
utterly at variance with it, in that here it is no longer forms of thought
and speech which enter into the designation, but merely different
classes of actual objects. Words so formed are now becoming quite
similar to those in which two elements constitute a compound
concept. What corresponds, on the other hand, in the inner shaping,
to the concept of inflection, differs precisely in that the duality we
started from in defining this concept is made up, not of two elements
at all, but only one, transposed into a specific category. The
characteristic feature here is precisely that this duality, when
analysed, is not of the same kind, but a different one, and pertains
to different spheres. Only so can purely organized languages achieve
the deep and firm combination of spontaneity and receptiveness,
from which there subsequently proceeds in them an infinity of
thought-couplings, all bearing the mark of a true form, which
satisfies, purely and fully, the demands of language as such. In
actuality, this does not preclude the possibility of finding, in words
so formed, a place for distinctions that have not been created simply
from experience. But in a language that once starts from the correct
mental principle in this part of its structure, such distinctions are then
conceived more generally, and are already placed on a higher level
by all the remainder of that language's procedure. Thus the concept
of gender-difference, for example, would not have been able to arise
without actual observation, though it is at once assigned, automatically as it were, to the original differences of imaginable forces,
by way of the general concepts of spontaneity and receptiveness. Now
it is actually exalted to this height in languages that utterly and
completely assimilate it into themselves, and designate it in just the

same way as they do words arising from the merely logical differences among concepts. We are not now coupling two concepts to each other, but are simply assigning one, by an inner mental relation, to a class whose concept runs through many things in nature, but could be regarded, even apart from particular observation, as a difference of reciprocally active forces.

What has been vividly sensed in the mind always makes itself felt, also, during the language-making periods of nations, in the corresponding sounds. As the feeling first inwardly arose, therefore, of having to attach a two-fold expression to the word, in accordance with the needs of changing speech or the word's enduring meaning, and without prejudice to its simplicity, so *inflection* emerged in languages, from a source within. But we can only pursue the opposite path, and penetrate into the inner meaning solely from the sounds and their analysis. Now here, where this feature has developed, we actually find a duality, a *designation* of the concept, and an *indication* of the category to which it is assigned. For in this way, perhaps, we can most definitely distinguish the two-fold striving, at once to mint out the concept, and to confer on it an indication of the kind under which it is actually to be thought. But the difference of intention here must emerge from the treatment of the sounds themselves.

The word admits of transformation in only two ways: by *internal change* or *external increment*. Both are impossible where the language rigidly encloses all words in their root form, with no chance of outer addition, and also leaves room for no change within them. Where *internal change* is possible, however, and is even promoted by the word-structure, the distinction of *indication* from *designation* – to retain these terms – is in this way easy and infallible. For the intention, inherent in this practice, of preserving the word's identity, and yet showing it as differently shaped, is best attained by internal change. With *external increment*, matters are altogether different. It is always composition in the broader sense, and here no harm is to befall the word's simplicity; we are not to couple two concepts into a third; one concept is to be thought in a particular relation. There is therefore required here a seemingly artificial procedure, though it appears automatically in the sounds, owing to the liveliness of intention felt in the mind. The indicating part of the word, with the phonetic incisiveness that is simultaneously imparted to it, must appear ranged against the dominance of the designating part, on a different line from the latter; the originally designative meaning of the increment, if it has harboured one, must be submerged in the intention of using it merely indicatively, and the increment itself, when combined with the word, must be treated merely as a necessary and independent part of it, not as something capable of existing on its own account. If this occurs, then in addition to internal change, and compounding, there arises a third transformation of words, by *accretion*, and we thereupon have the true concept of a *suffix*. Thus the continued influence of the mind upon the sound automatically transforms *compounding* into accretion. In each of them a contrary principle resides. Compounding is concerned to preserve the several stem-syllables in their meaningful sounds, whereas accretion endeavours to abolish whatever meaning they have in themselves; and under this conflicting treatment, language attains here its two-fold objective, by preserving and destroying the recognizability of the sounds. Compounding only becomes obscure if, as seen in the foregoing, language, following a different feeling, treats it as accretion. I have made mention here of compounding, however, more because accretion could have been erroneously confused with it, than because they actually belong together in a single class. This is always only seemingly the case; and accretion should in no way be thought of mechanically, as a deliberate coupling of the intrinsically separate, and obliteration of the traces of combination by verbal unity. The word inflected by accretion is no less a unit than are the different parts of a flower in bloom; and what occurs here in language is purely organic in character. However clearly the pronoun may adhere to the person of the verb, in truly inflected languages it would not be attached to it. The verb would not be thought of separately, but would stand before the mind as an individual form, and the sound would also cross the lips as one and indivisible. By the inscrutable spontaneity of language, the suffixes erupt from the root, and this happens as long and as far as the creative capacity of the language extends. Only if the latter is no longer active, can mechanical addition supervene. In order not to damage the truth of the real process, or reduce language to a mere procedure of the understanding, we must always keep in mind the mode of conception just adopted here. But we should not conceal from ourselves that, precisely because it leads into the inexplicable, this conception does not explain anything; that the truth lies only in the absolute unity of what is thought together, and in its simultaneous gestation, and in the symbolic agreement of the inward idea with the outward sound; but that for the rest it veils the unilluminable darkness in pictorial terms. For even though the sounds of the root often modify the suffix, they do not always do so, and it can never be said in anything but a pictorial sense that the latter erupts from the heart of the root. This can never mean anything other than that the mind conceives them as inseparably united, and that the sound, obedient to this uniting

[handwritten margin note:] suffixes erupt from the root of a word

[handwritten note:] absolute unity of inward idea and outward sound

in thought, presents them equally as a unity to the ear. I have therefore preferred the account chosen above, and will also adhere to it in the pages that follow. By preventing all admixture of a mechanical procedure, it can offer no occasion for misunderstandings. But for application to actual languages, the analysis into accretion and word-unity is more suitable, because language possesses technical means for both, but especially because in certain types of languages accretion does not differ purely and absolutely from true compounding, but only in degree. The term *accretion*, which befits only languages that truly inflect through increment, already assures, by comparison with the term *addition*, the correct view of the organic process.

Since the genuineness of accretion is primarily revealed in the fusion of the suffix with the word, the inflecting languages possess at the same time effective means for creating *word-unity*. The two tendencies, to give words an outwardly definite and distinct form by a firm coupling of syllables inside them, and to separate accretion from composition, mutually reinforce each other. Because of this combination, I have spoken here only of *suffixes*, increments at the end of the word, and not of *affixes* in general. What here determines the unity of the word, in sound and meaning, can proceed only from the stem-syllable, the designating part of the word, and its effectiveness in the sound can chiefly extend only over what *follows* it. The syllables that grow out at the *beginning* always merge with the word to a lesser degree, just as in emphasis, too, and metrical treatment, the indifferency of syllables principally lies in the initial ones, and the true pressure of metre only sets in with the stressed syllable that actually determines it. This observation seems to me particularly important in judging of those languages which generally annex the incremental syllables to words at the beginning. They proceed more by compounding than accretion, and the feeling of truly successful inflection remains alien to them. Sanscrit, which so perfectly reflects every nuance of the combination of sound with delicately allusive linguistic feeling, sets up different rules of euphony for the annexing of suffixed endings and prefixed prepositions. It treats the latter like the elements of compound words.

The *suffix* denotes the *relation* in which the word is to be taken; it is thus in this sense by no means meaningless. The same holds good of the *internal change* of words, and hence of inflection generally. But the important difference between internal change and suffix is that the former can originally have had no other meaning underlying it, whereas the incremental syllable may well have possessed one in most cases. Inner change is therefore always *symbolic*, even though we cannot always catch the feeling of it. In the *nature* of the change, the transition from a brighter to a darker sound, from a sharper to a longer one, there is an analogy to what is meant to be expressed in the two cases. The same possibility holds for the suffix. It can equally well be originally and exclusively symbolic, and this property may then reside purely in the sounds. But it is by no means necessary that this should always be so; and it is an erroneous misconception of the freedom and diversity of the paths that language takes in forming them, if we are willing to call inflectional only those incremental syllables which have never borne an independent meaning, and which owe their existence in languages solely to the intention of inflecting. Whenever the *intent* of the understanding is thought to be directly creative in languages, I am profoundly sure that this is always a mistaken view of the matter. Inasmuch as the prime mover in language must always be sought in the mind, everything in it, even to the utterance of articulated sound, must admittedly be called intention. But the way in which language proceeds is always a different one, and its formations emerge from the interaction of outer impression and inner feeling, related to the general linguistic aim of combining subjectivity with objectivity in the creation of an ideal, yet neither wholly internal nor wholly external world. What is now in itself neither merely symbolic nor merely indicative, but actually designative, loses this latter character, where the needs of language demand it, through the mode of treatment as a whole. We need only compare, for example, the independent pronoun with that which is built in to the persons of the verb. The sense of language rightly distinguishes pronoun and person, and conceives under the latter, not the independent substance, but one of the relations in which the basic concept of the inflected verb must necessarily appear. It treats the person simply as a part of the verb, therefore, and permits time to displace and wear it down, trusting to the sense of such indications established by its whole procedure for an assurance that the sound-displacement will still be no obstacle to recognition of the indicator. Now whether the displacement may actually have occurred, or the appended pronoun have largely remained unaltered, the case and the outcome are always as stated. The symbolic is not dependent here on a direct analogy to the sounds, but proceeds from the linguistic attitude more artfully infused into them. If it is an undoubted fact, not merely in Sanscrit, but in other languages as well, that the incremental syllables are taken, more or less, from the above-mentioned root-stems that refer directly to the speaker, then there the symbolic itself resides. For the relation to the categories of thought and speech, that is indicated by the incremental syllables, can find no more significant expression than in sounds which directly have the subject as the starting or terminal point of their meaning. Hence the analogy of tones may also be added to the foregoing, as Bopp has so admirably shown of the nominative and accusative endings in Sanscrit. In the third person pronoun, the light *s*-sound is obviously accorded symbolically to the living, and the dull *m* to the genderless neuter; and the same alternation of letters in the endings now distinguishes the subject considered as agent, the nominative, from the accusative, the object of agency.

The originally independent *significance of suffixes* is therefore no necessary obstacle to the purity of true inflection. Words formed with such inflectional syllables seem no less determinate than where internal change occurs, but to be merely simple concepts, cast in varying forms, and thus to fulfil exactly the aim of inflection. Such significance does indeed call for a greater strength of the inner sense of inflection and a more decided mental sound-mastery, which in this case must overcome a tendency for the grammatical form to degenerate into compounding. A language like Sanscrit, which chiefly employs such original, independent, meaningful syllables for inflection, shows by that very fact the confidence it reposes in the power of its animating spirit.

But in this part of language the *phonetic capacity* and associated *sound-habits* of nations also contribute a significant effect. The propensity to combine the elements of speech with one another, to couple sound to sound where their nature allows, to merge one into another, and in general to alter their contacts according to their make-up, assists the sense of inflection in its task of achieving unity, just as the stricter segregation of tones in some languages militates against its success. Now if the sound-capacity furthers the inner demand, the original sense of articulation becomes active, and in this way there arises that meaningful splitting of sounds, whereby even a single one of them can become the bearer of a formal relationship; and here, more than in any other part of language, such a thing is decisive, since in this instance a mental direction is to be indicated, not a concept designated. The sharpness of the *sense of articulation* and the purity of the *sense of inflection* therefore stand in a mutually reinforcing connection.

Between the want of all indication of the categories of words, as we find it in Chinese, and true inflection, there can be no third possibility compatible with pure organization of languages. The only conceivable intermediate is *compounding* used as inflection, an inflecting, therefore, deliberate but not brought to perfection – a more or less mechanical adding, not a truly organic accretion. This not always easily recognizable hybrid has lately been called *agglutination*. This way of annexing specificatory bye-concepts arises, on the one hand, invariably from weakness of the inwardly organizing sense of language, or from neglect of its true direction, but yet points, rather, on the other, to an endeavour, not only to confer phonetic validity upon conceptual categories as well, but also to treat this in the process as not altogether on a par with the true designation of concepts. Hence although such a language does not renounce grammatical indication, it does not effect this in pure fashion, but falsifies the very essence of it. It can therefore seemingly, and to some extent even actually, possess a mass of grammatical forms, and yet nowhere really achieve expression of the true concept of such a form. It can, moreover, also contain in some instances a genuine inflection by internal verbal change, and time can transform into seeming inflections its original true compoundings, so that it becomes difficult, and even remains in part impossible, to decide correctly in every single case. But what truly settles the whole thing is a survey of all cognate cases. From their general treatment it then appears how far the strength or weakness of the inner sense's tendency to inflection has exerted influence on the sound-structure. In this respect alone can the distinction be drawn. For these so-called agglutinating languages do not differ in type from the inflectional ones, as do those which reject all indication by means of inflection; they deviate only to the extent that their obscure endeavour in the same direction is more or less of a failure.

Where brilliance and acuity of the linguistic sense have struck out the right path during the formative period – and with such characteristics, no wrong path is taken – an inner clarity and distinctness are diffused over the whole linguistic structure, and the principal signs of their effectiveness are inseparably connected with one another. Thus we have observed the indissoluble combination of the *sense of inflection*, the striving for *verbal unity*, and the *power of articulation*, whereby sounds are meaningfully divided. The effect cannot be the same where the mind gives off only isolated sparks of the pure strivings; and, as we shall soon see below, the sense of language has then commonly taken a particular path that diverges from the right one, though it often testifies to equally great acumen and equally delicate feeling. This then often displays its influence on the individual case as well. Hence in languages of this sort, which we are not entitled to call inflectional, the inner transformation of words, where there is any, is mainly of the kind that follows the internally indicated procedure by a rough copying, as it were, in the sound. The plural and preterite, for example, are designated by a material halting of the voice, or by an aspiration forcibly expelled from the throat, and a return is made to the bounds of natural sound, with virtual abandonment of the realm of articulation, precisely where purely formed languages, like Semitic, exhibit the greatest acuity of the sense of articulation – not, indeed, in the cases actually mentioned, but in other grammatical transformations – by symbolic change of the vowel. No language, in my experience, is wholly agglutinative, and in particular cases there is often no deciding how much or how little the sense of inflection has contributed to the apparent suffix. In all languages that actually display a tendency to sound-fusion, or do not firmly reject it, a localized trend towards inflection is visible. But an assured verdict on the phenomenon as a whole can be rendered only by reference to the organism of the entire structure of such a language.

§15

Every peculiarity that arises from the inner conception of language enters into the total organism of the latter, and this is particularly the case with *inflection*. For it stands in most intimate connection with two different and seemingly opposed factors, which are actually in organic cooperation, namely *verbal unity*, and the appropriate *division* of the *parts* of the *sentence*, whereby its articulation becomes possible. The connection of inflection with verbal unity is self-evidently intelligible, since its endeavour is quite specifically directed to forming a *unity*, and is not merely satisifed with a *whole*. But it also demands an appropriate articulation of the sentence, and freedom in forming the latter, since in its own grammatical procedure it equips words with distinguishing marks, which can safely be trusted for recognition of how such a word is related to the whole sentence. It thereby removes anxiety about holding this word together as a unit, and encourages boldness in dismembering it into its parts. But what is far more important, by its inherent look backwards to the forms of thought, so far as these are related to language, it awakens a more accurate and perspicuous insight into the way that thoughts are put together. For in truth all the three peculiarities of language here alluded to arise from a single source, the living conception of the relationship of speech to language. Inflection, word-unity and appropriate division of the sentence should therefore never be separated in considering language. Only by addition of these other points does inflection appear in its true, beneficently operating power.

Speech demands elements adapted to the possibility of its limitless use, which cannot be measured at any moment; and this demand grows in scope, both intensively and extensively, the higher the level at which it is pitched. For at its most elevated, it becomes itself a *producing of ideas* and overall *development of thoughts*. But in man its tendency is invariably to this latter end, however many obstacles the actual development may encounter. Speech therefore always seeks that arrangement of linguistic elements which contains the liveliest expression of the forms of thought; and hence it is especially given to inflection, whose very nature is always to consider the concept simultaneously in both its internal and external relations, a practice which facilitates the progress of thought, owing to the regularity of the route carved out. But with these elements, speech is bent upon achieving the innumerable combinations of the winged idea, without being restricted in its boundlessness. The expression of all these connections is based upon *sentence-formation*; and this free flight of ideas is possible only if the parts of the simple sentence are associated or separated by a necessity arising from its nature, and not with a greater or lesser degree of arbitrariness.

The *development of ideas* requires a double procedure, a representing of particular concepts, and a linkage of them into *thoughts*. Both also occur in *speech*. A concept is enclosed in sounds that belong together and cannot be separated without destruction of meaning, and receives marks that indicate its relation to the construction of the sentence. The *word* so formed is uttered by the tongue, which separates it out as a whole from others that are conjoined to it in thought, but does not thereby abolish the simultaneous involvement of all words in the sentence. We here see word-unity in the narrowest sense, the treatment of each word as an individual, which without forfeiting its independence can enter into varying degrees of contact with others. But we have seen above, that even within the sphere of the same concept, and hence the same word, a different element is sometimes found; and from thence arises another type of word-unity, which in contrast to the external unity above-mentioned may be called an internal one. Now depending on whether the different factor is similar in type, and merely combines into a compound whole, or is dissimilar (designation and indication) in having to depict the concept as equipped with a definite stamp, the *inner word-unity* has a wider and a narrower meaning.

Word-unity in language has a twofold source, in the inner *linguistic sense* related to the need for developing thoughts, and in the *sound*. Since all thought consists in separating and combining, the linguistic sense's requirement, to depict all the different kinds of conceptual unity symbolically in speech, must automatically be roused, and show up in language in proportion to its alertness and ordered regularity. The sound, on the other hand, seeks to bring its various juxtaposed modifications into a relationship pleasing to utterance and ear. Often it thereby smooths out difficulties merely, or follows organically established custom. But it also goes further, forms rhythmical segments, and treats them as auditory wholes. Yet both of them, inner linguistic sense and sound, so far as it accedes to the former's demands, are in cooperation, and the treatment of *sound-unity* thereby becomes a symbol of the particular *conceptual unity* desired. The latter, thus embodied in sound, is diffused as a mental principle over speech, and the sound-formation, artistically treated in its melody and rhythm, reciprocally arouses in the soul a closer union of the ordering power of understanding with pictorially creative fantasy; so that the interweaving of the outgoing and ingoing forces, towards mind and nature, produces a heightened vitality and harmonious liveliness. The *means of designating* word-unity in speech are the *pause, change of letters*, and *accent*.

The *pause* can serve only to indicate *external unity*; within the word its effect, on the contrary, would be to destroy unity. But in speech it is natural, at the end of words, to insert a fleeting vocal break, perceptible only to the practised ear, in order to identify the elements of the thought. Moreover, the effort to designate the unity of the concepts runs counter to the equally necessary endeavour to elaborate the sentence – the audible unity of the concept conflicts with the unity of thought; and languages displaying a correct and delicate sensibility evince the dual intention and flatten this contrast, often, however, by reinforcing it, or again by other means. I shall always take the explanatory examples here from Sanscrit[1], since this language deals with verbal unity more happily and exhaustively than any other, and also possesses an alphabet more concerned than our own to present the exact utterance that strikes the ear in a graphic fashion to the eye as well. Now Sanscrit does not allow every letter to terminate a word, and by this already it acknowledges the independent individuality of the word, sanctioning its separation in speech by the fact that the changes of contiguous letters at the beginning and end are regulated differently from those in the middle of words. At the same time, however, more than in any other language of its kind, the *fusion of sounds* also follows the interweaving of the thought, so that at first sight the unity of the word seems to be destroyed by the unity of the thought. When terminal and initial vowels are changed into a third, there undeniably arises in this way a sonic unity of the two words. Where final consonants change before initial vowels, this admittedly does not occur, since the initial vowel,

---

[1] Even where I do not specifically cite the passages, I borrow the particular data on Sanscrit language-structure that are referred to in this treatise from Bopp's *Grammatik*, and gladly acknowledge that I owe a clearer insight into these matters solely to this classic work; for none of the earlier linguistic theories affords a like degree of understanding, however valuable some of them may be in other respects. Both the various editions of this *Sanscrit Grammar*, and the later *Comparative Grammar*, together with individual academic papers, contain a comparison of Sanscrit with its related languages which is as fruitful as it is talented; they will always remain true models of deep and successful penetration – often, indeed, of bold conjecture – into the analogy of grammatical forms, and even today, linguistics is indebted to them for the most significant advances upon what is in part a newly-opened road. In 1816, in his conjugation-system of the Indians, Bopp was already laying the basis for the inquiries which he subsequently pursued so successfully, and always in that same direction.

always accompanied by a slight aspiration, does not merge with the final consonant in the sense in which Sanscrit regards the consonant and following vowel in the same syllable as indissolubly one. This change of consonant does, indeed, always destroy the indication of separateness between individual words. But this mild disturbance can never truly abolish the latter in the hearer's mind, nor even weaken the recognition of it significantly. For on the one hand, the two main laws of change when words collide, the fusion of vowels and the transformation of voiceless into voiced consonants before vowels, do not actually occur within the word in question; while on the other, the inner word-unity in Sanscrit is so clear and definitely ordered, that in all the sonic intricacy of speech we can never mistake the fact that these are independent sound-units, which are merely coming into direct contact with each other. If the sonic intricacy of speech is evidence, moreover, for a fine sensitivity of ear, and for an active urge to indicate, symbolically, the unity of the thought, it is nevertheless remarkable that other Indian languages, notably the Telingic, to which no great degree of self-evolved culture can be attributed, also possess this feature, which is tied to the innermost sound-habits of a people, and hence, presumably, is not so readily passed on simply from one language to another. In itself, the interweaving of all speech-sounds is more natural in the uncultivated state of language, since the word must first be singled out from speech; but in Sanscrit this peculiarity has become an internal and external beauty of speech, which should not be the less prized because, like a luxury unnecessary to thought, it could be dispensed with. There is obviously a linguistic reverse action, distinct from the particular expression, upon the very mind that produces the thought, and for this purpose none of the advantages of the language are wasted, however dispensable they may seem in the particular case.

The inner unity of words can truly make its appearance only in languages which expand the sound into a polysyllable by clothing the concept with its modifiers, and permit a variety of *letter-changes* within the sound itself. The linguistic sense concerned with beauty of sound then handles this inner sphere of the word according to general and special laws of *euphony* and harmony. However, the *sense of articulation* also cooperates, and more particularly on these formations, in that sometimes it transforms sounds to a different significance, but sometimes also attracts to its domain sounds which themselves have independent validity, so that they are now used merely as signs of auxiliary modifications. For their original factual meaning now becomes symbolic; the sound itself, by subordination under a generic concept, is often reduced to a simple element, and thus even when different in origin acquires a shape like the purely symbolic one that is actually fashioned by the sense of articulation. The more active and vigorous the sense of articulation in constantly fusing concept to sound, the quicker this operation proceeds.

By means of these causes that are here in collaboration, there now arises a *word-structure* that is satisfying to understanding and aesthetic feeling alike; a structure in which precise analysis, starting from the word-stem, must endeavour to account for every added, ejected or altered letter, on grounds of significance or sound. It can genuinely reach this goal, moreover, at least insofar as it is able to set explanatory analogies alongside every change of this sort. The range and variety of this word-structure are greatest and most satisfying to mind and ear in those languages which impress no uniformly specific stamp on the original word-forms, and employ *accretion* to indicate auxiliary determinations, in preference to purely symbolic internal change of letters. This method, which originally seems rougher and less cultivated if we confuse it with mechanical addition, is undeniably able, through the power of the sense of inflection, raised to a higher level, to hold an advantage here over the intrinsically finer and more artistic one. It is certainly due largely to the disyllabic root-structure and aversion to compounding in the Semitic languages, that their word-structure is far from equalling the diversity, range and aptness to the overall purposes of language that we see in Sanscrit – notwithstanding the admirably diverse and pregnant sense of inflection and articulation that Semitic word-structure displays.

Sanscrit designates by sound the varying degrees of unity which the inner linguistic sense feels the need to distinguish. For this purpose it chiefly employs a differing treatment of syllables that come together as diverse conceptual elements in the same word, and of individual sounds in the letters wherein these sounds make contact. I have already pointed out above that separate words, and the inside of a word, are treated differently. The language now proceeds further along the same path; and if the rules for these two cases are regarded as forming two great mutually opposing classes, word-unity is indicated in the following stages, from the looser combination to the firmer one:

in compound words;
in words allied with prefixes, principally verbs;
in words formed by suffixes (*Taddhita*-suffixes) from basic words existing in the language;

[handwritten margin notes:] Semitic has diverse inflection and articulation of word structure but Semitic has an aversion to compounding

in words (*Kridanta*-words) derived by suffixes from roots, that is, from
words that actually lie outside the language;
in the grammatical forms for declension and conjugation.

The two first-named species of words follow, on the whole, the
addition-rules for *separate words*, the last three those for the *word-middle*.
Yet, as will be obvious, there are particular exceptions here; and the
whole sequence of stages just established is not, of course, based on
any absolute difference of rules for each class, but only on a greater
or lesser approximation to the two main classes, albeit a very decided
one. In the very exceptions, however, there is often betrayed once
more, in a meaningful way, the intention to unify more firmly. Thus
in separated words proper, if we discard one merely seeming
exception, the final consonant of a preceding word never occasions
a change in the initial letter of the succeeding one; yet this does occur
in some compound words, and in prefixes, in a manner that at times
has influence even on the second initial consonant, as when अग्नि *agni*,
fire, and स्तोम *stôma*, sacrifice, combine into अग्निष्टोम *agnishtôma*,
a burnt offering. By this departure from the addition-rules for
separate words, the language obviously indicates its feeling for the
requirement of word-unity. Yet it cannot be denied that in Sanscrit
the *compound* words are too much like the separate ones, owing to the
other and more general treatment of the final and initial letters that
are juxtaposed in them, and the want of combining sounds, which
the Greek language always employs in this case. The stress, admittedly
unknown to us, can hardly have eliminated this. Where the first
member of the compound retains its grammatical inflection, the
combination really lies solely in usage, which either always couples
these words, or never makes use of the last member in isolation. Yet
even the lack of inflections designates the unity of these words more
to the understanding only, without it acquiring validity to the ear
by fusion of the sounds. Where basic form and case-ending coincide
in the sound, the language omits to designate expressly whether a
word stands on its own, or is an element in a compound. A long
Sanscrit compound is therefore, by express grammatical indication,
less a single word than a series of uninflected words put together; and
it is a correct feeling of Greek, never to let its compound degenerate
thus by excessive length. Though Sanscrit, too, again shows in other
peculiarities, how meaningfully it sometimes knows how to indicate
the unity of these words; as, for example, when it assembles two or
more substantives, whatever their gender may be, into a single term
without gender.
    Among the classes of words which follow the addition-laws for the
middle of the word, the *Kridanta*-words and the grammatically inflected

ones are the most akin; and if there are traces of a still more intimate bond between them, such indications lie rather in the difference of the case and verb endings. The *krit*-suffixes behave entirely as the latter do. For they operate directly on the root, which in fact they first introduce into the language, whereas the case endings – in this resembling the *taddhita*-suffixes – attach to basic words already provided by the language itself. The intimacy of sound-fusion is properly at its firmest in the inflections of the verb, since to the mind as well, the verb-concept is least of all separable from its auxiliary determinations.

I have here aimed to show only, in what way the laws of euphony for contiguous letters diverge from one another according to the degree of internal word-unity. But we must certainly be wary of finding anything really intentional in this; in general, as I have already noted, the term *intention*, when used of languages, must be interpreted with care. Insofar as we conceive this as a sort of stipulation, or even merely as a striving that proceeds from the will towards a clearly envisaged goal, intention, as we cannot too often be reminded, is alien to languages. It always expresses itself merely in an original instinctive feeling. Now here, I am convinced, such a *feeling* of conceptual unity has actually passed over into the sound, and just because it is a feeling, not everywhere in the same measure or with equal consistency. Many of the particular deviations of the addition-laws from one another admittedly arise phonetically from the nature of the letters themselves. Now since all grammatically formed words invariably occur in the same combination of the initial and final letters of these elements, where in separate and even in compound words the same contiguity recurs only varyingly and individually, the former, of course, easily generate a special pronunciation that blends all elements more intimately, and we can therefore regard the feeling of verbal unity in these cases as having arisen from this, albeit in the opposite way to that I have adopted above. Yet the influence of this inner feeling of unity still remains the primitive one, since its outcome is that the grammatical additions, as such, are incorporated into the word-stem, and do not remain detached, as they do in some languages. For the phonetic effect, it is a major influence that both case-endings and suffixes begin only with certain consonants, and so can enter only into a certain number of combinations, which are at their most restricted in the case-endings, are larger in the *krit*-suffixes and verb endings, and in the *taddhita* suffixes are more extensive still.

Apart from the variety of addition-laws for *consonants* juxtaposed in the middle of words, languages contain yet another way of dealing with sound in the word, which designates its inner unity more

[handwritten margin note: intention alien to languages which are instinctive. see also p. 217]

definitely still; the method, that is, which allows the total structure to influence the change of individual letters, notably the vowels. This occurs when the annexing of more or less important syllables exerts influence on the vowels already present in the word; when an initial increment to the word produces abbreviations or elisions at the end of it; when accreting syllables assimilate their vowel to those of the word, or conversely; or when by reinforcement or change of sound a single syllable is given a preponderance that dominates the rest of the word to the ear. Each of these cases can, where it is not purely phonetic, be regarded as directly symbolic for the word's internal unity. In Sanscrit this sound-treatment appears in numerous guises, and always with remarkable concern for clarity of logical form and beauty of aesthetic configuration. Sanscrit does not, therefore, assimilate the stem-syllable, whose fixity must be preserved, to the endings; but it does allow lengthenings of the stem-vowel, from whose regular recurrence in the language the ear can easily recognize the original. This is an observation of Bopp's which evinces a fine linguistic sense, and which he very properly expresses by saying that in Sanscrit the change of the stem-vowel here alluded to is not qualitative, but quantitative.[2] Qualitative assimilation is due to carelessness of pronunciation, or to delight in uniformly sounding syllables; in the quantitative shift of metre, a higher and more delicate sense of euphony is expressed. In the former, the significant stem-vowel is well-nigh sacrificed to the sound; in the latter it remains, in its lengthened form, equally present to both mind and ear.

To give a syllable an emphasis in pronunciation that dominates the entire word, Sanscrit possesses, in *guna* and *vriddhi*, two methods so artfully fashioned, and so closely tied to the other sound affinities, that in this form and context they have remained peculiar to it alone. None of the sister languages has adopted these sound-changes, in either system or spirit; only individual fragments have passed over into some of them as finished results. *Guna* and *vriddhi* form a lengthening with *a*, and the diphthongs *ê* and *ô* from *i* and *u*; they change the vowel-*r* into *ar* and *âr*[3], and strengthen *ê* and *ô* by renewed

---

[2] *Jahrbücher für wissenschaftliche Kritik*, 1827, p. 281. Bopp makes this comment only in regard to directly appended derivatives. But the law seems to me generally valid throughout. Even the weightiest-seeming objection to it, the change of the *r*-vowel into *ur* in the non-*guna* inflections of the verb कृ, *kri* कुरुतस् *kurutas*), can be otherwise explained.

[3] Dr Lepsius, in a manner which ingeniously extends the analogy of these sound-transformations, construes *ar* and *âr* as diphthongs of the *r*-vowel Cf. his *Paläographie als Mittel für die Sprachforschung*, pp. 46–9, §36–9, a work which abounds in acute observations, and indicates a new path for linguistic research.

diphthonging to *ai* and *au*. If the *ê*, *ai*, *ô* and *au* produced by *guna* and *vriddhi* are followed by a vowel, these diphthongs resolve into *ay*, *ây*, *aw* and *âw*. Hence there arises a double series of five-fold sound-changes, which, through specific laws of language and the constant reversal of such changes by use of these laws, invariably lead back, nonetheless, to the same primal sound. The language thereby acquires a multitude of euphonious sound-associations, without the slightest prejudice to understanding. In *guna* and *vriddhi*, one sound is on each occasion replaced by another. Yet we should not regard them as mere vowel-changes, such as are commonplace in many languages. The important difference between the two is this, that in vowel-change the reason for the vowel substituted for another is always at least partly alien to the original reason for the syllable changed, and must be sought either in the endeavour to distinguish grammatically, or in the law of assimilation, or in some other cause, and that the new sound can therefore change under different circumstances; whereas in *guna* and *vriddhi* it always arises uniformly from the primal sound of the altered syllable itself, and belongs to it alone. So if we compare the *guna*-sound वेद्मि *vêdmi*, with तेनिम *tênima*, which on Bopp's explanation has arisen by assimilation, the adventitious *ê* in the first form has come from the *i* of the syllable changed, whereas in the second it has come from the *i* of the following syllable.

Guna and *vriddhi* are *reinforcements* of the basic sound, and not only of this, but also of one another; like comparative and superlative, they are reinforcements of the simple vowel which enhance it in equal quantitative measure. In breadth of enunciation, and of sound to the ear, this enhancement is unmistakeable; but it is also evident in meaning, of which a striking example is the future passive participle formed by appending *ya*. For there the simple concept requires only *guna*, but the reinforced concept, linked with necessity, demands *vriddhi*: स्तव्य *stavya*, a praiseworthy person; स्ताव्य *stâvya*, a person necessarily to be praised, and in every respect. But the concept of reinforcement does not exhaust the special nature of these sound-changes. The *vriddhi* of *a* must here, indeed, be excepted, for in grammatical application it belongs only somewhat to this class, and in sound not at all. In all other vowels and diphthongs, the characteristic of these reinforcements is that through them there arises an inflection of the sound, produced by combining dissimilar vowels or diphthongs. Since all *guna* and *vriddhi* is based on combining *a* with the other vowels or diphthongs, we may now take it that in *guna* a short *a* occurs before the simple vowel, and in *vriddhi* a long one, or that a short *a* always occurs, in *guna* before the simple vowel, in *vriddhi* before the vowel already reinforced by *guna*.[4] Apart from the solitary *a*, the mere production of lengthened vowels by combining similar ones is not, to my knowledge, counted as *vriddhi*, even by the Indian grammarians. Now since in *guna* and *vriddhi* a sound always arises which acts very differently on the ear, and has its basis exclusively in the primal sound of the syllable itself, the *guna* and *vriddhi* sounds come forth from the inner depth of the syllable itself in a manner that words cannot describe, though it is clearly perceptible to the ear. If *guna*, therefore, which so often changes the stem-syllable in the verb, were a definite characteristic of certain grammatical forms, we should be able to describe the latter – even in sensory appearance – as literal developments from within the root, and this in a more pregnant sense than in the Semitic tongues, where a merely symbolic vowel-change occurs.[5] But this is by no means the case, since *guna* is only one of the bye-formulations which Sanscrit confers by specific laws upon verbal forms, in addition to their true characteristics. It is by nature a purely phonetic phenomenon, and so far as we can discuss its basis, can also be explained from the sounds alone, without reference to particular meaning or symbolism. The sole case in the language which has to be seen as an exception to this is the *guna*-ing of the doubling-vowel in the intensive verbs. This is all the more evidence of the reinforcing impression which the language, in an otherwise unusual way, intends to impart to these forms, since doubling is elsewhere accustomed to shorten the long vowel, and since the *guna*

---

[4] Bopp (*Lateinische Sanskrit-Grammatik*, sec. 53) defends the first of these views. If I may be permitted to differ from so deep an investigator, I should like to declare for the second. On Bopp's assumption, it will hardly be possible to save the close connection of *guna* and *vriddhi* with the general sound-laws of the language, for dissimilar simple vowels, regardless of their length or shortness, are always transformed into the admittedly weaker diphthongs of *guna*. Since the nature of the diphthongs also lies essentially in the mere unlikeness of the tones, it is intelligible that the length and shortness of the new sounds should be swallowed up, without any surviving difference. Only if a new dissimilarity comes into play, is there a strengthening of the diphthongs. Hence I do not believe that the *guna*-diphthongs are originally fused directly from short vowels. That – unlike the *vriddhi* diphthongs – they take a short *a* on resolution (*ay*, *aw*, rather than *ây*, *âw*), can be otherwise explained. Since the difference of the two sound-extensions could not be made apparent in the semi-vowel, it had to fall into the quantity of the vowel in the new syllable. The same is true of the *r*-vowel.

[5] This made an essential contribution, perhaps, towards leading Friedrich Schlegel to his admittedly untenable theory for a classification of all languages (*Sprache und Weisheit der Indier*, p. 50). But it is worth noting, and too little recognized, in my opinion, that this deep thinker and gifted writer was the first German to draw our attention to the remarkable phenomenon of Sanscrit, and that he had already made significant progress in it at a period which lacked all the present numerous aids to learning the language. Even Wilkins' grammar appeared only in the same year as the aforementioned Schlegel work.

also occurs here, as it does not elsewhere, in long middle vowels of the root.

As against this, we can certainly regard *guna* in many cases as a symbol of internal *word-unity*, in that these sound-changes progressively operative in the sphere of the vowels produce a less material, more decisive and more tightly bound fusion of words than the changes of contiguous consonants. In this they bear some resemblance to accent, in that the same effect, the preponderance of a dominant syllable, is produced in accent by the pitch, and in *guna* and *vriddhi* by the extended inflection of sound. If they are thus an accompaniment of inner word-unity only in certain cases, they are nevertheless always one of the various expressions used to indicate such unity by language, which is far from always following the same course. This may also be why they are quite especially characteristic of the many-syllabled long forms of the tenth class of verbs, and of the causal verbs affiliated to them. If they are admittedly to be found, on the other hand, in quite short verbs as well, it cannot be denied on that account, that in the long verbs they prevent fragmentation of the syllables and oblige the voice to hold them firmly together. It also seems very significant, in this connection, that *guna* is predominant in word-types whose unity is firmest, the *kridanta* words and verb-endings, and normally affects the root-syllable in them, whereas it never appears in the stem-syllable of declensional inflections, or the words formed by *taddhita*-suffixes.

Vriddhi finds a twofold application. On the one hand, like *guna*, it is purely phonetic, and enhances the latter either necessarily, or at the speaker's will; on the other, it is meaningful and purely symbolic. In the former guise it chiefly affects final vowels, just as the long vowels among them also undergo *guna*, which does not happen elsewhere. This comes about in that the lengthening of a final vowel finds no limitation ahead of it. It is the same principle which in Javanese, under similar circumstances, allows the *a* incorporated into the consonant to terminate as a dull *o*. The meaningfulness of *vriddhi* is particularly evident in the *taddhita*-suffixes, and seems to have its original abode in the gender denominations, and in collective and abstract nouns. In all these cases there is an enlargement of the originally simple concrete concept. But the same extension is also carried over metaphorically to other cases, though not with the same constancy. This may be why the adjectives formed by *taddhita*-suffixes sometimes undergo *vriddhi*, and sometimes leave the vowel unchanged. For the adjective can be regarded as a concrete property, but also as comprehending within it the whole mass of things in which it appears.

In the *verb*, the presence or absence of *guna* creates, in precisely

guna-ed
and non-guna-ed
conjugations

defined grammatical instances, a contrast between *guna*-ed and
un*guna*-ed forms of conjugation. On occasion, but much more rarely,
a similar contrast is produced by the sometimes necessary, sometimes
voluntary, use of *vriddhi* rather than *guna*. Bopp was the first to explain
this contrast, as an effect of the sonic heaviness or lightness of the
endings on the root vowel, in a manner which certainly seems quite
satisfactory on the whole, though it must also disregard a few cases
as, in effect, exceptions. The heaviness, that is, prevents lengthening
of the vowel, which the lightness seems to elicit, and one or the other
occurs wherever the ending attaches directly to the root, or encounters
on its way there a vowel capable of *guna*. But where the influence of
the inflectional syllable is impeded by another intervening vowel, or
a consonant, so that the root-vowel's dependence on it ceases, the use
or non-use of *guna* can in no way be explained by the sounds, although
it regularly occurs even there, in particular cases; so this difference
in the root-syllable cannot be generally reduced in the language to
any universal law. The true explanation of the use or non-use of *guna*,
as such, can only be devised, it seems to me, from the history of the
conjugational forms of the verb. But this is still a very obscure area,
in which we can divine only fragmentary details. Perhaps there once
existed, in different dialects or periods, two types of conjugation, with
guna and without it, from whose mingling there has arisen the present
arrangement in the version of the language now before us. Such a
conjecture seems indicated, in fact, by some classes of roots, which
simultaneously allow derivation, and largely in the meaning referred
to, both with and without *guna*, or take it throughout, where the other
analogies of the language would require the contrast aforementioned.
The latter occurs only in isolated exceptions; but the former takes
place in all verbs that are simultaneously conjugated in the first and
sixth classes; as happens also in those of the first class, which frame
their multiform preterite on the pattern of the sixth, in complete
uniformity with their augment-preterite, even to the lack of *guna*. This
whole sixth pattern, corresponding to the second aorist in Greek,
might well be nothing but the true augment-preterite of a *guna*-less
conjugation, which has been joined by another that does employ *guna*
(our present augment-preterite of the roots of the first class). For to
me it is very probable that in the true sense of the word there are
only two preterites in Sanscrit, not three, as we now count them, so
that formations of the so-called third type, namely the multiform
ones, are merely bye-forms descended from other epochs of the
language.

If we thus assume in the language an originally two-fold conjugation, with and without *guna*, the question in some degree arises,

whether, where the weight of the endings produces a contrast, the *guna* has been suppressed or adopted; and we must unhesitatingly declare for the former. Sound-changes such as *guna* and *vriddhi* cannot be injected into a language; in the happy phrase that Grimm used of the German vowel-change, they go to the very bottom of it, and their origin can be explained from the dark and broad diphthongs that we also encounter in other languages. The feeling for euphony may have moderated and regulated them into a quantitatively definite relationship. But the same tendency of the vocal organs to lengthen the vowel may have burst out directly in a rhythmical style, where the people in question is fortunate in its organization. For it is not necessary, and scarcely even sensible, to imagine every excellence of a cultured language to have arisen gradually and by degrees.

The difference between raw natural sound and regulated tone is far more clearly evident still in another sound-form that makes an essential contribution to the inner verbal development, namely *reduplication*. The repetition of the initial syllable of a word, or even the whole word itself, either to reinforce significance for variety of expression, or as a mere sound-habit, is typical of the languages of many uncultured peoples. In others, such as some of the Malayan family, it already betrays an influence of the feeling for sound, that not always the root-vowel, but sometimes a related one, is repeated. In Sanscrit, however, reduplication becomes modified with such exact appropriateness to the internal word-structure on each occasion, that one may reckon five or six different patterns of it, distributed throughout the language. But all of them flow from the double principle of adapting this prior syllable to the particular form of the word, and of promoting internal word-unity. Some are at the same time indicative of specific grammatical forms. The adaptation is at times so ingenious that the syllable actually destined to precede the word divides it, and takes up a position between its initial vowel and final consonants; the reason may possibly be that these same forms also require a prefixing of the augment, and these two prefixed syllables could not have been distinguishably indicated as such in roots with an initial vowel. The Greek language, in which augment and reduplication actually coalesce, in these cases, in the *augmentum temporale,* has evolved similar forms to achieve the same purpose.[6] This is a remarkable example of how sound-formation, when the sense of

---

[6] In a paper that I read in 1828 at the French Institute, on the affinity of the Greek pluperfect, the reduplicating aorists and the Attic perfects with a Sanscrit tense-formation, I have discussed in detail the agreement and difference of the two languages in respect of these forms, and attempted to derive them from their sources.

[handwritten margin notes:] Sound changes go to the very bottom of language all the way down – not a superficial injection into them

in cultured peoples repeats syllables or even the whole word

Grimm's phrase-making

articulation is active and vigorous, blazes wondrous-seeming trails of its own, to accompany the internally organizing sense of language in all its various directions, keeping each one recognizable.

The intention of coupling the word firmly with the prefix is expressed in Sanscrit, in consonantal roots, by the brevity of the reiterated vowel, even against a long root-sound, so that the prefix shall be drowned by the word. The only two exceptions to this abbreviation in the language again have their own peculiar reason, which outweighs the general one; in the intensive verbs it is to indicate their strengthening; in the multiform preterite of the causal verbs it is the balance that euphony demands between the reiterated and root vowels. In roots that begin with a vowel, where reduplication is notified by lengthening that initial vowel, the preponderance of the sound falls upon the first syllable, and so promotes, as we have seen in *guna*, firm binding of the remaining syllables closely associated with it. The reduplication is in most cases a genuine index of specific grammatical forms, or at any rate a sound-modification that characteristically accompanies them. Only in a small portion of verbs (those of the third class) is it intrinsic to them as such. But here too, as with *guna*, we are led to surmise that in an earlier period of the language verbs could be conjugated with and without reduplication, and yet did not thereby undergo change, either in themselves or in their meaning. For the augment and multiform-preterites of certain verbs of the third class are distinguished solely by the employment or absence of reduplication. In this sound-form it seems even more natural than in *guna*. For the reinforcement of utterance through sound, by way of repetition, can originally be the effect only of the liveliness of individual feeling, and hence, even on becoming more general and regulated, can easily give occasion for varying use.

The *augment*, akin to reduplication in its indication of past time, is similarly treated, where the root has an initial vowel, in a manner that promotes word-unity, and in this displays a notable contrast to the like-sounding prefix that indicates negation. For where the *alpha privativum* takes position in front of these roots by simply inserting an *n*, the augment blends with the initial vowel, and already shows in doing so its decidedly greater intimacy of connection as a verbal form. In this blending, however, it oversteps the *guna* that results and extends into *vriddhi*, obviously because the sense of inner word-unity wishes to confer as much emphasis as possible on this initial vowel which holds the word together. In another verbal form, the re-duplicated preterite, we do indeed find in certain roots the insertion of *n* as well; but this occurs quite rarely in the language, and the addition is associated with a lengthening of the vowel-prefix.

Apart from those briefly referred to here, sonorous languages also possess a series of other methods, which all evince a sense of need, for giving the word an organic structure combining inner fullness and euphony. Among these we may reckon, in Sanscrit, the lengthening or change of the vowel, its transformation into a semi-vowel, the extension of the latter into a syllable by a following semi-vowel, and to some extent the insertion of a nasal tone; all this without considering the changes wrought by the general laws of the language in letters juxtaposed in the middle of the word. In all these cases the final form of the sound arises at once from the constitution of the root, and the nature of the grammatical additions. At the same time, however, independence and firmness, affinity and contrast, and the sonic weight of individual letters, find expression at one moment in original harmony, at another in a conflict that is always elegantly adjusted by the organizing sense of language. The care directed to the shaping of the whole word is still more clearly evinced in the *law of compensation*, whereby a strengthening or weakening that occurs in one part of the word gives rise to an opposite change in another part, to restore the balance. In this latter formation here, the qualitative character of the letters is disregarded. The sense of language stresses only the more immaterial quantitative element, and treats the word in quasi-metrical fashion, as a rhythmic series. Sanscrit, in this respect, contains forms so remarkable as would not be easily met with in other languages. The multiform preterite of the causal verbs (Bopp's seventh form), equipped at the same time with augment and reduplication, provides an example of this which is notable in every respect. Since, in the forms of this version of the tense, the always short augment in roots with an initial consonant is followed in immediate succession by the reiterated and root syllables, the language endeavours to give the vowels of these latter a specifically metrical relationship. With few exceptions, where these two syllables are sounded as a pyrrhic अजगदं *ajagadam*, ◡◡◡, from गद् *gad*, to talk, or spondee अदभ्राडं *adadhrâḍam*, ◡−−◡, from भ्राड् *dhrâḍ*, to fall off, fade, they either rise iambically अदुदूषं *adudûsham*, ◡◡−◡, from दुष् *dush*, to sin, defile oneself, or fall, as in most cases, in a trochee अचीकलं, *achîkalam*, ◡−◡◡, from कल् *kal*, to sling, swing, and for the same roots seldom allow pronunciation a choice between this pair of vowel-measures. If we now investigate the at first sight very complex quantitative relationship of these forms, we find that the language is following here an extremely simple procedure. For by effecting a change on the root-syllable it is merely applying the law of sound-compensation. Having undertaken to shorten the root-syllable, it simply restores the balance by lengthening the reiterative

[handwritten marginal note:] quantitative, rhythmical, values of Sanscrit words

syllable, and this is the source of the trochaic fall in which the language seemingly found a special pleasure here. The change of quantity in the root-syllable seems to violate the higher principle directed to preserving the stem-syllables. But closer investigation shows that this is by no means the case. For these preterites are formed, not from the primitive, but from the causal root, which has already been grammatically altered. The shortened length is therefore normally typical only of the causal root. Where the language alights, in these formations, upon a primitive stem-like length, or even upon a diphthong of this sort, it abandons its design, leaves the root-syllable unaltered, and now does not even lengthen the generally short reiterative syllable. From this difficulty, running counter to the procedure actually intended in these forms, there arises the iambic lilt which represents the natural, unaltered quantity-relationship. At the same time, the language is attentive to those cases where the length of the syllable does not arise from the nature of the vowel, but from its position in front of two successive consonants. It does not pile up two means of lengthening, and so even in the trochaic fall it leaves the reiterative vowel unlengthened before two initial consonants of the root. It is worth noting that true Malayan also takes a similar care to preserve the unity of the word under grammatical additions, and to treat it as a euphonious sound-whole by displacing the quantity of the root-syllables. Owing to their syllabic fullness and euphony, the Sanscrit forms referred to are the clearest examples of what a language is capable of evolving from monosyllabic roots, if it combine a rich alphabet with a solid sound-system, following the most delicate assonances of the letters through refinement of ear; and if to these be added accretion and internal change, again according to specific rules based upon a variety of finely distinguished grammatical principles.[7]

[7] What I say here about this form of the preterite of causal verbs has been extracted from a detailed paper already drawn up on these tense-forms some years ago. I there went through all the roots of the language, under the guidance of Forster's grammar, an excellent work for the purpose, attempted to trace the various formations to their sources, and also noted the individual exceptions. But the work has remained unprinted, since it seemed to me that so specialized an account of forms that occur very rarely could be of interest only to very few readers.

§16

Another word-unity common by nature to all languages, though in dead ones we can still know of it only where the transiency of pronunciation has been preserved by signs intelligible to us, resides in *accent*. For in the syllable, three kinds of phonetic properties are distinguishable: the individual type of its sounds, its quality, and its emphasis. The first two are determined by its own nature, and constitute, as it were, its bodily shape; but the tone (by which I always mean here the vocal tone, not the metrical stress) depends on the freedom of the speaker, is a force he imparts to the syllable, and resembles an alien spirit breathed into it. Like a principle more spiritual than the material language itself, it hovers over speech, and is a direct expression of the weight that the speaker wishes to confer upon it and each of its parts. Every syllable is intrinsically capable of emphasis. But if only one of a number actually receives the tone, the emphasis of those that directly accompany it is abolished, if the speaker does not also expressly sound forth one of them, and this abolition produces a combination of those syllables that become toneless with the one that is stressed and thereby prevails and dominates them. The two phenomena, the abolition of tone and the binding of syllables, condition one another, and each directly and automatically entrains the other. Thus arises the verbal accent, and the verbal unity it creates. No independent word can be conceived without an accent, and each can have no more than one main accent. With two, the word would fall apart into two wholes, and would thus become two words. In contrast, however, there can be auxiliary accents in a word, which arise either from its rhythmic constitution, or from nuancings of meaning.[1]

---

[1] The so-called accentless words in Greek do not seem, as I see it, to contradict this claim. But it would carry me too far from my main purpose, were I to try to show here how, as syllables preceding the accent of the subsequent word, they mostly attach to the front of it; though in word-positions that allow of no such explanation (as οὐκ in Sophocles: *Oedipus Rex*, v. 334–6, *Ed. Brunckii*), they doubtless possessed in pronunciation a weak emphasis that was simply not designated. That every word can have but one main accent is expressly stated by the Latin grammarians. Cicero, *Orat.* 18: *natura, quasi modularetur hominum orationem, in omni verbo posuit acutam vocem, nec una plus.* The Greek grammarians treat emphasis in general more as a property of the syllable than of the word. I know of no passage in them which sets forth the accent-unity of the latter as a universal rule. Perhaps they were led astray by those cases in which a word gets two accent-marks, on account of enclitic syllables, but where doubtless the one pertaining to the appendage always constituted a merely auxiliary accent.

need for strong emphasis in English reflects English character

More than any other part of language, emphasis is subject to the dual influence of the meaningfulness of speech and the metrical composition of sounds. Originally, and in its true shape, it undoubtedly proceeds from the former. But the more the taste of a nation is directed also to rhythmical and musical beauty, the more influence upon emphasis is also accorded to this requirement. But the urge to emphasize – if the term be allowed – contains far more than the significance directed to mere comprehension. Quite particularly expressed therein is also the impulse to designate the intellectual force of the thought and its constituents, far beyond the measure of mere necessity. In no other language is this so visible as in English, where the accent very often carries the quantity with it, actually altering the typical weight of the syllables. Only with extreme injustice could this be attributed to a deficient sense of euphony. On the contrary, it is only the intellectual energy associated with the national character, sometimes the rapid decisiveness of thought, sometimes the grave ceremoniousness, which strives, even in pronunciation, to designate beyond all else the element stressed by the mind. From the combination of this peculiarity with laws of euphony that are often apprehended with great purity and precision, there arises the English word-structure, which is truly wonderful in regard to stress and enunciation.[2] If the need for strong and sharply nuanced emphasis were not so deeply grounded in the English character, even the need for eloquence in public would not suffice to explain the great attention that is so visibly devoted in England to this portion of language. If all other parts of language are associated, rather, with the intellectual peculiarities of nations, emphasis, at the same time, is more nearly and intimately connected with character.

The couplings of speech also furnish instances where less weighty words are annexed by emphasis to weightier ones, but without merging into union with them. This is the case of enclisis, the Greek

need for strong and sharply nuanced emphasis grounded in the English character

emphasis is most closely related to character

Yet even among these writers there is no lack of specific allusions to this necessary unity. Thus Arcadius (περὶ τόνων, *Ed. Barkeri*, p. 190) says of Aristophanes; τὸν μὲν ὀξὺν τόνον ἐν ἅπαντι μέρει καθαρῷ τόνον ἅπαξ ἐμφαίνεσθαι δοκιμάσας.

[2] This interesting and at the same time most difficult part of English pronunciation, the emphasis, has been dealt with in detail, and largely himself created, by Buschmann, in his textbook of English pronunciation. He proposes essentially three tendencies therein: accentuation of the stem or first syllable (§ 2–15, § 26, 27 and 33), the retention of foreign accentuation (§ 16–22), and a notable attraction of the stress by endings (§ 22–25), between which tendencies, as is particularly brought out in § 28–32 and note 34, the language, in its non-Germanic vocabulary, often gropes about at a loss. Buschmann attempts (§ 75–8) to establish for English the bye-accent above alluded to, by a syllabic interval (of two syllables, and occasionally of three, for reasons connected with origins).

ἔγκλισις. The less weighty word then surrenders its independence, but not its self-sufficiency, as a separate element of speech. It loses its accent and falls into the accentual domain of the weightier word. But if, by such addition, this domain receives an extension running counter to the laws of the language, the weightier word, by taking on two accents, transforms its toneless final syllable into a sharply-stressed one and thereby annexes the less weighty word to itself.[3] But by this annexation the natural word-division is not to be disturbed; the procedure of *enclitic accentuation* demonstrates this clearly in a number of special cases. If two enclitic words occur in succession, the second, unlike the first, does not fall, by its stress, into the domain of the weightier word; the first, rather, itself takes over the sharp stress on behalf of the second. Thus the enclitic word is not skipped over, but respected as a self-sufficient word, and assimilates another to itself. The special individuality of such an enclitic word makes its influence felt on the very nature of the stress, as is further confirmed by the foregoing. For since a circumflex cannot change into an acute accent, the result, if the first of two successive enclitic words is circumflected, is a breakdown of the whole enclitic procedure, and the second enclitic word then retains its original stress.[4] I have alluded to these details merely to show how carefully nations whose mental bent has led them to fashion their language with great elevation and refinement, also indicate the different degrees of word-unity, down to cases where neither separation nor fusion is decisive and complete.

[3] The Greek grammarians called this *awakening the slumbering tone of the syllable*. They also employ the term *throwing back the tone* (αναβιβαξειν τὸν τόνον). But this latter metaphor is less happy. The whole context of Greek accent theory shows that what is actually going on here is the process described above.

[4] For example, Iliad I, v. 178. θεος που σοὶ τόγ' ἔδωκεν.

§17

The grammatically formed *word*, as we have so far examined it, in the composition of its elements, and in its unity as a whole, is destined to enter, again as an element, into the *sentence*. So language must here form a second, higher unity – higher, not merely because it is of greater extent, but also because it depends more exclusively on the ordering inner form of the sense of language, in that sound can only operate on it in an auxiliary fashion. Languages like Sanscrit, which already weave into the unity of the word its relations to the sentence, let the latter disintegrate into those parts wherein it presents itself, by its nature, before the understanding; from these parts, as it were, they build up its unity. Languages like Chinese, which incorporate every root-word into themselves with unaltered rigidity, do the same thing, in fact, and almost in a stricter sense, since the words occur totally isolated; but in building up the unity of the sentence, they assist the understanding, partly by merely soundless means, such as position, for example, and partly by special words that are again separate. But if we take these two together, there is opposed to them both a second method, which we here do better, however, to regard as a third, of preserving the unity of the sentence for the under-standing, namely to treat it, with all its necessary parts, not as a whole made up of words, but really as a single word.

If we start from the sentence, as is originally more correct, since every utterance, however incomplete, does really constitute a closed thought in the speaker's mind, then languages which employ this method by no means shatter the unity of the sentence, but try, rather, to knit its construction even more tightly together. But they manifestly derange the boundaries of verbal unity by carrying them over into the domain of sentential unity. Since the Chinese method is too feeble in conveying the feeling of sentential unity into the language, the correct distinction of the two unities emerges solely, therefore, from the truly inflectional languages; and languages only demonstrate that inflection, in its true spirit, has permeated their whole nature, when they develop the verbal unity to completion on the one hand, but simultaneously confine it, on the other, to its proper domain, divide the sentence into all its necessary parts, and from these alone again construct its unity. *Inflection, word-unity* and *sentential articulation* are thus to this extent closely allied, that an imperfect development of any one of these components always proves decisively that no one of them has predominated, in its utterly pure and unclouded sense, in the making of the language. This threefold procedure, therefore, the careful grammatical shaping of the word to unify the sentence, the quite indirect and largely soundless indication of the same, and the tight binding-together of the whole sentence, so far as can ever be done, into a single, collectively-uttered form, exhausts the manner in which languages compose the sentence from words. In the majority of languages, stronger or weaker traces of all three methods are to be found. But where one of them definitely prevails, and becomes the centre of the organism, it also draws after it the entire structure, with a more or less rigid consistency. As examples of an extreme predominance of each, we may instance Sanscrit, Chinese and the *Mexican language* which I am just about to discuss.

To bring about the union of the simple sentence into a single sound-linked form, this last-mentioned language[1] picks out the *verb* as the true centre, adjoins, so far as possible, the governing and governed parts of the sentence thereto, and gives this conjunction the

[1] I venture a remark here about the pronunciation of the name *Mexico*. If we give the *x* in this word the sound that is common among ourselves, this is plainly incorrect. But we should stray still further from the true native pronunciation if we followed the Spanish spelling, now become quite irrevocable in its latest and still more objectionable form *Mejico*, by using the gutteral *ch*. According to local pronunciation, the third letter of the name of the war-god *Mexitli*, and of the city-name *Mexico* derived from this, is a strong sibilant, even if one cannot say just how closely it approximates to our (German) *sch*. I was first led to this, in that *Castile* is written *Caxtil* in Mexican, and that in the related Cora language the Spanish *pesar*, to weigh, is written *pexuvi*. I found this surmise still more plainly confirmed by Gilij's practice of transliterating the *x* used in Mexican into Italian by *sc* (*Saggio di storia Americana*, III, 343). Since I also found this sibilant, or one like it, written *x* by the Spanish linguists in numerous other American languages, I explained this peculiarity to myself by the want of the *sch* sound in Spanish. Since the Spanish grammarians found nothing corresponding to it in their own alphabet, they chose to designate it by the *x* which for them is ambiguous, and itself foreign to their tongue. Later on I found the same explanation for this interchange of letters in the former Jesuit Camaño, who explicitly compares the sound written *x* in the Chiquitin language (from inland South America) with German *sch* and French *ch*, and offers the same reason for the use of the *x*. This statement is to be found in the manuscript of his very systematic and complete Chiquitin Grammar, which I owe to the kindness of State-Counsellor von Schlözer, as a gift from his father's estate. That the Spaniards' *x* does duty for such a sound in the American languages, was finally confirmed for me in so many words by Buschmann also, from observations made on the spot by himself; and he provides a more extended view of the matter by saying that the Spaniards use this letter to designate sounds which lie between German *sch* and the French *j*, which is likewise unknown to them, as well as for the latter two themselves. So in order to stay close to the native pronunciation, the capital of New Spain would have to be pronounced approximately in the Italian fashion, but more accurately still, as if the sound fell between *Messico* and *Meschico*.

stamp of a bonded whole by means of sound-formation: $\overset{1}{ni}$-$\overset{2}{naca}$-$\overset{3}{qua}$, $\overset{1}{I}$ $\overset{3}{eat}$ $\overset{2}{meat}$. This combination of the substantive with the verb might be regarded as a compound verb, like the Greek κρεωφαγέω; but the language obviously conceives it otherwise. For if, for any reason, the substantive itself is not incorporated, it is replaced by the third person pronoun, a clear proof that with the verb, and contained in it, the language demands to possess, at the same time, the schema of construction: $\overset{1}{ni}$-$\overset{2}{c}$-$\overset{3}{qua}$ $\overset{4}{in}$ $\overset{5}{nacatl}$, I eat it, the meat. In its form, the sentence is to appear already concluded in the verb, and is thereafter only determined more closely, as if by apposition. To the Mexican way of thinking, the verb simply cannot be conceived without these qualifiers to complete it. So if no particular object is present, the language combines with the verb a special indefinite pronoun, employed in dual form for persons and things: $\overset{1}{ni}$-$\overset{2}{tla}$-$\overset{3}{qua}$, $\overset{1}{I}$ $\overset{3}{eat}$ $\overset{2}{}$something; $\overset{1}{ni}$-$\overset{2}{te}$-$\overset{3}{tla}$-$\overset{4}{maca}$, $\overset{1}{I}$ $\overset{4}{give}$ $\overset{2}{somebody}$ $\overset{3}{something}$. The language betrays with the utmost clarity its intention of having these composite forms appear as a whole. For if such a verb, containing within it the sentence itself, or as it were the schema of this, is located in a past time, and thereby receives the augment o, this latter positions itself at the beginning of the composite, which clearly shows that these qualifiers always and necessarily belong to the verb, whereas the augment attaches to it only contingently, as an indication of pastness. Thus from ni-nemi, I live, which as an intransitive verb can bring no other pronouns with it, we have the perfect, o-ni-nen, I have lived, and from maca, give, we get o-ni-c-te-maca-c, I have given it to somebody. But it is still more important, that in words used for incorporation, the language very carefully distinguishes an absolute and an incorporative form, a precaution without which the whole method would become uncertain for the understanding, and which must therefore be regarded as basic to it. In incorporation, as in compound words, *nouns* drop the endings which always accompany them in the absolute state and characterize them as nouns. *Meat*, which we found incorporated above as *naca*, is called *nacatl* in its absolute form.[2] Of the incorporated *pronouns*, none is used separately

[2] The terminal sound of this word, which by its frequent recurrence becomes a sort of hall-mark of the Mexican language, is throughout written *tl* by the Spanish linguists. Tapia Zenteno (*Arte novissima de lengua Mexicana*, 1753, pp. 2–3) observes merely that at the beginning and in the middle of words the two consonants would indeed be pronounced as in Spanish, whereas at the end of a word they constitute but a single sound, which is very hard to learn. Having described it with great unclarity, he expressly censures the pronunciation of *tlatlacolli*, sin, and *tlamantli*, layer, as *claclacolli* and *clamancli*. But when, through the good offices of my brother,

in the same form. The two indefinite ones simply do not occur in the language in the absolute state. Those referring to a specific object have a form more or less different from their independent one. But the method described already shows automatically that the incorporative form must be dual, one for the governing and one for the governed pronoun. The independent personal pronouns can, indeed, be placed for special emphasis ahead of the forms here depicted, but the incorporated pronouns relating to them are not therefore absent. The subject of the sentence expressed in a particular word is not incorporated; but its presence is evinced in the form by the fact that in the third person thereof a governing pronoun indicating it is always lacking.

If we survey the diversity of ways in which even the simple sentence may be presented to the understanding, we readily perceive that the strict system of incorporation cannot be carried through all the different cases. So concepts in single words must often be extricated from the form, which cannot encompass everything. But in this the language always pursues the path once chosen, and invents new artificial aids where it runs into difficulties. Thus if, for example, one

I put questions in writing on this point to Mr Alaman and Mr Castorena, a native of Mexico, I was told in reply that the pronunciation of *tl* nowadays is generally and in every case that of *cl*. This is also evidenced by a word adopted into Spanish and quite common in Mexico, namely *claco*, a copper coin worth half a *quartillo*, that is, an eighth of a *real*, from Mexican *tlaco*, half. The Cora language lacks the *l*, and with Mexican words it therefore takes over only the first letter of the *tl*. But even the Spanish grammarians of this language then always put in a *t* (never a *c*), so that *tlatoani*, governor, is rendered *tatoani*. As I learn from Buschmann, the same *t* for the Mexican *tl* is also found in a language that displays a very notable affinity with Mexican, namely Cahita, from the Mexican province of Sinaloa, a language whose name I have not yet found mentioned anywhere, and only came to know about through Buschmann; here, for example, the aforementioned word *tlatlacolli*, for sin, has the form *tatacoli* (*Manual para administrar a los Indios del idioma Cahita los santos sacramentos*, Mexico 1740, p. 63). I wrote again to Messrs Alaman and Castorena, and confronted them with the foregoing objection from the Cora language. But the answer was the same as before. So the present-day pronunciation is not in doubt. We are simply at a loss whether to assume that the pronunciation has changed over time, has shifted from *t* to *k*, or whether the cause is that the sound preceding the *l* is an obscure one fluctuating between *t* and *k*. In the pronunciation of native Tahitians and Sandwich Islanders, I have myself confirmed that these sounds are scarcely to be distinguished from one another. I consider the last-mentioned reason to be the correct one. The Spaniards, who were the first to concern themselves seriously with the language, may have conceived the obscure sound as a *t*; and since they adopted it thus into their orthography, a standstill may then have occurred. Tapia Zenteno's statement seems likewise to evince a certain indecision over the sound, which he merely does not wish to see decay into a clear-cut *cl*, after the Spanish fashion.

thing is said to happen in relation to another, either for or against it, and the definite governed pronoun would now produce obscurity, since it would have to relate to two objects, the language forms a special class of such verbs, by means of an accreted ending, and otherwise proceeds as usual. The schema of the sentence now lies entirely once more in the coupled form, the indication of a thing done in the governed pronoun, and the bye-relation to another in the ending; and now, with certainty of understanding, the language can let these two objects follow on outside, without equipping them with marks of their relationship: *chihua*, to make, *chihui-lia*, to make for or against someone, with change of *a* into *i* by the law of assimilation, *ni-c-chihui-lia in no-piltzin ce calli*, I make it for the my son a house.

The Mexican method of incorporation testifies in this to a correct sense of sentence-formation, that it attaches the designation of its relations precisely to the verb, and thus to the point at which the sentence ties itself together into unity. It thereby differs essentially, and to its advantage, from the want of indication in Chinese, in which the verb cannot even be known with certainty from its position, but is often recognizable materially only, from its meaning. But in the parts standing outside the verb in more complicated sentences, it is again entirely on a par with the latter. For in projecting the whole of its indicative activity upon the verb, it leaves the noun completely uninflected. It approximates, indeed, to the Sanscrit procedure, insofar as it truly provides the threads that couple up the parts of the sentence; but for the rest, it stands in a remarkable opposition to the latter. In a wholly simple and natural way, Sanscrit designates every word as a constitutive part of the sentence. The incorporative method does not do this; where it cannot lump everything into one, it has markers emerging like arrows from the midpoint of the sentence, to show the directions in which particular parts must be looked for, in accordance with their relation to the sentence. We are not exempted from looking and guessing, being thrown back, rather, by this particular type of indication, into the opposite system of non-indication. But although this procedure thus has something in common with the other two, we would be mistaking its nature if we wished to regard it as a mixture of them, or to suppose that the inner linguistic sense had just not had the power to carry the system of indication throughout all parts of the language. This Mexican sentence-structure obviously harbours, on the contrary, a peculiar mode of conception. The sentence is not to be constructed, not to be built up gradually out of parts, but must be given all at once as a form stamped into unity.

If we venture to descend into the first beginnings of language, man certainly always couples internally a complete meaning, and thus a finished sentence, to every sound expelled as language; he does not merely put forth, by intent, an isolated word, even though his utterance, as we see it, contains but one of them. For this reason, however, we cannot conceive the original relation of sentence to word as though something already inherently complete and detailed were merely broken down afterwards, by abstraction, into words. If, as is after all most natural, we conceive of language-making as successive, we must base it, like all becoming in nature, upon a system of evolution. The feeling that finds vent in the sound contains everything in germ, but not everything is apparent at once in the sound itself. Only as the feeling develops more clearly, the articulation gains in freedom and distinctness, and the successful attempt at mutual understanding enhances courage, do the parts at first dimly enclosed become gradually brighter, and emerge in individual sounds. The Mexican procedure has a certain resemblance to this sequence. It first sets forth a bound totality, which is formally complete and sufficient; by means of the pronoun it expressly designates the not-yet-individually-specified as an undetermined somewhat, but subsequently portrays this undetermined residue in detail. It follows automatically from this sequence that, since the incorporated words do not have the endings they possess in a state of independence, we have to consider this, in the actual process of language-making, not as a dropping of the endings for purposes of incorporation, but as an adding of them in the independent state. I must not be misunderstood as supposing the Mexican language-structure to lie closer, for that reason, to those primeval beginnings. There is always something very dubious about applying temporal concepts to the development of a human characteristic that lies, as language does, so wholly in the region of innate mental powers beyond the reach of calculation. Moreover, the Mexican sentence-form is obviously already a most ingenious and often reworked construction, which has retained only the general type of those primeval forms, but otherwise already recalls, by the regular separation of the different kinds of pronoun, a period when a clearer mode of grammatical conception prevails. For these adjunctures to the verb have already been framed harmoniously, and to the same degree, as the composition into a verbal unit and the inflections of the verb itself. The difference is merely this, that what constitutes, as it were, the immature encapsulating bud in the primeval phase, is set forth complete and indivisible in the Mexican language as a compounded whole; whereas Chinese leaves it entirely to the listener to seek out a structure that is scarcely indicated by sounds at all, and the livelier and bolder Sanscrit, by firm designation, at once brings the part into view in its relation to the whole.

The Malayan languages do not, indeed, follow the system of incorporation, but have a certain resemblance to it in this respect, that they convey the directions taken by the course of the sentence through careful designation of the intransitive, transitive or causal nature of the verb, and thereby seek to make up for the lack of inflections in understanding the sentence. Some of them pile determinations of all kinds upon the verb in this fashion, so that they even to some extent express by this means whether it is singular or plural. Thus the hint is also given, by designation upon the verb, as to how the other parts of the sentence should be related to it. Nor is the verb, in these languages, entirely without inflection. Inflections, and a certain striving towards Sanscrit word-unity, cannot be denied to Mexican in the case of the verb, where tenses are designated by particular final letters, and in part by plainly symbolic means.

It represents, so to speak, a lesser degree of the incorporation process, when languages do not, indeed, constrain the verb to accept whole nouns into the midst of its inflections, but yet express by means of it, not only the governing pronoun, but also the governed one. In this, too, there are various nuances, depending on whether this method has been more or less deeply ingrained in the language and on whether this indication is also required where the express object of the action follows on its own. Where this mode of inflecting the verb, with its interwoven pronoun pointing in different directions, has attained its full development, as in some North American languages, and in Basque, there flourishes a wealth of verb-inflection forms which it is difficult to survey. But the analogy of their formation is adhered to with admirable care, so that the understanding runs through them by way of an easily recognizable guide-line. Since, in these forms, the same person of the pronoun frequently recurs in different relationships, as agent, or as direct and indirect object of action, and since these languages are mostly devoid of all declensional inflections, they must either contain pronominal affixes differing in sound, or prevent possible misunderstanding in some other way. This often produces a highly ingenious structuring of the verb. As an excellent example of this we may cite the Massachusetts language in New England, a branch of the great Delaware family. With the same pronominal affixes, which unlike Mexican it does not distinguish by sound, it defines all the inflections occurring in its complicated system of conjugation. In so doing it chiefly employs the method of prefixing the passive person in particular cases, so that once the rule has been grasped, the genus which that person belongs to can be recognized

[handwritten top margin: why are the first two pronouns of apparently greater importance than the 3rd person?]

[handwritten right margin top: There is then an ending showing the 3rd is active]

at once from the initial letters of the form. But since even this method is not perfectly adequate, the language combines it with others, notably an ending which, if the two first persons are passive, designates the third as active. This practice of indicating the varying significance of the pronoun by where it is positioned in the verb, has always seemed very remarkable to me, in that it either presupposes a specific mode of conception in the mind of the people, or leads one to conclude that the whole of the conjugation was obscurely present, as it were, to the linguistic sense, and that the latter then arbitrarily employed position as a means of distinction. But to my mind, the former is much the more probable. Yet at first sight it does in fact seem arbitrary, if the first person, as governed, is suffixed where the second person is the agent, and yet precedes the verb where the third person occurs as active; so that one always says *you seize me* and *me seizes he* and not vice versa. One reason, however, may be that the two first persons imposed upon the people's fancy with a higher degree of vividness, and that the nature of these forms proceeded from the affected, passive person, which is not unnatural to suppose. Of the two first persons, the second again seems to have priority; for the third, when passive, is never prefixed, and the second, in like case, never has any other position. But where the second, as active, comes together with the first, as passive, it still maintains its preferred position, in that the language continues to avoid confusion in another way. It also tells in favour of this view, that in the language of the main branch of the Delaware tribe, the Lenni Lenape dialect, the position of the pronoun in these forms is the same. Nor does there seem to be any departure from this in the idiom of the Mohicans (properly *Muhhekaneew*), made familiar to us by Cooper's spirited novel. But the weave of this conjugation always remains so ingenious, that one cannot avoid the impression that here, too, as was already remarked earlier about language in general, the forming of each part has been carried out with reference to the dimly sensed whole. The grammars give merely paradigms, and contain no analysis of the structure. But by an exact analysis of this sort, drawn up in extensive tables from Eliot's paradigms,[3] I have completely persuaded myself of the regularity prevailing in the apparent chaos. The want of aids does not always permit the analysis to permeate every part of each form, and more especially does not allow separation of what the grammarians regard as mere euphony-letters from all those that are

[handwritten right margin middle: why though is the 1st person suffixed if the 2nd person is the agent? Yet precedes the verb when the 3rd person is active?]

[handwritten right margin: Mohican language]

[handwritten right margin bottom: apparent chaos but he's persuaded of the regularity finally]

[3] John Eliot, *Massachusetts Grammar*, published by John Pickering, Boston 1822. Cf. also David Zeisberger's *Delaware Grammar*, translated by Du Ponceau, Philadelphia 1827 and Jonathan Edwards' *Observations on the Language of the Muhhekaneew Indians*, published by John Pickering, 1823.

characteristic. But the recognized rules conduct us through the great majority of the inflections; and where cases subsequently remain doubtful, we can still always show the meaning of the form, in that for definitely stateable reasons it can be no other. Yet it is not a happy outcome when the inner organization of a people, coupled with outer circumstances, leads the structure of language along this path. The grammatical forms assemble into masses too large and unwieldy for sound and understanding. The freedom of discourse feels constrained, since instead of compounding from particular elements the changing thought in its linkages, it must largely employ permanently stereo-typed expressions, of which it does not even need all the parts at every juncture. Yet in so doing, the bonding within these compound forms is still too loose and rickety for their individual parts to be able to merge together in true unity.

So when separation is not carried out with organic correctness, the bonding suffers. The objection here advanced applies to the whole procedure of incorporation. The Mexican language does, indeed, make word-unity stronger again, by weaving fewer determinations by pronouns into the verb inflections, and never indicates two definitely governed objects in this fashion, putting the designation of the indirect relation, if a direct one is simultaneously present, into the ending of the verb itself; yet it is also constantly linking what would better have been left uncombined. In languages betraying a high sense of verbal unity, the indication of the governed pronoun has also at times invaded the form of the verb; in Hebrew, for example, these governed pronouns figure as suffixes. But here the language itself lets us know what distinction it is making between these pronouns and those of the persons who are agents, which essentially belong to the nature of the verb itself. For while it combines these latter as tightly as it can with the stem, it attaches the former more loosely, and at times separates them entirely from the verb and sets them up on their own.

Languages which in this way run the boundaries of word- and sentence-formation into each other are commonly wanting in *declension*, and either have no case at all, or like Basque, do not always distinguish in sound between nominative and accusative. But this should not be regarded as the cause of such interpolation of the governed object, as if, so to speak, they wanted to avoid the unclarity arising from the lack of declension. This lack is a consequence, rather, of the procedure in question. For the reason behind all such confusion of what belongs to the part and what to the whole of the sentence, is that the right concept of particular parts of speech did not confront the mind when the language was being framed. From such a concept,

[handwritten margin note: Sanscrit has kept the pronouns out of the verb]

both the declension of the noun, and the restriction of the verb-forms
to their essential determinations, would have sprung directly of their
own accord. But if, instead of this, we have first taken the road of
holding tightly together in the word as well what is merely associated
in the construction, then development of the noun will naturally
appear less necessary. The image of it as part of the sentence did not
prevail in the people's imagination; it was merely brought in
afterwards as a clarifying concept. Sanscrit has kept itself entirely free
of this weaving of governed pronouns into the verb.

I have hitherto left unmentioned another coupling of the pronoun
in cases where it more naturally stands alone, namely that of the
possessive pronoun with the *noun*; this because the reason for it is at once,
and in the main, different from that under discussion here. The
Mexican language has an abbreviation specially reserved for the
possessive pronoun, and the pronoun thus gathers the two main parts
of the language into two separate forms. In Mexican, and not in that
language alone, this coupling has likewise a syntactical application,
and so is perfectly appropriate here. For the conjunction of the third
person pronoun with the noun is used as an indication of the genitive
relationship, in that the noun standing in the genitive is made to
follow, saying *his house the gardener,* rather than *the house of the gardener.* *[handwritten margin note: dem Dan sein Buch]*
We can see that this is precisely the same procedure as that with the
verb governing a substantive placed after it.

The couplings with the possessive pronoun are not merely far more
frequent in Mexican than appears necessary to our way of thinking;
with certain concepts, such as those of degrees of affinity and of the
parts of the human body, this pronoun has actually grown, as it were,
to be inseparable. Where no particular person is to be referred to,
the indefinite personal pronoun is appended to the degree of affinity,
and that of the first person plural to the bodily members. So we do
not just say *nantli*, the mother, but usually *te-nan*, somebody's mother,
and not just *maitl*, the hand, but *to-ma*, our hand. In many other
American languages the coupling of these concepts to the possessive
pronoun also goes so far as to make it seemingly impossible to
separate them. Now the reason here is pretty obviously not a
syntactical one, but lies, rather, more deeply implanted in the
people's way of thinking. Where the mind is still little accustomed
to abstraction, it grasps as a unit what it frequently conjoins
together; and what thought is able to separate with difficulty, or not
at all, is combined into a single word by language, where it has any
tendency whatever to such couplings. Such words acquire currency
thereafter, as a coinage minted for all time, and the speakers no longer
think of separating their elements. The constant relation of thing to

[margin, handwritten: The primeval human viewpoint]

[margin, handwritten: in all languages close to the primeval the personal pronoun retains an important role]

person is rooted, moreover, in a more primeval human viewpoint, and only with advancing culture is it restricted to cases where it is really necessary. In all languages, therefore, which retain stronger traces of that earlier state, the personal pronoun plays a more important role. Some other phenomena also confirm me in this view. In Mexican, the possessive pronouns take such control of the word that its endings are generally altered, and these compounds have throughout a plural ending that is peculiar to them. Such a transformation of the whole word is visible proof that even from within it is regarded as a new individual concept, not as a linkage of two different ones occurring merely casually in speech. In the Hebrew language, the influence of the varying firmness of conceptual coupling upon verbal linkage is displayed in especially significant nuances. As already observed above, the pronouns of the active person of the verb adhere most firmly and tightly to the stem, because the verb simply cannot be thought of without them. The firmer

[margin, handwritten: for Humboldt it is logical to have the object governed by the verb adhere to stem, not the active agent]

combination that ensues belongs to the possessive pronoun, and the pronoun of the verb's object attaches most loosely to the stem. On purely logical grounds, in the last two cases – if we wanted to concede any difference in them at all – the greater fixity should have been on the side of the object governed by the verb. For this is obviously more necessarily demanded by the transitive verb, than the possessive pronoun is in general demanded by the noun. That language here chooses the opposite way can have hardly any other reason save that this relationship, in the cases which it most frequently carries with it, presented itself to the people in individual unity.

If, as must strictly speaking be done, we assign to the system of incorporation all those cases where what might have formed a particular sentence is assembled into a word-form, we find examples of it even in languages to which it is otherwise foreign. But in that case they commonly occur in being used in compound sentences to avoid interpolations. Just as incorporation is connected in the simple sentence with lack of inflection in the noun, so here it is associated either with want of a relative pronoun and appropriate conjunctions, or with a lesser inclination to make use of this means of combination. In the Semitic languages the use of the *status constructus*, even in these cases, is less striking, since they are not indisposed to incorporation anyway. Yet even in Sanscrit, I need only recall here the so-called uninflected participles terminating in *twâ* and *ya*, and even the compounds which, like the *bahuvrîhis*, include whole relative clauses within them. The latter have passed over only in lesser degree into the Greek language, which in general also makes a less frequent use of this type of incorporation. It makes more use of the method of coupling conjunctions. It even prefers to increase the mental labour by leaving constructions unconjoined, when too much coupling together imposes a certain awkwardness on the sentence-structure – a fault from which Sanscrit, by comparison, cannot always be called entirely free. This is what happens when languages in general resolve into sentences word-forms that were minted as a unit. Though the reason for this procedure does not always have to be the blunting of forms as the languages weaken in constructive power. Even where no such thing can be supposed, the habituation to a more accurate and decisive division of concepts is able to dissolve what by sense and life had melted into one, for all that it was less adapted to express the change and flexibility in the coupling of ideas. To determine the limit of what and how much can be bound into a single form, there is need for a delicate and shrewd sense of grammar, and with this, of all nations, the Greeks were preeminently endowed, just as they carried it to the utmost refinement in a national life that was entwined throughout with a rich and meticulous employment of language.

Greeks had the shrewdest sense of grammar

§18

Grammatical formation arises from the *laws of thinking* in language, and rests on the *congruence of sound-forms* with the latter. Such a congruence must in some way be present in every language; the difference lies only in *degree*, and the blame for defective development may attach to an insufficiently plain emergence of these laws in the soul, or to an inadequate malleability of the sound-system. But deficiency on the one point always reacts back at once upon the other. The perfecting of language demands that every word be stamped as a specific *part of speech*, and carry within it those properties that a philosophical analysis of language perceives therein. It thus itself presupposes inflection. So the question now is as to how the simplest part of completed language formation, the minting of a word by *inflection* into a part of speech, can be supposed to proceed within the mind of a people? Reflective *consciousness* of the language cannot be presumed in connection with its origin, and would also harbour no creative power for the forming of sounds. Every advantage that a language possesses in this truly vital portion of its organism proceeds originally from the living *sensory world-outlook*. But because the power that is highest, and deviates least from truth, arises from the purest attunement of all mental capacities, whose most ideal blossom is language itself,. what is created from the world-outlook automatically reacts back upon the language. And that is also what happens here. The objects of outer *intuition*, as of inward *feeling*, are presented in a dual relationship: in their particular qualitative *constitution*, which distinguishes them as individuals; and under their general *category*, itself also always disclosed to a suitably alert intuition by something in the appearance and the feeling; the flight of a bird, for example, as this particular movement by wing-power, but simultaneously also as the immediately passing act, which can only be apprehended in this passage; and so too, in all other cases. An intuition proceeding .from the liveliest and most harmonious exertion of powers exhausts everything presented in the intuited, and does not confound the particular, but separates it out in clarity. Now from recognition of this dual relation of objects, from the feeling of their right relationship, and the vividness of the impression evoked by each one of them, inflection arises, as if automatically, as the verbal expression of what is intuited and felt.

At the same time, however, it is remarkable to see in what various

*incorporation is
in complete~~d~~
opposition to inflection*

ways the mental outlook arrives here at *sentence-formation*. It does not
set out from a prototype, does not laboriously put the sentence
together, but achieves this without any forethought, in that it merely
confers shape in sound upon the sharp and fully-registered impression
of the object. In that this happens correctly each time, and according
to the same feeling, the thought becomes coordinated out of the words
so formed. In its true inner nature, the mental feat we allude to is
an immediate effusion from the strength and purity of the primal
speech-capacity inherent in mankind. *Intuition* and *feeling* are merely the
handles, as it were, whereby this capacity is pulled over into the
external appearance; and hence we may see why its final result should
contain so infinitely much more than the latter seems to offer on its
own. Strictly speaking, the *method of incorporation* is by nature itself in
true opposition to inflection, in that the latter proceeds from the
particular, while the former sets out from the whole. Only in part
can it return again to inflection, through the victorious influence of
the inner linguistic sense. But incorporation always betrays the fact
that, owing to its lesser power, the objects are not presented to
intuition with a clarity and distinctness matching the points in those
objects which impinge individually upon feeling. Yet in that it
thereby adopts a different procedure, incorporation again achieves,
by actively pursuing this new path, a characteristic force and
freshness in the coupling of thoughts together. The relation of objects
to their most general categories, corresponding to the parts of speech,
is an ideal one, and the purest and most universal symbolic expression
of it is taken over from *personhood*, which presents itself likewise, even
to the senses, as the most natural way of designating such a relation.
So our earlier remarks about the meaningful interweaving of pronominal stems into grammatical forms are again applicable here.

Once inflection is truly predominant in a language, the further
evolution of the inflection-system follows automatically by a perfected
grammatical insight; and we have already pointed out above how
the further development sometimes creates new forms, sometimes
permeates into existing ones not hitherto employed with a varying
significance, even among languages of the same family. I have only
to recall here the origin of the Greek pluperfect, from a merely
variant form of a Sanscrit aorist. For amid the never-to-be-neglected
influence of sound-formation on this point, we still have to distinguish
whether it has operated to restrict the differentiation of a multitude
of grammatical concepts, or has merely failed to assimilate them
completely into itself. Even with the soundest linguistic insight, there
may exist, in earlier periods of the language, an excessive creation
of sensuous forms, in which one and the same grammatical concept

is matched by a multiplicity of forms. In these earlier periods, when the inner creative spirit of man was wholly steeped in language, the very words presented themselves as objects, seized the imagination with their ring, and asserted their special nature by imposing multiformity. Only later and by degrees did the precision and generality of the grammatical concept acquire force and weight, bring the words under control, and subject them to its uniformity. Even in Greek, and especially in the language of Homer, there are significant traces remaining of this earlier state of affairs. But on the whole we can discern on this very point the notable difference between Greek and Sanscrit, that the former confines the forms more accurately in accordance with grammatical concepts, and takes more care to utilize their diversity in designating the finer shades of such concepts; whereas Sanscrit puts greater stress on the technical means of designation, employing them more abundantly on the one hand, yet adhering to them better, more simply, and with fewer exceptions on the other.

§19

Since *language*, as I have often said already, always possesses a merely *ideal existence* in the hearts and minds of men, and never a *material* one, though engraved in stone or bronze, and since even the power of dead languages, so far as it is still discernible to us, depends largely on the strength of our own reanimating spirit, there can no more be a moment of true *stasis* in language, than in the ceaseless effulgence of human thinking itself. Its nature is to pursue a progressive path of development, under the influence of the *mental power*, at any time, of its speakers. In this progress there naturally arises two periods, which must be sharply distinguished: the one where the *sound-making impulse* of the language is still in a state of growth and lively activity; the other where, after completed *shaping* at least of the outer *speech-form*, a seeming halt occurs, and there then follows a visible decline in that creative sensuous impulse. Though even from the period of decline it is possible for new life-principles and novel transformations of the language to emerge, as I shall indicate more fully hereafter.

In the course of linguistic development as such, two mutually restrictive causes are working together, the original *principle* that determines the direction, and the influence of the *material* already brought forth, whose power always stands in an inverse relation to the operative force of the principle. There can be no doubt of the presence of such a *principle* in every language. Just as a people, or a human power of thought in general, assimilates *linguistic elements* into itself, so it must combine them, even involuntarily and without attaining clear consciousness of this, into a *unity*, since without this operation neither linguistic thinking in the individual, nor mutual comprehension, would be possible. We would have to suppose just this, if we were able to ascend to the first gestation of a language. But such unity can only be that of an exclusively dominating *principle*. If this principle approximates to the general *language-making principle* in men as nearly as their necessary individualization permits, and if it permeates the language in full and unmitigated force, it will run through every stage in the latter's *development*, in such wise that a fading force will always be replaced by a new one, appropriate to the onward-creeping path. For it is typical of any intellectual development, that its force does not really die away, but merely alters in its functions, or replaces one of its organs by another. But if the first principle is already adulterated by something not rooted in the necessity of the speech-form, or if the principle does not truly permeate the sound, or if a not purely organic material conjoins with something equally misshapen to produce even greater deviance, then the natural course of evolution is opposed by an alien influence, and the language is unable to gain new strength by pursuing its own path, as must otherwise be the case in every proper development of the intellectual powers. Here, too, as in designating the manifold connections among thoughts, language requires *freedom*; and it can be seen as a sure sign of the purest and most successful language-structure, if the formation of words and word-patterns therein is subject to no other restraints than are necessary to couple *regularity*, too, with freedom, that is, to assure freedom its own existence by keeping it within bounds. The proper evolution of language is in natural accord with that of the *intellectual capacity* as such. For since the need to think awakens language in man, the successful advance of thought must also necessarily call for what emanates purely from the concept of language. Yet were even a nation endowed with such a language to lapse, for other reasons, into mental torpor and weakness, it would always be able to extricate itself more easily from this state by means of its language. Conversely, the intellectual capacity must find means for advancement from its own resources, if accompanied by a language that deviates from this correct and natural line of development. Through its self-created means it will then react upon the language, not indeed creatively, since such creations can only be the work of the language's own vital impulse, but by building itself into the language, lending a meaning and allowing an application to the forms of the latter, which that tongue itself had not imparted and to which it had not led.

Among the numberless multiplicity of existing and extinct languages we can now establish a distinction of decisive importance for the progressive cultivation of mankind, namely that between languages which have evolved forcefully and consistently from *pure principle in regulated freedom*, and those which cannot boast of this advantage. The former are the ripe fruits of the linguistic impulse luxuriating in manifold endeavour among mankind. The latter have a deviant form, in which two things come together: a weakness of the *linguistic sense* that at first is always surely inherent in man, and a one-sided deformation arising from the fact that to a *sound-form* not emanating necessarily from the language, others, thereby drawn to it, become annexed.

The foregoing inquiries provide us with a clue by which to examine this in actual languages, and present it in simple form, however much we may initially seem to find in them a bewildering mass of details.

For we have tried to show what the highest principles are concerned with, and thereby to establish points which the *analysis of languages* may ascend to. For all that this path may yet be capable of further illumination and levelling, we can grasp the possibility of discovering in every language the form from which its structural pattern emanates, and can perceive in what has just been outlined the measure of its virtues and defects.

If I have succeeded in depicting the *method of inflection* in all its completeness, how it alone imparts true inner fixity to the word for both mind and ear, and likewise separates with certainty the parts of the sentence, in keeping with the necessary ordering of thought, then there can be no doubt but that it harbours exclusively the sure principle of language-structure. In that it takes every element of speech in its two-fold significance, its objective meaning and subjective relation to thought and language, and designates this duality in its relative weight by sound-forms appropriate thereto, it elevates the most primary essence of language, viz. articulation and symbolization, to their highest degree. So it is merely a question of determining in which languages this method is most consistently, completely and freely preserved. No actual language may have reached the summit in this respect. But we observed above a difference of degree between the *Sanscrit* and *Semitic* languages: in the latter, inflection in its truest and most unmistakable form, and coupled with the most refined symbolization, yet not carried through all parts of speech, and limited by more or less accidental laws, the two-syllable word-form, the vowels used exclusively to denote inflection, the reluctance to compound; in the former, inflection redeemed by the firmness of word-unity from any suspicion of agglutination, carried through all parts of speech, and prevailing there with the utmost freedom.

Compared with the *incorporative procedure*, and that of loose *addition* without true word-unity, the *method of inflection* appears as a principle of genius, born of a true intuition of language. For in that such languages earnestly endeavour to unite every particular into the sentence, or to present the latter all in one piece, inflection immediately stamps the parts of every thought-sequence accordingly, and is by nature quite incapable of detaching from the part its verbal relation to the whole. Weakness of the language-forming impulse at times, as in Chinese, does not allow the inflectional method to enter into the sound; at times, as in languages which solely pursue an incorporative procedure, it is not permitted to operate freely and alone. But the action of the pure principle can also, at the same time, be impeded by one-sided malformation, as when in Malayan, for example, a single pattern, the determining of the verb by modifying prefixes, becomes dominant to the neglect of all others.

But however various the *deviations* from the *pure principle* may be, we shall still always be able to characterize every language by the extent to which it evinces a lack of connectives, the endeavour to append them and raise them to inflections, and the expedient of branding as a word what speech should present as a sentence. The nature of such a language will result from a *mixing* of these principles, through as a rule it will evolve from their appliation a form more individual still. For where the full energy of the guiding power does not preserve the correct balance, it is easy for one part of the language to attain, improperly, a development out of keeping with the rest. From this and other factors, *particular excellences* may also arise in languages in which we cannot otherwise recognize precisely the character of being exceptionally suitable organs of thought. Nobody can deny that old-style Chinese possesses a striking dignity, in that manifestly weighty ideas approach each other directly, and that it acquires a simple grandeur by seeming, as it were, in rejecting all useless auxiliary relations, to escape entirely into pure thought by way of language. The Malayan language proper is not unjustly renowned for its agility and the great simplicity of its verbal arrangement. The Semitic languages preserve an admirable artistry in the fine distinctions of meaning they attach to numerous gradations of the vowel. In its word-construction and speech-ordering, Basque has a special power arising from its brevity and boldness of expression. The Delaware and other American Indian languages combine within a single word a number of concepts that we would need many words to express. But all these examples merely show that whatever the path it strikes out, even in a one-sided fashion, the human mind is always capable of producing something great, and both fruitful and inspiring in its reverse action upon the mind itself. These particular points decide nothing, however, as to the *advantage* that languages have over one another. The true advantage of a language is simply that of developing from a principle, and with a freedom, which enable it to maintain all the intellectual capacities of man in busy activity, to serve the capacities as an adequate organ, and to act as an eternal stimulus upon them, through the sensuous richness and mental orderliness it preserves. In this *formative* character lies everything producible from language that is beneficial to the mind. It is the riverbed down which the latter may course with certain assurance that the sources thus fed to it will never run dry. For the mind really hovers over language as over a fathomless abyss, from which, however, it can always create the more, the more it has already been replenished from that source. So this formal yardstick can be applied to languages only if we endeavour to subject them to a general process of comparison.

mind hovers over language as over a
fathomless abyss

mind = god
Language = The material that
needs to be whipped
into shape?
The tools by which
Things are whipped into
shape?

The *grammatical framework* of language, as we have so far broadly surveyed it, and its *external structure* in general, by no means exhaust its nature, however, and its real and true *character* still depends upon something far more subtle, more deeply hidden and less accessible to analysis. What has mainly been examined up to now continues, nevertheless, to be the necessary assured foundation, in which the finer and nobler elements can take root. To present this more clearly, we must again look back for a moment at the general course of linguistic *development*. In the period of *form-creation*, the nations are more concerned with language than with its purpose, that is, with what it is meant to designate. They struggle to express their thoughts, and this urge, together with the inspiring stimulus of success, engenders and sustains their creative power. Language arises, if the simile be allowable, in much the same way that, in physical nature, one crystal builds up upon another. The formation occurs gradually, but according to a law. This initially more predominant tendency of language, as the living creation of the mind, lies in the nature of the matter; but it is also apparent in languages themselves, which possess an ever richer abundance of forms, the more primitive they are. In some of them this plainly exceeds the requirements of thought, and is therefore moderated in the transformations undergone by languages of the same family, under the influence of a maturer mental cultivation. Once this crystallization is at an end, the language is in effect a finished product. The instrument is at hand, and it now falls to the mind to make use of it and establish itself therein. This actually takes place; and the language acquires colour and character through the various ways in which the mind employs it for self-expression.

It would be a great mistake, however, to suppose that what I have here kept sharply separate for purposes of clear distinction, is equally distinct in Nature. The persistent *work of the mind* in using language has a definite and continuing influence even on the true structure of language and the actual pattern of its forms; but it is a subtle influence, and sometimes escapes notice at first sight. Nor can any period of mankind, or of a people, be regarded as exclusively and deliberately given over to the developing of language. Language is formed by speaking, and speaking is the expression of thought or feeling. The mode of thinking or sensing in a people, by which – as I was just saying – its language acquires colour and character, is already at work upon it from the very outset. It is certain, on the other hand, that the further a language has advanced in its grammatical structure, the fewer become the cases requiring a new decision. The struggle to express thought becomes weaker, therefore; and the more the mind now employs what has already been created, the more its creative urge relaxes, and with that also its creative power. As against this, the mass of material produced in the edifice increases, and this external mass, now reacting upon the mind, imposes its own characteristic laws, and hampers the free and independent operation of the intelligence. In these two points there lies what belongs, in the above-mentioned distinction, not to the subjective aspect, but to the real essence of the matter. So in order to follow out more accurately the entwining of mind into language, we still have to distinguish the latter's grammatical and lexical make-up, as the fixed and external structure, from the *inner character* which dwells therein like a soul, and produces the effect which every language typically exerts upon us, as soon as we begin to master it. We by no means wish to imply here that such an effect is alien to the *external structure*. The individual life of a language extends through all its fibres, and permeates every element of its sound. We merely wish to draw attention to the fact that this realm of forms is not the only territory which the linguistic researcher must deal with, and that at least he must not fail to recognize in language the presence of something still higher and more original, of which he must retain an inkling, even where cognition is no longer adequate. In languages of a widespread and numerously divided family, the foregoing can be demonstrated by simple examples. Sanscrit, Greek and Latin have a system of word-construction and word-ordering that is closely related and on very many points the same. But everyone feels the difference of their individual character, which is not just a national characteristic becoming visible in the language, but, deeply rooted in the languages themselves, determines the specific make-up of each. I shall therefore dwell here upon this distinction between the principle from which, as aforesaid, the *structure* of language develops, and the true *character* of the language, and flatter myself that I shall be able to ensure that this distinction is neither seen as too sharply drawn, nor misconstrued, on the other hand, as a purely subjective one.

In order to examine more closely the *character* of languages, insofar as we are contrasting it with their organization, we must look to the situation after their structure is completed. The joyous astonishment at language itself, as an ever new creation of the moment, gradually diminishes. The nation's activity switches from language more to the

literature arises

use of it, and this begins a career with the typical spirit of the people, in which neither of the two components can call itself independent of the other, but each rejoices in the other's inspiring help. The admiration and pleasure are now directed to the felicitous expression of particulars. Songs, prayers, sayings and stories excite the desire to rescue them from the transiency of fleeting discourse, are preserved, altered and imitated. They become the foundation of *literature*; and this forming of spirit and language gradually passes from the nation as a whole over to individuals, and the language lapses into the hands of the *poets and teachers* of the people, who gradually come to confront the latter. The language thereby acquires a dual shape from which, so long as the contrast retains its proper proportion, there spring for it two mutually complementary sources of power and purity.

Alongside these creators who give vital shape to the language in their works, there then arise the *grammarians* proper, who put the final touches to the perfecting of the organism. It is not their business to create; in a language that otherwise lacks such things, they can popularize neither inflection nor the assimilation of terminal and initial sounds. But they reject, generalize, smooth out irregularities, and fill up remaining gaps. In inflected languages they can justly be credited with the schemata of conjugations and declensions, in that they first bring to light, in consolidated form, the totality of the cases involved. In themselves creating from the infinite treasure of the language confronting them, they become, in this area, legislators. Since they are actually the first to introduce the concept of such schemata into consciousness, it is thereby possible for forms that have lost all real significance to again become meaningful, merely by the position that they occupy in the schema. Such treatments of one and the same language may succeed one another in different epochs; but if the language is to remain at once popular and cultivated, the regularity of its flow from the people to the authors and grammarians, and from the latter back to the people, must always continue without a break.

grammarians become the unacknowledged legislators of the world (not poets)

So long as the mind of a people is at work in living individuality within it, and upon its language, the latter receives refinements and enrichments which in turn have a stimulating effect upon the mind. But here, too, in course of time, an epoch may ensue in which the language, as it were, outgrows the mind, and the latter, in its own languor, having ceased to be self-creative, plays an increasingly empty game with idioms and forms of the language that originated from truly meaningful use. This, then, is a second *wearying* of language, if we consider the extinction of its external formative urge to be the first. In the second, the bloom of its character withers,

the second wearying of language

[handwritten margin notes: commonplaces of material life — to pure evolution of thought via literature]

though languages and nations can again be aroused and uplifted from this condition by the genius of particular great men.

Language develops its character primarily during the periods of its *literature*, and in the preparatory phase that leads to this. For it is then withdrawing more from the commonplaces of material life, and raising itself to the pure evolution of thought, and to free expression. It seems strange, however, that languages should be able to possess an individual character – apart from what is furnished by their outer organization – since each is destined to serve as a tool for the most varied individualities. For leaving aside differences of sex and age, a nation surely embraces every nuance of human idiosyncrasy. Even those who start from the same point and pursue the same occupation differ in their mode of apprehension and response. But this difference grows greater still with language, since it enters into the most secret recesses of mind and temperament. Now everyone uses language to express his most particular individuality; for it always proceeds from the individual, and each uses it primarily for himself alone. Yet it suffices everyone, insofar as words, however inadequate, fulfil the urge to express one's innermost feelings. Nor can it be claimed that language, as a universal medium, reduces these differences to a common level. It does indeed build bridges from one individuality to another, and is a means of mutual understanding; but in fact it enlarges the difference itself, since by clarifying and refining concepts it produces a sharper awareness of how such difference is rooted in the original cast of mind. The possibility of serving to express such diverse individualities seems, therefore, to presuppose in language itself a perfect lack of character, with which, however, it can by no means be reproached. It actually combines the two opposing properties of dividing itself, as one language in the same nation, into an infinity of parts, and as such an infinity, of uniting itself, as one language of a particular character, against those of other nations. How differently each man takes and uses the same mother-tongue, we find – if it were not already obvious in daily life – on comparing major writers, each of whom creates his own idiom. But the difference of character among various languages, such as Sanscrit, Greek and Latin, for example, is apparent at first sight on comparing them.

If we examine more closely how language unites this opposition, we find that the ability to serve as a medium for the most varied individualities is rooted in the deepest essence of its nature. Its element, the *word* – to which, for simplicity, we may confine ourselves – does not, like a substance, purvey something already produced, nor does it contain an already *closed concept*; it merely provokes the user to form such a concept under his own power, albeit in a particular way. Men do not understand one another by actually exchanging signs for things, nor by mutually occasioning one another to produce exactly and completely the same concept; they do it by touching in one another the same link in the chain of their sensory ideas and internal conceptualizations, by striking the same note on their mental instrument, whereupon matching but not identical concepts are engendered in each. Only within these limits, and with these divergences, do they come together on the same word. In naming the commonest of objects, such as a horse, they all mean the same animal, but each attaches to the word a different idea, more sensuous or more rational, more vivid than a thing, or nearer to the dead sign, and so on. Hence, in the period of language-making, there arises in some languages the multitude of terms for the same object. There are likewise many properties under which the object has been thought, and whose expression has been put in place of it. But now if the link in the chain, the note on the instrument, is touched in this fashion, the whole vibrates; and what issues from the soul as a concept is attuned to everything that surrounds the individual link, even to the remotest distance. The idea evoked by the word in different people bears the stamp of each one's individuality, but is designated by all of them with the same sound.

But the individualities to be found in the same nation fall within the *national uniformity*, which again distinguishes each particular turn of thought from those that resemble it in another people. From this uniformity, and that of the special stimulus peculiar to every language, the *character* of that language arises. Every language receives a specific individuality through that of the nation, and has on the latter a uniformly determining reverse effect. The *national character* is indeed sustained, strengthened, and even to some extent engendered by community of habitat and action; but in fact it rests on a likeness of *natural disposition*, which is normally explained by community of *descent*. And in this, too, assuredly lies the impenetrable secret of the thousandfold diversity of connection between body and mental power, which constitutes the essence of each human individuality. It can only be a question of whether there might be no other way of explaining the likeness of natural disposition; and in no case can *language* be ruled out here. For there the coupling of the sound with its meaning is a thing no less inscrutable than the disposition alluded to. We can split up concepts, dismember words, as far as we are able, and we still get no closer to the secret of how the thought actually couples with the word. In their most primal relation to the nature of individuality, therefore, language and the

[margin handwritten note: language and nationality directly resemble each other]

basis of all nationality have a direct resemblance to one another. But the effect of the former is stronger and more evident, and the concept of a nation must chiefly be founded upon it. Since the development in man of his human nature depends on that of his language, the very concept of the nation is thereby directly given, as that of a body of men who form language in a particular way.

[margin handwritten note: development of human nature depends on language]

But language also has the power to estrange or assimilate, and itself communicates the national character, even where descent is different. This in fact distinguishes a *family* from a *nation*. In the former there is a relation among the members that can be factually known; the same family can even flourish in two different nations. Among nations it can still appear doubtful – and in widely dispersed races is a matter of importance – whether all those who speak the same languages have a common origin, or whether this uniformity of theirs has arisen from a primordial natural disposition, coupled with distribution over the same territory, under the influence of uniformly operating causes. But whatever be the situation with these first causes beyond our ken, it is certain that the *development of language* first conveys *national differences* into the brighter region of the mind. They are thereby brought to consciousness, and receive from this development objects in which they must necessarily be embodied, which are more accessible to clear insight, and by which at the same time the differences themselves appear more finely and definitely spun out. For in that language intellectualizes man up to the point he can attain, the dark region of undeveloped feeling is left increasingly behind him. Now by this the languages, which are the tools of this development, themselves acquire so definite a character, that that of the nation can be better recognized therein than by its manners, customs and deeds. This is why peoples who lack a literature, and whose linguistic usage we do not plumb deeply enough, often seem to us more uniform than they are. We do not recognize their distinguishing traits, because they are not conveyed to us by the medium that would enable us to see them.

[margin handwritten note: language first brings national differences into brighter regions of the mind]

[margin handwritten note: dark region of undeveloped feeling gradually left behind]

If we separate the *character of languages* from their outer *form*, under which alone a particular language is conceivable, and contrast the two together, then character consists in the way that the *thought* is combined with the *sounds*. Character, in this sense, is the spirit, as it were, which takes up its abode in the language and animates the latter like a body it has produced. It is a natural consequence of the continued operation of the nation's mental individuality. In that this individuality always takes up the general meanings of words in the same individual way, accompanies them with the same associations and feelings, combines ideas from the same angles, and employs its

[margin handwritten note: character is a spirit animating a body it has produced]

freedom of construction in the same proportion as the ratio of its intellectual boldness to the capacity of its understanding, it imparts to the language a characteristic colour and shading which the latter fixes and so works back along the same track. From every language, therefore, we can infer backwards to the national character. Even the languages of rude and *uncultured* peoples bear these traces within them, and can thereby often allow us to catch glimpses of intellectual peculiarities that were not to be expected at this level of defective culture. The languages of the native inhabitants of America are rich in examples of this kind, in bold metaphors, correct – though unexpected – juxtapositions of concepts, cases where inanimate objects are transposed, by a fertile, imaginative view of their nature, into the field of the animate, and so on. For since these languages pay no attention, grammatically, to the difference of genders, though they do, and on a most extensive scale, to that of the living and the dead, their view of the matter results from the practice of their grammar. If they misplace the constellations, grammatically, into the same class with men and animals, they obviously regard the former as beings endowed with personality, moving under their own power, and probably also guiding human destinies from above. To peruse in this light the dictionaries of the dialects of such peoples, is a source of special pleasure, leading to thoughts of the most various kind; and if we recall at the same time that attempts, such as those seen above, to analyse assiduously the forms of such languages, allow us to discover the mental pattern from which their structure springs, then all that is dry and dreary vanishes from linguistic study. In every one of its parts it leads back to that inner mental configuration which in every age sustains the deepest insights, the richest stock of ideas, and the noblest emotions of mankind.

But with peoples among whom we can discover the marks of their individuality only in the particular *elements* of their language, we are seldom or never able to project a *coherent picture* of what is peculiar to them. Although this is everywhere a difficult task, it only becomes truly possible where nations have set down their world-view in a more or less extensive literature and imprinted it on their language in *connected discourse*. For even with regard to the validity of its particular elements, and in those nuances of its constructions which cannot be exactly reduced to grammatical rules, speech contains an infinity of what can no longer be observed there, once it is broken down into these elements. A word, for the most part, acquires its full validity only by the context in which it appears. This type of linguistic research requires, therefore, a critically exact editing of the *literary monuments* existing in a language, and finds material prepared in a

[margin notes:]
infer backwards from language to national character

rude uncultured defective native americans

boldly poetic inanimate transposed mov animate (all so unexpected) though

no attention to gender but great attention to living and dead constellations are living for Indians

helps to have literature connected discourse otherwise hard to extract a world view

masterly fashion in the philological treatment of the *Greek and Latin authors*. For although in such treatment the study of the whole language is itself the ultimate aim, it still starts initially from the monuments extant therein, attempts to restore and preserve them as purely and faithfully as possible, and seeks to use them for obtaining reliable knowledge of antiquity. However closely the analysis of the language, the examination of its connection with related languages, and the explanation of its structure (alone attainable by this route), must remain associated with the editing of literary monuments, they are still obviously two different branches of linguistic study, demanding different talents and directly productive, also, of different results. It would not, perhaps, be improper to distinguish in this way between linguistics and philology, and to reserve exclusively to the latter the narrower meaning that was formerly attached to the term, though in recent years, especially in France and England, it has been extended to cover every kind of concern with a given language. It is at any rate certain that the linguistic research we are talking of can be founded only on a treatment of literary monuments that is truly philological, in the sense here proposed. In that the great men who have adorned this branch of scholarship in recent centuries are establishing, with scrupulous fidelity, and down to the smallest modifications of the sound, the linguistic usage of every author, the language is shown to be constantly under the dominant influence of mental individuality, and preserves a view of this connection which enables us, at the same time, to seek out the particular points to which it attaches. We learn all at once what pertains to the period, the place and the individual, and how all these differences are embraced within the common language. But the knowledge of details is always accompanied by the impression of a whole, without the phenomenon losing anything of its individuality as a result of analysis.

Language is obviously affected, not only by the original cast of the national individuality, but by every *change of internal direction* brought about by *time*, and by every external circumstance which uplifts or depresses the nation's soul and energy of mind; especially, however, by the impact of *exceptional intellects*. As eternal mediator between mind and nature, it remakes itself at every stage in the mind's progress, albeit the traces of this become ever more subtle and hard to detect in detail, and the fact is revealed only in the total effect. No nation could animate and fertilize the language of another with the spirit peculiar to itself, without *ipso facto* transforming it into a different one. But our earlier remarks concerning all individuality are likewise applicable here. Although each of a variety of languages excludes every other, because it follows one particular path, a number

differences of nat. character need not necessarily mean absolute advantages

of them may nevertheless agree in a *common goal*. The *difference of character* among languages need not necessarily consist, therefore, in any absolute *advantages* of one over another. But to see how the formation of such a character is possible, we need to examine more closely the standpoint from which a nation must deal internally with its language, in order to set such a stamp upon it.

If a language were used simply and solely for the *daily needs* of life, the words would serve merely to represent the decision or desire to be expressed, and within it there could be no question whatever of any *inner conception*, allowing the possibility of diversity. The material thing or action would at once and directly replace the word in the speaker's or respondent's mind. Now fortunately there can be no actual language of this sort among men who continue to think and feel. One could at best compare it to the linguistic medleys produced here and there, especially in seaports, by commerce among people of quite different nationalities and dialects – such as the *lingua franca* around the shores of the Mediterranean. Aside from that, individual *attitude* and *feeling* always assert their rights. It is, indeed, very probable, could one trace it back so far, that the first use of language was a mere expression of feeling. I have already spoken out above (p. 60) against attributing the origin of language to the *helplessness* of the individual. Not even among animals does the *social* impulse arise from helplessness. The strongest animal, the elephant, is at the same time the most sociable. Everywhere in nature, life and activity evolve from inner *freedom*, whose source we seek in vain within the realm of appearances. But in every language, even the most cultivated, the use here referred to does at times occur. A person ordering a *tree* to be felled thinks of nothing by that term but the trunk he designates; but things are very different if the same word appears, without qualification or comment, even, in a description of nature or a poem. The difference of conceptual *attitude* confers on the same sounds a *significance* enhanced in various ways, and it is as if from every expression there was a sort of overspill of something not absolutely determined thereby.

This difference obviously depends on whether language is used in relation to an inner whole of thought-association and feeling, or one-sidedly employed for a limited *purpose* in a *localized activity of the soul*. In this respect it is not less severely restricted by purely *scientific* use, if the latter be not subject to the guiding influence of higher ideas, than it is by the *daily needs* of life; more so, indeed, since feeling and passion play some part in the latter. Neither in concepts, nor in language itself, does anything exist in *isolation*. But concepts actually acquire *associations* only if the mind acts in inner unity, if full *subjectivity* is directed upon a completed *objectivity*. No angle from which the object can impinge is then neglected, and each of these impacts leaves behind a slight trace on the language. If the feeling truly awakens in the soul, that language is not just a medium of exchange for mutual comprehension, but a true *world* which the *mind* must insert, by its own inner labour, between itself and *objects*, then it is on the right road towards continually finding more and depositing more in its language.

Where such an interaction obtains between language, enclosed in specific sounds, and the inner conception, which by nature is always reaching further, then the mind, seeing language to be actually engaged in endless creation, no longer regards it as *closed*, but strives unceasingly to import *new matter*, so as to have this, once patched into the language, *react* upon itself. But this presupposes two things: a feeling that there is something which the language does not directly contain, but which the mind, spurred on by language, must supply; and the impulse, in turn, to couple everything felt by the soul with a sound. Both arise from the living conviction that the nature of man has intimations of a region that *transcends* language, and is actually constricted by language; but that language in turn is the only means of exploring and fertilizing this region, and that precisely by technical and sensuous improvement it is capable of assimilating an ever larger proportion thereof to itself. This attitude is the basis of *character-expression* in languages; and the more vigorously it acts in both directions, upon the *sensuous form* of language, and into the depths of the *soul*, the more clearly and distinctly does *individuality* make its presence in language felt. It gains, so to speak, in perspicuity, and permits us to see into the speaker's mind.

What shows through in this fashion, by way of language, cannot be anything that is singly, objectively and qualitatively *indicative*. For every language would be able to indicate everything, if the people it belongs to were to traverse every stage of their culture. But each language has a part that is either still hidden as yet, or, in the case of dead languages, remains so for ever. Each, like man himself, is an *infinity* gradually developing in time. What glimmers through is therefore something that *modifies* all indications subjectively and even quantitatively. It does not appear there as an effect; rather, the *operative force* is vented directly, as such, and hence as merely caressing the effects with its breath, so to speak, in a peculiar way that is harder to recognize. *Man* is always confronting the *world* in *unity*. The direction, the goal, the amount of motion, wherewith he grasps and deals with objects, are always the same. Upon this unity his *individuality* is based. But there is a duality in this unity, though again

language is a world between itself and objects (see p.70)

nature of man has intimations of a region that transcends language, nature of man is constricted by language but language is only means of exploring that region

each language is an infinity developing over time like man himself

there is a duality between operative force and activity just like the difference between a moving body and what impels, propels it — being vs action

a mutually determining one, namely the character of the *operative force* and that of its *activity*, just as in the physical world the moving body is distinguished from the impulse that determines the intensity, velocity and duration of its motion. We have the former in mind when we attribute to a nation a more lively concreteness and creative imagination, a greater inclination to abstract ideas, or a more specifically practical bent; the latter, when we call a nation more vehement than others, more changeable, more rapid in its train of thought, or more constant in its feelings. In both, therefore, we distinguish *being* from *action*, and contrast the former, as invisible cause, to the thinking, feeling and acting which enter the realm of appearance. We are not then thinking, however, of this or that particular being of the individual, but rather of the *universal* being that emerges as a determining factor in every single one of them. Every exhaustive *depiction of character* must have this being in view as the terminal point of its research.

how deeply does man strike his roots into reality? does reality split apart from the inner life?

If we now follow out the total inner and outer *activity of man* to its simplest endpoints, we find them in the way he either couples *reality* to himself, as an object he accepts or a material he shapes, or else makes his own way independently thereof. The original characteristic mark of man's individuality is the depth to which he strikes his roots into reality, and his manner of doing so. The modes of this connection may be numberless, depending on whether reality or the *inner life* – neither of which can wholly do without the other – attempt to split apart, or combine together in various degrees and directions.

are the cries of whooping savages driven by appetite or is this the flowing of song and poetry?

But we are not to suppose that such a yardstick is applicable only among nations already *intellectually cultivated*. In the cries of joy of a troop of *savages*, it will be possible to distinguish how far this differs from mere satisfaction of appetite, and whether, as a true divine spark, it breaks out from the inner man as a genuinely human feeling, destined to flower one day in song and poetry. But though it cannot be doubted that the *character of a nation* is revealed in everything truly peculiar to it, such character is primarily disclosed in *language*. In its interfusion with all expressions of the mind, language, for that very reason, more often recalls that individual stamp which always remains the same. Yet it is also itself tied to *individuality* by such tender and intimate links, that it must repeatedly attach the same links to the mind of the listener, in order to be fully understood. The whole individuality of the speaker is therefore carried over by language into the other, not to repress the latter's own individuality, but in order to fashion from ownness and otherness a new and fruitful contrast.

The sense of difference between the material that the soul absorbs and engenders, and the power that impels and modulates in this

absorbed material vs impelling power

two-fold activity – between the *effect* and the *being* that occasions it – together with the correct and proportionate estimation of both, and the more vivid presence, as it were, to consciousness, of whichever is the higher in degree, is not found equally strongly in every national character. If we look more deeply into the reason for variation here, we find it in the more or less clearly apprehended necessity of a connection between all the *individual's* thoughts and feelings throughout his entire lifetime, and the same pattern divined and demanded in *Nature*. Whatever the soul may produce, it is merely a fragment; and the more nimble and lively its activity, the more stir there is among everything that relates, at various levels, to its product. Thus beyond the *particular* there is always a surplus of something less definitely expressible, or rather, there attaches to the particular a demand for more presentation and *development* than it directly contains; and by expression in language this demand is transferred to the listener, who is bidden, as it were, in his own mind to supply the missing element in harmony with what is given. Where there is a lively sense of this, language appears defective and inadequate for full expression, while in the opposite case there is scarcely a suspicion that anything could still be lacking, over and above the given. But between these two extremes there are innumerable intermediate stages, themselves obviously based on the prevailing tendency towards the mind's interior, or to outer reality.

The Greeks, who in all this area provide the most instructive example, combined the words in their poetry generally, but especially in lyric poetry, with song, instrumental music, dance and gesture. But they did not just do this in order to increase and multiply the sensuous impression, as can be clearly seen from the fact that to all these particular contributions they imparted a uniform character. Music, dance and dialect speech had to be subjected to one and the same original national style, to be Dorian, Aeolian or in some other mode and dialect. Thus they sought out the impelling and modulating force in the soul, in order to keep the thoughts of the song in a particular path, and to enliven and strengthen them in this path by a mental stimulus not amounting to an idea. For as in poetry and song the words and their thought-content predominate, and the accompanying mood and impetus are merely an adjunct to them, so the opposite is the case in music. The mind is merely triggered and inspired to thoughts, sensations and actions. The latter must emerge of their own accord from the heart of this inspiration, and the notes merely govern them to the extent that only certain things can develop on those paths into which they direct the stimulus. But – as is evident here among the Greeks – the feeling of a force in the soul that impels and modulates is necessarily always a feeling of individuality, present or called for, since the power that embraces all mental activity can only be a definite one, and can work only in a definite direction.

So when I referred above to something *surplus to expression*, and actually lacking there, this should by no means be construed as anything indeterminate. On the contrary, it is the most determinate of all, since it imparts the final touches of individuality, which the word by itself, being always less individualizing, owing to its dependence on the object, and the general validity required of it, is unable to do. So even if this same feeling presupposes a more *internal* mood, not restricted to reality, and can only arise from such a mood, it does not on that account lead back from the living intuition into abstract thought. Since it proceeds from the subject's own individuality, it awakens, rather, the demand for a maximum *individualization of the object*, attainable only by penetration into every detail of sensory conception, and by the utmost concreteness of presentation. This, too, is shown by the Greeks. Their attention was directed primarily to what things are and how they appear, and not, one-sidedly, to what they count for in the usage of reality. Their bent was therefore originally an *internal* and *intellectual* one. The whole of their private and public life confirms this, since everything in it was in part treated ethically, in part attended by art, and mostly, indeed, the ethical became woven into the art itself. Thus almost every outer shape recalls, in their case, an inner one, often in a manner dangerous, and even truly detrimental, to practical utility. Now for that very reason, they started in all intellectual activities from the conception and presentation of *character*, though always with the feeling that only a complete penetration into intuition is able to recognize and depict it, and that the totality of this, which intrinsically is never entirely expressible, can only arise from a coupling of details by means of a correctly ordered tact which is striving for precisely such unity. This, in particular, is what makes their *earlier poetry*, that is, the Homeric, so *plastic* in every respect. It sets before us Nature as it is, and action, even of the smallest kind, for example the donning of armour, as it gradually progresses; and it is always character that emerges from the description, without the latter ever descending to a mere narration of what took place. Yet this is effected not only by selection of the material portrayed, but also in that the powerful energy of the singer, animated by the sense of individuality, and striving towards individualization, suffuses his poetry and is conveyed to the listener. In virtue of this mental trait, the Greeks were led by their intellectuality into the whole living multiplicity of the sensuous world, and since they were looking there for something that can only belong to the Idea, were again driven back into intellectuality. For their goal was always character, and not just the characteristic, and the divining of the former differs entirely from hunting after the latter. This bent for the true individual character then turned at the same time towards the *ideal*, since the collaboration of individualities at the highest level of conception leads to an endeavour to abolish the individual as a restriction, and to preserve it only as a faint outline of determinate shape. From thence arose the perfection of Greek *art*, the portrayal of nature from the median of the living organism of every object, which succeeded, not only in its maximally complete scrutiny of reality, but also through the striving that inspired the artist, towards supreme unity of the ideal.

But there is also something in the historical development of the Greek race which directed them especially to cultivation of the characteristic, namely the division into particular tribes of differing dialect and temperament, and the *mingling* of these produced by numerous migrations and an inherent tendency to move about. The general Hellenism embraced them all, and at the same time set its special imprint on each, in every manifestation of activity, from the constitution of the state to the strains of the flute-player. Now historically annexed to this was the other favourable circumstance, that none of these tribes was dominant over the rest, and all of them flourished in a certain equality of endeavour; that none of the individual *dialects* of the language was reduced to a mere vernacular or elevated into a higher common tongue; and that this equal burgeoning of individuality was strongest and most decisive precisely during the period when language and nation were most vitally and forcefully in process of formation. And from this came the Greek propensity, in all things to let the highest emerge from the most specifically individual, a thing that cannot be seen to the same degree in any other people. For the Greek habit was to treat these original ethnic features as *kinds* of art, and in this way they were introduced into architecture, music, poetry and the nobler uses of language.[1] The

---

[1] The close connection between the folk-character of the various Greek peoples and their poetry, music, dance and mime, and even their architecture, has been set in a clear and full light by A. Boeckh, in the essays accompanying his edition of Pindar, where a rich hoard of variegated and till now largely recondite learning is brought to the reader's attention, in a methodically intelligible arrangement. For he is not content to depict the character of the tonalities in general terms, but goes into the particular metrical and musical points relating to the differences between them, a thing that had never previously been done in this thoroughly historical and exactly scientific manner. It would be uncommonly desirable that this philologist, who combines the most extensive knowledge of the language with a rare insight into Greek antiquity in all its parts and propensities, should very

merely folk element was removed from them, sounds and forms in the dialects were purified and subordinated to the sense of beauty and concord. Thus ennobled, they became elevated into specific features of style and poetic diction, capable, in their complementary contrasts, of working ideally together. I need hardly say that here, in the matter of dialect and diction, I refer only to the use of different tonalities and dialects in lyrical poetry, and to the distinction of choruses and dialogue in tragedy, not to the cases where, in comedy, different dialects are put into the mouths of the characters. The latter cases have nothing whatever in common with the former, and are doubtless to be found, more or less, in the literatures of all peoples.

Among the Romans, so far as their individuality is also displayed in their language and literature, there is far less evidence of any feeling for the necessity of furnishing the utterances of their mind with any simultaneous direct influence of the impelling and modulating force. Their perfection and greatness develop on another route, more in keeping with the imprint they laid upon their external destinies. By contrast, that feeling speaks out no less plainly, perhaps, in the German temperament than in that of the Greeks, save only that where the latter tended to individualize outer *intuition*, we do so more with inner *sensation*.

I have the feeling that everything engendered in the *mind*, as the outflow of a single *force*, constitutes a great *totality*, and that the detail, as if by the breath of that force, must bear marks of its connection with this whole, which has so far been considered more in its influence upon particular utterances. But the totality also exerts a no less significant reverse effect on the way that this force, as first cause of all the mind's productions, attains to consciousness itself. The image of his original force can, however, appear to man only as a striving on a particular course, and such a striving presupposes a goal which can be nothing other than the *human ideal*. In this mirror we discern the self-intuition of nations. Now the first proof of their higher intellectuality and more deeply penetrating inwardness is when they do not enclose this ideal within the confines of fitness for specific purposes, but regard it as a thing that can seek its purpose only in its own perfection, as a gradual flowing into unending *development*; and so to regard it is the source of inner freedom and many-sidedness. Though even when this first condition is presupposed in equal purity,

soon execute his plan to devote a separate work to the influence of the character and customs of the various Greek peoples upon their music, poetry and art, in order to treat of this important topic over its full range and extent. Cf. his remarks upon such a project in his edition of Pindar, vol. I, *de metris Pindari*, p. 253, n. 14, and more especially p. 279.

different phenomena arise from the differences of individual approach to sensory *intuition*, inner *feeling*, and abstract *thought*. In each of them the *world* surrounding man, assimilated into him from another angle, streams back out of him in a different form. To single out one such feature here, everything in external Nature forms a constant sequence, simultaneously presented to view, and following successively in the development of circumstances one from another. This is no less the case in the plastic arts. Among the Greeks, who had the gift of always drawing the fullest and most delicate meaning from sensuous outer intuition, the most characteristic trait, perhaps, of their mental activity is their distaste for everything excessive and exaggerated, the inherent tendency, for all their liveliness and freedom of imagination, their seeming extravagance of feeling, their volatility of temper, their readiness to switch from one decision to another, still always to keep everything that took shape inside them within the bounds of moderation and harmony. To a higher degree than any other people, they had tact and taste; and what is evident in all their works is still further distinguished by the fact that violation of the delicacy of feeling is never avoided at the expense of its strength or of truth to nature. Even without departing from the proper course, their inner sensitivity permits stronger contrasts, abrupter transitions, cleavage of the mind into fissures beyond repair. All these phenomena, therefore – and this already begins with the Romans – are exhibited in cultures of a later age.

The field of *diversity in mental individuality* is of measureless extent and unfathomable depth. But the course of these introductory observations has not allowed me to leave it wholly untouched. It may seem, on the contrary, that I have too largely been looking for the *character of nations* in the inner *temper of the mind*, when it is actually more vividly and palpably disclosed in *reality*. If we leave out language and its products, this character is expressed in physiognomy, body-structure, dress, customs, life-style, domestic and civic arrangements, and above all in the impress that peoples stamp, over a span of centuries, upon their works and deeds. This living picture seems transformed into a shadow, if we seek the pattern of character in the temper of mind underlying these vivid manifestations. But in order to demonstrate the influence of character upon language, it did not seem possible for me to avoid this procedure. Language cannot everywhere be directly linked to these concrete manifestations. We have to find the medium in which both make contact, and, emanating from a single source, pursue their different ways. But this is plainly just the inmost core of the mind itself.

No less difficult than the delimiting of *mental individuality* is the problem of finding out how it takes root in languages, what the *character* of languages attaches to therein, and in which of their parts it can be recognized. In that they make use of languages, the individuality of nations becomes visible in every stage of their life. The influence of this individuality *modifies* the languages of different races, many languages of the same stock, the idioms of a particular language, and even, in the end, the same externally constant idiom, as times and authors vary. The character of the language then mingles with that of *style*, but remains always peculiar to the language, since only certain kinds of style are easy and natural in each. If, among the cases here enumerated, we distinguish as to whether the *sounds* in the words and inflections are different, as is seen in ever-diminishing degree from languages of different stocks down to dialects, or whether the influence lies only in the *use* of words and constructions, while the *outer form* remains wholly or substantially the same, then the mind's operation is more evident, but finer, in the latter case, since here the language must already have attained to a higher intellectual development, while in the former it is mightier but more obscure, since only in a few cases can the connection of sounds and temperament be clearly and distinctly recognized and described. Yet even in dialects, small modifications of particular vowels, producing but little change in the language as a whole, may justly be referred to the temper of the people, as the Greek grammarians already observe of the more masculine Dorian *a*, in contrast to the more effeminate Ionian *ae* (η).

In the period of original language-making, to which, from our standpoint, we must consign those languages of different families which are underivable from each other, the endeavour first of all to create language truly from the mind, in a manner perspicuous to one's own consciousness and intelligible to the listener, a sort of creation of its *technique*, prevails too strongly not to obscure to some extent the influence of the individual *temper*, which shines out more calmly and clearly from later *usage*. Yet the original *character* of the peoples undoubtedly contributes most powerfully and influentially to this very purpose. We see this alike at two points, which, since they characterize the entire disposition of the intellect, at once determine a multitude of others. The various ways pointed out above, in which languages effect the *coupling of clauses*, constitute the most important part of their technique. Now precisely in this there is revealed, firstly, the clarity and distinctness of logical arrangement, which alone provides a secure basis for the free flow of thought, and at the same time supplies orderliness and an enlargement of intellectuality; and secondly, the more or less evident need for sensuous richness and euphony, the mind's demand also to clothe externally with sound whatever is perceived and felt within. Yet within this technical form of languages there certainly also lie further proofs of other and more special mental individualities of nations, even if they can be less certainly derived therefrom. Should not, for example, the fine distinction of numerous modifications and positionings of the vowel, and the meaningful use of these, coupled with a restriction to this procedure and a rejection of compounding, betray and promote an excess of (clever and crafty) analytical understanding among the peoples of Semitic descent, especially the Arabs? The wealth of imagery in Arabic does indeed seem to conflict with this. But if it does not itself represent a (cunning) division of concepts, I would say that this pictorial abundance lies in the words once formed, whereas the language itself, by comparison with Sanscrit and Greek, contains a far smaller stock of means for allowing literature of every kind to keep burgeoning forth from it. To me, at least, it certainly seems that we must distinguish a state of language in which, as faithful portrait of such a period, it contains many poetically formed elements, from one in which its very organism is implanted, in sounds, forms, untrammelled constructions and turns of speech, with imperishable seeds of ever-springing literary art. In the first case, the form once minted gradually cools off, and its poetic content is no longer felt to inspire. In the second, the poetic form of the language can appropriate self-created material with ever-renewed freshness, depending on the mental cultivation of the age and the genius of its poets. The remarks already made earlier about the system of inflection also find confirmation here. The true advantage of a language consists in tempering the mind, throughout the whole sequence of its developments, to orderly activity and cultivation of its particular capacities, or, to put it in terms of mental efficacy, in bearing the stamp of such a pure, orderly and vital energy within itself.

Yet even where the *form-system* of several languages is on the whole the same, as in Sanscrit, Greek, Latin and German, in all of which the prevailing method is that of inflection, by both vowel-change and affix – rarely by the former and commonly by the latter – important differences due to mental individuality may lie in the *application* of this system. One of the most important is the more or less visible prevalence of correct and complete *grammatical concepts*, and the distribution of the various sound-forms under them. Whenever this becomes dominant in a people, as its language is elaborated, attention reverts from the sensuous abundance of sounds and multiplicity of forms to the definiteness and sharply demarcated refinement of their use. This can also be found, therefore, in the same

youthful sensuousness later suitability for expression of inward ness

language at different times. Such a careful relation of forms to grammatical concepts is apparent throughout in Greek; and if we also take account of the difference between some of its dialects, it betrays at the same time a tendency to rid itself of the over-abundant sound-stock of excessively sonorous forms, to condense them or replace them by shorter ones. The youthful efflorescence of the language in its *sensuous* aspect becomes concentrated more upon its suitability for the *expression of inner thoughts*. Time makes a two-fold contribution to this, in that on the one hand the mind in its progressive development inclines increasingly towards inner activity, while on the other the language becomes worn down and simplified, wherever mental individuality does not preserve all the originally significant sounds intact. Even in Greek, compared with Sanscrit, the process of simplification is already visible, though not to the extent that a sufficient ground of explanation might be found in this alone. If in the Greek use of forms there is actually, as I think, a maturer intellectual tendency, it arises in truth from the nation's inherent feeling for a rapid, delicate and sharply separated evolution of thought. The higher stage of German culture, on the other hand, found our language already at a point where meaningful sounds had become worn and blunted, so that in our case the lesser inclination to sensory concreteness and greater withdrawal towards feeling may well have been due to this too. In Latin a plethora of sounds, and *Latin more manly and practical* great freedom of imagination, were never expended on sound-formation; the more manly and serious temper of the people, directed far more towards reality, and that portion of the intellectual immediately relevant to this, presumably allowed no such exuberant and free proliferation of sounds. In consequence of the great variety *Greek variety of imagination* of the Greek imagination, and the delicacy of their sense of beauty, we may doubtless also, without going astray, attribute to Greek grammatical forms a greater nimbleness, pliancy and more pleasing grace, exceeding that of the other members of the family.

Even the degree to which nations make use of the *technical* means of their languages is different in accordance with their varying individuality of mind. I merely allude here to the formation of compound words. Sanscrit employs it within the widest limits that any language could readily allow itself, the Greeks in a far more restricted fashion, determined by differences of dialect and style. In Latin literature it is found especially among the oldest authors, and is increasingly excluded as the culture of the language advances.

Only on closer examination, but then plainly and palpably, do we find the character of a people's distinct *world-view* attaching to the *significance* of its *words*. I have already brought out above (pp. 152, 156), that no word is readily understood in the same way by different

[handwritten marginal note: no true synonyms between languages]

individuals, unless it were to be used for a moment simply as the material sign of its concept. We can therefore positively maintain that each of them harbours something that cannot in turn be verbally distinguished, and that the words of various languages are never true synonyms, even when they designate, on the whole, the same concepts. A definition cannot encompass them, in any strict and exact sense, and often we can only point, as it were, to the place they occupy in the area to which they belong. I have already mentioned, too, how this is even the case in the designation of *physical objects*. But the true field of differing word-value is the designation of *mental concepts*. It is seldom here that a word expresses the same as a word from another language, without very obvious differences. Where we have no notion of the finer nuances of words, as in the languages of rude and uncultured peoples, the opposite does, indeed, often seem to occur. But attention directed to other, highly cultivated languages preserves us from any such over-hasty view; and we could set up a fruitful comparison of such expressions, a dictionary of synonyms for several languages, of the same kind as we have for this one or that. Among nations of great mental vivacity, however, this significance, if pursued into its finest shadings, remains, as it were, in constant flux. Every age, every independent author, involuntarily adds to it, or diverges away, since he cannot avoid imposing his individuality upon his language, and thus presents the latter with another need for the term. It becomes instructive in these cases to undertake a double comparison, of the words used for much the same concept in several languages, and of those in one and the same language which belong to the same category. In the latter case the mental individuality is depicted in its uniformity and unity; it is always the same individuality, which is infused into the objective concepts. In the former we recognize how the same concept, e.g., that of the *soul*, is apprehended from different angles, and thereby gain acquaintance, as it were, in a historical way, with the range of man's presentational modes. These can be extended by particular languages, and even by particular authors. In both cases the result comes about partly through the variously exerted and collaborative activity of the mind, partly through the manifold ways whereby the mind – in which nothing ever exists alone – brings concepts into connection. For here we are speaking of the expression emanating from the abundance of *mental life*, not of the shaping of concepts by the *school*, which confines them to their *necessary characteristic marks*. From this systematically exact limitation and fixing of concepts and their signs, there arises *scientific terminology*, which in Sanscrit we find developed in every period of philosophizing and in all areas of knowledge, since the Indian mind was especially prone to the separating and enumeration of concepts. The dual comparison aforementioned brings the specific and delicate separation of subjective and objective into the light of consciousness, and shows how both always interact with each other, and how the uplifting and ennobling of creative power goes hand in hand with the harmonious integration of knowledge.

Erroneous or defective construals of concepts have been excluded from the view developed here. It was a question only of the different lines pursued in the communally regulated and energetic effort to express concepts, of the framing of these concepts, as reflected from infinitely many angles, in the individuality of the mind. But in seeking out the mental idiosyncrasies in language the correct *demarcation of concepts* is also, of course, the primary concern. Thus if, for example, two concepts often but not necessarily connected are combined, in language, into the same word, a pure expression for either of them, taken alone, may be lacking. We find an example, in some languages, in the terms for *willing, wishing* and *becoming.* As to the influence of the mind upon the mode of designating concepts, in accordance with the affinity between the latter produced by likeness of sounds, and in regard to the metaphors employed in this connection, we hardly need to make special mention of it here.

Far more, however, than in individual words, the intellectual diversity of nations is exhibited in the *constructions of speech*, in the range that they are able to give to *sentences*, and in the multiplicity attainable within these limits. In this lies the true picture of the train and *linkage of thoughts*, to which speech cannot truly approximate, if the language does not possess the appropriate richness and inspiring liberty of construction. Everything that, in form, is the work of the mind *per se*, appears here in language, and likewise reacts in turn upon the internal. The gradations here are beyond number, and the detail produced by the effect cannot always be exactly and determinately presented in words. But the different mind so engendered hovers, like a gentle breeze, over the whole.

I have hitherto been dwelling on particular points in the *reciprocal influence of national character and language*. But there are two phenomena in the latter wherein not only do they all most decisively come together, but where the influence of the whole is also so far in evidence, that the very concept of the particular vanishes from the scene, namely *poetry* and *prose*. We must call them *phenomena of language*, since even the original disposition of the latter gives a predominant tendency to one or the other, or, where the form is truly a great one, to an equal development of both in regular proportion, and also reacts upon this in turn in its own course. But in fact the two are primarily *paths of development* for *intellectuality* itself, and if their approach is not defective, and their course undisturbed, must necessarily evolve from this. They therefore call for the most careful study, not only in their mutual *relationship* as such, but especially in regard to the *time* at which they *arise*.

If both are simultaneously viewed from their most concrete and ideal aspect, they pursue different paths to a similar end. For both move out from *reality* toward something that does not belong there. *Poetry* grasps reality in its *sensuous appearance*, as outwardly and inwardly experienced, but has no interest in that which makes it reality, indeed deliberately repulses this aspect of the real. It thereupon conjoins the sensuous appearance before the *imagination*, and proceeds by means of it to intuition of an artistically *ideal whole*. *Prose* seeks in reality for the very roots whereby the latter attaches to existence, and the threads which connect it to this. It thereupon couples intellectually fact with fact and concept with concept, and strives towards an *objective nexus* in an *Idea*. The difference between the two is here depicted as it declares itself in the mind according to its true nature. If we look merely to a possible manifestation in *language*, and here only to an aspect of this that is very powerful in combination, but of virtually no account in isolation, then the inner tendency of prose can be carried out in bound, and that of poetry in free diction, but in most cases only at the expense of both, so that the prosaic, poetically expressed, has the character neither of prose entirely, nor that of poetry, and likewise with poetry clothed in prose. Poetic content also forcibly engenders a poetic dress; and there is no lack of examples of authors, who, feeling this power, have completed in verse what they began in prose. What both have in common – to revert to their true nature – is the tension and range of the spiritual powers, which calls for a combination of the complete penetration of *reality* with the attainment of an ideal nexus of infinite multiplicity, and the bending of the mind to consistent pursuit of the path laid down. Yet this in turn must be so conceived as not to exclude, but rather to promote, the pursuit of the opposite in the nation's mind. Both, the poetic and the prosaic temper, must complement each other for the common purpose of allowing man to strike roots deep into reality, but only so that his growth may be no less joyfully uplifted beyond the real, into a freer element. The poetry of a people has not attained the highest summit, if, in its many-sidedness and the free flexibility of its impulse, it does not simultaneously proclaim the possibility of a corresponding development in prose. Since the human mind, conceived in power and freedom, must arrive at the fashioning of both, we recognize the one from the other, as we see from the fragment of a sculpture whether it has been part of a group.

But prose can also stop at mere presentation of the *actual*, and at wholly *external aims*, can to some extent be merely a conveyor of facts, not a stimulant of ideas or feelings. In that case it does not depart from *ordinary speech*, and fails to reach the summit of its true nature. It cannot then be called a path of intellectual development, and has no formal connections, but only material ones. Where it pursues the higher path, it also needs means that sink deeper into the mind in order to reach the goal, and then elevates itself to that *ennobled speech* which is alone in question if we consider it as the companion of poetry in the intellectual career of nations. It then demands to embrace its object with all powers of the mind in unison, from which there at once ensues a treatment showing the latter as radiating in every direction where it can exert an effect. The analysing understanding is not active alone – the other powers join in, and form the conception which in heightened terms is called mentally vivacious. In this unity the mind, besides dealing with the object, also conveys the impress of its own temper into speech. The language, uplifted by the sweep of thought, makes its own merits felt, but subdues them to the governing purpose in hand. A tone of moral feeling is imparted to it, and the soul gleams out in the style. In a manner quite peculiar to itself, however, there is revealed in prose, through subordination and contraposition of clauses, that *logical eurhythmy*, answering to the sequence of thought, which is expected of prose diction in the general enhancement occasioned by its particular purpose. If the poet succumbs to this too much, he gives poetry the semblance of rhetorical prose. Now in that everything here separately enumerated is collectively at work in *vivid prose*, there is depicted in the latter the whole living growth of thought, the wrestling of mind with its object. Where the object allows it, thought takes shape as a free, direct inspiration, and mimics in the realm of truth the self-sufficient beauty of poetry.

It follows from all this that *poetry and prose* are subject to the same *general requirements*. In both, an impulse arising from within must uplift and support the mind. Man in all his individuality must move in thought towards the outer and inner world, and in grasping detail must also allow it the form which connects it to the whole. Poetry and prose are different, however, in their *directions* and *means* of operation, and can really never be intermingled. In regard to *language* it must also be particularly noted that *poetry*, in its true nature, is inseparable from *music*, whereas *prose* relies exclusively on *language*. It is well-known how precisely the poetry of the Greeks was linked to instrumental music, and the same is true of the lyrical poetry of the Hebrews. The effect of the various tonalities on poetry has also been mentioned above. However poetic thought and language may be, we do not feel ourselves in the true realm of poetry, if the musical element is lacking. Hence the natural bond between great poets and composers, although the propensity of music to evolve in unrestricted independence also aims, no doubt, to put poetry in the shade.

Strictly speaking, it can never be said that *prose results from poetry*. Even where this appears to be historically[2] true of them, as in Greek literature, the correct explanation can only be that the prose originated from a mentality conditioned for centuries by the truest and most varied poetry, and in a language formed in that way. But essentially the two are different. The germ of Greek prose, like that of poetry, already lay originally in the Greek mind, through whose individuality, too, they match one another in their particular character, each with its essential nature unscathed. Greek poetry exhibits the broad, free soaring of the mind which engenders the need for prose. The development of both was the perfectly natural outcome of a common original, and an intellectual urge embracing both at once, which only external circumstances could have prevented from reaching full maturity. Still less can the *higher levels of prose* be explained as arising from an admixture of *poetic elements*, however much diminished by the specific purpose and taste of speech. The intrinsic differences of both exert their effect, of course, upon the *language* as well, and the poetic and the prosaic each have their peculiarities in the choice of *terms, grammatical forms and constructions*. Much more than by these details, however, they are kept apart by the *tone of the whole* residing in their deeper nature. However infinite and inexhaustible within itself, the sphere of the poetic is nevertheless always a *closed* one, which does not take in everything, or does not allow what is taken in to retain its original nature; thought, unfettered by any external form, can move onwards in free development to every side, both in grasping the particular and in constructing the univeral Idea. To that extent the need to cultivate *prose* is rooted in the abundance and freedom of *intellectuality*, and makes the prose of certain periods a unique sign of mental culture. But it also has another aspect, by which it charms and engages the mind: its close affinity with the affairs of *ordinary life*, which can be spiritually heightened by its ennobling power, without any loss of truth or natural simplicity. In this connection even *poetry* may choose a *prosaic dress*, to render feeling, as it were, in all its purity and truth. As a

---

[2] The introduction to G. Bernhardi's *Wissenschaftliche Syntax der griechischen Sprache* provides a most intelligent review, attesting a deep and thorough reading of the ancients, of the course of Greek literature in regard to construction and style.

man may himself be averse to language, conceiving it to limit the mind and distort the purity of his utterance, and may yearn to feel and think without such a medium, so, by laying all its ornament aside, he may betake himself, even in the highest poetic mood, to the simplicity of prose. Poetry, by nature, is always clothed in an outer artistic form. But the soul can have a bent towards *nature*, rather than *art*, yet of such a kind that its whole ideal content is kept for the feeling of nature; and this seems in fact to be peculiar to the *more recently cultured peoples*. It can certainly be found, at all events, in our *German cast of mind*, and this is directly connected with the equally deep but less sensuous way in which our language has been formed. The poet can then deliberately stay close to real-life situations, and, if the power of his genius suffices, create a truly poetic work in the vesture of prose. I need only refer here to Goethe's *Werther*, of which every reader will feel how necessarily the outer form is related to the inner content. But I mention this only to show how quite different frames of mind can engender postures of *poetry* and *prose* to one another, and connections of their inner and outer nature, which all have an influence on the *character of language*, but also in turn undergo its *reverse effect*, which is even more visible to us.

But *poetry* and *prose* themselves also take on, each for itself, a peculiar *coloration*. In *Greek poetry*, in keeping with the general intellectual individuality, the *outer artistic forms* predominated over everything else. This arose initially from its lively and pervasive attachment to music, but also primarily from the delicate tact with which this people knew how to weigh and adjust the inner effects upon the mind. Thus it clothed the *old comedy* in the richest and most varied rhythmic dress. The more deeply this comedy would often descend, in its portraiture and diction, to the commonplace and even to the low, the more it felt the necessity of securing firmness and vigour through the tightness of the outer form. The combination of a high poetic tone with the utterly practical, old-fashioned solidity of the dense-packed *parabases*, devoted to simplicity of manners and civic virtue, now seizes the mind, as we vividly feel on reading Aristophanes, in an opposition which at bottom again finds unity. To the Greeks, moreover, the intrusion of prose into poetry, such as we find among the Indian writers, and in Shakespeare, was utterly foreign. The felt need to approximate to conversation on the stage, and the correct feeling that even the fullest narration, put into the mouth of an actor, would have to differ from the epic recital of the rhapsode, while always vividly recalling this, gave rise to special metres for these parts of the drama, to mediate, as it were, between the artifice of poetry and the natural simplicity of prose. But the same general temper worked on these as well, and gave them also an outwardly more artistic shape. The national individuality is particularly evident in the critical attitude to the great prose-writers, and the judgement they receive. Where we take an altogether different line, the cause of their excellence is primarily sought in refinements of pulse, elegant figures of speech, and external features of sentence-structure. In reading such writings, for instance the in this case pioneering works of Dionysius of Halicarnassus, the collective effect of the whole, the intuition of an inner evolution of thought – of which style is merely a reflection – seem from our point of view to utterly vanish. It cannot be denied, however, that discounting the biasses and pedantries of this type of criticism, the beauty of these great exemplars does partly depend on such details; and a closer examination of this viewpoint at once leads us more deeply into the idiosyncrasy of the Greek mind. For works of genius exert their effect only through the manner in which nations conceive them; and it is precisely the effect upon languages, our present topic of concern, which chiefly depends on this conception.

The progressive *cultivation of the mind* leads to a stage at which, ceasing, as it were, to divine and conjecture, it struggles to establish knowledge and to assemble the essence of it into unity. This is the period of the rise of *science*, and of the *learning* which results, and this stage cannot fail to influence language in the highest degree. I have already spoken earlier (p. 167) of the terminology that grows up in the schools of science. But it is here the place to allude to the general influence of this phase, since science in the strict sense demands a *prosaic* garb, and only by accident can acquire a poetic one. Now in this area the mind deals exclusively with the *objective*, and with the subjective only insofar as the latter contains necessity; it is seeking *truth* and the banishment of all outer and inner seeming. Thus only by this labour does language acquire final precision in the separating and fixing of *concepts*, and the purest consideration of *sentences* and their parts, which are together pushing toward a single goal. But since by the scientific form of the edifice of knowledge, and the fixing of its bearings, the cognitive capacity of the mind is confronted with something quite new, which surpasses all particulars in *sublimity*, this operates at the same time on *language*, giving it a character of higher *seriousness*, and a *strength* that brings concepts to maximum clarity. But its use in this area demands, on the other hand, *coldness* and *dryness*, and in *constructions* the avoidance of any more artificial *complexity*, which would hamper ease of understanding and be unsuited to the simple purpose of presenting the object. The scientific tone of prose is therefore quite unlike that depicted so far. Without exhibiting its own independence, language has merely to adhere to, accompany and present the thought as closely as it can. In the history of man's mind accessible to us, Aristotle may justly be called the founder of science, and of the attitude directed towards it. Although the impulse to this arose, of course, much earlier, and advances were gradually made, it was only with him that the concept came to fruition. As though it had suddenly burst out in him with a clarity hitherto unknown, his lectures and methods of investigation are separated from those of his immediate predecessors by a palpable gulf which cannot be traversed in stages. He sought out facts, collected them and strove to nurture them into general ideas. He examined the systems created before him, showed that they were untenable, and endeavoured to give his own a basis that rested on a deeper inquiry into man's cognitive powers. At the same time he brought all the knowledge encompassed by his giant intellect into a relationship ordered by concepts. From such a procedure, at once deeply penetrating and broadly comprehensive, directed equally strictly to the matter and form of knowledge, wherein the pursuit of truth was primarily marked by a sharp detachment from all misleading sham, there was bound to arise, with Aristotle, a language that presented a striking contrast to that of his immediate predecessor and contemporary, Plato. We cannot in fact put both of them into the same period of development, and must look upon Platonic diction as the culmination of an epoch which did not subsequently recur, and that of Aristotle as beginning a new one. But here we have a striking glimpse of the effect of the peculiar way in which philosophic cognition goes to work. We should certainly be much mistaken in seeking to attribute Aristotle's more charmless, unadorned and undeniably often hard language to a natural dryness and meagreness, as it were, of his mind. Music and poetry had occupied a large part of his studies. Their effect, as we can already see from his few remaining pronouncements in this field, had penetrated him deeply, and only a native inclination could have led him to this branch of literature. We still possess a hymn of his, full of poetic ardour; and if his exoteric writings, especially the dialogues, had come down to us, our judgement on the range of his style would probably turn out quite different. Individual passages from his extant writings, especially the *Ethics*, show the heights he was capable of rising to. A truly deep and well-distilled philosophy also has its own ways of reaching a peak of high eloquence. Where the teaching comes from a genuinely creative mind, the solidity and even the finality of the concepts gives the language, too, a sublimity that matches the inner depth.

[handwritten top margin: Alexander von Humbolt mentioned here]

A version of philosophical style of quite peculiar beauty is also to be found among us in the pursuit of fine-drawn concepts in the writings of Fichte and Schelling, and though only here and there, but then to truly gripping effect, in Kant. The results of factual scientific investigations are for the most part not only capable of a fine prose that is well-worked-out and proceeds automatically from a deep and general view of the whole of nature; such a prose is actually demanded by scientific inquiry itself, since it fires the spirit which alone can lead to great discoveries there. If at this point I mention the works of *my brother* which enter this domain, I believe I am only reiterating a general opinion that has often been expressed.

The field of knowledge can coalesce into universality from every angle; and this enhancement, and the most accurate and complete treatment of the factual basis, are in fact very intimately connected. Only where learning, and the effort to extend it, are not suffused with the authentic spirit, does language also suffer; this, then, is one of the quarters from which prose is threatened with decay, just as it is by the decline of cultivated, thoughtful conversation into commonplace or conventional talk. The works of language can prosper only so long as they are carried upward by a mental ardour, directed to the enlargement of its own culture, and to conjoining the world to its own essential nature. Such ardour appears in numberless gradations and guises, but by its own inherent impulse is always ultimately striving – even where man is not individually aware of the fact – towards this grand conjunction. Where a nation's intellectual individuality does not rise powerfully enough to this altitude, or where language, in the intellectual decline of a cultured people, is deserted by the spirit to which its power and vitality are solely due, a prose of distinction never arises, or else falls to pieces, when the mind's creativity relapses into scholarly compilation.

[handwritten right margin: you've got to have mental ardour in any writing and is always fusion ~ the world ~ the outside]

Poetry can belong only to certain moments of life, and certain frames of mind; prose is man's constant companion, in all the utterances of his mental activity. It clings to every thought and feeling; and if it has evolved in a language, by precision, lucidity, fluency, euphony and concord, to the point where it can spring into the freest action from every angle, yet also has a fine sense of where and how far such ebullience becomes it in each particular case, then it attests and fosters a turn of mind that is no less free and lightsome, yet likewise wary in its advance. This is the highest peak that language can attain in the forming of its character, and which therefore, from the first seeds of its outer form onwards, requires the broadest and surest of foundations.

When prose takes shape in this way, poetry cannot have remained behind, since both emanate from a common source. It can however, reach a high degree of excellence, without prose having also achieved a similar development in the language. The circle of the latter is always completed only by both at once. In *Greek literature*, albeit with great and lamentable gaps, the career of the language in this respect is more fully and purely presented to us than we see it anywhere else. Without discernible influence from foreign works, though that of foreign ideas is not thereby ruled out, it develops through every phase of its course, from Homer to the Byzantine writers, entirely from within itself, and from transformations of the national mind through the inner and outer vicissitudes of history. The peculiar nature of the Greek peoples consisted in a national restlessness that was always struggling at once for freedom and supremacy, though happy for the most part to preserve the appearance of freedom for the conquered as well. Like the waves of the inland sea about them, this temperament produced within the same modest boundaries incessant changes of dwelling-place, size and dominance, providing the mind with constant new nourishment and incentive to vent itself in every kind of activity. Where the Greeks operated at a distance, as in the founding of colonial cities, the same national spirit prevailed. So long as the situation lasted, this inner national principle permeated the language and its works. Throughout this period we have a lively sense of the intimate progressive interconnection of all the mind's products, the active interlinking of poetry and prose, and of every species of both. But when, after Alexander, the Greek language and literature had been spread by conquest, and later, as the possession of a defeated people, had combined with the world-dominating culture of the victors, outstanding minds and poetic talents did indeed continue to arise, but the animating principle had expired, and with it the living creativity that sprang from the fullness of its own power. In a truly world-historic association between two extraordinary men, one rich in deeds, the other in ideas, the knowledge of a large part of the earth's surface was now truly disclosed for the first time, and, by the teaching and example of Aristotle, the scientific observation and systematic analysis of the entire field of knowledge had been made clear to the mind. With overwhelming force, the world of objects bore down upon subjective creativity; and the latter was still further oppressed by the earlier literature, which, since its animating principle had vanished with the freedom it sprang from, was bound all at once to appear as a power that brooked no real competition, though many imitations were attempted. So from this period onwards there begins a gradual decline of the language and literature. But scientific activity now turned to the treatment of both, so far as they

survived from the purest state of their prime, and hence there have
come down to us, at the same time, a large proportion of works from
the best periods, and the way in which these works were reflected
in the consciously directed scrutiny by later generations of the same
people, who, though cast down by outward misfortunes, remained
always what they were.

As for Sanscrit, our knowledge of its literature permits no reliable
judgement of the level and extent to which *prose* was also developed
therein. But the condition of civil and social life in India hardly
offered the same incentives to such development. More, perhaps,
than was ever the case in any other nation, the Greek mind and
character were intrinsically given to associations in which conversation, if not the sole purpose, was at any rate the main seasoning. The
proceedings in courts and the popular assembly demanded eloquence
to convince and sway the mind. It may be due to these and similar
causes, if even in the future, we find nothing among the relics of
Indian literature which is comparable in style to the Greek historians,
orators and philosophers. The rich, flexible language, equipped with
all the means whereby speech acquires solidity, dignity and grace,
obviously harbours within it all the seeds for this purpose, and in the
higher treatment of prose would have evolved quite different
characteristics from those we now know in it. The simple, graceful
tone of the *Hitôpadêśa* stories, wonderfully attractive alike by accurate
and elegant description and a wholly individual sharpness of understanding, is already proof of this.

Latin prose was related to poetry in a way quite different from the
Greek. The Romans were equally strongly affected here by their
imitation of Greek models, and by their own originality, which is
everywhere apparent. For their language and style manifestly bear
the imprint of their inner and outer political development. Set down,
with their literature, in an altogether different temporal context,
there could be among them no original and natural development,
such as we perceive in the Greeks from Homeric times onward, and
through the lasting influence of those earliest songs. The great
original prose of the Romans springs directly from mind and
character, from manly seriousness, moral rigour and all-exclusive
patriotism, sometimes intrinsically, sometimes in contrast to later
decadence. It has far less of a purely intellectual tinge, and for all
these reasons together, is bound to lack the simple charm of some
Greek authors, which occurs among the Romans only in the poetic
mood, since poetry is able to throw the mind into any and every state.
More generally, in virtually every comparison that can be made
between Greek and Latin authors, the former appear less pompous,

simpler and more natural. From this there arises a major difference between the prose of the two nations; and it is scarcely credible that an author like Tacitus should have been truly appreciated by the Greeks of his day. Such a prose would have had to operate all the more differently upon the language too, in that both received the same impulse from the same national individuality. An equally unbounded pliancy, yielding to every thought, pursuing every avenue of mind with equal nimbleness, and finding its true character precisely in this versatility and mobility, to which nothing came amiss, could not have arisen from such prose, and could equally little have engendered it. A look at the *prose of more recent nations* would lead to considerations more complicated still, since where not themselves original, these peoples have been unable to avoid being differently attracted by the Romans and the Greeks, while at the same time quite new conditions have also produced in them an originality not known before.

Since the masterly investigations of F. A. Wolf on the origin of the *Homeric poems*, it is doubtless generally acknowledged that the *poetry* of a people can still remain unrecorded long after the invention of *writing*, and that the two epochs by no means necessarily coincide. Designed to add lustre to the present moment, and to help in the celebrating of festive occasions, poetry in the earliest ages was too intimately connected to life, too spontaneously engendered alike by the fancy of the poet and the apprehension of his audience, for the deliberation of cold recording not to have remained alien to it. It flowed from the lips of the poet, or the school of singers which had made his poems their own; it was a living recital, accompanied with song and instrumental music. The words comprised only a part of this, and were inseparably conjoined with it. This whole recital was likewise transmitted to posterity, and it could not have occurred to anyone to wish to dissever what was so firmly intertwined. Through the whole way in which poetry took root, during this period, in the mental life of the people, the notion of inscribing it never arose at all. This first called for reflection, which always develops from the art that is practised for a time in a merely natural fashion, and for a greater extension of everyday living conditions, which provokes the wish to separate activities, and to let their products work enduringly together. Only then could the association of poetry with recitation, and the pleasure of the moment, become less close. The fixity of poetic word-ordering, and the presence of metre, also made it largely unnecessary to help out transmission by memory with the aid of script.

With *prose*, this was all quite different. Yet in my view the main difficulty is not to be sought here in the impossibility of committing to memory the longer passages of unstructured speech. There certainly exists among peoples a purely national prose, preserved by oral tradition, in which the garb and expression are assuredly not due to chance. In the folk-tales of nations which possess no writing at all, we find a use of language, a kind of style, from which it is evident that they have certainly been passed on with minor changes from one narrator to another. Even children, in repeating the tales they have heard, are normally careful to employ the same turns of speech. I need only recall here the story of *Tangaloa* on the Tonga islands.[3] Among the Basques, such unrecorded tales are in circulation even to this day, and in manifest proof that the outer form here is also, and quite specially, attended to, we are assured by native speakers that these narratives lose all their charm and natural elegance when translated into Spanish. The people are so devoted to these stories that they have been divided into various categories, according to content. I myself heard one told, which was very like our own Pied Piper of Hamelin; others, simply altered in various ways, present the myths of Hercules, and a purely local one from a small offshore island[4] tells the tale of Hero and Leander, carried over to a monk and his beloved. Yet the *written record*, of which no thought even arises in the earliest poetry, is still a necessary and immediate part of the original purpose of prose, even before it rises to a truly artistic level. Facts must be looked into or presented, concepts developed and conjoined, i.e. something objective be ascertained. The mood which attempts to achieve this is a sober one, directed to inquiry, separating truth from illusion, handing control of the business over to the understanding. It therefore begins by rejecting metre, not just because of the burden of its fetters, but rather because the need for it cannot here be justified – on the contrary, a form that constrains language in accordance with a particular feeling is not suited to the many-sidedness of the understanding, as it pries and couples, this way and that. Through this, and in virtue of the whole undertaking, a written record now becomes desirable, and even indispensable. The topic of inquiry, and even the very course of research, must be safely and surely set down in every detail. The aim itself is maximum possible unification: history must preserve what would otherwise slip away in the course of time, doctrine connect one generation with the next, to ensure further development. Prose also first makes possible the emergence of named individuals from the mass in mental productions, since inquiry implies personal investigations, visits to foreign countries, and self-chosen methods of connecting

---

[3] W. Mariner, vol. II, p. 377.
[4] Izaro, in the Bay of Bermeo.

things; truth, especially in times when other proofs are lacking, has need of an authority, and the historian cannot, like the poet, derive his credentials from Olympus. The disposition towards prose that develops in a nation must therefore seek ways of facilitating writing-methods, and may be stimulated by those already available.

In *poetry*, through the natural course of cultivation among peoples, there are two different species[5] that arise, to be distinguished precisely by their use or avoidance of *writing*; one, as it were, predominantly *natural*, emanating from enthusiasm, without thought or consciousness of art; the other later and more *artistic*, though pertaining no less, on that account, to the deepest and most genuine poetic spirit. In *prose* this cannot occur in like fashion, and still less so in the same periods. But in another way, the same is also true of it. For if, in a people fortunately endowed for prose and poetry, occasions arise where life has need of free-flowing *eloquence*, there is here a similar linkage of prose with the life of the people, such as we found above in connection with poetry; it just happens in a different way. Then, too, so long as it persists without consciousness of deliberate art, it rejects the dead, cold, written record. This was very likely the case during the great age of Athens, between the Persian and Peloponnesian wars, and even later on. Orators such as Themistocles, Pericles and Alcibiades undoubtedly showed for-midable talents as speakers; this is expressly emphasized of the latter two. Yet none of their speeches has come down to us – for those in the historians naturally belong only to the latter – and even antiquity seems to have possessed no writings that could safely be ascribed to them. In Alcibiades' time there were, indeed, ready-written speeches, and even speeches that were meant to be delivered by others than their authors; but it was part of the whole complexion of political life in that period, that those who were the real leaders of the state found no occasion to write down their speeches, either before or after delivery. Yet no less than the poetry, this natural eloquence assuredly harbours, not merely the seed, but in many passages the unsurpassed model for the later, more artistic, style. Here, however, where our subject is the influence of the two styles upon language, a closer

---

[5] The discussion of the earliest poetry of the Greeks and Indians, in the Preface to A. W. von Schlegel's *Ramayana*, is incomparably expressed and perceived with a poet's own feeling. What a boon it would be to the philosophical and aesthetic assessment of both literatures, and to the history of poetry, if this author, so preeminently endowed with the necessary gifts for it, would consent to write the history of Indian literature, or at least to treat particular parts of it, namely the dramatic poetry, and to subject it to as happy a critique as the drama of other nations has received from his truly masterful hand.

consideration of the matter could not be dispensed with. The later orators received the language from an age when great and splendid achievements in the plastic and literary arts had already aroused the genius of orators and moulded popular taste; and they received it, therefore, in a very different state of fullness and refinement from what it had been able to boast of earlier on. The live discussion in the schools of philosophy must have had something very similar to show.

§21

It is marvellous to see what a long series of languages, equally happy in their structure and equally stimulating in their effect upon the mind, has been engendered by that language which we must place at the summit of the *Sanscrit family*, if in every such family we are to assume a primeval or mother language at all. To enumerate at this point only the factors that chiefly concern us, we first find Zend and Sanscrit in close affinity, though also notably different, yet both of them permeated by the liveliest principle of fecundity and regularity in the creation of words and forms. From this stock there subsequently emerged the *two languages* of our *classical* scholarship, and – albeit in a later development, scientifically speaking – the entire *Germanic group*. Finally, when *Latin* degenerated through decadence and mutilation, there blossomed from it, as if with renewed vitality, the *Romance languages*, to which our present-day culture is so infinitely indebted. This primeval language therefore harboured a life-principle by which the thread of mankind's intellectual development was able to spin itself out for at least three thousand years, and which itself had the power to regenerate new linguistic forms, even from the collapsed and the exploded.

In the history of nations, the question may well have been raised as to what would have happened in the world if Carthage had defeated Rome and conquered the European West. One might equally well ask what the present state of our culture would be if the Arabs had remained, as they were for a time, the sole possessors of scientific knowledge, and had spread throughout the Western world. A less favourable outcome seems to me, in both cases, beyond doubt. It is to the same causes which produced the world-dominance of Rome, namely the *Roman spirit and character*, rather than to external and more accidental circumstances, that we owe the powerful influence of this world-dominion upon our civil institutions, laws, language and culture. Through the turn toward this culture, and through inner kinship, we became genuinely receptive to the Greek mind and language, where the Arabs only adhered, for the most part, to the scientific results of Greek inquiry. Even on the basis of the same antique heritage, they would not have been capable of erecting the edifice of science and art which we may justly boast today.

Assuming this to be correct, we may ask whether such a pre-eminence of the peoples of *Sanscrit origin* is to be sought in their

[handwritten marginalia, left margin:] what if Carthage had defeated Rome

[handwritten marginalia, left margin:] if arabs had retained science

[handwritten marginalia, left margin:] bad outcome in both cases!

[handwritten marginalia, left margin:] arabs would have been able to erect scientific knowledge in the same way

[handwritten marginalia, bottom:] is Sanscrit preeminence to be sought in intellect. endowment, or in the language, or in more favorable history? none of these alone

[margin handwritten notes: intellect. endowment and language are not to be seperated]

intellectual endowments, or in their language, or in more favourable
historical circumstances. It is obvious that none of these causes can
be regarded as working alone. *Language* and *intellectual endowment*, in
their constant interaction, admit of no separation, and even *historical
destinies* may not be so independent of the inner nature of peoples and
individuals, for all that the connection is far from being evident to
us on every point. Yet this superiority must be discernible from
something in the language; and so here, too, starting from the
example of the Sanscrit family, we must look into the question of why
one language should possess a stronger and more variously creative
life-principle than the rest. As is plainly visible here, the cause lies in
two points, namely that we are speaking of a *family of languages*, not
a single one, and beyond that in the individual make-up of the
language-structure itself. I shall first dwell on the latter at this point,
since only later on can I come back to the special relationships of those
languages that form a single stock.

   It is self-evident that the language whose structure is best adapted
to the *mind,* and which gives the liveliest incentive to its activity, must
also possess the most enduring power of giving birth to all the *new
configurations* occasioned by lapse of time and the destinies of nations.
But such an answer to our question, pointing to the total *linguistic
form,* is much too general, and strictly speaking merely echoes the
question in other words. But our need here is for an answer that
directs us to special points; and that, too, seems possible to me.
Language, in the isolated word and in connected discourse, is an *act,*
a truly creative *performance of the mind*; and in every language this act
is an *individual* one, proceeding in a way that is determined from every
angle. *Concept* and *sound,* combined in a manner commensurate with
their true nature, and recognizable only in the fact itself, are uttered
as *word* and *speech,* and by this something different from both is
created between the *external world* and the *mind.* Upon the *strength* and
regularity of this act depends the *completion* of language in all its
particular excellences, whatever names they may go by, and upon
this, therefore, there also rests the living principle in it which leads
to further creation. It is not even necessary, however, to refer to the
regularity of this act as well; for it is already inherent in the concept
of strength. The full power always develops only in the correct way.
Every wrong way runs into a boundary that restricts perfect
development. So if the Sanscrit languages have given proofs of their
creative power for at least millenia, this is simply an effect of the
strength of the language-creating act in the peoples to which they
belonged.

   We have spoken at length above (§12) of the compounding of the

[margin handwritten notes: historical destinies and inner nature of peoples may not be so independent of each other; yet there is something in the language that shows a stronger life principle; full power can unfold in the correct way only; the wrong way shows restricted development]

inner thought-form with the *sound*, and perceived in it a *synthesis* which – as is possible only through a truly creative act of the mind – engenders from the two elements to be combined a third, in which the particular nature of each vanishes. It is this *synthesis* whose *strength* is at issue here. In the language-making of nations, that race will wrest the palm, which executes this synthesis with the greatest vitality and most unweakened power. In all nations with more imperfect languages, this synthesis is by nature feeble, or is hampered and crippled by some adventitious circumstance. Yet even these observations are still unduly general in their indication of what is actually specified in the languages themselves, and can be demonstrated as a fact.

For there are points in the grammatical structure of languages at which this synthesis, and the power that produces it, come nakedly and directly to view, as it were, and with which all the rest of the language-structure is then also necessarily most intimately connected. Since the synthesis we are speaking of is not a state, nor even properly a deed, but itself a real action, always passing with the moment, there can be no special *sign* for it in the words, and the endeavour to find such a sign would already in itself bear witness to a lack of true strength in the act, in that its nature was misunderstood. The real presence of the synthesis must reveal itself *immaterially*, as it were, in the language; we must become aware that, like a flicker of lightning, it is illuminating the latter, and like a fireflash from regions unknown, has fused the elements that needed combination. This point is too important not to require an example. If, in a language, a root is marked out by a suffix as a substantive, the suffix is the material sign of the relating of the concept to the category of substance. But the synthetic act whereby, as soon as the word is uttered, this transposition actually occurs in the mind, has no single sign of its own in the word itself; its existence is revealed, rather, by the unity and interdependence to which suffix and root have been fused, and hence by a different and indirect designation, though one which flows from the endeavour in question.

We may call this act in general – as I have done here in this particular case – the act of *spontaneous positing* by bringing-together (synthesis). It recurs everywhere in language. We see it most clearly and manifestly in *sentence-formation*, then in *words derived* by inflection or by affixes, and finally, in general, in all *couplings* of the *concept* to the *sound*. In each of these cases, something new is created by combination, and actually posited as a thing existing (ideally) for itself. The mind creates, but by the same act opposes itself to the created, and allows this, as object, to react back upon it. Thus from the world reflected in man there arises, between them, the language which unites him with it, and fructifies it through him. It becomes clear in this fashion how the whole life that animates a particular language through all periods is dependent on the *strength* of this act.

Now if, for purposes of the historical and practical evaluation and judgement of languages, from which I never stray far in this inquiry, we look into how the strength of this act is discernible in linguistic structure, three points emerge in particular, to which it attaches, and in which we find the lack of its original strength evinced by an endeavour to replace it in another fashion. For here, too, as has already been mentioned several times in the foregoing, it emerges that the correct demand of the language (e.g., in Chinese, for a demarcation of the parts of speech) is always present in the mind, though not always in so incisively vivid a manner as to call for depiction in the sound as well. In the outer grammatical structure there then arises a gap to be filled in by the mind, or a replacement by inadequate analogues. So here, too, it comes down to a discovery of the synthetic act in the speech-structure, sufficient to demonstrate not only its efficacy in the mind, but its true passage into the forming of the sound. Now these three points are the *verb*, the *conjunction*, and the *relative pronoun*; and we must dwell a few moments longer on each of them.

The *verb* (to speak first of this by itself) differs in a sharply determinate way from the noun, and from the other parts of speech that might possibly occur in a simple sentence, in that to it alone is assigned the act of *synthetic positing* as a grammatical function. Like the declined noun, it arose through such an act, in the fusion of its elements with the stem, but it has also received this form in order to have the office and capacity of itself again performing this act with regard to the sentence. Between it and the other words of the simple sentence there is therefore a difference which forbids us to count it along with them in the same category. All the other words of the sentence are like dead matter lying there for combination; the verb alone is the centre, containing and disseminating life. Through one and the same synthetic act, it conjoins, by *being*, the *predicate* with the *subject*, yet in such a way that the being which passes, with an energetic predicate, into an action, becomes attributed to the subject itself, so that what is *thought* as merely capable of conjunction becomes, in *reality*, a state or process. We do not just think of the lightning striking: rather, it is the lightning itself that falls. We do not just bring together the mind and the immortal, as capable of conjunction; the mind, rather, is immortal. The thought, if one may put it so concretely, departs, through the verb, from its inner abode, and steps across into reality.

Now if this be the distinctive nature and peculiar function of the verb, the *grammatical conformation* of it in each individual language must inform us whether and how this particular characteristic function is indicated in the language. It is certainly the custom, in order to give an idea of the make-up and differences among languages, to point out how many tenses, moods and conjugations the verb has in them, to enumerate the different kinds of verb, and so on. All these points are of unquestionable importance. But as to the true nature of the verb, insofar as it is the nerve-centre of the whole language, they tell us nothing. The root of the matter is whether and how, through the verb of a language, expression is given to its synthetic power, the function in virtue of which it is a verb;[1] and this point is only too often left quite untouched. In this fashion we do not get deep enough, and do not go back to the true inner endeavours of language-making, but stop short at the externals of linguistic structure, without considering that the latter only acquire significance when their connection with these more deep-lying tendencies is simultaneously brought out.

In Sanscrit the indication of the verb's conjoining power rests solely on the grammatical treatment of this part of speech, and since it follows the nature of the verb completely, there is absolutely nothing to complain of here. Since, on the point here in question, the verb in Sansrit is by nature distinct from all other constituents of the simple sentence, it has nothing at all in common with the noun; the two remain perfectly pure and separate. It is indeed possible, in certain cases, to create derived verbs from the formed noun. But this amounts to no more than a treatment of the noun as a root, without regard for its own special nature. In the process, its ending, that is, the very part that is grammatically designative, undergoes a number of changes. It also commonly happens that, in addition to the verbal treatment involved in inflecting, a further syllable or letter is appended, whereby a second concept, that of an action, is added to the concept of the noun. This is immediately evident in the syllable कास्य, *kâmy*, from काम, *kâma*, desire. But even if the other interpolations of a different sort, such as *y*, *sy*, etc, should possess no real meaning, they still give formal expression to their verb-type associations, in that they likewise occur in the primitive verbs, arising from true roots, and do so, when we enter into examination of particular cases, in very much the same way. For nouns to be turned into verbs without such an addition is by far the rarest case.

---

[1] I have attempted to answer this question, with regard to the American languages whose grammar is known to us, in a paper of my own, presented at one of the class-sessions of the Berlin Academy.

Moreover, in the older form of the language, this whole process of converting nouns into verbs was only very sparingly used.

Secondly, just as the verb, in the function here under consideration, is never at rest like a substance, but always appears in a particular action, determined in every respect, so the language also allows it no rest. Sanscrit does not first create a basic form, as it does with the noun, to which it attaches relations; and even its infinitive is not verb-like in nature, but a palpable noun derived, not from a part of the verb, but from the root itself. Now this, to be sure, must be called a defect in the language, which seems really to misconstrue the whole peculiar nature of the infinitive. But it merely proves once more how carefully Sanscrit endeavours to remove every semblance of noun-like character from the verb. The noun is a thing, and can enter as such into relations and take on the signs for them. The verb, as an action of the passing moment, is nothing but the very essence of relations; and that is how the language actually presents it. I need scarcely mention here that it can probably occur to nobody to regard the class-syllables of the special tenses of the Sanscrit verb as corresponding to the basic forms of the noun. Omitting the verbs of the fourth and tenth classes, to be discussed in due course below, there remain only vowels, with or without inserted nasals, and thus obviously mere phonetic additions to the root that is translated into verb form.

Third and last, insofar as the inner shaping of a part of speech is declared at all in languages, by the symbolic sound-unity of the grammatical form, without a direct sound-sign, it can truly be claimed that in the Sanscrit verb-forms this unity is far more tightly closed than in those of the noun. I have already drawn attention above to the fact that the noun, on inflection, never enhances a stem-vowel by the use of *guna,* as the verb so often does. In this respect the language seems obviously willing, at all events, to tolerate in the noun a separating of the stem from the suffix, which it entirely effaces in the verb. With the exception of the pronominal suffixes in personal endings, the meaning of the not-merely-phonetic elements of verb-formations is also much harder to discover than in that of at least certain points of noun-formation. If the line between those languages (the inflecting), that proceed from the true concept of grammatical forms, and those (the agglutinating) that are imperfectly struggling towards it, is drawn on the double principle of either creating from the form a single quite unintelligible sign, or merely fastening two significant concepts tightly together, then in the whole of Sanscrit the verb-forms exhibit the clearest evidence of the former. In accordance with this procedure, the designation of each particular relation is not the same, but merely analogically similar in form, and the individual case is specially treated, according to the sounds of the designator and stem, though the general analogy is preserved. Hence the individual designators have different characteristics, to be employed always in specific cases only, as I have already pointed out above (pp. 121–2) in connection with the augment and reduplication. The simplicity of means whereby the language engenders such an uncommonly large number of verb-forms is truly to be marvelled at. It is, however, only possible to distinguish them in that all sound-changes, whether merely phonetic or designative, are coupled in different ways, and among these many combinations the specific change marks only that particular case of inflection which thereupon remains designative, if only because it occupies precisely this position in the conjugational schema, even when time has actually eroded its significant sounds. Personal endings, symbolic designations by augment and reduplication, and the sounds probably related only to euphony, whose insertion indicates the verb-classes, are the main elements of which the verb-forms are composed. Apart from these, there are only two sounds, i and s, which, where not just of purely phonetic origin, must rank as genuine designations of the types, tenses and moods of the verb. Since they seem to me to contain an especially refined and significant use of words grammatically designated, though originally meaningful in themselves, I shall dwell upon them a moment longer.

Bopp was the first to demonstrate, with great acuity and incontestable certainty, that the first future and one of the formations of the multiform augment-preterite were made up of a stem-word and the verb अस् *as*, to be. Haughton, in equally shrewd fashion, believes he has discovered in the *ya* the passive of the verb *to go*, इ *i*, or या *yâ*. Even where *s* or *sy* appear, without the presence of the verb *as* being so visible in its own inflection as in the tenses aforementioned, we can regard these signs as originating from *as*; and this has in part been done already by Bopp as well. If we ponder on this, and at the same time assemble all the cases where i, or sounds deriving from it, appear to be significant in the verb-forms, there emerges something similar in the verb to what we have found earlier on in the noun. Just as the pronoun there, in various versions, forms cases of inflection, so here the same thing is done by two verbs of the most general meaning. In accordance both with this meaning, and with the sound, there is betrayed in this choice the intention of the language to employ compounding not for a true combination of two specific verb-concepts, as when other languages indicate verb-character by addition of the concepts *do* or *make*, but, relying only lightly on the actual meaning of the appended verb, to make use of its sound as a mere indication of which category of the verb the particular form in question is to be put into. *Go* could be applied to an unspecifiable number of relations of the concept. Motion towards something can be viewed, from the side of its cause, as voluntary or involuntary, as an active willing or passive becoming, and from the side of its effect as a production, attainment, and so on. But from a phonetic aspect, the *i*-vowel was the very one best suited to serve by nature as a suffix, and to play this hybrid role between significance and symbolization precisely in such a fashion, that the former was put entirely in the shade here, even though the sound proceeded from it. For in the verb it already serves intrinsically, for the most part, as an intermediate sound, and its euphonic changes into *y* and *ay* increase the multiplicity of sounds in the construction of forms; *a* did not provide this advantage, and *u* has a sound too peculiarly heavy to serve so frequently for immaterial symbolization. Of the *s* of the verb *as*, to be, we can say, not the same, but still something similar, since it is also in part phonetically employed, and changes its sound in accordance with the vowel that precedes it.[2]

---

[2] If I try here to give greater scope to Haughton's claim (Manuscript edition, Pt I, p. 329), I flatter myself that this distinguished scholar would perhaps have done as much himself, if in the passage cited he had not, so it seems, been less concerned with this etymological conjecture than with the logical fixation of the *neutral verb* and *passive*. For it must be frankly admitted that the concept of *going* by no means agrees precisely with that of the passive as such, but does so to some extent only if we regard the latter as a *becoming*, in conjunction, rather, with the conception of the neutral verb. It appears this way also, on Haughton's showing, in Hindustani, where it stands opposed to *being*. The more modern languages, which lack a word expressing the transition to *being* directly and without metaphor, such as Greek γίνεσθαι, Latin *fieri* and German *werden*, also take refuge in the picturesque term for *going*, except that they conceive it more meaningfully, locating themselves at the end-point of the going, so to speak, as a *coming*: *diventare, divenire, devenir, to become*. In Sanscrit, therefore, even assuming the correctness of this etymology, the main force of the passive must always lie in the neutral conjugation (that of *Atmanêpadam*), and the combination of this with *going* must designate the 'going', in and by itself, as an internal change, not to be externally actuated. It is not unworthy of note, in this connection, and could have been cited by Haughton in support of his view, that the *intensives* only take the intermediate syllable *ya* in *Atmanêpadam*, which betrays a special affinity of the *ya* for this inflectional form. At first sight it is striking that in both passive and intensive the *ya* drops out in the general tenses, on which the distinction of classes has no effect. But this seems to me just a further proof that the passive evolved from the neutral verb of the fourth verb-class, and that the language, predominantly pursuing the course of the forms, did not wish to carry outside them the marker-syllable taken from that class. The *sy* of the *desideratives*, whatever its meaning may be, also adheres to the forms in those tenses, and is not subject to the limitation of the class-tenses, since it has no connection with them. Far more naturally than to the passive, the concept of *going* is suited to

That in languages one development always proceeds from another, so that the earlier thereby comes to determine the later, and that in Sanscrit, above all, the thread of these developments is primarily to be spun out from the sound-forms, is strikingly evidenced by the *passive* of Sanscrit grammar. By correct grammatical concepts, this species of verb is always a mere correlate of the active, and indeed an actual reversal thereof. But although, by sense, the agent becomes the patient, and *vice versa*, the patient ought nevertheless, by grammatical form, to be the subject of the verb, and the agent to be governed by it. Grammatical form-creation has not viewed the passive in Sanscrit from this, the only correct angle, as is evident throughout, but most clearly where the infinitive of the passive is meant to be expressed. At the same time, however, the passive designates something occurring with the person, relating inwardly to him apart from his activity. Now since Sanscrit had directly arrived at separating outward action from inward experiencing throughout the inflection of the verb, it also conceived the passive, in terms of form, from this point of view. It was doubtless due to this that the class of verbs which predominantly followed that internal mode of conjugation also gave rise to the syllable marking the passive. But now if the passive is hard to conceive correctly, as the union, so to speak, of a contradiction that holds between meaning and form, and remains unresolved, then it cannot be adequately construed in annexing it to the action inhering in the subject himself, and can hardly be kept clear of secondary ideas. In the former connection, we see how some languages, such as the Malayan – and Tagalic the most ingeniously amongst them – struggle laboriously to create a sort of passive. In the latter case it becomes clear that the pure concept,

the *denominatives* formed by addition of a *y*, which indicate a desire, appropriation or imitation of a thing. The same concept may also have predominated in the *causal verbs*; and it might therefore, perhaps, be no matter for disapproval, but could serve, rather, as a reminder of the derivation, when the Indian grammarians consider *i* as the marker-syllable of these verbs, and *ay* as merely the necessary phonetic extension of this. (Cf. Bopp's Latin *Grammar of Sancrit*, p. 142, n. 233). Comparison with the quite regularly constructed denominatives makes this very probable. In the verbs formed from nouns by काम्य *kâmy*, this additional syllable seems to consist of a compounding of काम *kâma*, craving, and इ *i*, to go, and is thus itself a complete denominative verb on its own. If a further extension of conjecture be permitted, then the *sy* of the desiderative verbs could be explained as a going into position, which would likewise find application to the etymology of the second future. What Bopp, very acutely and correctly, was the first to point out about the affinity of *potential* and *second future*, can be very well combined with this ('On the Conjugation-System of Sanscrit', *Annals of Oriental Literature*, pp. 29–33, 45–50). The denominatives with the marker-syllables *sya* and *asya* seem modelled on the desideratives.

which was correctly grasped, as we see from its literature, in later Sanscrit, did not find its way into the earlier form of the language at all. For instead of giving the passive a mode of expression that runs uniformly or analogously through all the tenses, early Sanscrit attaches it to the fourth class of verbs, and allows it to drop its marker-syllable at the boundaries of that class, being content with imperfect designation in the forms that do not lie within those limits.

In Sanscrit, therefore – to return to our main topic – the feeling for the *gathering-power of the verb* has completely permeated the language. It has created in the verb not merely a decisive expression, but indeed the only one appropriate to it, namely a purely *symbolic* one – a proof of its strength and vitality. For I have already often remarked in these pages, that where the linguistic form is clearly and vividly present in the mind, it enters into the outer process of development which otherwise guides external language-making, makes its influence felt, and, in the mere elaboration of lines once started, does not permit makeshifts, as it were, to be produced, instead of pure forms. Sanscrit provides us here with apt examples of both success and failure on this point. The function of the verb gives pure and decisive expression to the feeling; in designating the passive, the same feeling lets itself be misled into pursuing the external path.

One of the most natural and universal consequences of inner misconception, or rather an incomplete conception, of the function of the verb, is a blurring of the boundaries between *noun* and *verb*. The same word can be used for both parts of speech; every noun can be moulded into a verb; the marks of the verb do more to modify its concept than to characterize its function; the signs of tense and mood accompany the verb in an independence of their own, and the coupling of the pronoun is so loose that we are compelled in our minds to put in the verb *to be* between it and the alleged verb, which is more of a noun form with a verb-like meaning. The natural result of this is that true verb-relations are attracted towards noun-relations, and both become intermingled in the most variegated fashion. All the above statements are nowhere, perhaps, so much to the purpose as in the *Malayan family of languages*, which suffers, on the one hand, with few exceptions, from the Chinese lack of inflection, and on the other does not, like Chinese, reject grammatical formation with scornful resignation, but seeks it out, attains it in a one-sided manner, and wondrously multiplies it in this one-sidedness. Constructions carried through as complete by the grammarians, throughout entire conjugations, can be clearly proved to be true noun-forms; and although the verb cannot be lacking in any language, yet he who seeks the true

one feels that the malayan verb is absent?

expression of this part of speech is reduced, in the Malayan languages, to a sort of feeling that it is absent. This is true not only of the language of Malacca, whose structure is in general of still greater simplicity than that of the rest, but also of Tagalic, which in the Malayan manner is very rich in forms. It is worth noting that in Javanese, by mere change of the initial letters into another of the same class, noun- and verb-forms are reciprocally transformed into one another. This seems at first sight a truly symbolic designation; but I shall show further on (vol. 2) that this change of letters is due merely to the wearing-away of a prefix in the course of time. I shall not elaborate more fully on this matter here, only because it must be dealt with in detail, and in its proper place, in the second and third volumes of this work.

In languages where the verb possesses no indications whatever of its true function, or very imperfect ones, it coincides automatically, more or less, with the *attributive*, that is, with a *noun*, and the verb proper, which indicates the actual positing of what is thought, must be literally supplied to the subject and this attributive, as the verb *to be*. Such an omission of the verb, where a property has merely to be attached to something, is not unfamiliar even in the most sophisticated languages. We encounter it frequently, that is, in Sanscrit and Latin, more rarely in Greek. Alongside a perfectly formed verb, it has nothing to contribute to the characterization of the verb, but is merely a way of forming sentences. By contrast, some of those languages which in their structure manage only with an effort to express the verb, give a special form to these constructions, and thereby draw them, after a fashion, into the structure of the verb. Thus in Mexican *I love* can be equally well expressed by *ni-tlazotla*, as by *ni-tlazotla-ni*. The former is the coupling of the verb-pronoun with the stem of the verb, the latter, the same with the participle, insofar, that is, as certain Mexican verb-adjectives, though they do not contain the concept of continuing action (the element from which true tense first arises, by means of combination with the three stages of time),[3] can still be called participles in the sense that they are active, passive or reflexive in meaning. Vetancourt, in his Mexican

---

[3] I am following, in fact, the theory of the Greek grammarians, now too often, I think, unjustly neglected, whereby every tense consists of a combination of one of the three times with one of the three stages in the course of action; a theory admirably set forth by Harris, in his *Hermes*, and by Reitz in academy papers that are unfortunately too little known, though Wolf has extended it by giving an exact definition of the three aorists. The verb is the coupling of an energetic attributive (not a merely qualitative one) with *to be*. The energetic attributive contains the stages of the action, the *to be* those of time. Bernhardi, in my opinion, has correctly established and demonstrated this.

grammar,[4] makes the second of the above forms into a tense indicating custom. Yet this is an obviously mistaken view, since such a form in the verb could not be a tense, but would have to be inflected throughout the tenses, which is not the case. But from Vetancourt's more exact account of the meaning of the expression, we see that it is nothing else but the combination of a pronoun and a noun, with the verb *to be* omitted. *I love* is a pure expression of the verb; *I am a loving* [person] (that is, *I am accustomed to love*) is, strictly speaking, not a verb form but a sentence. Yet the language stamps this construction to some extent as a verb, by attaching to it the words that it governs: *ni-te-tla-namaca-ni*, I (am) one selling something to someone, that is, I am accustomed to sell, am a merchant.

The Mixteca language, which also comes from New Spain, distinguishes the cases where the attributive, as already dependent on the substantive, is designative, and where it is only connected to the substantive via the verb-expression, by the positioning of the two parts of speech. In the former, the attributive must follow the substantive; in the latter, precede it: *naha quadza*, the wicked woman, *quadza naha*, the woman is wicked.[5]

The impossibility of putting the term for the copula (*to be*) directly into the form of the verb, which in the cases just mentioned causes the entire absence of this term, can also, on the contrary, lead to the wholly material introduction of it, where it ought not to appear in this way. This happens when, to a truly attributive verb (*he goes, he flies*), *to be* is appended as a genuine auxiliary verb (*he is going, he is flying*). Yet this expedient does not really assist the perplexity of the language-making mind. Since this auxiliary verb must itself have the form of a verb, and again can be only the coupling of *to be* with an energetic attributive, the aforesaid perplexity continues to arise, and the difference is merely this, that whereas the same trouble otherwise recurs with every verb, it is here confined only to one. The feeling that such an auxiliary verb is necessary also shows that language-making, even if it has not had the power to create a correct expression for the true function of the verb, has nevertheless been aware of the concept of this. It would be useless to want to cite examples for a thing that frequently occurs in languages, sometimes in the whole fashioning of the verb, sometimes in particular inflections. Instead, I shall dwell for a few moments on a more interesting and rarer case, where the function of the auxiliary verb (the addition of *to be*) is allotted to another part of speech than the verb itself, namely the pronoun, in an otherwise very similar manner.

[4] *Arte de lengua Mexicana*, Mexico 1673, p. 6.
[5] *Arte Mixteca, compuesta por Fr. Antonio de los Reyes*.

In the language of the Yarura, a community on the Casanare and lower Orinoco rivers, the whole conjugation is formed in the simplest way by coupling the pronoun with the particles of tense. These combinations themselves make up the verb *to be*, and when suffixed to a word, the conjugational syllables thereof. The verb *to be* entirely lacks any root sound of its own, that would not belong to the pronoun or the tense-particles; and since the present tense has no particle to itself, the persons of it consist merely in the persons of the pronoun itself, which differ only as abbreviations from the independent pronoun.[6] So the three persons of the singular of the verb *to be* are *que, mé, di*,[7] and in literal translation are simply *I, thou, he*. In the imperfect these syllables are prefixed by *ri, ri-que*, I was, and coupled with a noun, *ui ri-di*, water was (present), but as a true verb we have *jura-ri-di*, he ate. Thus *que*, on this showing, meant *I am*, and this form of the pronoun actually expressed the function of the verb. However, this combination of the pronoun with the temporal particles can never be used all by itself, but always in such a way only that by means of another word, which may be any part of speech, a sentence is formed. *Que* or *di* alone never mean *I am, he is*, but *ui di* does mean *it is water*, and *jura-n-di*, with a euphonic *n*, *he eats*. When carefully looked at, therefore, the grammatical form of these idioms is not the one here under discussion, an incorporation of the concept of *to be* into the pronoun, but rather the case referred to earlier, of an omission and supplying of the verb *to be* through a coupling of the pronoun with another word. The foregoing time-particle *ri*, for that matter, is nothing else but a word indicating distance. Its opposite is the particle *re*, which is said to mark the subjunctive. But this *re* is merely the preposition *in*, which finds a similar application in many

---

[6] Between the independent pronoun *coddé*, I, and the corresponding verb marker *que*, the difference, to be sure, is seemingly greater. But in the accusative, the independent pronoun is *qua*; and on comparing *coddé* with the demonstrative pronoun *oddé*, we see clearly that the root-sound of the first person consists only in the *k*-sound, and that *coddé* is a composite form.

[7] The information on this language has been secured for us by the diligent industry of the estimable Sr Hervas. He had the praiseworthy idea of getting the Jesuits who had settled in Italy, after banishment from America and Spain, to describe their recollections of the languages of American natives to whom they had been missionaries. He collected their reports, and revised them where necessary, so that the result was a series of manuscript grammars of languages, some of which are otherwise quite unknown to us. When I was Ambassador in Rome, I had this collection copied for me, and through the good offices of the present Prussian envoy in Rome, Herr Bunsen, these versions have since been accurately compared once more with the original manuscript, deposited after Hervas' death in the Collegio Romano. The data on the Yarura language are due to the former Jesuit, Father Forneri.

American languages. It forms an analogue to a gerund: *jura-re*, in eating, *edendo*; and by prefixing of the independent pronoun, this gerund is then turned into a subjunctive or optative: *were I to eat*, or *that I would eat*. Here the concept of *to be* is coupled with the mark of the subjunctive, and hence the verb-suffixes for persons, which are otherwise invariably attached to it, drop out, in that the independent pronoun is prefixed. Forneri, in fact, takes *re*, *ri-re* to be present and past gerunds, in his paradigm of the verb *to be*, and translates them: *if I were, if I were to have been*.

Thus the language here does indeed specify a peculiar form of the pronoun, constantly and exclusively associated with the concept of *to be*; yet it was not a pure instance of the case at present under discussion, namely the incorporation of this concept into the pronoun itself; and the same holds, though in yet another fashion, of the Huasteca language, spoken in a part of New Spain. There too the pronouns, though only the independent ones, combine with a temporal particle, and thereupon constitute the verb *to be*. They approximate the more closely to the latter, in its true conception, in that these combinations, as was not the case in Yarura, can also stand entirely alone. *nânâ – itz*, I was, *tâtâ – itz*, thou wast, etc. In the attributive verb, the persons are indicated by other pronominal forms, which come very close to the possessive pronoun. But the origin of the particle coupled with the pronoun is too little known to allow us to decide whether a verb-root of its own is not contained in it. By now, at all events, it serves in the language to characterize past tenses – constantly and exclusively for the imperfect, and in the other tenses by special rules. The mountain dwellers, among whom the oldest form of the language is doubtless preserved, are said, however, to make a more general use of this syllable, and to add it also to the present and future. At times it is also attached to a verb, to indicate vigour of action; and in this sense, as an intensifier (as reduplication, also, in so many languages, accompanies the perfect to strengthen it), it could well have become by degrees an exclusive feature of the past tenses.[8]

In the Maya language, spoken on the Yucatan peninsula, we find, however, the case we are talking of, pure and complete.[9] It possesses

---

[8] *Noticia de la lengua Huasteca que dà Carlos de Tapia Zenteno*, Mexico, 1767, p. 18.

[9] What I know of this language has been taken from Hervas' manuscript grammar. He constructed this partly from written reports by the former Jesuit, Domingo Rodriguez, and partly from the printed grammar of the Franciscan cleric, Gabriel de S. Buenaventura (Mexico, 1684), which he found in the library of the Collegio Romano. I have tried in vain to rediscover this grammar in the aforesaid library. It seems to have been lost.

pronoun constitutes
The verb "to be"

a pronoun which, used alone, itself constitutes the verb *to be*, and attests to a most notable concern for indicating the true function of the verb in every case by a unique element specially designed for the purpose. The pronoun, in fact, is a dual one. One version carries with it the concept of *to be*, the other does not have this property, but also combines with the verb. The first version divides into two sub-species, of which one provides the meaning of *to be* only in combination with another word, while the other contains this meaning directly in itself. This latter sub-species forms the verb *to be* perfectly, since it also combines with the particles of tense (though these are lacking in the language for the present and perfect). In the two first persons of the singular and plural, these pronouns are *Pedro en*, I am Peter, and so on by analogy: *ech*, *on*, *ex*; on the other hand, *ten*, I am, *tech*, thou art, *toon*, we are, *teex*, you are. Apart from the three types mentioned here, there is no independent pronoun, but the one (*ten*) which serves simultaneously as the verb *to be* is used for this purpose. The one which does not carry with it the notion of *to be* is always affixed, and *en* has throughout no other use than that referred to. Where the verb dispenses with the first type of pronoun, it regularly combines with the second. But in that case we find in the forms of it an element (*cah* and *ah*, which alternate by definite rules) which remains over when the verb is analysed, i.e., when all the elements that normally accompany it (person, tense, mood, etc) are taken away. *En*, *ten*, *cah* and *ah* appear, therefore, in all forms of the verb, yet always in such a way that one of these syllables excludes the others, from which it is already apparent that they all express the function of the verb, so that one of them cannot be lacking, whereas each makes the use of the others superfluous. Their application is now subject to specific rules. *En* is used only with the intransitive verb, and even there, not in the present and imperfect, but only in the other tenses; *ah*, in the same tenses, with transitive verbs; and *cah* with all verbs alike, but only in the present and imperfect. *Ten* occurs merely in a supposedly anomalous conjugation. If we examine this more closely, it carries with it the meaning of a custom or enduring state, and if *cah* and *ah* are discarded, the form contains endings which in part also constitute the so-called gerunds. So here a transformation is occurring, of a verb-form into a noun-form, and this noun-form now requires the true verb *to be*, in order to become a verb again. To that extent these forms agree entirely with the above-mentioned Mexican tense of custom. But I must further note that in this way of looking at it the concept of the transitive verb is confined to those which really govern an object outside themselves. Indefinitely used true actives, e.g. *love*, *kill*, like those such as the Greek οἰκοδομέω, which contain the governed object within them, are treated as intransitive.

The reader will already have noticed that the two sub-categories of the first pronominal type are distinguished only by a prefixed *t*. Since this *t* occurs precisely in that pronoun which has the significance of a verb on its own account, it is natural to suppose that it constitutes the root-sound of a verb, so that, to put it more exactly, it is not the pronoun that is used in the language as the verb *to be*, but rather this verb that is used as a pronoun. The inseparable coupling of existence with the person would then remain the same, but the viewpoint would nevertheless be different. That *ten*, and the other forms dependent on it, are actually used also as quite self-sufficient pronouns, may be seen from the Mayan *Paternoster*.[10] In fact, I consider this *t* a stem-sound, though not that of a verb, but of the pronoun itself. The expression that stands for the third person supports this view. For the latter is quite different from the first two, and in the singular is *lai-lo*, for both categories expressing the verb *to be*, and in the plural *ob* for the category that does not serve as a verb, and *loob* for the others. Now if *t* were the root-sound of a verb, this would be quite inexplicable. But since a number of languages find it difficult to grasp the third person in its pure concept, and to separate it from the demonstrative pronoun, it cannot appear surprising that the two first persons should have a stem-sound peculiar to them alone. In Mayan, actually, a supposed relative pronoun *lai* is introduced, and other American languages also possess stem-sounds that run through several or all the persons of the pronoun. In the language of the Maipure, the third person, though with a different attachment, is found again in the first two, so that if the third, perhaps, originally meant *man*, the first two would be saying, as it were, *I-man* and *thou-man*. Among the Achaguas, all three persons of the pronoun have the same final syllable. Both these communities live between the Rio Negro and the upper Orinoco. Between the two main types of the Mayan pronoun there is a sound-affinity only in some persons, whereas in others there are great differences. The *t* is nowhere found in the affixed pronoun. The *ex* and *ob* of the second and third person plural of the pronoun connected with the meaning of *to be*, have gone over entirely into the same persons of the other pronoun, which does not carry this meaning. But since these syllables are attached merely as endings here to the second and third persons singular, we see that, having been taken from this possibly older pronoun, they are merely serving the other one as signs for the plural.

Cah and *ah* likewise differ only by the added consonant, and this

[10] Adelung's *Mithridates*, Pt III, sec 3, p. 20, where Vater, however, has not recognized the pronoun correctly, and has wrongly assigned the German words to the Mayan ones.

seems to me a true verb-root, which in combination with *ah* forms an auxiliary verb *to be*. Where *cah* is permanently incorporated into a verb, it conveys the notion of vigour; and this may be why the language has employed it to designate all actions, since force and movement are inherent there throughout. With a truly refined tact, however, *cah* has been kept only for the vitality of the continuing action, and thus for the present and imperfect. That *cah* is really treated as a verb-stem, is shown by the differing positions of the affixed pronoun in the forms with *cah* and *ah*. In the former, this pronoun always appears immediately before the *cah*; in the latter, not before the *ah*, but in front of the attributive verb. Now since it is always prefixed to a stem-word, noun or verb, this clearly proves that *ah* in these forms is neither, but has, on the contrary, a different role from *cah*. Thus the first person present singular of *canan*, to watch over, is *canan-in-cah*, whereas the same person in the perfect is *canan-t-ah*. *In* is the first person singular pronoun, the interpolated *t* a euphonic sound. As a prefix, *ah* has a multiple function in the language, being a mark of the male gender, of the inhabitant, and lastly of the nouns formed from active verbs. It may therefore have evolved from a substantive to a demonstrative pronoun, and finally an affix. Since by origin it is less adapted to indicate the vigorous movement of the verb, it is left to designate tenses that lie further from immediate appearance. The same tenses of intransitive verbs require still more of the purely static concept of *to be*, in order to make entry into the verb, and are therefore content with the pronoun to which this concept is always attached in thought. Thus the language designates different degrees of vitality among phenomena, and thence creates its conjugation-forms in a more artistic fashion than even the highly cultivated languages do, though not in a way so simple, natural and correct in delimiting the functions of the different parts of speech. The verb-structure is therefore always deficient; but there is visibly evident in it a feeling for the true function of the verb, and even an anxious endeavour not to let it lack for an appropriate means of expression.

The affixed pronoun of the second main type also serves as a possessive pronoun with substantives. It betrays a total misapprehension of the difference between noun and verb, to assign a possessive pronoun to the latter – to confuse *our eating* with *we eat*. But in languages that are guilty of this, it seems to me due, rather, to a want of proper separation among the various categories of pronoun. For obviously the error is smaller if the concept of the possessive pronoun is itself not apprehended with appropriate precision; and this, I think, is the case here. In almost all American languages, the understanding

Centrality of the pronoun in some Indian languages

of their structure starts, as it were, with the pronoun, and this twines in two great branches, as possessive pronoun around the noun, and as governing or governed around the verb, and both parts of speech remain, for the most part, tied to the pronoun throughout. The language also normally possesses a variety of pronominal forms for this. But where this is not so, the concept of person is coupled in a wavering and uncertain manner with the one part of speech or the other. The difference between the two cases is felt, no doubt, but not with the formal precision and determinacy which the transition into sound-designation requires. At times, however, the sense of difference is indicated otherwise than by accurate separation of a dual pronoun. In the language of the Betoi, who also live around the Casanare and lower Orinoco, the pronoun, if it conjoins with the verb, as governing, has a position different from that of the possessive pronoun combined with the noun. For the possessive pronoun is attached in front, while that which accompanies the person of the verb follows behind; the difference of sound consists only in a shortening produced by the attachment. Thus *rau tucu* means *my house*, but *humasoi-rrù* means *man am I*, and *ajoi-rrù*, *I am*. In the latter word the meaning of the root-syllable is unknown to me. But this suffixing of the pronoun only occurs where the latter is coupled as an aorist with another word, without special determination of tense. In that case the pronoun then forms with this word a single word-sound, and in fact a verb-form arises. For the accent, in these cases, shifts from the coupled word to the pronoun. This is therefore, as it were, a symbolic sign of the mobile nature of the action, as also occurs in English, where the same disyllabic word can be used as noun and verb, and the oxytonic shift indicates the verb-form. In Chinese, there is also, indeed, a designation by accent of the passage from noun to verb, and *vice versa*, but not in any symbolic relation to the nature of the verb, since the same accent, without change, expresses both transitions, and indicates merely that the word is becoming the part of speech opposite to its natural meaning and customary use.[11]

I did not want to interrupt the foregoing discussion of Mayan conjugation by mention of an exception, to which, however, I will now briefly recur. For the future differs entirely in its formation from the remaining tenses. It does, indeed, couple its marker-syllables with *ten*, but never takes either *cah* or *ah*, has its own suffixes, and yet in certain changes of its form dispenses with all of them. It is especially averse to the syllable *ah*, for it even excises the latter where this syllable is a real ending of the root-verb. It would take us too far afield here

[11] Cf. my *Lettre à Monsieur Abel-Rémusat*, p. 23.

to enter into an examination of whether these aberrations arise from the nature of the suffixes peculiar to the future, or from other causes. But this exception can prove nothing against what was said above. Rather, the repugnance for the particle *ah* confirms the meaning attributed to it above, since the uncertainty of the future does not evoke the vivacity of a pronoun, and contrasts with that of a phenomenon that has actually taken place.

Where languages do actually set out to indicate the function of the verb symbolically, by a closer linkage of its ever-changing modifications with the root, then, even if they do not perfectly achieve the goal, it is a favourable sign of their correct feeling for this function, if they seek this closeness of connection predominantly with the *pronoun*. They then come ever closer to transforming the pronoun into the person, and hence to the true form of the verb, whose most essential point is the formal indication of the person (which is not attained by merely putting the independent pronoun out in front). All other modifications of the verb (apart from the moods, which belong more to sentence-formation) can also characterize that part of the verb which has first to be set in motion by verb-function, and has more resemblance to the noun. This is the main reason why, in the Malayan languages, which are somewhat like Chinese in this respect, the nature of the verb comes so relatively little into view. The decided tendency of the American languages to affix the pronoun in some way, leads them on to a more correct path here. If all modifications of the verb are really attached to the root-syllable, the perfection of verb-forms rests solely on the closeness of the connection, on the question of whether the verb's inherent power of positing is more energetically displayed, by inflection, or more ponderously, by agglutination.

No less strongly than the verb, the correct and adequate formation of *conjunctions* in languages is founded on the activity of this same force we are discussing, on the part of the language-making spirit. For the conjunction, properly speaking, shows the *relations of two clauses* to one another; and a *twofold coupling*, a more *complex synthesis*, is therefore inherent in it. Every clause must be taken as a unit, but these units must again be connected into a larger one, and the preceding clause kept hovering long enough before the mind for its successor to impart complete determinacy to the total utterance. The formation of clauses extends here to the *sentence*, and the conjunctions divide up into the easier ones, which merely *connect* and *separate* clauses, and the harder ones, which make one clause *dependent* on another. In this seemingly straightforward or involved march of the sentence, the Greek grammarians had already located the characteristic marks of

the simpler or more artistically aspiring styles. The merely connected
clauses run one after another in an indeterminate sequence, and do
not form a whole in which beginning and end are mutually related,
whereas those that are truly united into a sentence reciprocally hold
and support each other, like the stones of an arch.[12] The less
cultivated languages are normally deficient in conjunctions, or
employ for the purpose words not exclusively dedicated thereto, and
only indirectly suited to such use, and very often let clauses follow
each other without connection. Even those that do depend on one
another become converted, so far as can be done, into straightforward
sequences; and cultivated languages themselves still bear traces of
this. When we say, for example: *I see that you are ready* [fertig bist],
this is certainly nothing else but: *I see that: you are ready* [bist fertig],
except that in later times correct grammatical feeling has symbolically
indicated the dependency of the following clause by transposition of
the [German] verb.

less cultivated language don't have conjunctions just let clauses follow each other without connection

The most difficult thing to grasp grammatically is the synthetic
positing that occurs in the *relative pronoun*. Two clauses have to be
united in such a way that the one constitutes a mere *expression of the
attributes* of a *noun* in the other. The word by which this is effected
must therefore be at once both *pronoun* and *conjunction*, representing
the noun by substitution, and governing a clause. Its nature is
straightway lost, if the two mutually modifying parts of speech
combined in it are not linked indivisibly in thought. The mutual
relation of the two clauses requires, finally, that the conjunction-
pronoun (the relative) should take the case which the verb of the
relative clause demands, but yet, whatever this case may be, should
govern the clause itself, standing at its head. Here the difficulties
obviously mount up, and the clause carrying a relative pronoun can
only be grasped completely by means of the other one. The only
languages that can match up entirely to the concept of this pronoun,
are those in which the noun is declinable. But even apart from this
requirement, it will be impossible for the majority of less cultivated
languages to find a true expression for this clause-designation; the
relative pronoun is really lacking in them, and they circumvent the
use of it so far as possible; but where this cannot be done, they employ
more or less skilful *constructions* to take its place.

relative pronoun

One of these, though in fact a clever one, is common in Quichua,
the general language of Peru. The sequence of clauses is reversed,
with the relative preceding as an independent and simple statement,
while the main clause follows it. But in the relative, the word to which

---

[12] Demetrius, *De elocutione*, §11–13.

the relation attaches is omitted, and this same word, with a demonstrative pronoun in front of it, is put at the head of the main clause, and in the case governed by its verb. So instead of saying: 'The man who trusts in God's grace shall receive it; that which you now believe, you will hereafter see revealed in heaven; I shall walk in the path where thou leadest me', we say: 'He trusts in God's grace, this man receives it; you believe now, this will you see hereafter revealed in heaven; thou leadest me, this path shall I walk in.' In these constructions, the essential meaning of the relative clause, namely that a word is to be thought of only under the determination contained in the relative clause, is not only preserved, but even to some extent symbolically expressed. The relative clause, to which attention has first to be drawn, takes precedence, and likewise the noun it determines is placed at the head of the main clause, even if the latter's construction would otherwise assign it a different position. Yet all grammatical difficulties of word-order are obviated. The dependency of both clauses remains unexpressed; the artificial method of having the relative clause always governed by the pronoun, even if the latter is actually governed by its own verb, drops out entirely. There is simply no relative pronoun at all in these constructions. But the noun is given the common and easily-grasped demonstrative pronoun, so that the language has visibly felt in an obscure way the mutual relation of the two pronouns, though it has indicated this from the easier point of view. Mexican proceeds more briefly on this point, but in a way that does not come so close to the true significance of the relative clause. It precedes the relative clause with the word *in*, which simultaneously replaces the demonstrative pronoun and the article, and thereby attaches the relative to the main clause.

If a people preserves in its language the power of *synthetic positing*, up to the point of giving an adequate and precisely fitting *expression* to it in the language's structure, there immediately follows from this a happy ordering of its *organism*, which remains the same in every part. If the *verb* is rightly construed, then in view of the way it governs the sentence, the other parts of speech must equally be so as well. The same power, putting thought and expression into their correct and most fruitful relationship, suffuses the language in all its parts; and it cannot go astray in easier matters, once it has overcome the greater difficulty of the synthesis that forms the sentence. The true expression of this synthesis can therefore be proper only to truly *inflected languages*, and among these always to those alone which are inflected to a higher degree. Factual denotation and relation must find a correctly ordered expression; word-unity, under the influence of rhythm, must possess the greatest firmness; and the sentence, on the other hand, must display in turn the separation of individual words which assures its freedom. The whole of this happy disposition of the organism is engendered in language, as a necessary consequence, by the power of synthesis.

Within the mind, however, this power also brings about a complete *agreement* between the onward march of *thought* and the *language* that accompanies it. Since thinking and speaking invariably complement each other, the correct course operates to guarantee in both an uninterrupted progression. Insofar as it is material, and dependent, at the same time, on external influences, language, when left to itself, puts difficulties in the way of the inner form that works upon it, or in the absence of forceful intervention by the latter, it steals off in its formations towards analogies peculiar to itself. Where permeated, however, by an energetic inner power, it feels carried along by this, uplifts itself with joy, and now responds in turn through its own material self-sufficiency. It is here, precisely, that its enduring and independent nature works to advantage, when – as manifestly happens, if the organism be fortunate – it serves as an *inspiring instrument* to new generations that are forever coming to birth. In addition to inner national disposition, and the character of the language, the success of *mental activity in science and literature* depends, at the same time, on a variety of external influences, which may or may not be present. But since the *language-structure* persists independently of these, it needs only a fortunate impulsion to make the people that possesses it aware that they have in their language an implement adapted to quite different trends of thought. The *nation's talents* awaken, and from their interaction with the *language* a new period comes into bloom. If we compare the history of peoples, we certainly find it rare for a nation to have undergone two different and unconnected *flowerings* of its *literature*. But in another respect we cannot, I think, do other than attribute such an efflorescence of peoples into higher mental activity to a situation wherein, both in mental abilities and in language itself, the seeds of strong development were already lying sleeping, as it were, and preformed. Were we even to suppose entire ages of bards before Homer, it is certain, nonetheless, that the Greek language was merely elaborated by them as well, and not originally formed. Its fortunate organic pattern, its truly inflectional character, its synthetic power, in a word everything that constitutes the basis and nerve-centre of its structure, had certainly belonged to it already for a countless lapse of centuries. In a contrary fashion, we also see peoples in possession of the noblest languages, without a corresponding literature having ever, to our knowledge,

[handwritten margin annotations at top: "Lithuanian Sanscritically very loyal"]

developed among them. So here the cause lay in a want of *impulsion*, or *hampering circumstances*. I may allude here merely to Lithuanian, which with far more fortune than others of its sisters has stayed loyal to the Sanscrit stock it descends from. If I call the hampering or promoting influences external and contingent, or better, historical, this expression is perfectly accurate, in view of the real power which their presence or absence exerts. But in essence the effect can still only proceed from within. A spark must be struck, a bond that prevents, as it were, the soul from spreading its wings, must somehow be loosed; and this can happen in a moment, without any slow preliminaries. The true and forever incomprehensible upsurge is made no easier to explain by shifting its first moment further back.

[handwritten margin annotation: "but something has held it back, something historical"]

The concurrence of *language-making* with the overall *development of thought*, of which we have considered the apt expression of *synthetic positing* in the concrete language-structure to be a happy sign, leads at once to that mental activity which alone is creative from within. If we view the *successful language-structure* as merely working backwards, and forget for the moment that whatever it imparts to the mind, it has itself first received from thence, then the benefits it confers are power of intellectuality, clarity of logical arrangement, a sense of something deeper than can be reached by mere analysis of thought, and the craving to fathom it, the intimation of a mutual relation between the mental and the sensuous, and finally a rhythmically melodic treatment of tone, related to a general notion of the artistic – or else an enhancement of all this, where it is already present on its own. Through the collective endeavour of mental forces in the appropriate direction, there arises, therefore, like the gleam of a reviving spark, an activity of purely mental *thought-development*; and hence a vitally-felt, fortunate language-structure evokes, by its own nature, *philosophy* and *literature*. But the flourishing of both permits, on the other hand, a reverse inference to the vitality of this influence on the part of language. The self-aware language is readiest to move where it deems itself dominant, and mental activity likewise puts forth its greatest effort and achieves its highest satisfaction, where in intellectual contemplation or spontaneous fashioning it creates from its own fullness, or ties up the loose ends of scientific research. But in these areas also, *intellectual individuality* comes most vividly to the fore. So in that a highly perfected language-structure, sprung from fortunate beginnings, and continuing to nourish and stimulate them, keeps the life-principle of the language secure, it occasions and furthers at the same time the diversity of directions revealed in the above-mentioned differences of character among languages of the same linguistic group.

[handwritten margin annotation: "a fortunate language structure evokes by its own nature philosophy and literature"]

But how can the claim here put forward, that the fruitful *life-principle* of languages resides primarily in their inflectional nature, be reconciled with the fact that the wealth of inflections is always greatest in the most *youthful period* of languages, but gradually diminishes in the course of time? It seems strange, at least, that the declining principle should be the very one that preserves. The *wearing-down of inflections* is an undeniable fact. From various causes, and at various stages, the language-forming faculty at times lets them lapse through indifference, and at times deliberately discards them; and it is actually more correct to describe the phenomenon in this fashion, than to fasten the blame solely and exclusively upon time. Even in the forms of declination and conjugation, which have certainly undergone much decay, visibly characteristic sounds are always carelessly thrown away, the more the concept is established of the whole schema, automatically assigning its position to each particular case. Bolder sacrifices are made to euphony, and the piling-up of markers is avoided, where the form is already assured by one of them against confusion with others. If my observations do not deceive me, these sound-changes that are normally attributed to time occur less frequently in the supposedly ruder languages than in the *cultured* ones, and this phenomenon might well have a very natural explanation. Among all the influences at work upon language, the most volatile of all is the *human mind* itself; and so language also undergoes the most changes from the mind's very lively activity. But it is precisely in keeping with the mind's progress, that increasing trust in the firmness of its inner vision should lead it to consider superfluous a too-careful modification of sounds. From this very principle, the inflected languages are threatened, at a very much later period in their career, with a transformation which affects their nature far more deeply. The more mature the mind feels itself to be, the more boldly it works in combinations of its own, and the more confidently it casts away the bridges that language constructs for the understanding. This mood is then readily conjoined with a lack of feeling for the poetic charm that resides in sonority. Poetry itself then plots out more internal paths, on which it can forego such advantages with less risk. It is thus a transition from a more sensuous to a more purely intellectual frame of mind, whereby language is here reshaped. Yet the primary causes are not always of the nobler kind. Cruder organs, less adapted to the pure and more delicate separation of sounds, an ear by nature less sensitive and musically untrained, lay the foundation for *indifference* to the *tonal principle* in language. In like fashion, the predominantly *practical tendency* can impose on language abbreviations, omissions of relating terms, ellipses of every kind, since when understanding is the only goal, everything not directly necessary for that purpose is disdained.

In general, the relation of the *popular mind* to the language must be entirely different, so long as the latter is still in the tumult of its *first formation*, and when what has already been formed is serving merely for the *uses of daily life*. So long as the elements, in this early period, are still clearly present, even by origin, to the mind, and the latter is occupied in assembling them, it takes pleasure in this fashioning of the instrument of its activity, and omits nothing that is seized upon by any expressive nuance of feeling. Thereafter the aim of *understanding* comes more to the fore, the meaning of the elements becomes dimmer, and the ingrained habit of usage takes no trouble over details of construction and the accurate preservation of sounds. The imaginative pleasure at a clever combination of indicative signs with a sonorous march of syllables is replaced by convenience of understanding, whereby forms are dissolved into auxiliary verbs and prepositions. The aim of a readier clarity is thus elevated at once above the other merits of language, since this analytic method does indeed diminish the effort of comprehension, and even in some cases increases accuracy, where the synthetic method has more difficulty in attaining it. But by the use of these grammatical *auxiliary terms* the inflections become more dispensable, and gradually lose their importance for the vigilance of the linguistic sense.

Now whatever the cause may be, it is certain that in this way true inflectional languages become poorer in *forms*, frequently put grammatical words in their place, and may thereby approach in detail to those languages which differ from their family by an utterly distinct and more imperfect principle. Our present-day German, and the English language, contain numerous examples of this, though many more in the latter; but its admixture of Romance material does not seem to me responsible for this, since the latter exerts little or no influence upon its grammatical structure. Yet I do not believe that any objection can be drawn from this against the fruitful influences of the inflectional principle, even down to the latest stage in a language's career. Were there even a Sanscrit language which had approximated in the way here described to the Chinese practice of dispensing with the signs relating parts of speech, the case would remain, nevertheless, entirely different. The Chinese structure, however we may explain it, is obviously founded on an imperfection in the making of the language, probably a custom, peculiar to that people, of isolating sounds, coinciding with an insufficient strength of the inner linguistic sense that calls for their combination and mediation. In such a Sanscrit language, on the other hand, the truest inflectional character, with all its beneficial influences, would have been established for a countless number of generations, and given its shape to the linguistic sense. In its true nature, such a language would therefore have always remained Sanscritic; its difference would lie only in particular features, which would be unable to erase the stamp impressed by the inflectional nature of all the rest of the language. The nation, moreover, since it would belong to the same race, would bear within it the same national characteristics to which the noble language-structure owed its origin, and would regard its language in a similar sense and spirit, even if certain portions of the tongue in question were to be outwardly less in keeping with that spirit. Furthermore, as is actually the case in English conjugation, certain genuine inflections would always have remained extant, and would not have let the mind go astray as to the true origin and real nature of the language. *A smaller stock of forms* and *simpler structure*, arising in this way, do not therefore render languages – as we actually see in English and German – by any means incapable of *superior merits*, but merely endow them with a different *character*. Their *poetry*, admittedly, forfeits thereby the full power of one of its main elements. But if poetry in such a nation were really to founder, or even decline in its fruitfulness, this would certainly be due to deeper internal causes, without the language being to blame.

The *daughter-languages of Latin* also owe their pure grammatical structure to the firm, one might well say the indelible, attachment of the true organism to those languages which have once made it their own. It seems to me a major requirement, for a correct assessment of the remarkable phenomenon of their emergence, to lay stress on the fact that, if we consider only grammatically formal features, the reconstruction of the ruined language of Rome was not affected in any essential way by *foreign material*. The *indigenous languages* of the countries in which the new idioms sprang up seem to have had no part in it at all. Of Basque this is certain; but it is likewise exceedingly probable of the languages originally prevailing in Gaul. The foreign immigrant peoples, largely of German or German-related stock, have contributed a great many *words* to the reshaping of Latin; but on the grammatical side it is difficult to find any significant traces of the tongues they spoke. Peoples do not readily remodel the form in which they are accustomed to cast their thoughts. The foundation from which the grammar of the new languages arose was therefore essentially and principally that of the destroyed language itself. But the causes of destruction and downfall must already be sought for much earlier than in the period when the results became plain. Already in the heyday of the Empire, Latin in the *provinces* was being differently spoken, according to their own differences, from the way it was in Latium and the capital. Even in this original seat of the nation, the *vernacular language* could have had peculiarities of its own, which only came more generally to view later on, after the educated speech had declined. There would naturally have arisen departures in pronunciation, solecisms in construction, and probably already an easing of formal constraints by auxiliary terms, where the cultivated language permitted them not at all, or only as quite particular exceptions. The popular idiosyncrasies must have become dominant when the latter, as the community declined, no longer felt itself buoyed up by literature and the spoken use of it in public.[13] The provincial degeneracy spread the more widely, the looser became the ties attaching the provinces to the whole.

This twofold decay was finally carried to its highest point by *foreign immigrations*. It was now no longer a mere corruption of the language formerly predominant, but a rejection and destruction of its most essential forms, often a real misunderstanding of them, but always at the same time an interpolating of new means for preserving the unity of speech, created from the existing stock, though often connected in perverse ways. But amid all these changes, the declining language held on to the essential principle of its structure, the pure distinction between thing- and relation-concept, the need to create the appropriate expression for each of them, and the feeling for this in the people, deeply ingrained by the habit of centuries. This mark adhered to every fragment of the language; it could not have been erased, even if the peoples had failed to perceive it. Yet it was their own responsibility to seek it out, to solve the riddle of it, and to employ it for reconstruction. In this uniformity of the new remaking, arising from the general nature of the linguistic sense itself, coupled with the unity of the mother-language, which had remained uncontaminated from a grammatical viewpoint, we must seek an explanation for the fact that the procedure of the Romance languages remains so much alike in quite distant regions, and often surprises us by quite isolated coincidences. *Forms* declined, but not *the form*, which continued, rather, to pour out its old spirit over the new transformations.

For if, in these newer languages, a *preposition* replaces a case, the situation is not like that where a word indicates the case in a language that merely adds particles. Even though the original factual meaning of it may have been lost, it still does not purely express a relation

[13] Cf. on this, and for this whole section, Diefenbach's treatise, which is very well worth reading, on the Romance literary languages of today.

merely as such, since this mode of expression is alien to the whole
language, its structure has not emanated from the inner linguistic
viewpoint which purely and energetically insists on a sharp demarcation of the parts of speech, and the national spirit does not assimilate
its constructions from this point of view. In Latin this latter situation
was exactly and perfectly realized. The prepositions formed a totality
of such relations, each one demanding, according to its meaning, a
case appropriate to it; only in conjunction with this did it designate
the relationship. This elegant agreement was not adopted by the
languages of degenerate origin. But the feeling of this, the acknowledgement of the preposition as a distinct part of speech, the true
significance of it, did not go under as well; and this is no mere
arbitrary assumption. It is unmistakeably visible in the shaping of
the whole language, which in spite of a plethora of gaps in particular
forms, has preserved an overall formality, and is itself, in its principle,
no less of an *inflectional language* than its parent. The same is to be found
in the usage of the verb. However defective its forms may be, its
synthetic power of positing is still the same, since the language still
bears the indelible imprint of a separation between verb and noun.
Even the *pronoun*, employed in innumerable instances where the
mother-language gives no independent expression to it, still corresponds in feeling to the true concept of this part of speech. Whereas
in languages that lack any designation for persons in the verb, it is
placed as a descriptive concept in front of the verb, in the daughter-
languages of Latin it is taken, in fact, to be simply the person,
detached and located elsewhere. For the inseparability of verb and
person has been firmly rooted in the language from the parent
tongue, and is actually evinced in the daughter-language by various
residual end-sounds. In the latter, as in all inflected languages, the
representative function of the pronoun becomes more generally
evident; and since this leads to a pure apprehension of the relative
pronoun, the language is also guided thereby into a correct use of
the latter. The same phenomenon therefore recurs everywhere. The
ruined form is reconstructed in quite a different manner, but the spirit
of it still hovers over the new formation, and shows how hard it is
to destroy the persistence of the *life-principle*, in language-stocks that
have truly been fashioned in a grammatical way.

Amid all the uniformity of treatment given to the transformed
material, which the Latin daughter-languages adhere to on the
whole, a *special principle* of individual apprehension still underlies each
particular one. As I have repeatedly indicated in the foregoing, the
numberless details which the use of language makes necessary must
be gathered into unity, wherever and however the spoken word is

to occur; and since language sinks its roots into every fibre of the human mind, this unity can only be an individual one. By the very fact that an altered principle of unity, a new conception of a people's mind, has been adopted, a new language actually comes into being; and where a nation experiences radical changes that operate powerfully upon its language, it must incorporate the changed or novel elements by *new formation*. We have spoken above of that moment in a nation's life, when the possibility becomes clear to it of employing the language, independently of external usage, to construct a whole of thought and feeling. Even though the emergence of a *literature*, which we have here defined in its true nature, and from the standpoint of its ultimate completion, proceeds, in the event, only gradually and from obscurely felt impulses, the inception of it is always a unique upswing, the pressure emanating from within towards a joint action of the *form of the language* and the individuality of the *mind*, from which the true and pure nature of both is reflected, and which has no other purpose but this very reflection. The manner in which this pressure develops becomes the *highway of ideas* which the nation traverses until its language collapses. It represents, as it were, a second and higher coupling of the language into unity; and how this is related to the fashioning of the outer, technical form, we have touched on more closely above, in speaking of the character of languages.

In the transition of Latin into the newer languages that arose from it, this dual treatment is very clearly distinguishable. Two such, Rhaeto-Romansh and Daco-Rumanian, have taken no part in *scientific* matters, though it cannot be said that their technical form lags behind the others. On the contrary, Daco-Rumanian has actually kept the most inflections from the mother-tongue, and approximates, moreover, to Italian in dealing with them. Thus the defect here was due merely to external circumstances, to the want of events and situations that could cause the upswing to utilize the language for higher ends.

Passing to a similar kind of case, the same was incontestably the reason why the downfall of Greek did not give rise to a language distinguished by new individuality. For in other respects the formation of modern Greek is in many ways very like that of the Romance languages. Since these transformations lie largely in the natural course of the language, and both mother-languages have the same grammatical character, this similarity is easy to explain, but makes even more striking the difference in the final result. Greece, as the province of a declining empire, often exposed to the ravages of foreign tribesmen, was unable to acquire the flourishing power of resilience which produced in the West the freshness and stimulus of new-forming inner and outer circumstances. With new social institutions, the total lapsing of ties with a decrepit body politic, and reinforcement through the arrival of staunch and sturdy races, the Western nations were bound to tread new paths in all activities of mind and character. The new pattern that evolved from this at once brought with it a combination of the religious, the warlike and the poetic mentalities, which exerted the most happy and decisive influence upon the language. For these nations there blossomed a new, poetically creative youth, and their condition became, in that respect, somewhat similar to that which is otherwise separated from us by the dimness of the preceding dark age.

As surely, however, as this outer historical turn of events must be held responsible for the flowering of the newer Western languages and literatures into an individuality wherein they were able to emulate the parental stock, so also, in my view, was there yet another cause quite essentially at work, to which passing reference has already been made above (p. 208), and whose estimation is quite properly included in the course of these reflections, since it relates especially to language. The transformation undergone by Latin was beyond comparison more penetrating, powerful and sudden than that experienced by Greek. It was like a true destruction, whereas that of Greek remained more within the confines of mere individual mutilations and the dissolution of forms. We perceive from this example a dual possibility, confirmed also by other cases in linguistic history, for the passage from a form-rich language to a more formless one. In one, the artistic structure collapses, to be recreated on a less perfect level. In the other, the declining language receives only individual wounds, which again heal; no purely new creation occurs, the antiquated language persists, but in a lamentable state of disfigurement. Since the Byzantine empire, for all its decrepitude and weakness, still endured for a long time, the old language also lasted longer, and continued to stand there as a treasury that could still be drawn upon, a canon one could always come back to. There is no more convincing proof of the difference, on this point, between the neo-Hellenic and Romance languages, than the fact that the method attempted, till the very last, for elevating and refining the former, has always been that of a maximal approximation to Ancient Greek. The thought of such a possibility could not have occurred even, to a Spaniard or Italian. The Romance nations saw themselves really flung off into new paths, and since no retreat was possible, the sense of imperative necessity gave them the courage to level these paths and conduct them to the goal in directions suited to their own individual mentalities. From another viewpoint, however, neo-

Hellenic is placed by this very difference in a more favourable position. There is a major distinction between those languaes which, as related shoots of the same stock, spring apart from each other in the course of their inner development, and those which grow up from the downfall and ruin of others, by the operation, that is, of external circumstances. In the former, undamaged by mighty revolutions and significant admixtures of foreign matter, we can go back, more or less, from every expression, word or form, into unfathomable depths. For they largely preserve in themselves the foundation of this; and they alone can boast of being self-sufficient and possessing demonstrable consistency within their own bounds. *Daughter-languages*, like those of the Romance group, are obviously not in this position. They rest wholly, on the one hand, upon a language no longer extant, and on the other, upon foreign tongues. So all expressions, as we pursue their origin, lead us mostly through a quite short series of intermediate forms, into an alien region unknown to the people. Even in the grammatical portion, little if at all contaminated by foreign elements, the consistency of structure, so far as it actually exists, is always demonstrable only by reference to the alien mother-language. The deeper understanding of these languages, and even the impress produced in every language by the inner harmonious connection of all its elements, is therefore always but halfway possible through the language itself, and needs for its completion material that is inaccessible to those who speak it. In both types of languages we can be compelled to go back to the *earlier* tongue. But the difference in the way this happens can be accurately sensed if we compare how the want of self-sufficient explanation leads back, in Latin, to Sanscritic foundations, and in French to Latin ones. The transformation in the latter case obviously has a greater degree of arbitrariness, due to external influences, and even the natural sequence of analogy, which does, indeed, recur even here, depends on a presumption of this influence from outside. Now this situation, as depicted here of the *Romance languages*, is one to which *neo-Hellenic*, just because it did not really become an authentically new language, is subject not at all, or at least to an infinitely lesser degree. It can free itself, in course of time, from admixture with foreign words, since these, with but few exceptions, have not penetrated so deeply into its true life as they have in the Romance languages. Its real parent, however, the Greek of antiquity, cannot even appear foreign to the people. Though the latter may no longer be able to enter in thought into the whole of its artistic structure, they must still recognize the elements as belonging, for the most part, to their own language as well.

The difference here referred to is certainly noteworthy in regard to the *nature of language* itself. Whether it also exerts a significant influence on the *national mind* and *character*, may well seem doubtful. We may justly object to it that every consideration transcending the current state of the language at any time is alien to the people, that hence the self-sufficient explicability of a language that is self-enclosed in a purely organic way remains unfruitful for them, and that every language which has arisen, in whatever manner, from another one, but has already been cultivated for centuries, acquires by that very fact a consistency which is perfectly adequate in its effect upon the nation. It is actually conceivable that among the earlier languages which to us appear as parent tongues, there may be some that arose in much the same way as the Romance languages did, though a careful and exact analysis would probably soon betray that they could not be explained from within their own bounds. But in the secret darkness of the soul's formation, and the inheritance of mental individuality, there undoubtedly resides an infinitely powerful connection between the tonal fabric of the language and the totality of thought and feeling. So it cannot possibly be a matter of indifference whether sensation and mood have been entwined in unbroken sequence with the same sounds, and have suffused the latter with their content and warmth, or whether this self-sufficient series of effects and causes has been subject to violent disturbances. Even here, however, a new consistency does take shape, and time has more power of healing wounds in languages than elsewhere in the human soul. But nor should it be forgotten, that this consistency is restored only gradually, and that the generations who live before it is solidly established also enter the sequence already as causative agents. It seems to me, therefore, by no means without effect upon a people's depth of intellect, sensitivity of feeling and power of emotions, whether it does or does not speak a wholly self-sufficient language, or one that has at least come about through a purely organic process of development. In the description of nations that fall into the second category, we should not, therefore, neglect to examine whether and how far the equilibrium disturbed, as it were, by the influence of their language, has been restored in them in other ways – indeed, whether and how a new advantage has perhaps been wrested from the imperfection which cannot be denied.

§22

We have now reached one of the destinations to which the present inquiry was designed to lead.

To recall briefly what has been said already, so far as it needs to be linked with what follows, the entire view of *language* here presented depends essentially on the fact that it is at once the necessary *completion of thought*, and the natural *development* of a disposition that characterizes man as such. But this development is not that of an *instinct*, which could be explained on merely physiological grounds. Without being an act of immediate consciousness, indeed of instant spontaneity and freedom, it can still belong only to a being endowed with *consciousness* and *freedom*, and proceeds in such a being from the unfathomable depth of his *individuality*, and from the *activity* of the forces within him. For it depends throughout upon the *energy* with which man, unbeknownst to himself, provides, from his entire *mental individuality*, the driving *impulse*, and upon the *form* in which he does it.[1] Through this connection with an *individual reality*, and from other accessory causes, such a development is at the same time subject, however, to the *conditions* that surround man in the world, and exert influence even on the acts of his freedom. Now in language, insofar as it actually appears in man, two constitutive principles may be distinguished: the *inner linguistic sense* (by which I understand, not a special power, but the entire mental capacity, as related to the formation and use of language, and thus merely a tendency); and *sound*, insofar as it depends on the constitution of the organs, and is based on what has been handed down already. The inner linguistic sense is the principle which dominates language from within outwards, and everywhere supplies the guiding impulse. Sound, in and for itself, would resemble the passive matter which receives form. But since permeation by the linguistic sense transforms it into *articulate* sound, containing both intellectual and sensuous power, inseparably united and in constant mutual interaction, it becomes, in its perpetual symbolizing activity, the actual *creative principle* in language, and seemingly even an independent one. Just as it is a general law of man's existence in the world, that he can project nothing from himself that does not at once become a thing that reacts upon him and conditions his further creation, so sound also modifies in its turn the outlook and

[1] Cf. above, pp. 24, 43–4, 46–7.

214

procedure of the inner linguistic sense. Thus every subsequent creation does not maintain the simple direction of the original force, but is subject to a composite influence, made up of this and the force supplied by the product created earlier. Since the *natural disposition* to language is universal in man, and everyone must possess the key to the understanding of all languages, it follows automatically that the *form* of all languages must be essentially the *same*, and always achieve the universal purpose. The *difference* can lie only in the means, and only within the limits permitted by attainment of the goal. It is multifariously present in languages, however, and not in the mere *sounds* alone, so that the same things are just differently designated; it also occurs in the *use* which the linguistic sense makes of sounds, with a view to the form of language, and even in its own conception of this form. Through it alone, indeed, so far as languages are purely formal, should mere *uniformity* be able to arise in them. For it must demand in all of them the *correct* and *regular* structure, which can only be one and the same. But in reality matters are not like this, partly owing to the *retroactive effect* of *sound*, partly because of the *individuality* of the inner sense, as manifested in appearance. It is a matter, that is, of the *energy* of the force whereby it acts upon the sound, and transforms the latter in every nuance, even the finest, into a living expression of thought. But this energy cannot everywhere be the same, cannot everywhere display a like intensity, vivacity and regularity. Nor is it always supported by a similar inclination to treat the thought symbolically, or a similar aesthetic pleasure in sonic abundance and euphony. Yet the striving of the *inner linguistic sense* remains always directed to *uniformity* in languages, and its authority seeks always to lead even deviant forms back, in some way, to the right course. *Sound,* on the other hand, is truly the principle that increases *diversity.* For it depends upon that constitution of the *organs* which mainly fashions the *alphabet,* the latter, as a suitably conducted analysis demonstrates, being the foundation of every language. The *articulated* sound, moreover, also possesses its own peculiar *laws* and *customs,* founded partly on ease and partly on euphony of pronunciation, which admittedly again engender uniformity, but necessarily create differences in their particular application. Since we nowhere encounter an isolated language, making an entirely fresh start, the articulated sound must always, in the end, attach itself to *what has gone before,* or to an alien source. In all of this, taken together, lie the grounds for the necessary *diversity of structure in the languages of man.* Languages cannot contain it in themselves, since the nations who speak them are different, and have an existence governed by different circumstances.

[margin notes, handwritten:] form of all languages are essentially the same (what differs is the means by which each language realizes grammatical functions deriving from universal principles of thought.)

[margin:] inner linguistic sense tends toward uniformity

[margin:] sound tends toward diversity

[margin:] how to account for diversity of structure of languages of man

[margin:] nations are different, different circumstances

In the consideration of *language as such*, a form must be disclosed, which of all those imaginable *coincides the most* with the *aims of language*, and we must be able to judge the merits and defects of existing languages by the *degree* to which they approximate to this one form. Following this route, we have found that this form is necessarily that which is most in keeping with the general *course of the human mind*, promotes its growth by the most regulated activity, and not only facilitates the relative concord of all its tendencies, but evokes them more vividly in reaction to its stimulus. But mental activity does not aim simply at its own internal *enhancement*. In following this path it is also necessarily driven outward to erect a scientific edifice in the form of a *world-view*, and again to work creatively from this standpoint. This, too, we have taken into consideration, and it has unmistakeably emerged that such an enlargement of man's outlook prospers best, or rather solely, under the guidance of the *most perfect linguistic form*. We have therefore gone into this in more detail, and I have tried to point out the nature of this form on those points in which the procedure of language marshals itself for the direct attainment of its *ultimate aims*. The question of how language manages to present thought in *simple sentences*, and in *periods* involving many clauses, seemed to offer here the simplest solution to the task of assessing it, in both its inner and outer purposes. But from this procedure we could at once revert to the necessary constitution of the *individual elements*. That a given linguistic family, or even just a single language from one, should coincide throughout and on all points with the perfect form of language, is not to be expected, and is at all events not to be found within the range of our experience. But the *Sanscritic languages* come closest to this form, and are likewise those in which the mental cultivation of mankind has evolved most happily in the longest sequence of advances. We can therefore regard them as a fixed *point of comparison* for *all the rest*.

These latter cannot be depicted with equal simplicity. Since they strive toward the same objectives as the purely regular languages, but do not reach this goal to the same degree, or in the correct way, there can be no such clearly evident consistency prevailing in their structure. Apart from Chinese, which dispenses with all grammatical forms, we previously postulated in languages *three possible forms* for the attainment of sentence-making, the *inflectional*, the *agglutinating* and the *incorporative*. All languages carry one or more of these forms within them; and in assessing their relative merits, it becomes a question of how they have assimilated these abstract forms into their concrete ones, or rather, of what the principle of such assimilation or mixture may be. This distinction of *abstract* possible forms of language from

[handwritten marginal notes:]
There must be an ideal language by which we judge the rest

the one that best conforms to human mind is the best

The world-view

Sanscritic languages are the fixed point of reference for all the rest

Chinese has no grammar apart from Chinese — inflectional agglutinating incorporative

Does creation of any language depend on human capacity at all? See also p. 115

[handwritten top margin: denies that he is claiming certain languages are illegitimate and imperfect]

the *concrete* ones that are actually present, will already contribute, I fancy, to a lessening of the uncongenial impression that I am singling out certain languages as the only legitimate ones, which automatically stamps the remainder as *more imperfect*. For that among *abstract* forms, the *inflectional ones* can alone be called correct, is not easily to be disputed. But the judgement thereby passed upon the others does not apply in equal measure to *concrete* existing languages, in which no one of these forms prevails exclusively, but a striving towards the correct one is always, on the contrary, visibly at work. This point, however, still needs to be vindicated by more detailed discussion.

[handwritten right margin: hard to dispute inflectional perfection — in other languages there is this striving toward correct solution]

Among those having knowledge of several languages, there may well be a very general feeling that, so far as these tongues are on the same level of *culture*, *each* can claim *merits peculiar* to itself, without our being able to attribute to any a decisive *advantage* over the rest. Now the view put forward in the present considerations is in direct opposition to this; yet to many it may seem all the more repugnant, in that the endeavour of these very reflections has been largely devoted to demonstrating the lively and inseparable *connection* between *languages* and the *mental capacity of nations*. This same adverse judgement about languages appears, therefore, to refer to *peoples* as well. But here a more accurate distinction is needed. We have already remarked earlier, that the *merits* of languages are indeed in general dependent on the *energy of mental activity,* and in fact are quite especially due to the latter's peculiar propensity for elaborating *thought* by means of *sound*. A more *imperfect language* is therefore initially proof only of the smaller *impulse* the nation has directed to this, without implying any decision as to its other *intellectual merits*. We have everywhere set out at first from the *structure* of languages alone, and in forming a judgement about it have also confined ourselves solely to this. Now that this structure is better in one than another, is more excellent in Sanscrit than in Chinese, and in Greek than in Arabic, could hardly be disputed by any impartial scholar. However we might try to weigh off their respective virtues, we should always have to admit that one of these languages is animated by a *more fruitful principle of mental development* than the other. But now we should inevitably have misconstrued all the mutual relations of *mind* and *language,* if we were unwilling to extend the various consequences thereof to the *reverse action* of these languages, and to the *intellectuality* of the peoples who created them (so far as this lies within human capacity at all). So from this point of view our proposed approach is perfectly justified. Yet it could still be objected to this, that the *particular virtues* of a language are also capable of fostering *particular intellectual characteristics*, and that the *mental dispositions* of nations are

[handwritten right margin: "is not referring to peoples"]

[handwritten right margin: "more imperfect" means a nation has directed a smaller impulse to elaborate thought via sound – nothing here about its other intellec. merits]

[handwritten bottom margin: still languages have more fruitful principles of mental development than others]

[handwritten bottom margin: these have had consequences on the mental development of peoples and their intellectuality]

themselves far more various in their *mixture* and *composition* than could be measured off in *degrees*. Both observations are undoubtedly correct. But the *true merit* of languages must still be sought in the *versatility* and *harmony* of their activating *power*. They are tools that *mental activity* requires, tracks on which it rolls forward. They are therefore truly beneficial only when they accompany this activity in every direction, with assistance and encouragement, putting it at the centre from which each of its varieties harmoniously unfolds. So although we gladly concede that the form of Chinese exhibits, more perhaps than any other language, the power of pure thought, and directs the mind more exclusively and urgently to this, precisely because it lops off all the small distracting sounds of connection, and although the reading of just a few Chinese texts reinforces this conviction to the point of admiration, still, even the most resolute defenders of this language can hardly maintain that it guides the mind's activity to the true centre, from which poetry and philosophy, scientific research and eloquent discourse, spring forth with equal readiness.

Thus whatever the viewpoint I start from, I can never avoid a clear and open adoption of the decisive contrast between languages of *purely regular* form, and those of a form that *deviates* from this. It is my sincere conviction that what is expressed thereby is just an undeniable fact. The excellence even of these deviant languages, with the *particular advantages* it confers, the artistry of their technical construction, is neither misapprehended nor despised; we simply deny them the capacity to act, of themselves, in so ordered, so versatile and so harmonious a fashion upon the mind. To pass sentence of condemnation on any language, even of the rudest savages, is a thing that nobody can be further from doing than myself. I would consider it not merely a disparagement of man in his most individual talent, but also as incompatible with any correct view provided, through reflection and experience, by language itself. For every language always remains a *copy* of that *original talent* for language as such; and to be capable of reaching even the simplest objectives that every language must necessarily attain, there is invariably need of a *structure* so *artful*, that the study of it is bound to attract research, without even considering the fact that every language, apart from its already *developed part*, has an incalculable capacity, alike for internal flexibility and for the assimilation of ever richer and loftier ideas. In all that I have said here, I have presupposed the nations to be *confined solely to themselves*. But they also attract *foreign culture*, and their mental activity receives from this an *accession* which is not due to their *language*, and which serves, on the contrary, to provide the latter with an *enlargement* of its own particular scope. For every language is malleable enough to be able to assimilate everything, and to lend everything expression again from its own resources. It cannot ever, under any circumstances, become an absolute *restraint* upon man. The difference consists only in whether the starting-point for enhancement of powers and enlargement of ideas is located in the language itself, or is alien to it; whether, in other words, it provides the inspiration for this, or merely gives in to it, as it were, in a passive and cooperative way.

Now if there is such a *difference* between languages, we may ask by what *signs* it can be recognized, and it may seem one-sided, and out of keeping with the richness of the concept, that I should have sought it precisely in the grammatical *method of constructing sentences*. It was by no means my intention to confine it to this, since it is assuredly no less actively at work in *every element* and *every construction*. I have, however, deliberately reverted to that which constitutes, as it were, the foundation of language, and is likewise of quite decisive effect upon the evolution of *concepts*. Its logical arrangement, its clear discrimination, the accurate portrayal of its relationships one to another, constitute the indispensable foundations of all expressions of mental activity, even the highest; but this, as must be evident to everyone, is essentially dependent on these various linguistic methods. With correct methods, correct thinking also goes on in an easy and natural fashion, but with others it finds difficulties to overcome, or at least does not enjoy any similar aid from language. The same temper of mind which gives rise to these three different modes of procedure also extends automatically to the formation of *all other linguistic elements*, and is merely more especially recognizable in sentence-formation. Lastly, these very characteristics are at the same time particularly well suited to factual display in the linguistic structure, a circumstances of much importance in an inquiry quite specifically devoted to discovering, from the *actual, historically recognizable features* in languages, the form which they impart to the mind, or in which they are inwardly presented to it.

The routes that *deviate* from the path mapped out by the pure necessity of *regularity* can be of infinite diversity. The languages enclosed in this area cannot, therefore, be exhaustively derived or classified according to *principles*; at best one may group them by *likenesses* in the major portions of their structure. But if it is true that the *natural* structure depends, on the one hand, upon fixed *word-unity*, and on the other, upon proper *separation* of the *members* that constitute the *sentence*, then all the languages at present under discussion must either narrow down the *unity of the word* or the *freedom* to *couple thoughts*, or else combine both of these drawbacks within them. In comparing even the most diverse languages, we shall always be able to find here a general yardstick of their relation to mental development. Investigation of the *reasons* for such *departures* from the *natural course* is attended with peculiar difficulties. The course itself can be traced by way of *concepts*, but the *abberation* is due to *individual* factors, which, amid the darkness that shrouds the earlier history of every language, can only be conjectured and divined. Where the imperfection of the organism is due merely to the fact that the inner linguistic sense has not been everywhere able to create *sensuous expression* in the *sound*, and the *formative power* of the latter has therefore wearied before the attainment of complete formality, this difficulty is at all events less in evidence, since the ground of imperfection then lies in the weakness itself. But even such cases seldom present themselves in so simple a fashion, and there are others, and these in fact the most notable, which are by no means explicable merely in this way. Yet the inquiry must be pursued without flagging to this point, if we are not to forego discovery of the *language-structure* in its *first foundations*, so to speak, where it takes root in the organs and the mind. It would be impossible to go into this matter at all exhaustively here. I shall therefore be content to dwell for a few moments only upon two examples, and select for the first of them the Semitic languages, though again with reference primarily to Hebrew.

This family of languages is obviously of the *inflecting* type, and we have, in fact, already noted above that *inflection of the truest kind,* in contrast to meaningful appending, is actually indigenous there. Hebrew and Arabic also bear witness to the inner *excellence* of their *structure*, the former by works of the highest poetical inspiration, and the latter by a rich, comprehensive scientific literature, as well as a poetic one. Even in itself, from a merely technical viewpoint, the *organism* of these languages is not only second to none in rigour of consistency, artistic simplicity and ingenious adaptation of sound to thought, but perhaps excels all others in that respect. Yet these languages have *two* inherent *peculiarities* which do not lie in the natural requirements of language, and, we may certainly add, are scarcely within the tolerances of language as such. For at least in their present form, they call throughout for *three consonants* in each word stem, and *consonant* and *vowel* do not together contain the meaning of words, *meaning* and *relation* being exclusively assigned, rather, to the consonants and vowels respectively. From the first of these peculiarities there arises a *constraint* upon *word-form*, which is plainly less preferable than the freedom of other languages, namely those of the Sanscrit group. And in regard to the second of them, we find obstacles to *inflection* by the addition of suitably subordinated sounds. In these respects, I believe, we must therefore still count the Semitic languages as deviants from the most appropriate path of mental development. But if we now try to trace the *reasons* for this phenomenon, and its connection with the *national linguistic aptitudes*, we shall have difficulty in arriving at any quite satisfactory results. It seems doubtful right away as to which of these two peculiarities should be seen as the *determining ground* of the other. Both are obviously most intimately *connected*. The range of syllables possible with three consonants was an invitation, as it were, to indicating the manifold relations of words by means of vowel change; and if it was decided to utilize the vowels exclusively for this purpose, the necessary abundance of meanings could be secured only by using several consonants in the same word. But the *interaction* here described is more suited to explaining the inner connection of the language in its present-day form, than to serving as a basis for the origin of such a structure. The indication of grammatical relations by mere vowels cannot reasonably be taken as the primary determining ground, since everywhere in languages the meaning naturally comes first, and hence the exclusion of the vowels from this would already have to be explained. The *vowels*, indeed, must be viewed in a dual capacity. In the first place they serve only as *sounds*, without which the *consonants* could not be pronounced; but we then encounter the *difference of sound* which they take on in the vocalic series. In the first connection there are no vowels, but just one general vowel-sound that stands adjacent, or, if you will, really no true vowel at all, but an indistinct schwa-sound that is not yet developed in detail. Something similar occurs with the *consonants*, in their combination with vowels. Even the vowel, to become audible, requires the consonantal aspirate; and so

far as the latter merely has the character needed for this purpose, such
a vowel differs from the tones which stand mutually contrasted, in
the sequence of consonants, by difference of timbre.[1] From this it
already follows automatically that in expressing concepts the vowels
merely attach to the consonants, and as the deepest linguists have
already recognized,[2] serve mainly to *define* more accurately the word
shaped by the consonants. It is also inherent in the phonetic nature
of vowels, that they indicate something finer, more penetrating and
intimate, than the consonants, and are less bodily, as it were, and
more spiritual. They are therefore more suited to *grammatical indication*,
and their acoustic lightness and capacity for attachment reinforces
this. Yet the *exclusively grammatical use* of them in the Semitic languages
is still very different from all this, presents, I believe, a unique
phenomenon in linguistic history, and therefore needs a special
reason to explain it. If, in order to find it, we set out in the other
direction, from the *disyllabic root-structure*, the attempt comes up
against the fact that this root-structure, though constitutive for the
state of these languages as we know it, was probably not the truly
original one. As will be explained in more detail later, it was
underlain by a *monosyllabic* structure – probably to a greater extent
than it is now customary to suppose. But perhaps the peculiarity in
question can still be derived from this very fact, and from that
transition to the disyllabic forms, to which we are led by comparing
the disyllables one to another. These monosyllabic forms had two
consonants, which enclosed a vowel between them. Perhaps the vowel
so enclosed, and drowned out by the sound of the consonants, then
lost the capacity for suitable development on its own, and thus took
no part in expressing the meaning. Perhaps the subsequently
emerging need for grammatical designation thereupon evoked this
development, and brought about the addition of a second syllable,
to give greater scope for grammatical inflection. But still there must
always have been some other reason for not letting the vowels occur
freely in final position; and this should doubtless be looked for in the

---

[1] Lepsius, in his *Palaeography*, has set forth these principles in the clearest and most
satisfying way, and demonstrated the difference between the initial *a* and the *h*
in Sanscrit script. I had noticed in the Bugi and some other related alphabets,
that the sign which in all treatments of the languages possessing these alphabets
is called an initial *a*, is actually no vowel at all, but a weak consonantal breathing,
analogous to the *spiritus lenis* of Greek. But all the phenomena that I there pointed
out (*Nouveau Journal Asiatique*, IX, pp. 489–94), can be better and more correctly
explained by what Lepsius has worked out on the same point in the Sanscrit
alphabet.

[2] Grimm, in his happily pregnant style, expresses this as follows: the consonant
shapes, the vowel defines and illuminates the word (*Deutsche Grammatik*, II, p. 1).

constitution of the organs, and the individuality of pronunciation, rather than in the inner linguistic viewpoint.

It seems to me, however, more certain than the foregoing, and more important for determining the relation of the Semitic languages to mental development, that the inner linguistic sense of these peoples still lacked the necessary sharpness and clarity of distinction between material *meaning* and the *relations* of *words*, partly in its general *forms* of *speaking* and *thinking*, partly in *sentence-making*, so that even the purity of the distinction between consonants and vowel-character is thereby put at risk. I must first call attention here to the special nature of those sounds that are called *roots* in the Semitic languages, but which are essentially different from the root-sounds in other languages. Since the vowels are excluded from material significance, the three consonants of the root must, strictly speaking, be vowelless, i.e., accompanied merely by the sound required to expel them. But in this condition they lack the sound-form necessary for their appearance in speech, since even the Semitic languages do not tolerate a number of consonants following hard upon one another, connected merely by a schwa. With vowels appended, they express one definite relation or another, and cease to be relationless roots. So where the roots actually appear in the language, they are already true word-forms; in their root-format proper they still lack an important factor for completing their sound-form in speech. Hence even *inflection*, in the Semitic languages, takes on a meaning different from that which this concept has in other languages, where the root appears, free of all relation, genuinely perceptible to the ear, as at least part of a word in speech. In the Semitic languages, inflected words do not undergo modifications of the original tones, but completions into the true sound-form. Now since, in the context of speech, the original root-sound cannot become perceptible to the ear alongside the inflected one, the living distinction between *semantic* and *relational expression* is thereby vitiated. Yet precisely because of this, the combination of the two becomes still more intimate, and as Ewald astutely and correctly observes, the application of the sounds becomes apter than in any other language, since the more intellectual elements are apportioned to the readily mobile vowels, and the more material to the consonants. But the sense of necessary unity in the word that encompasses both meaning and relation at once, is greater and more energetic if the elements fused can be divided in pure independence; and this is appropriate to the purpose of language, which forever separates and combines, and to the nature of thinking itself. Yet even on looking into the various *kinds* of relational and semantic expression, we find that language is not without a certain mingling of both. Through lack of *inseparable prepositions*, it loses an entire class of relational designations, which form a systematic whole, and can be set out in a complete schema. In the Semitic languages this deficiency is partially remedied, in that special words are assigned for these verb-concepts modified by prepositions. But this can assure no completeness, and such apparent wealth is even less able to mitigate the drawback, that since the contrast is now less palpably presented, the totality, too, does not comprehensively meet the eye, and the speakers lose the possibility of an easy and certain extension of language, by particular applications that have hitherto remained untried.

Nor can I pass over here a difference that strikes me as important, in the designation of various kinds of relations. The indication of the *cases of the noun*, so far as they admit of expression, and are not merely distinguished by position, is effected by adding prepositions, whereas the *persons of the verb* are shown by adding pronouns. The meaning of the words is in no way affected by these two relations. They are expressions of quite generally applicable relationships. But the grammatical *method* is addition, and that of such letters or syllables as the language recognizes to be self-subsistent, and also combines with the words up to only a certain degree of fixity. So far as vowel-change also plays a part, it is a consequence of these accessions, whose addition cannot remain without effect on the word-form in a language which possesses such firmly-defined rules for the structure of words. The other expressions of relation, whether they consist in pure vowel-change, or in simultaneous addition of consonantal sounds, as in *hifil*, *nifal*, etc, or in duplication of one of the consonants of the word itself, as in most of the comparative forms, have a closer affinity with the material meaning of the word, affect this more or less, and may also change it entirely to some extent, as when the verb 'educate' is produced from the stem 'great', precisely through such a form. Originally and principally they do indeed designate real grammatical relations, the difference of noun and verb, the transitive, intransitive, reflexive and causative verbs, etc. The change of the original meaning, whereby derived concepts arise from the stems, is a natural consequence of these forms themselves, without the need for any mingling in it of relational and semantic expressions. This is also confirmed by the same phenomenon in the Sanscritic languages. Yet the whole difference of these two classes (case and pronominal affixes on the one hand, and inner inflections of the verb on the other), and their differing designation, is intrinsically striking. It does in fact embody a certain appropriateness to the difference of the cases themselves. Where the concept is subject to no change, the relation becomes external, merely, but is internally designated, in the stem itself, where the grammatical form, extending merely to the single word, affects the meaning. In the latter case the vowel takes on the attribute of fine delineation and more detailed modification that we referred to earlier on. All cases of the second class are in fact of this kind, and – to confine ourselves to the verb – can already be applied to mere participles, without alluding to the actual force of the verb itself. In the Burmese language this actually happens, and in this type of designation the verb-prefixes of the Malayan languages also describe approximately the same circuit as do those of the Semitic. For all such cases can actually be traced to something that alters the concept itself. This holds even of the indication of tenses, insofar as it occurs by inflection and not by syntactical means. For in this way it merely distinguishes reality from the uncertainty that cannot yet be specified with confidence. It seems strange, however, that precisely those relations, such as case, which mostly put the unaltered concept into another relation, merely, and those, such as the persons, which are most essential in forming the nature of the verb, are less formally designated, and almost incline towards agglutination, in defiance of the concept of inflection; whereas the relations that modify the concept itself are those that are most formally expressed. The course of the nation's linguistic sense does not seem here to have been that of any sharp separation of relation and meaning, but rather that of deriving, by a systematic classification of grammatical form, the concepts flowing from the original meaning into their different nuances, according to a regular plan. Otherwise the common nature of all grammatical relations would not have been somewhat obliterated by treating the expression of it in two ways. If this argument is sound and appears to tally with the facts, this case is evidence of how a people can handle its language with admirable shrewdness, and an equally rare sense of the reciprocal demands of concepts and sound, and yet miss the path that is most naturally suited to language as such. The Semitic languages' aversion for compounding can be readily accounted for by their overall form, whose main features have here been outlined. Even if it had been possible to overcome the difficulty of imparting to polysyllabic words the verbal form that by then had taken firm root in the language – a possibility demonstrated by the compound proper names – such compounding would still have had to be avoided, for preference, given the people's habituation to a shorter word-form, permitting an inner structure that was strictly articulated and readily surveyed. There were also fewer inducements to form compounds, however, since the abundance of stems made it easier to dispense with them.

[margin top left, handwritten: In Delaware compounds the elements don't contain all the original word — only parts of it]

[margin top right, handwritten: horse = "es" from "awesis", animal]

In the Delaware language of North America, the habit of forming new words by *compounding* is more prevalent, perhaps, than in any other tongue. But the elements of these composites seldom contain all the original word; only parts of it, and even just single sounds, go over into the compound. From an example given by Du Ponceau[3] we are actually obliged to conclude that it rests with the speaker to assemble such words, or rather whole phrases coined into words, out of fragments, as it were, of simpler words. From *ki*, thou, *wulit*, good, beautiful, pretty, *wichgat*, paw, and *schis*, a word used as an ending to mean smallness, there is fashioned, in talking to a kitten, *k-uli-gat-schis*, your pretty little paw. In the same way, turns of phrase are transformed into verbs, and thereupon completely conjugated. *Nad-hol-ineen*, from *nalen*, to fetch, *amochol*, boat, and the concluding governed pronoun of the first person plural, means: Fetch us with the boat!— across the river, that is. It will already be seen from these examples that the changes in the words that make up these compounds are very significant. Thus *wulit*, in the above example, becomes *uli*;

[margin left, handwritten: sometimes wulit becomes uli, sometimes wul can also be ola]

in other cases, where no consonant precedes in the compound, it is *wul*, but with a preceding consonant can also be *ola*.[4] The shortenings are also very violent at times. From *awesis*, animal, only the syllable *es* is taken up into the compound, to form the word 'horse'. At the same time, since the word-fragments are now combined with other sounds, euphonic changes occur, which make these fragments even less recognizable. Apart from the *es* ending, the above-mentioned word for 'horse', *nanayung-es*, is based only on *nayundam*, to bear a burden on the back. The *g* appears inserted, and the strengthening by reduplication of the first syllable seems applied only to the compound. A mere initial *m*, from *machit*, back, or *medhick*, evil, gives the word a vile and contemptuous sense.[5] These word-mutilations have therefore been very severely censured, on occasion, as barbaric crudities. But one would need to possess a deeper knowledge of the Delaware language, and the kinship of its words, in order to decide whether the stem-syllable has really been abolished in the shortened words, or whether it has not actually been preserved. That the latter

[margin left, handwritten: Humbolt is not so quick as some to call these mutilations hopeless and damaging to etymology]

3 Preface to Zeisberger's *Delaware Grammar*, Philadelphia 1827, 4, p. 20.
4 *Transactions of the Historical and Literary Committee of the American Philosophical Society*, Philadelphia 1819, Vol. 1, p. 405 *et seq.*
5 Zeisberger (*op. cit*) remarks that *mannitto* forms an exception to this, since the word means God himself, the great and good spirit. But it is very common to find the religious ideas of uncultured peoples starting from the fear of evil spirits. The original meaning of the word could therefore quite easily have been of this sort. For lack of a Delaware dictionary, I can find no information on the rest of the word. The resemblance of this remainder to the Tagalic *anito*, idol, is striking, though perhaps due merely to chance (Cf. *Über die Kawi-Sprache*, Vol. 1, p. 75).

is in fact the case, in some instances, is evidenced by a remarkable example. *Lenape* means 'man'; *lenni*, which together with the word just mentioned makes up the name (*Lenni Lenape*) of the main tribe of the Delawares, has the meaning of something original, unmixed, long resident in the country, and thus also means *common* or *customary*. In this latter sense the term serves to designate everything indigenous, given to the country by the great and good spirit, as opposed to what has only been brought in from outside by the white man. *Ape* means to walk upright.[6] In *lenape,* therefore, the characteristic marks of the erect-walking native are quite accurately contained. That in this way the word stands in general for *man*, and to become a proper name, again couples with itself the concept of the original, are phenomena it is easy to explain. In *pilape,* youth, the word *pilsit*, chaste, innocent, is compounded with that part of *lenape* which designates the characteristic property of man. Since the words conjoined in the compound are largely polysyllabic and are themselves already compounds in turn, it is all a matter of which of their parts is used as an element in the new compound; only the more accurate knowledge of the language to be gathered from a complete dictionary could enlighten us on this point. It can also, no doubt, be taken for granted that usage will have circumscribed these abridgements within specific rules. We can see as much already from the fact that, in the examples given, the modified word always comes after the modifying one in the compound, as the final element. The procedure employed in this seeming mutilation of words might well deserve a milder judgement, therefore, and not be so damaging to the etymology as a superficial glance could lead one to fear. It is closely connected with the tendency, already cited above as distinctive of the American languages, to couple the pronoun with the verb and the noun in an abridged or still more divergent form. What has just been said of the Delaware tongue betrays an even more general endeavour towards combining several concepts in the same word. If we compare a number of those languages which indicate grammatical relations by particles, without inflection, we find that some of them, such as Burmese, the majority of South Sea Island dialects, and even Manchu and Mongolian, prefer to keep the particles apart from the words governed by them, whereas the American languages evince a tendency to conjoin them. The latter is already a natural outcome of the incorporative procedure described earlier (§17). I have depicted this in the foregoing as a limitation on sentence-formation,

---

[6] So, at least, I understand Heckewelder (*Transactions*, op. cit. [n.4] I, 411). *Ape* in any case, is merely an ending for 'being that walks upright', as *chum* is for 'quadrupeds'.

and explained it as due to the anxiety of the linguistic sense to bind the sentence-parts closely together, for purposes of comprehension.

At the same time, however, yet another aspect can be extracted from the Delaware method of word-making that we are considering here. The latter is obviously inclined to take the concepts associated in thought and present them to the mind all at once, and also coupled through the sound, instead of enumerating them one by one. It is a graphic treatment of language, closely connected with the pictorial handling of concepts that is elsewhere evinced in all the Delaware designations. The acorn is called *wu-nach-quim*, the nut of the leaf-hand (from *wumpach*, leaf, *nach*, hand, and *quim*, the nut), because the lively imagination of the people compares the indented leaves of the oak-tree to a hand. Again one should notice here the twofold compliance with the above-mentioned law in the placing of the elements, first in the last one, then in the first two, where again the hand, being formed, as it were, from a leaf, comes after this latter word, and not the other way round. It is manifestly of great importance, how much a language includes within a single word, instead of using several to circumscribe the idea. The good writer also exercises careful discrimination in this, where the language allows him a free choice. The correct balance that Greek observes in this respect is certainly one of its greatest beauties. What is combined into a single word is also presented as more of a unity to the mind, since the words in a language are what individuals are in reality. It arouses the imagination more vividly than what is enumerated piecemeal. Hence enclosure in a single word is more a matter for the imagination, and separation more the concern of the understanding. Both, indeed, can be opposed in this, and at least proceed in this respect according to their own laws, whose difference is betrayed here in language in a clear-cut example. Understanding demands of the word that it should evoke the concept in a complete and purely determinative way, but should also, at the same time, indicate within it the logical relation in which it figures in both language and speech. The Delaware language meets these requirements of the understanding only in its own fashion, which does not satisfy the higher linguistic sense. Conversely, it becomes the living symbol of the imagination that strings images together, and preserves in this respect a most individual beauty. In Sanscrit, too, the so-called indeclinable participles, which so often serve to express parenthetical clauses, contribute essentially to the vivid presentation of thought, whose parts they bring before the mind with a greater degree of simultaneity. But since these words designate grammatically, they combine the rigour of the understanding's demand with the free effusion of the imagination. This is their commendable aspect. For they also have an opposite side, if by clumsiness they put fetters on the freedom of sentence-making, and if their incorporative method suggests a defective variety of means for expanding the sentence in a suitable way.

It seems to me not unworthy of notice, that this boldly pictorial compounding of words should actually be typical of a *North-American* language, though I would not, however, care to draw any confident conclusions from this as to the character of these peoples, in contrast to those of South America, since for this purpose we would need to have more information about both groups, and their earlier history. It is certain nonetheless, that in the speech and behaviour of these North American tribes we perceive a greater elevation of mind and a bolder flight of imagination, than anything we have knowledge of in South America. Nature, climate, and the *hunting way of life* that is more typical of the peoples of this part of America, with the extensive forays through the loneliest forests that this entails, may likewise contribute to these traits. But if the facts are as stated, then undoubtedly the great *despotic régimes,* especially the concurrently *theocratic* government of Peru, with its suppression of free individual development, exerted a most damaging influence, since these hunting tribes always lived merely in free confederations, at least so far as we know. Even since their *conquest* by *Europeans,* the two races have undergone a different fate, and one of the most crucial character, in that very respect which is here under discussion. The foreign settlers along the North American coastline pushed back the native inhabitants, and no doubt deprived them of their possessions, even in unjust ways; but they did not subdue these peoples, since even their missionaries, imbued with the freer and milder spirit of protestantism, had no thought of imposing an oppressive monastic régime of the kind systematically introduced by the Spaniards and Portuguese.

Whether, in other respects, the rich *imagination*, whose visible traces are present in such languages as that of the Delawares, also harbours a sign that we find preserved in them a *more youthful* state of *language,* is a question difficult to answer, since we are too little able to separate what is due here to time, and what pertains to the mental tendency of the nation. I merely observe here, on this subject, that such compounding of words, of which in our present-day versions only single letters may often have remained behind, is also readily to be found even in the most beautiful and cultivated languages, since it lies in the nature of things to ascend upwards from the simple; and in the course of so many thousands of years, during which the language has been propagated in the mouth of peoples, the meanings of the primeval sounds have naturally been lost.

Chinese consigns grammatical work to the mind
Sanscrit consigns grammar to sound

Among all known languages the most violent contrast obtains between Chinese and Sanscrit, since the former consigns all *grammatical form* of the language to the *work of the mind*, whereas the latter seeks to incorporate it, even to the finest shadings, in the *sound*. Thus the difference of the two languages obviously lies in defective, and visibly luminous, *designation*. Apart from the use of a few particles, which, as will be seen below, it is again largely able to dispense with, Chinese marks all grammatical form, in the widest sense, by *position*, by a *word-usage* just fixed in one specific form, and by the connection of the sense – by means, that is, whose application calls for inner effort. Sanscrit, on the other hand, puts into the *sound* itself, not only the *sense* of the grammatical form, but also its more intellectual aspect, its *relationship* to material *meaning*.

On this showing, we ought at first sight to consider Chinese as departing the furthest from the natural demands of language, as being the *most imperfect* of all. But this attitude evaporates on closer inspection. Chinese, on the contrary, has a high degree of excellence, and exerts a powerful, albeit one-sided, *influence* on the *mental faculties*. One might, indeed, seek the reason for this in its *early scientific treatment* and abundant *literature*. But it is obviously, on the contrary, the language itself, as a challenge and an aid, which has contributed essentially to these advances in culture. In the first place, there is no contesting the great *consistency* of its *structure*. All the other uninflected languages, however much endeavour they display towards inflection, remain stuck on the way to it, without reaching their goal. Chinese, by abandoning this route entirely, carries its basic principle through to the end. And there the very nature of the means employed in it, for the understanding of everything formal, without the support of significant sounds, provided an impulse towards stricter attention to the various formal relationships, and a systematic method of ordering them. In the end, the difference between material *meaning* and formal *relation* automatically becomes all the clearer to the mind by this, in that the language, as the ear perceives it, contains only *materially significant sounds*, while the expression of formal relations attaches to the sounds only as a relationship in *position* and *subordination*. By this almost entirely *soundless designation* of formal *relations*, the Chinese language differs from all others that we know of, insofar as the general resemblance of all languages allows for difference within a single

230

[marginalia]: is Chinese the most imperfect language then? — no

[marginalia]: The drawbacks of the language have contributed to its cultural advances(?.)

[marginalia]: 'its consistent in its structure

[marginalia]: completely abandoned the notion of inflection

[marginalia]: almost soundless designation of formal relations

[marginalia]: containing only materially significant sounds

inner form. This is evidenced most clearly if we try to compel any one of its parts into the form of these other languages, as Abel Rémusat, one of the greatest of Chinese scholars, did in compiling a complete Chinese declension.[1] It is quite understandable that in every language there has to be a means of distinguishing the different relations of the noun. But they can by no means always be regarded, therefore, as cases in the true sense of the word. Chinese gains nothing whatever from such an approach. As Rémusat also very properly remarks in the same passage, its characteristic merit lies, on the contrary, in the system whereby it deviates from other languages, even if, precisely through this system, it also forgoes a variety of advantages, and lags, in any case, behind the Sanscrit and Semitic tongues as a language and instrument of the mind. But the want of any sound-designation of formal relations should not be taken by itself. We must simultaneously, and indeed principally, take account of the reaction which this deficiency necessarily exerts upon the mind, by compelling it to couple these relations in a subtler fashion with the words, and yet not actually to lodge them therein, but rather, in a true sense, to discover them there. However paradoxical it may sound, therefore, I consider it established nonetheless, that the seeming absence of all grammar in Chinese is precisely what enhances, in the national mind, the acuteness of the ability to recognize the formal linkage of speech; whereas, on the contrary, those languages which attempt, without success, to designate grammatical relationships, are liable, rather, to put the mind to sleep, and to cloud the grammatical sense by a mingling of the materially and formally meaningful.

The peculiar *structure of Chinese* must undoubtedly be due to the sound-idiosyncrasy of the people in earliest times, to the custom of keeping the syllables sharply distinct in pronunciation, and to a lack of that mobility whereby one tone acts upon another to alter it. For if the mental oddity of the inner linguistic form is to be explained, this sensuous idiosyncrasy must be made the reason for it, since every language can only proceed from the unlettered idiom of the people. If, through the questing and inventive temper of the nation, its sharp and active understanding, which took precedence over fancy, there now arose a philosophical and scientific *treatment of the language*, it could only take the road actually manifested in the *older style*, and adhere to the separation of tones as it existed in the mouth of the people, while fixing and carefully distinguishing everything demanded in the higher usage of the language for the luminous presentation of thought, albeit divested of the emphasis and gesture

[1] *Fundgruben des Orients.* III, p. 283.

that come to the aid of the understanding. But that such a treatment had already begun *very early* is historically demonstrated, and evident also in the unmistakeable though slender traces of pictorial representation in the *Chinese script*.

It can doubtless be maintained, in general, that once the mind begins to ascend to *scientific thinking*, and such a tendency enters into the treatment of language, a pictographic script simply cannot survive for long. Among the Chinese, this must have been doubly true. Like all other peoples, they would have been led to an *alphabetic script* by distinctions in the articulation of the sound. It is intelligible, however, that in their case the invention of writing did not follow this path. Since in the spoken language the tones were never intertwined, their individual designation was less called for. Just as the ear perceived monograms of sound, so the script was patterned upon these monograms. Starting out from pictography, without any approach to an alphabetic notation, an artistic, arbitrarily fashioned sign-system was created, not without interconnection of particular symbols, but always in a merely ideal sense, never a phonetic one. For since, in both nation and language, the propensities of the understanding took precedence over the pleasure in sound-change, these signs became indicators of *concepts* rather than *sounds*, except that a definite *word* still corresponds to each of them, since only in the word does the concept obtain its fulfilment.

In this way, across the whole area of language known to us, Chinese and Sanscrit represent two fixed *extremes*, unequal to each other in their aptness for mental development, but alike in internal consistency and complete execution of their systems. The Semitic languages cannot be regarded as lying in between them. In virtue of their decided tendency to inflection, they belong in the same class with Sanscrit. We can, however, consider *all other languages* to be located in between these two *end-points*, since they all must approximate either to the Chinese divestiture of words from their grammatical relations, or to the firm annexation of the sounds that designate such relations. Even incorporating languages, such as Mexican, are in this case, since incorporation cannot indicate all relationships, and where it does not suffice, these languages have to use particles, that are appended, or may remain separate. But beyond the negative properties, of not dispensing with all grammatical designation, and of possessing no inflection, these multifariously diversified languages have nothing in common with each other, and so can only be thrown quite indiscriminately into a single class.

So the question arises whether, in the *making of language* (not in the same family, but generally), there might not be an *ascent in stages* to an ever *more perfect* state. This question may be taken factually, from the actual genesis of language, as though in various epochs of mankind there have simply been successive creations of language at different levels, each presupposing and conditioning one another in their origin. In that case, Chinese would be the oldest language, and Sanscrit the youngest. For time could have preserved for us forms from different epochs. I have already argued sufficiently above – and it represents a major element in my view of language – that, considered merely from a conceptual viewpoint, there is no need for the more perfect to be also the later in time. Historically, nothing can be decided on this issue; but in one of the sections to follow, concerning the factual genesis and mixing of languages, I shall attempt to determine the point more precisely. Yet even without reference to what has actually taken place, we may ask whether those languages that lie in the middle are related to one another, by mere structure, as ascending stages of this sort, or whether their diversity does not permit us to apply so simple a yardstick to them. Now on one side the former does actually seem to be the case. If Burmese, for example, has real sound-designations, in the form of particles, for the majority of grammatical relations, but does not interlace them either with one another, or with the main words, by means of sound-changes, whereas the American languages, as I have shown, combine shortened elements, and confer upon the resulting words a certain phonetic unity, then the latter procedure does seem a closer approach to genuine inflection. But if, on comparing Burmese with true Malayan, we see in turn that the former certainly designates many more relations, whereas the latter adheres to the Chinese lack of designation, yet that Malayan, however, treats the syllables it does attach with careful attention, both to their own sound and to that of the main word, we may hesitate as to which of the two languages should be awarded the palm, though on judging in another way, it undoubtedly belongs to Malayan.

We see, therefore, that it would be one-sided to define linguistic stages in such a fashion, and by such criteria. And this is perfectly understandable. If the foregoing considerations have rightly recognized a single linguistic form as the sole regular one, the merit of it rests only on the fact that, by a happy coincidence of a rich and fine organ with lively energy of the linguistic sense, the whole of man's mental and physical endowment for language is completely and genuinely developed in the sound. A language-structure evolving under such favourable circumstances then appears to have sprung from a correct and energetic intuition of the relation of speech to thought, and of all parts of language to one another. The truly regular language-structure is possible, in fact, only where such an intuition, like a life-giving flame, runs gleaming through the formative process. Without a principle working outward from within, it remains unattainable by mechanical, gradually operating means. Yet even if such a favourable conjunction of circumstances does not everywhere occur, still, all peoples always have just one and the same tendency in their language-making. All desire the correct, the natural, and hence the highest. The language evolving in and about them produces this automatically, and without their aid, nor is it conceivable that a nation should as it were deliberately designate the material meaning alone, for example, but withhold the grammatical relations from designation by sound. To repeat here an observation already used earlier, man does not so much frame language, as discover it in himself, with a sort of joyous astonishment, in all its seemingly spontaneous developments; and since its creation is conditioned by the circumstances under which it makes its appearance, it does not everywhere attain the same goal, but feels itself inadequate before a boundary that is not of its own making. Yet the necessity, nevertheless, of always fulfilling its general purpose, impels it, in one way of another, beyond that boundary towards a configuration appropriate to this end. Hence arises the *concrete form* of the various languages of mankind; and so far as it deviates from a regular structure, this form, therefore, always contains at the same time a negative portion, indicating the boundary to creation, and a positive component which carries the incomplete achievement to the general goal. Now on the *negative* side we might well suppose an *ascent by stages*, depending on the degree to which the language's creative power had been adequate. But the *positive* aspect, containing the often very ingenious individual structure of even the more imperfect languages, is by no means always susceptible of being so simply defined. In that greater or lesser degrees of conformity and remoteness to the regular structure are here simultaneously present, we must often be content with a mere weighing of *merits* and *defects*. In this anomalous method (if I may so call it) of linguistic production, a particular *portion of the language* is often fashioned with a certain preference over the rest, and here, indeed, the characteristic feature of certain languages is frequently found to lie. But in that case, the true purity of the correct principle cannot, of course, find expression in any part. For that demands an equitable treatment of all parts, and if it could truly permeate any one of them, it would also spill over spontaneously to the rest. A want of true inner *consistency* is therefore a feature common to all these languages. Even Chinese is unable to achieve it perfectly, since it, too, in certain cases, though

want of inner consistency is characteristic of defective language structure

admittedly not many, has to help out the principle of word-order by using particles.

If the more imperfect languages lack the true *unity* of a single *principle,* irradiating them uniformly from within, it is still inherent in the procedure here outlined, that each, nonetheless, possesses a firm *connection,* and a *unity* resulting, not indeed always from the nature of language as such, but at least from their special indivi- duality. Without unity of form, no language would be conceivable at all; and as men speak, they necessarily gather up their speaking into such a unity. This happens with every inner or outer accession that the language receives. For in its inmost nature it constitutes a coherent web of analogies, in which the foreign element can hold firm only by attachment on its own account.

[margin handwritten note: even if there is no true unity of a single principle, there can be a unity of special individuality]

Our present observations show at once what a *variety* of different structure man's language-making is able to embrace, and lead us therefore to doubt the possibility of an exhaustive *classification* of languages. For specific *purposes,* and if particular phenomena in languages are adopted as the basis for division, such classification could well be carried out, but it gets into insoluble difficulties if, on more thorough investigation, the division is also to enter into the essential constitution of languages, and their inner connection with the mental individuality of nations. Even if the aforesaid general difficulties did not stand in the way, the establishment of any kind of complete system of their connection and differences would still be impossible in the present state of our linguistic knowledge. A not inconsiderable number of inquiries, such as have never yet been undertaken, would necessarily have to precede such a work. For correct insight into the nature of a language demands investigations far deeper and more persistent than the majority of languages have yet had devoted to them.

Yet even between unrelated languages, and on points most decidedly connected with the mental aspect, there are differences whereby a number of genuinely distinct *classes* seem to form. I have spoken above (§21) of the importance of giving to the *verb* a designation that formally characterizes its true function. Now in this particular there are differences between languages which seem otherwise, in the whole of their formation, to stand on the same level. It is natural that no original distinction between *noun* and *verb* should be established by the *particle languages,* as we might call those tongues which do indeed designate the grammatical relations by syllables or words, yet attach them but loosely and variably, or not at all. Even if they designate some individual categories of the noun, this happens only in relation to specific concepts, and in specific cases – not consistently, as a mode of grammatical segregation. It is therefore not uncommon in them for every word to be stamped without distinction as a verb, whereas every verb-inflection may equally well rank at the same time as a participle. Now languages which are alike in this respect may yet differ again, in that some do not furnish the verb with *any expression whatever* to characterize its peculiar function of conjoining the sentence, whereas others at least do this by means of the *pronouns* attached to it in abbreviated or modified form, preserving that distinction between pronoun and person of the verb which has already been frequently referred to above. The first procedure is followed by Burmese, for example, so far as I can tell at all accurately; by Siamese, Manchu and Mongolian, to the extent that they do not curtail the pronouns into affixes; by the South Sea Island languages; and largely also by the rest of the Malayan dialects of the western archipelago. The second course is taken by Mexican, the Delaware language, and other American tongues. In that Mexican attaches to the verb the governing and governed pronouns, sometimes in a concrete sense, sometimes in a general one, it really expresses in a cleverer way the unique function of the verb, by directing it towards the other main parts of the sentence. In the first of these two procedures, subject and predicate can only be conjoined by indicating the force of the verb through addition of the verb *to be*. But for the most part this is simply understood; what is called a verb, in languages that so operate, is merely a participle or verb-noun, and can be perfectly well used in this way, so long as verb-genus, tense and mood are expressed in it. But *mood*, for these languages, covers only those cases where the concepts of wishing, fearing, being able to, having to, etc. find application. The pure *subjunctive* is normally foreign to them. The uncertain and conditional positing it expresses, without addition of a material auxiliary concept, cannot be aptly designated in languages where simple positing of the actual finds no formal expression. This part of the so-called verb is then more or less carefully dealt with and fused into word-unity. But the difference here outlined is precisely a question of whether the verb is resolved into its *context*, or employed in its living *unity*. The former is more of a logically ordered procedure, the latter a sensuously pictorial one; and on immersing oneself in the peculiar character of these languages, it is possible to imagine what must go on in the mind of peoples for whom only the resolving process is typical. The other languages, such as those of regular construction, employ both methods, depending on difference of circumstances. Language, by its very nature, cannot forego a sensuously pictorial expression of the function of the verb, without incurring great disadvantages. And even in languages which suffer, as must be candidly admitted, from genuine absence of the true verb, the drawback is in fact diminished, in that for a good proportion of verbs their verb-like nature lies in the *meaning* itself, so that the deficiency of form is made up for in a material way. If it should happen, furthermore – as in Chinese – that words which could take on the functions of both noun and verb are marked out by *usage* for only one of these roles, or can indicate their significance by *emphasis*, then language has been still more restored to its rights, albeit in another way.

Of all the languages with which I am at all familiar, none is so utterly lacking in formal designation of the *function of the verb* as Burmese.[2] Carey, in his *Grammar*, expressly remarks that in Burmese verbs are hardly used in anything but participial forms, though he adds that this is sufficient to indicate every concept that needs expression by a verb. In another passage he denies that Burmese has any verbs at all.[3] But this peculiarity becomes quite easy to understand, once we view it in connection with the remaining structure of the language.

The Burmese *stem-words* do not undergo any change by the addition of *grammatical syllables*. The only *letter-changes* in the language are the conversion of the first aspirated letter into an unaspirated one, wherever an aspirated letter is reduplicated; and, in coupling two monosyllabic stem-words into a single word, or in repetition of that word, the transition of the mute initial consonant of the second into the sounded non-aspirate. In Tamil, also,[4] *k, t* (both lingual and dental) and *p* in the middle of words become *g, d* and *b*. The difference is merely that in Tamil the consonant remains mute if it occurs

[2] The name which the Burmans give to themselves is *Mranmâ*. But the word is commonly written *Mrammâ*, and pronounced *Byammâ* (Judson, s.v.). If it be permissible to explain this name directly from the meaning of its elements, it designates a *strong and hardy race of men*. For *mran* means *swift*, and *mâ* to be *hardy, healthy and robust*. From this indigenous word there have doubtless arisen the various current spellings for the people and the country, of which Barma and Barman are correct. When Carey and Judson write Burma and Burman, they are referring to the same sound inherent in the consonant, and merely designate this by a false method, now generally abandoned. *Cf.* also H. Berghaus, *Atlas of Asia*, Gotha 1832, Pt I, No. 8, Further India, p. 77, and J. Leyden, *Asiatick Researches*, x, p. 232.

[3] *A Grammar of the Burman Language*, Serampore 1814, p. 79 §1, p. 181. Especially also the Preface, pp. 8–9. The author of this grammar was Felix Carey, eldest son of William Carey, teacher of various Indian languages at the College in Fort William, to whom we are indebted for a series of grammars of Asian languages. Felix Carey died, unfortunately, as early as 1822 (*Journal Asiatique*, III, p. 59). His father followed him in 1834.

[4] R. Anderson: *Rudiments of Tamul Grammar*, London 1821, in the 'Table of the Alphabet'.

doubled in the middle of the word, whereas in Burmese the change also takes place if the first of the two stem-words ends with a consonant. Burmese therefore achieves in each case a greater word-unity through the greater liquidity of the added consonant.[5]

Apart from the pronouns and grammatical particles, the Burmese word-structure rests upon *monosyllabic stem-words* and the *compounds* formed from them. Of the *stem-words*, two classes can be distinguished. The first denote actions and properties, and relate therefore to a *variety of objects*. The second are names of *particular* objects, living

---

[5] In both languages, this change of *pronunciation* occasions no change of letter in the *script*, although Burmese, unlike Tamil, has signs for all sounded letters. It is common in Burmese for pronunciation to depart from the script. As to the most important of these deviations in the monosyllabic stem-words, where the written *kak*, for example, is pronounced *ket*, I have ventured the conjecture, in my letter to M. Jacquet on the *Polynesian Alphabets* (*Nouveau Journal Asiatique*, IX, p. 500), that the retention of a spelling different from the pronunciation has an etymological basis, and am still of this opinion today. For the situation seems to me this, that the pronunciation deviated gradually from the script, but that in order to keep the original pattern of the word recognizable, these deviations were not followed in the written word. Leyden seems to have had the same view on this point, since (in *Asiatick Researches*, x, p. 237) he attributes to the Burmese a pronunciation more gentle, less articulated, and less in keeping with the current orthography of the language than that of the Rukhéng, the inhabitants of Aracan (*Rariñ* in Judson). It lies, however, in the nature of the case that it cannot very well be otherwise. If *kak*, in the aforementioned example, had not actually been said earlier on, this ending would not be found in the script either. For it is an assured principle, and one sufficiently expounded of late by Herr Lepsius in his treatise on *Paleography as a Method of Philological Inquiry* (pp. 6, 7, 89), a work abounding in acute remarks and subtle observations, that nothing is represented in writing that was not at some time to be found in pronunciation. It is only the converse of this statement that I hold to be more than dubious, since there are examples not easily refutable, to show that writing, however perspicuous it may be, does not always exhibit the complete pronunciation. That in Burmese these sound-changes have arisen only by growing carelessness of pronunciation, is shown by Carey's express remark, that the endings of monosyllabic words which depart from the script are by no means purely uttered, but are pronounced in a very obscure manner, and one that can scarcely be distinguished aright by the ear. In such cases it is by no means uncommon for the palatal nasal sound to be totally omitted in pronunciation at the end of the words. Hence it comes about that the syllable written *thang*, which figures in a number of grammatical contexts, is said by Carey to be pronounced sometimes as *theen* (where the *ee* serves as a long *i*. Table following p. 20 [in Carey, op. cit.]), and sometimes as *thee* (p. 36 § 105), and by Hough, in his English-Burmese dictionary, to be normally sounded as *the* (p. 14), so that the curtailment seems to be now greater and now less. On another point, it can be proved historically that the script preserves the pronunciation of another, and presumably older, dialect. The verb *to be* is written *hri*, and pronounced *shi* by the Burmese. In Aracan, however, they say *hi*; and the ancestry of the people of this province is held to have been older and sooner civilized than that of the Burmese (Leyden, *op. cit*, x, pp. 222, 237).

creatures or inanimate things. Thus verb, adjective and substantive are in this case inherent in the meaning of the stem-words. The aforementioned difference of these words also resides merely in their *meaning*, not in their form; *ê*, to be cool or get cold, *kû*, to surround, combine or help, *mâ*, to be hard, strong or healthy, are formed no otherwise than *lê*, wind, *rê* (pronounced *yê*),[6] water, and *lû*, man. Carey has listed the *stem-words* denoting properties and actions in a special alphabetical index appended to his Grammar, and treated them just like the *roots* of Sanscrit. From one point of view, they are indeed comparable. For in their original form they belong to no single part of speech, and even in discourse appear only with the grammatical particles which confer their definition upon them there. A great many words are also derived from them, which already follows naturally from the type of concepts they designate. Yet on closer consideration, these stem-words are entirely different in kind from the Sanscrit roots, since the grammatical treatment of the whole language merely strings together stem-words and grammatical particles, does not create any fused word-wholes, and also, for that very reason, does not combine mere derivational syllables with stem-sounds. In this way the stem-words appear in speech, not as inseparable parts of combined word-forms, but actually in quite unaltered shape, and there is no need to extract them artificially from larger internally fused forms. Derivation from them is likewise no true derivation, but mere compounding. Finally, the substantives, for the most part, have nothing to distinguish them from stem-words, and are mostly not derivable from them. In Sanscrit, except in rare cases, the form of the nouns is at least distinct from that of the root, even if it may justly be deemed inadmissible to derive all nouns from the roots by means of *unâdi*-suffixes. The alleged *Burmese roots* therefore really behave in themselves like Chinese words, but when taken in

---

[6] According to Hough, that is; the *r* is sometimes pronounced as *r*, sometimes as *y*, and there seems to be no assured rule on this point. Klaproth (*Asia Polyglotta*, Paris 1823, p. 369) writes the word *jî*, in the French pronunciation, but does not give the source from which he has taken his Burmese words. Since the pronunciation often departs from the orthography, I write the Burmese words exactly according to the latter, so that every word I cite can be reconverted accurately into the Burmese characters, according to the explanation given at the outset of this work concerning the transliteration of the Burmese alphabet. I then give the pronunciation in parentheses, wherever it deviates and is definitely known to me. An H at such a point indicates that Hough supplies the pronunciation. Whether Klaproth, in *Asia Polyglotta*, is following the script or the pronunciation, is not clearly apparent. Thus on p. 375, he writes *la* for *tongue*, and *lek* for *hand*. But the first word is written *hlyâ* and pronounced *shyâ*, the second written *lak* and pronounced *let*. The word *ma*, which he gives for *tongue*, I do not find in my dictionaries at all.

conjunction with the rest of the language-structure, they do indeed betray a certain approximation to Sanscrit roots. Very often the supposed root – without any change at all – has additionally the meaning of a *substantive*, in which its specific verb-meaning emerges more or less clearly. Thus *mai* means *to be black, to threaten, to frighten* and the *indigo-plant; nê* means *to remain, to continue* and the *sun; pauñ*, for emphasis, *to add*, hence *to pledge*, and the *haunch* or *hind-leg* in animals. Only in one case do I find the grammatical category merely modified from the root, and designated, by a *derivational syllable*; at least this case alone seems to differ in appearance from the otherwise normal compounding. For substantives, and according to Hough (*Voc.*, p. 20) also adjectives, are formed from the root by the prefixing of an *a: a-châ*, food, nourishment, from *châ*, to eat; *a-myak* (*amyet* in Hough), anger, from *myak*, to be or become angry; *a-pan:*, a wearisome business, from *pan:*, to breathe with difficulty; *chang* (*chî*), to put in an unbroken line, and *a-chang*, order or method. But this preceding *a* is again dropped if the substantive figures as one of the final elements in a compound. However, as will later be seen with *ama*, this elimination also occurs in cases where the *a* is certainly no derivational syllable from a root. There are also substantives which, without alteration of meaning, sometimes have and sometimes dispense with this prefix. Thus the aforementioned *pauñ*, haunch, is also at times rendered *apauñ*. So this *a* cannot be equated with any true derivational syllable.

In compounds, sometimes two property or action words (Carey's roots) are combined, sometimes two nouns, and sometimes, lastly, a noun and one of these roots. The first case is often employed in place of a mood of the verb, e.g., the optative, by combining some verb-concept with *to wish*. However, two roots are also compounded merely to modify the sense, and in that case the latter of them sometimes adds scarcely a minor nuance; at times, indeed, the cause of the compounding cannot be guessed from the meaning of the individual roots. Thus *pan, pan-krâ:* and *pan-kwâ* mean to *request permission, to ask; krâ: (kyâ:)* means *to give and receive news*, but then also *to be separated; kwâ to separate*, and after prior combination, *to be divided*. In other compounds the composition is easier to explain; thus *prach-hmâ:* means *to sin against something, to overstep*, and *prach (prich)*, by itself, *to throw at something; hmâ:* is *to err, be on the wrong track*, and so, also by itself, *to sin*. Thus by means of the compounding a strengthening of the concept is attained here. Similar cases occur quite frequently in the language, and clearly show it to possess the peculiarity of very often forming, alongside a simple and therefore *monosyllabic root*, a *verb* composed of two roots, and hence *disyllabic*;

and this it does in such a way that the additional root either merely reiterates the concept of the other in a somewhat different fashion, or quite simply repeats it, or lastly, appends an entirely general concept.[7] I shall later on return to this phenomenon, which is important for language-structure. Some of these roots are never used singly, even when they are the first terms in a compound. An instance of this type is *tuñ·*, which always occurs only in conjunction with *wap* (*wet*), although both roots themselves carry the meaning of the compound, *to bow in respect*. One may also say, conversely, *wap-tuñ·*, though in a reinforced sense: *to creep upon the ground, to lie prostrate before superiors*. At times also roots are so used to form compounds, that only a part of their meaning is carried over to the composite, and no heed

---

[7] Carey's grammar does not single out this type of compound, and makes no special mention of it. But it appears automatically, if we go through the Burmese dictionary to check. Judson also seems to be pointing to this species of compounding when he remarks of *pañ* that this word is used only in compounds with words of similar meaning. To establish the fact precisely, I append here some further examples of such words:

chî: and *chî:-nañ:*, to ride or travel on something; *nañ:* (*neñ:*H) by itself: to tread on something.

tup (*tôk*. According to Carey, the *o* is pronounced as in English *yoke*, and according to Hough, as in English *go*) and *tup-kwa*, to kneel; *kwa* by itself: to be low.

nâ and *nâ-hkañ* (*nâ-gañ*), to listen, attend; *hkañ* by itself: to take, receive.

pañ (*peñ* H.) and *pañ-pan:*, to be tired, exhausted; *pan:* by itself means the same, as does *pañ-hrâ:*; *hrâ:* (*sha:*) by itself means to recede, but also to be present in small quantity.

rang(*yi*), to remember, concentrate on something, observe, reflect about something; *rang-hchauñ*, the same, with a still more definite meaning of aiming at something, of emphasizing a thing; *hchauñ* by itself: to carry, hold, complete; *rang-pê:* same as the foregoing; *pê:* by itself: to give.

hrâ(*shâ*), to seek, look after something; *hrâ-krañ* (*shâ-gyañ*), the same; *krañ* by itself: to think, consider, look into, intend.

kan and *kan-kwak*, to hinder, obstruct, thwart; *kwak* (*kwet*) by itself: to enclose in a circle, set bounds to.

chang (*chi*) and *chang-kâ:*, numerous, to be present in abundance; *kâ:* by itself: to expand, extend, scatter.

ram: (*ran*, the vowel as in English *pan*) and *ram:-hcha*, to guess at something, try, investigate; *hcha* by itself: to consider, be doubtful. *Taû*, by itself, and in combination with *hcha*, also means *to guess*, but is not used alone.

pa and *pa-tha*, to make offering or sacrifice to an evil spirit; *tha* by itself: to renew, restore, but also: to bring along, offer up.

In the above examples I have been careful always to compare only words equipped with the same accent. But if, perhaps, words of different accent may also stand in etymological combination – a point on which my sources are silent – then many more cases of this compounding would show up, and at times it would be possible to derive them from roots whose meanings correspond even better to the compound in question.

is given to the fact that the remaining portion is in conflict with the other term of the compound. Thus *hchwat*, to be very white, is also used, as Judson expressly remarks, as an intensive with words for other colours. How powerfully compounding affects the individual word can also be seen, finally, from Judson's observation on *hchauñ*, the word just alluded to, that at times it acquires 'a specific meaning' through the combination in which it stands.

Where nouns are coupled with roots, the latter generally follow the former: *lak-tat* (*let-tat* Hough), an artist or maker, from *lak* (*let* Hough), the hand, and *tat*, to be skilled at something, to understand it. These compounds therefore compare with those of Sanscrit, where as in धर्मविद् *dharmavid*, a root is appended as final term to a noun. But often in these compounds, even the very root is taken in the sense of an adjective, and then a composite arises only inasmuch as Burmese always considers an adjective coupled with its substantive to be one: *nwâ-kauñ*, cow good (i.e. to be good). A composite of this type in the properer sense of the word is *lû-chu*, a crowd of people, from *lû*, man, and *chu*, to collect. In the compounding of *nouns with one another*, there are cases where the one that serves as final term is so far removed from its original meaning as to become a suffix of general significance. Thus *ama*, wife, mother,[8] becomes shortened to *ma* by dropping the *a*, and then supplies to the first term of the compound the meaning of great, foremost, chief: *tak* (*tet*), the oar, but *tak-ma*, the main oar, the steering oar.

Between *noun* and *verb* in the language there is no original difference. Only in speech does it come to be defined, by the *particles* attached to the word; but the noun cannot be recognized, as it is in Sanscrit, by particular *derivational syllables*, and in Burmese the concept of a basic form, lying between the root and the inflected noun, is totally absent. At best there is an exception to this in the substantives formed by prefixing an *a*, of which mention has already been made. All grammatical formation of *substantives* and *adjectives* consists of palpable *compounding*, in which the second term adds a more general meaning to the concept of the first, whether the latter be a root or a noun. In the first case the roots give rise to nouns, in the second, several nouns are put together under one concept, as if under a class. It is evident that the last term of these compounds cannot properly be called an *affix*, although in Burmese grammar it always bears that name. The true affix shows, by the treatment of sound in the word-unit, that it displaces the meaningful part of the word into

---

[8] So Judson (under *ma*) explains the word *ama*. But to this word itself he assigns only the meaning *woman, older sister* or *sister* as such; *mother*, he says, is actually *ami*.

a specific category, without appending anything material to it. Where, as here, such a sound-treatment is absent, this displacement has not been symbolically translated into sound, and the speaker has first to impart it from the meaning of the supposed affix, or from the usage implied. This difference must certainly be kept in mind when evaluating the Burmese language as a whole. It expresses all or most of what can be indicated by inflection, but is everywhere lacking in that true symbolic expression, whereby form passes over into language, and again returns from thence into the soul. Hence in Carey's grammar, under the title of noun-formation, the most various cases are found in juxtaposition – derived nouns, purely compound ones, gerunds, participles, etc. – nor is it even possible, in truth, to fault this tabulation, since in all these cases words are conjoined under a single concept through a so-called affix, and – so far as the language has word-unity – into a single word as well. Nor can it be denied that the constantly recurring use of these compounds brings the final terms therein closer to true affixes in the speaker's mind, especially when, as is actually the case at times in Burmese, the so-called affixes either have no stateable meaning of their own, or possess one in independence that does not reappear under affixation, or does so only in a very remote way. As we see on perusing the dictionary, both cases occur in the language with some frequency, though they are not of the commonest either, and though the second of them cannot always be decided on with complete certainty, since the combinations of ideas can be so various. This tendency to compound the affixation is also evinced in the fact that, as already seen, a significant number of roots and nouns are never used independently outside the composite state, a situation that is also found in other languages, notably Sanscrit. A widely-used affix which always involves conversion of a root, and thus a verb, into a noun, is *hkyañ:*[9]. It elicits the abstract state-concept contained in the verb, the action conceived as a thing: *chê*, to send, *chê-hkyañ: (chê-gyeñ:)*, sending. As a self-subsistent verb, *hkyañ:* means to bore, transfix or penetrate, between which, and its sense as an affix, no connection whatever is discoverable. But unquestionably these contemporary concrete meanings are based upon general meanings that have been lost. All other noun-forming affixes, so far as I can discern, are of a more particular nature.

The treatment of the *adjective* is explicable solely through *compounding*, and quite obviously demonstrates how the language always has this method in view for grammatical formation. In and by itself,

---

[9] Carey, p. 144, §8, writes *hkrañ*, and gives the word no accent. I have followed Judson's spelling.

the adjective can be nothing but the root itself. It fulfils its grammatical nature only in combination with a *substantive*, or when postulated *absolutely*, where, like the nouns, it takes a prefixed *a*. In combining with a substantive it may either precede or follow, but in the former case must be attached by means of a connective particle (*thang* or *thau*). The reason for this difference is to be found, I believe, in the nature of the compounding. The second term of this must be of a more general nature, and be able to include the first within its larger scope. But in coupling an adjective with a substantive, the former has the larger scope, and therefore needs an addition suitable to its nature in order to attach itself to the substantive. These connective particles, to be more fully discussed below, fulfil this purpose; and now the combination does not so much mean *a good man*, for example, as *a good-being one*, or *a man who is good*, save that in Burmese these concepts (good, which, man) follow in reverse order. The supposed adjective is thereby treated entirely as a verb; for if, on the one hand, *kauñ:-thang-lû* means *the good man*, then the first two elements of the compound would mean, on their own, *he is good*. This appears more clearly still, in that, instead of a mere adjective, the substantive can be preceded, in precisely the same fashion, by a perfect verb that is actually furnished with the word it governs; *the bird flying in the air* is rendered in Burmese word-order: *air-space in to fly* (connective particle) *bird*. Where the adjective follows, the positioning of the concepts conforms to that of those compounds, where a root standing as final term, such as *possess, weigh, be worthy*, joins other words to form nouns modified by their meaning.

In *connected speech*, the mutual *relations* of words are indicated by *particles*. It is intelligible, therefore, that these should be different for *noun* and *verb*. Yet this is not even so in all cases, and noun and verb thereby tend to fall still further into one and the same category. The connective particle *thang* is at the same time the true *sign of the nominative*, and also forms the *indicative* of the verb. In the short phrase *ñâ-thang pru-thang*, I do, it occurs in both these functions, one hard upon the other. The use of the word is obviously founded upon a view that differs from the normal meaning of grammatical forms, and we shall examine this later on. But the same particle is said to be an ending for the *instrumental* case, and occurs thus in the following phrase: *lû-tat-thang hchauk-thang-im*, the house built by a skilled man. The first of these two words contains the compound of *man* and *skilled*, followed by the supposed sign for the instrumental. The second contains the root *to build*, here in the sense of *to be built*, prefixed as an adjective to the substantive *im* (*ieng* Hough), house, by means of the connective particle *thang*, in the manner previously described.

Now I am very much in doubt as to whether the concept of the instrumental is in fact originally present in the particle *thang*, or whether it was only later imported by grammatical opinion, since originally the first of these words contained merely the concept of the skilled man, and left it to the listener to supply, in thought, the relation in which this word was here put in front of the second word. *Thang* is also stated, in similar fashion, to be a *genitive sign*. If we collect together the large number of particles which allegedly give expression, as cases, to the relationships of the noun, it is plainly evident that *Pali grammarians*, to whom Burmese is generally indebted for its scientific arrangement and terminology, have been at pains to distribute these particles under the *eight cases* of Sanscrit and their own language, and thereby to form a declension. But strictly speaking, such a thing is alien to Burmese, which uses the so-called case-endings merely with an eye to the meaning of the particles and with no reference at all to the sound of the noun. A number are assigned to each case, but each gives expression, in turn, to particular nuances of the relational idea. Even Carey, having established his declension, lists a number of them separately afterwards. Some of these case-signs also have others annexed to them, sometimes in front and sometimes behind, to determine the sense of the relation more exactly. Moreover, they always follow the noun; and between it and them there stand, if present, the designations of *gender* and of the *plural*. The latter, like all case-signs, also serves with the pronoun, and there are no special pronouns for *we, you* and *they*. Thus the language distinguishes everything by significance, combines nothing by means of sound, and so visibly rejects the natural and original endeavour of the inner linguistic sense, to turn gender, number and case into unified sound-modifications of the materially meaningful word. Hence the original meaning of the case-signs can be demonstrated only in a few instances; even of the plural sign *tô·* (*do* Hough), we can do it only if, by ignoring the accent, we undertake to derive it from *tô:*, to increase or add to. The *personal pronouns* always appear in independent form only, and never serve, shortened or modified, as affixes.

The *verb*, if we consider merely the stem-word, can be recognized only through its material *meaning*. The *governing pronoun* invariably precedes, and shows that it does not belong to the form of the verb, by the very fact of its entire separation from the *verb-particles*, which always follow the stem-word. Such verb-forms as the language possesses depend exclusively on these particles, which indicate the plural, if applicable, the mood and the tense. Such a verb-form is the same for all three persons; and the simple view of the whole verb, or rather of sentence-formation, is therefore this, that the stem-word with its verb-form constitutes a *participle*, which combines with the independently existing subject by means of a mentally appended verb *to be*. The latter does, indeed, explicitly occur in the language as well, but seems to be seldom resorted to for normal expression of the verb.

Reverting now to the verb-form, the *expression for the plural* attaches directly to the stem-word, or to that part of it which is regarded as constituting one and the same whole with it. It is noteworthy, however – and this represents a means for recognizing the verb – that the plural sign for conjugation is entirely different from that for declension. The never-failing monosyllabic sign for the plural, *kra* (*kya*) is normally, though not always, followed immediately by a second, *kun*, related to *akun*, fully, completely;[10] and here, too, the language displays its double peculiarity, of designating grammatical relationship by compounding, and in so doing, of reinforcing the expression by addition of another term, even where one word would already be enough. And here, indeed, we have the not unremarkable case, that a word of known meaning is attached to one that has become an affix, its original meaning having been lost.

As has already been mentioned above, the *moods* depend largely on combining roots of *more general* meaning with concrete ones. Being directed thus to material significance only, they utterly transcend the logical range of this verb-form, and their number becomes to some extent indefinable. The tense-signs follow them, save for a few exceptions, in their attachment to the verb proper; but the plural sign is adjusted according to how firmly the root indicating the mood is considered to be coupled to the concrete term, as to which there seem to be two views prevailing in the people's linguistic sense. In a few cases the plural sign occurs between the two roots, but for the most part it follows the last of them. It is obvious that the mood-indicating roots are accompanied more in the first case by a dim feeling of grammatical form, whereas in the second, both roots, in the union of their meanings, are taken in effect to be one and the same stem-word. Under the heading of what is here called mood by combining of roots, we find forms of quite different grammatical meaning, such as the *causal verbs*, which are constructed by addition of the root *to send, order* or *command*, and verbs whose meaning is modified in other languages by *inseparable prepositions*.

Among *tense-particles*, Carey gives five for the present, three for both present and preterite, two belonging exclusively to the latter, and then several for the future. He calls the verb-inflections so constructed forms of the verb, though without giving the difference in usage of

[10] Hough writes *a-kun:*. The meaning of this word comes from that implicit in the verb *kun*, to come to an end, which is used, however, of exhaustion.

those that designate the same tense. That a distinction is nonetheless made between them, is evident from his passing remark that two of those he alludes to have but little variance in meaning, one from another. Judson notes of *thê:* that it indicates that the act has not yet ceased to go on at the present moment. But apart from those cited, there are also others, such as one for the whole completed past. Now strictly these tense-signs belong to the *indicative*, to the extent that, in and by themselves, they indicate no other mood; but some of them also serve in fact to designate the imperative, though this likewise has particles of its very own, or is indicated by the bare root. Judson calls some of these particles merely euphonic, or expletive. If traced in the dictionary, the majority prove at the same time to be genuine roots, albeit in a meaning that has no kinship whatever, or only a distant one; and so here, too, the language employs the practice of meaningful compounding. As the language intends it, these particles obviously comprise a single word with the root, and the whole form must be regarded as a composite. But this unity is not indicated by letter-change, except that in the aforementioned cases the mute letters are converted, in pronunciation, to their unaspirated voiced equivalents. This, too, is not expressly noted by Carey; but it seems to follow from the generality of his rule, and from the orthography of Hough, who employs this conversion for all words used as particles in this fashion, and writes *byî:*, for example, when giving the pronunciation of *prî:*, the sign for the completed past. In the future of the causal verbs, I even find a contraction of the vowels of two such monosyllables that actually occurs in the written language. The causal sign *chê* (the root *to command*), and the particle *an·* of the future, become *chim·*[11]. The same thing seems to happen with the compound future particle *lim·-mang*, where the particle *lê* has been contracted with *an·* into *lim·*, and another future particle, *mang*, is then appended. The language may yet exhibit other such cases, but they cannot possibly be frequent, since otherwise we should necessarily have been bound to meet them more often. The verb-forms here depicted can again be declined by the addition of *case-signs*, which are either attached directly to the root, or to the accompanying particle. Now although this conforms to the nature of the gerunds and participles in other languages, we shall see further on, however, that Burmese continues to treat verbs and verb-clauses as nouns, in a manner quite peculiar to itself.

From the mood and tense particles here referred to, we must distinguish another which exerts a most essential influence on the

[11] Carey, p. 116, §112. Judson, under *chim·*.

creation of verb-forms, but also belongs to the *noun*, and plays an important part in the grammar of the whole language. It will already be gleaned from the foregoing that I refer to the word *thang*, which was mentioned earlier as a nominative sign. Carey, too, has felt this difference. For though he cites *thang* as forming the first of the present tense forms of the verb, he still invariably treats it quite separately, under the name of a 'connective increment'. Unlike the other particles, *thang* does not append a modification to the verb,[12] being actually inessential to its meaning; but it shows in what grammatical sense we are to take the word it is annexed to, and delimits – if we may so express it – its grammatical forms. With respect to the verb it belongs, therefore, not to the meaningful words, but to those that guide the understanding in coupling together the elements of speech, and conforms entirely to the notion of what in Chinese are called empty or hollow words. Where *thang* accompanies the verb, it is either positioned directly after the root, if no other particle is present, or else it follows the particles that are so situated. In both positions it can be inflected by attachment of case-signs. But here we find the remarkable difference, that in declining the noun, *thang* is merely the nominative sign, and no longer appears when the other cases are attached, but yet retains its position in declining the participle (for here, indeed, that is all we can take the verb to be). This seems to show that in the latter case its function is to indicate the linkage of the particles with the root, and thus the delimitation of the participial form. It finds its regular usage only in the *indicative*. From the subjunctive it is wholly excluded, as also from the imperative; and in certain other particular constructions it also drops away. According to Carey, it serves to link the participial forms with a following word, which agrees with my contention, insofar as it constitutes a delimitation of these forms from those that follow them. If we take all this together, and couple it with the usage of the word in connection with the noun, we soon feel that it cannot be explained by the theory of the parts of speech, and that, as with the Chinese particles, we have to go back to the word's original meaning. Now in that sense it expresses the idea of *this* or *thus*, and is in fact called a demonstrative pronoun and adverb by Carey and Judson (who merely fail to connect this meaning with the use of the word as a particle). In both functions it forms a number of compounds, as the first term thereof. In the coupling of verb-roots, indeed, where one, of more general meaning, modifies the sense of the others, Carey cites

---

[12] Carey expressly states this at several points in his grammar. Pp. 96, §34, 110, §92, 93. But how far he is justified in his still more comprehensive claim, that the word has no meaning at all of its own, we shall see in a moment.

thang in a sense related to its adverbial meaning: *to correspond* or *agree* (hence *to be like*), but he has not included it in his list of roots, and unfortunately gives no example, either, of this meaning.[13] Now in this sense it seems to me to be used as a means of guiding the understanding. In that the speaker is emphasizing certain words, which he wants to have taken in close association, or is particularly stressing the substantives and verbs, he follows them up with a *this!* *thus!*, and turns the listener's attention to what he has said, in order now to couple it further with what follows, or also, if *thang* is the last word of the sentence, to round off the completed utterance. Carey's account of *thang*, as a particle uniting a preceding with a subsequent phrase, does not fit this case, and this may be why he says that the root or verb-form coupled with *thang* has the force of a verb, when it is located at the end of the sentence.[14] In mid-discourse, the verb-form coupled with *thang* is in Carey's view a participle, or at least a construction in which the true verb is recognizable only with difficulty, whereas at the end of a sentence it is a genuine inflected verb. This distinction strikes me as unfounded. Even at the end of a sentence, the form under discussion is merely a participle, or – to speak more accurately – a form merely modified in the likeness of a participle. In both positions the true *force of a verb* must always be mentally supplied.

But to really express this, the language has yet another method; though neither Carey nor Judson provides a perfect elucidation of its true nature, it does in fact have much resemblance to the force of an appended auxiliary verb. For if it is truly desired to end a sentence with a genuinely inflected verb, and to sever all connection with what follows, the word *êng* (*î* Hough) is put after the root or verb-form, in place of *thang*. All misunderstanding that might arise from the connective nature of *thang* is thereby prevented, and the series of successively linked participles really brought to an end; *pru-êng* now really means *I do*, no longer *I am doing; pru-prî:-êng, I have done*, not *I have been doing*. Neither Carey nor Judson gives the proper meaning of this little word. The latter merely says that it is 'equivalent' to *hri* (*shi*), to be. But it then seems strange that it should be used for conjugating that very verb itself.[15] According to Carey and Hough it is also a case sign for the *genitive: lû-êng*, of the man. Judson does not record this meaning.[16] But as Carey tells us, this

---

[13] p. 115, §110. The other passages for comparison are pp. 67; 74, §75; 162, §4; 169, §24; 170, §25; 173.

[14] p. 96, §34.

[15] Cf. in St John's Gospel, 21.2, *hri-kra-êng* (*shi-gya-î*), they are or were.

[16] Carey, pp. 79, §1; 96, §37; 44; 46. Hough, p. 14. Judson, under *êng*.

terminal sign is rarely used in conversation, and even in writing is found chiefly in translations from Pali; a difference attributable to the tendency of Burmese to hang the clauses of speech one upon another, and to the regular sentence-structure of a daughter-language of Sanscrit. Another and better reason why it should be precisely translations from Pali that are fond of this auxiliary word is to be found, I think, in the fact that Pali combines participles with the verb *to be*, in order to indicate a number of tenses, and then always causes the auxiliary verb to follow, with a sound-change.[17] The Burmese translators, sticking close to the words, might have looked for an equivalent to this auxiliary verb, and chosen *êng* for the purpose. But the word is nonetheless a genuinely Burmese one, not a borrowing from Pali. A true rendering of the Pali auxiliary form was in any case impossible, in that the Burmese verb includes no designation of the persons. It is an oddity of the language, that this terminal word can be used after all other verb-forms, but not those of the future. The Pali construction referred to seems primarily to occur in past tenses. But the reason can hardly lie in the nature of the future particles, since they accept *thang* without difficulty. Carey, who gives praise-worthy attention to the distinction between participial forms and the inflected verb, remarks that the imperative and interrogative forms of the verb are the only ones in the language to have any appearance of this latter part of speech.[18] But this seeming exception also lies merely in the fact that the forms alluded to cannot be coupled to case-signs which would not combine with the particles peculiar to such forms. For these particles close the form, and in the interrogative verbs the connective *thang* comes before them, to couple those very verbs to the tense-particles.

The connective particle *thau* is very similar in nature to the *thang* we have just been considering. But since my purpose here is merely to outline the character of the language as a whole, I pass over their particular points of agreement and difference. There are still other connective particles which are likewise attached to the verb-form, without adding anything to the sense, and which then usurp the place of *thang* and *thau*. But some of them are also used, on other occasions, to designate the subjunctive, and only the context of utterance betrays their function at any time.

The sequence of the *parts of the sentence* is such that the subject comes first, then the object, and lastly the verb: 'God the earth created'; 'the king to his general spoke'; 'he to me gave'. The place of the *verb* in this construction is obviously not the natural one, since in the

---

[17] E. Burnouf and C. Lassen: *Essai sur le Pali*, pp. 136, 137.

[18] p. 109, §88.

sequence of ideas this part of speech is interposed between subject and object. But in Burmese the explanation for it is that the verb is properly a mere participle, which expects its terminating clause only later, and also contains within it a particle whose function is to connect with something that follows. Now without giving form to the sentence like a real verb, this verb-form includes within it everything that has gone before, and carries it over into the sequel. Carey observes that by means of these forms the language is able, to any extent it pleases, to *weave* sentences into one another without reaching a conclusion, and adds that in all purely Burmese works this is very largely the case. Now the further it defers the keystone of a whole argument conducted in interlinked sentences, the more careful the language must be, always to round off the individual sentences with each subordinated end-word. To this form it remains faithful throughout, and always makes the determining term precede what is to be determined. It therefore does not say: 'The fish is in the water', 'The herdsman goes with the cows', 'I eat rice cooked with butter', but: 'In the water the fish is', 'With the cows the herdsman goes', 'I with rice cooked butter eat.' In this way, at the end of each intermediate sentence, there is always a word which can expect no further determination after it. On the contrary, the broader determination regularly precedes the narrower one. This becomes particularly clear in translations from other languages. Where the English Bible says, in St John's Gospel, 21.2: *and Nathanael of Cana in Galilee*, the Burmese translation turns the phrase around and says: 'Galilee of the district Cana of the town citizen Nathanael'.

Another method of coupling many sentences together, is to transform them into parts of a *composite*, where each individual sentence forms an adjective that precedes the substantive. In the locution: 'I praise God, who has created all things, who is free of sin...' etc., each of these sentences, however numerous they are, is coupled to the substantive by the word *thau* (already noted earlier in this role), though it only follows after the last of them. These individual relative clauses therefore precede the substantive that follows them, and are regarded as forming a compound word with it; the verb (I praise) concludes the sentence. But as an aid to understanding, the Burmese script divides each individual element of this long composite by its inter-punctuation sign. The regularity of this positioning actually makes it easy to follow the structure of the period, for one merely has to progress, in sentences of the kind described, from the end towards the beginning. Only in listening must attention be laboriously strained, before it finds out to whom the endless foregoing predicates are supposed to refer. But everyday discourse presumably avoids such a large number of serried phrases linked to one another.

It is by no means typical of Burmese *construction* to order the individual *parts of the periods* in proper separation, so that the governed clause follows the governing one. The attempt, rather, is always to absorb the former into the latter, where it must then of course come first. In this way, whole clauses are there treated like individual *nouns*. To say, for example: 'I have heard that you have sold your books', the language turns the phrase around, makes *your books* come first, has the perfect of the verb *to sell* follow afterwards, and now adds to this the accusative sign, to which *I have heard* is finally appended in turn.

If the present attempt at an analysis has succeeded in discovering the true path on which Burmese endeavours to gather up thought into speech, we see that on the one hand it is by no means totally devoid of *grammatical forms*, though on the other it does not manage to give *shape* to them. To that extent it truly falls midway between types of language-structure. Its original word-construction already hampers it in arriving at truly grammatical forms, since it is one of the *monosyllabic languages* of the peoples dwelling between China and India. This peculiarity of word-formation does not, indeed, produce on the deeper structure of these languages the precise effect of enclosing every concept in single, tightly-coupled sounds. Yet since, in these languages, the monosyllabic character does not arise by chance, in that the organs cling to it deliberately and by virtue of their individual tendency, it comes to be linked with the individual enunciation of each *syllable*, which then of course extends to the inmost depths of the language-structure, owing to the impossibility of blending *suffixes*, indicating relational concepts, with the materially meaningful words. The Indo-Chinese nations, says Leyden,[19] have adopted a multitude of Pali words, but adapt them all to their own peculiar pronunciation, in that they emit every individual syllable as a specific word. So this feature must be considered, as with Chinese, to be a characteristic idiosyncrasy of these languages, and kept firmly in mind when examining their structure, if not actually treated as basic – since all language sets out from sound. A second feature, far less typical of other languages, is coupled with it, namely the diversification and increase of lexical abundance by the various *accents* accorded to the words. The Chinese accents are well-known; but some Indo-Chinese languages, notably Siamese and Annamese, have such a large multitude of them that it is well-nigh impossible

[19] *Asiatick Researches*, x, 222.

for our ear to distinguish them aright. Speech is thereby transformed into a sort of singing or recitative, and Low considers the Siamese version of it perfectly comparable to a musical scale.[20] These accents give occasion, at the same time, to still larger and more numerous dialectal differences than do the true letters; and we are assured that in Annam every notable locality has its own dialect, and that neighbouring communities, to understand one another, must at times have recourse to the written language.[21] Burmese possesses two such accents, the long and gentle one, designated in the Burmese script by a colon at the end of the word, and the short curtailed one, indicated by a dot set below [or after] the word. If we add to this the accentless pronunciation, then the same word can be found in the language in *three* forms, each with a more or less different meaning: *pô*, to halt, to pour on, to overfill, a long oval basket; *pô:*, to fasten or bind together, to hang up, an insect or worm; *pô·*, to carry or fetch, to teach or instruct, to offer (a wish or blessing), to be thrown into or on to something; *ñâ*, I; *ñâ:*, five, a fish. But not every word is capable of this varied accentuation. Some final vowels take neither of the two accents, others only one of them, and they can always attach only to words that end with a vowel or nasal consonant. The latter clearly shows them to be modifications of the vowels, and inseparably connected to them. When two Burmese monosyllables come together as a compound, the first does not lose its accent on that account, from which it may well be inferred that even in compounds, pronunciation keeps the syllables apart as if they were distinct words. These accents are customarily attributed to the need for monosyllabic languages to increase the numbers of possible sound-combinations. But so deliberate a procedure is hardly conceivable. It seems, on the contrary, far more natural to suppose that these manifold modifications of pronunciation were rooted first and foremost in the organs and sound-habits of the peoples, that in order to enunciate them clearly the syllables were doled out singly and with small pauses to the ear, and that this very habit offered no inducement to the formation of polysyllabic words.

Hence, even without postulating any historical relationship between them, the monosyllabic languages of Indo-China have, by their very nature, a number of properties in common, both with one another and with Chinese. I confine myself here, however, to Burmese alone, since for the others I have at my disposal no manuals that would furnish sufficient data for investigations such as the

---

[20] *A Grammar of the Thai or Siamese Language*, pp. 12–19.
[21] *Asiatick Researches*, x, 270.

present.[22] Of Burmese we must first of all acknowledge that it never *modifies the sound* of the stem-words to express their *relationships*, and does not make the grammatical categories a basis for its *construction of speech*. For we have seen above that it does not originally distinguish such categories by words, that it assigns the same word to several of them, mistakes the nature of the verb, and even uses a particle simultaneously with both verb and noun, in such a way that only the meaning of the word, and where even this is not enough, the context of utterance, allows us to determine which of the two categories is intended. The principle of its speech-construction is to indicate which word in discourse determines the other. In this it concurs entirely with Chinese.[23] Just to bring this about, it resembles Chinese in having among its particles one that is designed solely to order the construction, and which simultaneously separates and combines, with the same object in view; for the similarity, in this use in the construction, between *thang* and the Chinese *tchi*, is too striking to be overlooked.[24] Burmese, on the other hand, again departs very significantly from Chinese, alike in the sense in which it takes the *determining*, and in the means for indicating it. For the determining here alluded to covers two cases, which it is most essential to distinguish carefully from one another: the *government* of one word by another, and the *completion* of a concept that has remained undetermined in certain respects. The word must be delimited qualitatively, in its scope and nature, and relatively, in terms of its causality, as dependent on the other or itself in control thereof.[25] Chinese, in its construction, distinguishes the two cases exactly, and employs each of them *where* it truly belongs. It puts the governing word before the governed, the subject before the verb, the verb before its direct object, and the direct before the indirect object, if there is one. It cannot

[22] J. Low provides, indeed, some very important information on Siamese, which becomes incomparably more instructive when taken in conjunction with Burnouf's excellent review of his work in *Nouveau Journal Asiatique*, IV, 210. Yet on most parts of the grammar he is too brief, and too much content to give mere examples, instead of rules, without even analysing these examples in a proper way. On Annamese, I have before me only Leyden's valuable discussion (*Asiatick Researches*, x, 158), inadequate though it is for the present position of linguistic studies.

[23] My *Letter to Abel Rémusat*, p. 31.

[24] *Ibid.*, pp. 31–34.

[25] In my letter to Abel Rémusat (pp. 41, 42), I have designated the case of completion as the limitation of a concept of wider to one of lesser scope. But both expressions refer here to the same thing. For the adjective completes the concept of the substantive, and is limited in its use at any time from its broad meaning to a single case. So it is also, with the adverb and the verb. With the genitive, the situation seems less clear. Yet here, too, the words contraposed in this relation are regarded as restricted, from the many relations possible among them, to one particular case.

properly be said here that the preceding word contains the completion of the concept; rather, the verb is completed in its concept by both subject and object on either side of it, and the direct object likewise, by the indirect. The language, on the other hand, always puts the completing word before what is still undetermined by the concept thereof, the adjective before the substantive, the adverb before the verb, the genitive before the nominative, and thereby follows a practice somewhat opposed to that which has just been outlined. For this still undetermined word, which here comes second, is in fact the governing one, and on the analogy of the previous case, it ought, as such, to precede. Thus the Chinese construction rests upon two great general laws, which are, however, intrinsically different, and it obviously does well to single out the relation of the verb to its object by means of a special position, since the verb is the governing factor in a sense far more important than that of any other word in the sentence. The first law it applies to the *main articulation of the sentence*, the second, to its *subordinate parts*. Had it framed the latter on the model of the former, so as to have adjective, adverb and genitive following the substantive, verb and nominative, then the harmony of sentence-structure, which arises from the very contrast we have here been expounding, would assuredly have suffered, nor would the placing of the adverb after the verb have allowed it to be clearly distinguished from the object; though no harm would have been done to the mere ordering of the sentence itself, to the conformity of its course with the inner sequence of the linguistic sense. The essential thing was to pin down the concept of *governing* correctly; and to this the Chinese construction adheres, with the few exceptions which in all languages give more or less justification for departures from the normal rule of word-order. Burmese makes next to no distinction between these two cases, retains in fact one *law of construction* only, and neglects, indeed, the more important of the two. It simply has the subject preceding the object and verb, while the latter is made to follow the object. This inversion makes it more than doubtful whether the precedence accorded to the subject is intended to present it as actually governing, and does not regard it, rather, as a completion of the subsequent parts of the sentence. The governed object is obviously viewed as a completive determination of the verb, which, being in itself undetermined, follows after the complete enumeration of all determinations by its subject and object, and concludes the sentence. That subject and object each in turn attach ahead of themselves the bye-determinations that complete them, is both self-explanatory, and is evident from the examples cited above.

This difference between the Burmese and Chinese *constructions* is obviously due to the correct view of the *verb* that prevails in Chinese, and the defective notion of it in Burmese. The Chinese construction betrays a feeling for the true and characteristic function of the verb. This finds expression in the fact that Chinese puts the verb in the middle of the sentence, between subject and object, that the verb dominates the sentence, and is the soul of the entire speech-pattern. Even in the absence of sound-modifications to the verb, the language imparts to the sentence, by mere position, the life and movement that proceed from the verb, and demonstrates the actual positing of the linguistic sense, or at least betrays the inner feeling of this. In Burmese, the whole situation is utterly different. The *verb-forms* vacillate between inflected *verb* and *participle*, are properly the latter in a material sense, and cannot attain to a formal one, since the language possesses no form for the verb itself. Not only does its essential function find no expression in the language; the peculiar formation of the so-called verb-forms, and their obvious affinity to the noun, give evidence that the speakers themselves are in no way vitally imbued with feeling for the true force of the verb. If we recall, on the other hand, that Burmese makes such incomparably greater use than Chinese of *particles* to characterize the verb and distinguish it from the noun, it will seem all the more remarkable that it nonetheless evicts the verb from its true category. But not only is this undeniably the case; it also makes it easier to explain the fact that the language should designate the verb merely by modifications which can also be taken materially, without betraying even a suspicion of the purely formal element in the verb itself. Chinese seldom employs this material indication, and often refrains from it entirely, but recognizes, in the correct placing of words, a form that adheres invisibly to speech. One might say that the less it possesses of an outer grammar, the more it is possessed by an inner one. Where a grammatical conception takes hold there, it is the logically correct one. This conception imparted its first ordering into the language, and was bound, by the use of so rightly tuned an instrument, to take root in the mind of the people. It might be objected to the view just put forward here, that even the inflected languages by no means uncommonly place the verb after its object, and that Burmese, as we know, preserves, as they do, the case of the noun by means of specific particles. But since on many other points the language shows clearly that it relies upon no clear idea of the parts of speech, but merely pursues in its reconstructions the modifications of words by one another, it cannot in fact be acquitted of such a mistaken view of the true nature of *sentence-formation*. It evinces this also by the inflexible way in which it always relegates its supposed verb to the end of the sentence. This is all the more clearly apparent, when it also becomes plain from the second reason for this positioning, already stated above, namely to enable another new sentence to be attached to the verb-form, that the language is imbued neither with the true nature of *period-structure*, nor with the power of the verb at work in it. It has a manifest lack of *particles* which, like our conjunctions, give life and variety to sentences by the intertwining of clauses. Far superior in this respect is Chinese, which also observes here its general law of word-order, in that, as with genitive and nominative, it likewise makes the more closely determinative and completive clause precede the one that it modifies. In Burmese the clauses run one after another, as it were, in a straight line. But even so they are seldom given a sequential arrangement by coupling conjunctions which, like our own *and*, preserve the independence of each. They conjoin in a way that does more to weave together the material content. This is already implicit in the particle *thang*, which is normally used at the end of each of these on-running clauses, and which, by summarizing what has gone before, invariably applies it at once to the understanding of what comes next. It is evident that the outcome of this must be a certain clumsiness, in which, moreover, a tedious uniformity seems to be inevitable.

In their methods for indicating *word-sequence*, the two languages agree to this extent, that they both make use of *position* and special *particles*. Burmese would not actually need such rigid laws for the former, since a large number of particles indicating relationships is sufficient to ensure understanding. Yet it is even more conscientious in adhering to placements that have once been established, and on one point only is not so consistent in arranging them, in that it allows the *adjective* to be put either before or after the *substantive*. But since the first of these placements always calls for the addition of a particle needed to determine the word-sequence, we see from thence that the second is regarded as the truly natural one; and this, no doubt, must be put down to the fact that adjective and substantive together form a *compound*, in which the case-inflection that is never supplied when the adjective precedes must be considered to belong only to the substantive, modified in its meaning by the adjective. Now in its *composites*, both of nouns and verbs, the language normally sets the word that serves it each time as species-concept to precede in the first component, while the specifying, more general term (insofar as it can find application to several species) follows in the second. In this way it forms moods of the verb, creates, with the word *fish* preceding, a large number of fish-names, etc. When in other cases it seems to take the opposite route, forming words for craftsmen with the general word *to make*, standing as second term behind the names of their tools, we remain doubtful whether it is really following another method in doing so, or merely taking a different view of what counts, on each occasion, as a species-concept. In coupling the following adjective, it likewise now treats the latter as qualifying a species-concept. Here, too, Chinese remains faithful to its general law; the word to which a more special determination is to accrue forms the last term, even in the compound. When the verb *to see* is used, in what is admittedly an intrinsically less natural fashion, to form, or rather to replace, the passive, it precedes the main concept: *see kill*, i.e. to be killed. Since so many things can be seen, *to kill* should really have come first. But the reverse positioning shows that *to see* has to be considered here as a modification of the following word, and thus as a state of *kill*; and hence, in what seems at first sight a curious idiom, the grammatical relationship is indicated in an intelligently precise way. *Husbandman, book house*, etc. are formed in a similar manner.

The Burmese and Chinese languages are alike in resorting to *particles* for the articulation of word-order. They also resemble one another in assigning some of these particles purely to indication of the construction, in such a way as to add nothing to the material meaning. But it is precisely in these particles that we find the turning-point at which Burmese abandons the character of Chinese and takes on one of its own. The anxiety to designate, by mediating concepts, the relation in which one word is to be taken along with another, increases the number of these particles, and produces in them a certain completeness, albeit not a wholly systematic one. But the language also evinces an endeavour to bring these particles into closer proximity to the stem-word than to the other words in the sentence. Yet given the syllable-dividing pronunciation, and the whole spirit of the language, true word-unity cannot in fact occur. We have seen, however, that in some cases the effect of a word is to bring about a consonantal change in the one immediately appended to it; and in the verb-forms the terminating particles *thang* and *êng* fuse the verb-particles into a whole with the stem-word. In one particular case there is even a merging of two syllables into one, a thing that already in the Chinese script could be rendered phonetically only, that is, in a foreign way. A feeling for the true nature of the suffixes is also inherent in the fact that even those members of this particle-group which could be regarded, like the plural signs, as determining adjectives, are never found preceding the stem-word, but always following it. In Chinese it is sometimes the one position that is customary, and sometimes the other, depending on differences among the plural particles.

To the extent that Burmese departs from the Chinese structure, it approaches that of Sanscrit. But it would be superfluous to depict in further detail what a true chasm again divides it from the latter. The difference here does not consist merely in the more or less close attachment of the *particles* to the main word. It emerges quite especially from a comparison of these to the *suffixes* of the Indian language. The former are just as much *significant words* as all others in the language, even if the meaning has admittedly been largely erased already in the memory of the people. The latter, for the most part, are *subjective sounds*, appropriate to relations, albeit of a merely internal kind. The Burmese language in general, even if it does seem to stand in the middle between the two others, can never be regarded as a crossing-point from one to the other. The life of each language rests upon the inner intuition of the people concerning the method of clothing thoughts in sound. But this differs entirely in the three language-families under comparison here. Even though the number of *particles*, and the frequency of their use, may betray a gradually ascending approach to *grammatical indication*, from old-style Chinese, through modern, up to Burmese, still, the latter of these languages is quite unlike the first in its basic intuition, which even in modern Chinese remains essentially the same. Chinese relies solely on *word-order*, and on the imprint of *grammatical form* within the mind. Burmese, in its construction, does not depend on word-order, though it clings even more firmly to what is apt to its mode of thought. It relates *concepts* by the addition of *new* ones, and is itself necessarily led to this by its own method of positioning, which is liable to ambiguity in the absence of such aid. Since the mediating concepts are perforce expressive of *grammatical forms*, the latter do indeed also figure in the language. But the intuition of them is less clear and distinct than it is in Chinese and Sanscrit; less so than in the former, because it possesses those very supports, in the way of mediating concepts, which diminish the need for true concentration of the linguistic sense; less so than in Sanscrit, because it does not have command of the sounds in the language, does not push on to the creation of genuine word-unity and authentic forms. But nor, on the other hand, can we reckon Burmese among the agglutinating languages, since, on the contrary, it assiduously keeps the syllables apart in pronouncing them. It is purer and more consistent in its system than languages of that type, even if it also, for that very reason, is still less prone to any kind of inflection, albeit that the latter, in agglutinating languages, does not spring from any authentic source, but is merely a chance phenomenon.

Sanscrit, or the dialects that descend from it, have implanted themselves, more or less, in the languages of all the peoples on the borders of India; and it is fascinating to see how, by means of such linkages, which owe more to the spirit of religion and science than to political affinities or living conditions, these different languages bear comparison to one another. Thus in upper India the Pali language, an inflected tongue that has lost many sound-distinctions among its forms, has come in contact with languages that are essentially akin to Chinese – at the very point, that is, where the contrast between a wealth of grammatical indication, and an almost total lack of it, is at its greatest. I cannot subscribe to the view that Burmese, in its true form, and so far as it belongs to that nation, has been reshaped by Pali in any significant way. The polysyllabic words therein have arisen from the native propensity to compounding, and had no need of Pali as an example; and the use of particles in approximation to forms is likewise indigenous to Burmese alone. The Pali scholars have merely clothed the language externally in its grammatical vesture. We see this from the multiplicity of case-signs, and from the classes of compound words. What they here equate to the Sanscrit *Karmadhâraya* is utterly different from this, since the preceding adjective in Burmese is always in need of a connective particle. To judge by Carey's grammar, they do not seem ever to have ventured to apply their terminology to the verb. Yet we cannot deny the possibility, that through continued study of Pali the style, and to that extent also the character of Burmese, may be shifted towards an approximation to Pali, and might continue increasingly to be changed in that direction. The truly physical form of language, which rests upon the sounds, permits of such an influence only within very restricted limits. The inner intuition of the form, however, is very susceptible to such influence; and by intimacy with more perfect languages, the grammatical conceptions, and even the strength and vivacity of the linguistic sense, are rectified and enhanced. This then has a reverse effect upon the language, insofar as it submits to the authority of usage. Now in Burmese this reverse effect would be particularly strong, since major portions of its structure already approach that of Sanscrit, and the main thing they lack is merely to be taken in the proper sense, which the language itself cannot bring them to, since it has not arisen from that sense. Now in this respect the alien viewpoint would come to its assistance. To this end it would merely be necessary, by degrees, to appropriate the accumulated particles to specific grammatical forms, discarding many in the process; to make more frequent use, in construction, of the existing auxiliary verb; and so on. Though whatever the care devoted to such endeavours, it will never succeed in eliminating the fact that the language is still inherently subject to a totally different form; and the results of such a procedure would always have an un-Burmese ring to them, since, to stress just this one point, the numerous particles available for one and the same form find their application, not indifferently, but by delicate nuances implicit in linguistic usage. So there would always be a sense that something alien to the language had been injected into it.

According to all the evidence, there seems to be no *historical affinity* between Burmese and Chinese. The two languages are said to have only a few *words in common.* Still, I do not know whether this point might not call for a more careful assessment. One is struck by the great resemblance in sound of some words, drawn precisely from the class of grammatical terms. For those who are better acquainted with both languages, I cite them here. The Burmese plural signs for nouns and verbs are *tô·* and *kra* (pronounced *kya*), and *toû* and *kiâi* are Chinese plural signs in the old and new style: *thang* (pronounced *thi* Hough) corresponds, as we have already seen above, to *ti* in the new and *tchî* in the older style; *hri* (pronounced *shi*) is the verb *to be*, and in Chinese, according to Rémusat, it is likewise *chi*. Morrison and Hough write both words perfectly alike, in the English manner, as *she*. However, the Chinese word is simultaneously both a pronoun and an affirmative particle, so that its verb-meaning has doubtless merely been taken from this. But this origin would contribute nothing to the relationship of the two words. Finally, the general type-expression used in both languages for specifying numbered objects, analogous in this respect to our word *piece*, is *hku* in Burmese, and in Chinese *ko*.[26] Though the number of these words may be small, they belong to precisely those parts of the structure of the two languages which betray their kinship to the greatest extent; and even the differences between Chinese and Burmese grammar, great as they are, and deeply as they penetrate into the language-structure, are still not of such a kind as to make all affinity impossible, as is the case, for example, between Burmese and Tagalic.

[26] See further *Über die Kawi-Sprache*, I, p. 253, n. 3.

§25

The inquiries just inaugurated are closely related to the question of whether the difference between *mono-* and *polysyllabic languages* is an *absolute* one, or merely *relative* according to degree; and whether this form of the words is essentially constitutive of the *character* of languages, or whether the *monosyllabic structure* is merely a *transitional phase* from which the *polysyllabic languages* have gradually evolved.

In the earlier days of language study, Chinese and a number of South East Asian languages were roundly declared to be monosyllabic. Later on there came to be doubts about this; and Abel Rémusat expressly denied this claim concerning Chinese.[1] But such a view appeared to be too much at variance with the observed facts; and it can legitimately be argued that we have now returned, and not without reason, to the earlier assumption. The whole dispute was based, however, on a number of misunderstandings; and the first thing needed is therefore an appropriate account of what we call a *monosyllabic word-form*, and of the sense in which mono- and polysyllabic languages are distinguished from one another. All examples of polysyllabic form in Chinese that were adduced by Rémusat turn out to be *compounds*; and there can really be no doubt that compounding is something altogether different from an originally polysyllabic form. In compounding, even the concept that is regarded as entirely simple arises from two or more concepts coupled together. The resultant word is thus never a simple one; and a language does not cease to be monosyllabic because it possesses compound words. It is obviously a question of those simple words in which we can distinguish no elementary concepts forming the idea, but where the sign for this consists of the sounds of two or more syllables that have *no meaning* of their own. Even when we find words in which this is seemingly the case, we always need a closer inquiry as to whether each individual syllable did not originally possess a meaning of its own that has merely become lost there. A proper counterexample to the monosyllabic character of a language would have to carry proof that *all* the word's *sounds* are *meaningful* only *collectively* and *together*, not by themselves in isolation. Abel Rémusat did not have this clearly enough in mind, however, and hence, in the essay above-cited, he

---

[1] *Fundgruben des Orients*, III, p. 279.

in fact mistook the original character of Chinese.[2] From another side, however, Rémusat's view was indeed founded on something true and correctly observed. For he adhered to the division of languages into mono- and polysyllabic, and it did not escape his acuteness that this division, as it is commonly understood, is not in fact to be taken in a precise sense. I have already remarked earlier that such a dichotomy cannot rely on the mere fact of a preponderance of mono- and polysyllabic words, but is founded on something far more essential, namely the dual circumstance of a lack of *affixes*, and the bent of pronunciation to keep the *syllabic sounds separate*, even where the mind unites the concepts. The reason for the *want of affixes* lies deeper, and truly in the mind. For if the latter has a vivid sense of the dependency of the affix upon the main concept, the tongue cannot possibly give it an equal weight of sound in a word of its own. The merging of two different elements into verbal unity is a necessary and immediate consequence of this feeling. So Rémusat seems to me to have been at fault only in this, that instead of assailing the monosyllabic character of Chinese, he did not attempt rather to show that even the *other languages* proceed from a *monosyllabic root-structure*, and only arrive at a *polysyllabic* form, partly through their characteristic

[2] M. Ampère (*De la Chine et des travaux de M. Abel Rémusat*, in the *Revue des deux mondes*, vol. 8, 1832, pp. 373–405) has correctly sensed this. But he recalls at the same time that this treatise dates from the early years of Abel Rémusat's Chinese studies, though observing on this point that even later he never wholly abandoned this view. Rémusat, in fact, was certainly too much inclined to consider the Chinese language-structure to be less deviant from that of other languages than it actually is. To this he may first have been led by the venturesome ideas, concerning Chinese and the difficulty of learning it, which still prevailed at the time he began his studies. But he was also insufficiently aware that the lack of certain finer grammatical designations, although doubtless at times innocuous in detail to the sense as such, is never so to the more definite nuancing of the thought as a whole. Yet otherwise he was plainly the first to depict the true nature of Chinese; and one only learns to recognize truly the great value of his *Grammar*, now that that of Father Prémare, also very valuable in its own way, has appeared in print (*Notitia linguae Sinicae auctore P. Prémare*, Malacca 1831). Comparison of the two works shows unmistakably how great is the service rendered to the subject by that of Rémusat. From it, the individuality of the language it deals with beams out upon the reader, in easy arrangement and limpid clarity, at every point. The work of his predecessor furnishes exceedingly valuable material, and certainly embraces every feature of the language in detail; but its author hardly entertained an equally clear picture of the whole, and at least did not succeed in conveying such a thing to his readers. Profounder students of the language may also yearn for the filling of many gaps in Rémusat's *Grammar*; but this admirable author will forever be accorded the great credit of having first truly reached the vantage-point for a correct view of the language, and beyond that, of having made the study of it generally accessible, and so really become the first founder thereof.

method of *affixation*, and partly by way of *compounding*, which is also not foreign to Chinese; but that they actually reach this goal, since the aforementioned obstacles did not stand in their way, as they do in Chinese. This is the path that I now wish to open up, and to pursue under the guidance of a factual investigation of certain languages which call for prime consideration here.

However difficult, and in part impossible, it may be, to trace back *words* to their true *origin*, a carefully conducted analysis still leads us, in most languages, to *monosyllabic* stems; and particular cases of the opposite cannot constitute a proof of *originally pollysyllabic* stems as well, since the cause of the phenomenon can be sought with much greater probability in an analysis that has not been carried sufficiently far. But if the question be considered in a purely conceptual fashion, we also assuredly do not go too far in making the general assumption, that every concept was originally designated by *one syllable* alone. In the invention of language, the concept is the *impression* made upon man by the *object*, either external or internal; and the *sound* evoked from the breast by the vividness of this impression is the *word*. In this way two sounds cannot easily correspond to a single impression. If two sounds were really to arise in immediate succession, they would be evidence of two impressions proceeding from the same object, and would constitute *compounding* already in the genesis of the word, without the monosyllabic principle being thereby impaired. This is in fact the case with the *reduplication* which we find in all languages, but especially in those that are less cultivated. Each of the repeated sounds expresses the whole object; but by repetition the expression acquires a further nuance, either a mere strengthening, as a sign of the greater vivacity of the impression received, or in order to indicate the recurrence of the object; reduplication therefore occurs primarily in adjectives, since with a property it is especially noticeable that it does not appear as a single body, but is spread like a surface everywhere in the same space. In many languages, of which I will here cite only those of the South Sea Islands, reduplication is really associated predominantly, indeed almost exclusively, with adjectives and with the substantives that were formed from them, and thus originally felt in an adjectival way. To be sure, if we conceive of the original linguistic designation as a deliberate *parcelling-out* of *sounds* among *objects*, then the matter certainly appears very different. The concern not to give exactly the same signs to different concepts could then have been the likeliest reason for having annexed a second and third syllable to the first, quite regardless of any new significance. But this way of thinking, in which it is utterly forgotten that language is no dead mechanism, but a living creation from

[margin note: original linguistic designation was not deliberate]

within itself, and that the first speakers were far more sensuously responsive than ourselves, who have been dulled by culture and knowledge that rests on the experience of others, is obviously false. All languages certainly contain words which are liable to produce ambiguity, in that exactly the same sound has quite different meanings. But that this is infrequent, and that a differently stressed sound normally corresponds to each concept, has certainly not been due to deliberate comparison of words already extant, of which the speaker could not even have been aware; it is because both the *impression* of the object, and the *sound* it evoked, were always *individual*, and no individuality coincides completely with any other. From another point of view, the word-store was admittedly also augmented by *extension* of the particular *designations on hand*. As man became acquainted with more objects, and got to know them better, he encountered in many *specific difference* amid *general likeness*; and this new impression naturally occasioned a new sound, which, when attached to the previous one, became a *polysyllabic word*. But here, too, conjoined concepts operate with conjoined sounds as designations of one and the same object. At most we might think it possible, so far as the original designation is concerned, that the voice could have made quite *meaningless* additions, from a merely sensuous delight in tonal sonority, or that merely sounded breathings should have become true syllables, once pronunciation had achieved a greater regularity. I would not wish to deny that sounds without any meaning do actually persist in languages, for merely sensuous reasons; but this is so only because their significance has become lost. Originally the breast emits no articulate sound that was not aroused by a feeling.

In the course of time, matters also go quite differently with regard to *polysyllabicity*. There is no denying it, as a *fact*, in the developed languages – it is contested only in the *roots*, and beyond this sphere, as may generally be assumed and very often proved in detail, it relies for its origin upon *compounding*, and thereby forfeits its peculiar nature. For it is not just because we lack the *meaning* of particular *word-elements*, that they seem *unmeaning* to us; there is often something positive at the bottom of the phenomenon as well. Language begins by combining *concepts* that really *modify* one another. It then attaches to a *main concept* another one, metaphorically only, or with only a part of its meaning operative, as when Chinese, to mark the distinction in kinship of older and younger, employs the word *son* in compounded kinship-names, where neither direct descent nor gender is apposite, but solely the fact of being junior in age. Now if some such concepts, owing to the possibility for this that is furnished by their greater generality, have become largely *word-elements* for the *specification* of concepts, then language doubtless also becomes accustomed to employing them where their relation is merely a quite distant one that is hardly traceable, or where it has to be freely admitted that no genuine relation is present, and hence the significance in fact amounts to nothing. This phenomenon, whereby language, following a general analogy, applies sounds from cases where they truly belong to others that they are alien to, is also to be found in other parts of its procedure. Thus it cannot be denied that in many inflections of the Sanscrit declension pronominal stems are concealed, but that in some of these instances no reason is really discoverable for precisely this stem and no other being assigned to this or that case, or even for saying how a pronominal stem can constitute the expression of this particular case-relation at all. Yet even in those cases that seem to us the most striking, there may still be quite individual, finely conceived *conjunctions* between the *concept* and the *sound*. But these are then so divested of general necessity, and though not accidental, are so far open to historical recognition merely, that for us their very existence is lost. I deliberately omit mention here of the incorporation of *foreign polysyllables* from one language to another, since, if the claim here put forward is correct, the polysyllabic character of such words is never original, and the lack of meaning of their individual elements, for the language they take root in, remains of a merely relative kind.

In the non-monosyllabic languages, albeit in very varying degree, there does, however, exist, owing to a concurrence of inner and outer causes, a *striving* towards a purely *polysyllabic character*, without regard to the origin of this in compounding, whether it be still known or lost in darkness. The language then demands range of sound for the expression of *simple concepts*, and allows the elementary concepts coupled therein to dissolve into these simple forms. In this two-fold fashion there then arises the designation of a single concept by several syllables. For just as Chinese resists the polysyllabic character, and as its script, which has manifestly originated from this resistance, confirms it in this, so other languages have the opposite tendency. Through delight in euphony and the urge towards rhythmical proportions, they proceed towards the forming of larger word-wholes, and in response to an inner feeling go on to distinguish the mere compounding that arises simply through *talk*, from that which can be confounded with the expression of a simple concept by several syllables, whose individual meaning is no longer known or no longer attended to. But since everything in language is always inwardly connected, even this endeavour, which at first seems merely sensuous, has a broader and firmer basis. For the tendency of the mind, to combine the concept and its relations into the unity of the same word, makes an obvious contribution to this, whether the language, as a truly inflected one, should have actually reached this goal, or as an agglutinating one, have stopped half way. The creative power whereby language itself (to employ a figure of speech) pushes forth from the root the whole of what pertains to the inner and outer fashioning of the word-form, is here the originally operative factor. The further such creation extends, the greater the degree of this endeavour; the earlier it wearies, the less. But in the sound-range of the word that arises from this, the necessary limits are set by the completed rounding-off of this endeavour, in accordance with laws of euphony. Precisely those languages that are less happy in the fusion of syllables into unity, string a larger number of them unrhythmically together, where the completed urge to unity conjoins fewer in a harmonious way. Thus here, too, both inner and outer success are closely and exactly in agreement with one another. But in many cases the concept itself occasions an attempt to couple some syllables merely with a view to giving a simple concept an appropriate sign, and without any precise wish to preserve recollection of the particular syllables so conjoined. From this there then naturally arises an even greater degree of true polysyllabicity, when the concept so compounded lays stress upon its simplicity alone.

Among the cases here referred to, two different classes chiefly stand out. In one, the *concept* already given by a *sound* is merely to be *fixed* more definitely, or *elucidated* more fully, by attachment of a second sound, so that uncertainty or unclarity may be avoided in the whole. In this way languages often combine together concepts having just the same meaning, or differing only in very small nuances; also general concepts annexed to special ones, and often coined into such generality from the special only by way of this usage, as when in Chinese the concept of striking is virtually transformed, in these compoundings, into that of doing as such. The other class includes those cases where from *two different concepts* a *third* is actually formed, as when the *sun*, for example, is called the *eye of day*, or *milk* the *water of the breast*, etc. The first class of combinations is based on a mistrust of the clarity of the expression used, or a lively haste to amplify it. It should rarely be found in very evolved languages, but in some that are aware, in their structure, of a certain indefiniteness, it is very common. In cases of the second class, the two concepts to be combined are the direct portrayal of the impression received, and are thus in their special meaning the actual word. In and for themselves they would remain two. But since they do designate only one thing, understanding insists upon their maximally close association in the verbal form; and as its power over the language grows, and the original conception lapses therein, even the most pregnant and attractive metaphors of this kind come to lose their retroactive influence, and disappear from the speaker's attention, however clearly it may still be possible to point them out. Both classes also occur in the *monosyllabic* languages, save that there the inner need to combine the concepts is unable to overcome the propensity for keeping the syllables apart.

It is thus, I believe, that we must construe and judge the phenomenon of mono- and polysyllabic character in languages. This general argument, which I was not willing to interrupt by enumerating facts, I will now try to confirm with some examples.

The *newer style* of Chinese already possesses a not insignificant number of words composed of *two elements*, such that their compounding is aimed solely at the formation of a third simple concept. In some of them it is even apparent that the addition of the one element has only become *habitual* on the strength of actually meaningful cases. The enlargement of concepts and languages must bring it about that new objects are designated by comparison with others already known, and that the mind's method of forming its concepts is carried over into the languages as well. Such a method must gradually replace the earlier one, of symbolically reproducing the impression by way of the analogy residing in the articulated tones. But in peoples of great liveliness of imagination and keenness of sensuous apprehension, even the later method goes back to a very distant epoch, and hence those languages which still give most evidence of the early days of their formation, possess, for the most part, a large number of such words that depict in pictorial fashion the nature of the objects. But modern Chinese displays here, in fact, a deformity that only pertains to a later culture. The words made up of two elements consist very largely of playfully witty, rather than truly poetic, descriptions of objects, in which these latter often lie concealed like riddles.[3] Another class of such words appears at first sight very strange, namely those where *two* mutually *opposing concepts* express by their combination the general concept that covers them both, as when *the younger and older brothers*, or *the high and low mountains*, are used to speak of *the brothers* and *the mountains* as such. The universality that resides, in such cases, in the definite article is here more intuitively indicated by the opposing extremes in a manner that

---

[3] Saint Julien, of Paris, was the first to draw attention to this terminology of the poetic style, as one might call it, which calls for a broadly-based study on its own account, and leads into the greatest misunderstandings without it.

admits of no exception. Properly speaking, this type of word is really more a figure of speech than a formative method of languages. But in a language where the otherwise merely grammatical expression must so commonly be inserted into the content of speech, it is not unreasonable to count it as a method. Particular compounds of this sort are to be found, moreover, in all languages; in Sanscrit they remind one of the स्थावरजङ्गमम् *sthâwara-jaṇgamam* [the unmoving and the moving, the inanimate and the animate], which frequently occurs in philosophical poetry. But in Chinese there is also the fact that in some of these cases the language has no word at all for the simple general concept, and so must necessarily make use of these circumlocutions. The condition of age, for example, is inseparable from the word *brother*, and hence one may speak only of *older* and *younger brothers*, not of brothers in general. This may still be a legacy from an earlier uncultivated phase. The desire to present the object intuitively in the word, along with its properties, and the want of abstraction, lead to neglect of the general expression that covers a variety of differences; the individual sensuous approach takes precedence over the generalizing method of the understanding. This phenomenon is also common in the American languages. From a totally different angle, and precisely through an artificially-pursued method of the understanding, this type of word-construction is also still further emphasized in Chinese, in that the symmetrical arrangement of concepts that stand contrasted in certain respects is considered a merit and an ornament of style – a view influenced also by the nature of a script that encloses every concept in a single sign. There is thus an endeavour to weave such concepts deliberately into speech, and since no relation is so definite as that of pure contrariety, Chinese rhetoric has made a special business of enumerating the *contrasting* concepts in the language.[4] The older Chinese style makes no use of *compounded* words, whether it be because in earlier times – as is very understandable for certain classes of them – this procedure had not yet been arrived at, or because such practices were ruled out by this stricter style, which to some extent disdained, in general, to assist the exertions of the understanding by linguistic means.

I can here pass over the Burmese language, since in my previous general description of its structure I have already shown how it creates polysyllabic words from monosyllables, by conjoining either synonymous or modifying stems.

[4] In the supplements to Basile's large dictionary, Klaproth has provided such a list, and one very considerably augmented over those that till now have been known in Europe. It also excels the one to be found in Prémare's *Grammar*, by its exceedingly valuable notes throwing light on the Chinese systems of philosophy.

In the Malayan languages, after dropping the *affixes*, we are left very frequently – one might well say mostly – with a *disyllabic stem* which cannot be further divided in grammatical relation to the speech-structure. Even where the stem is a monosyllable, it is often reduplicated, and this is actually normal in Tagalic. So we often find mention of the *disyllabic structure* of these languages. But so far as I know, an analysis of these word-stems has never yet been undertaken. I have made the attempt; and though I may not yet have succeeded in giving a fully adequate account of the nature of the elements in all these words, I am nonetheless persuaded that in very many cases *each* of the two united *syllables* can be shown to be a *monosyllabic stem* in the language, and that the cause of the coupling is intelligible. Now if this be so even with our incomplete aids and defective knowledge, we may doubtless infer a greater extension of this principle, and conclude that these languages also were *originally monosyllabic*. More difficulty, to be sure, is created by words such as Tagalic *lisà* and *lisaỳ*, from the root *lis* (see below), which end in mere vowel sounds; but these, too, will no doubt become explicable on future investigation. By now at least this much is apparent, that in the majority of cases the *final syllables* of the Malayan disyllabic stems should not be regarded as *suffixes* adjoined to meaningful words, but that in them we may recognize genuine *roots*, exactly like those that form the first syllable. For they also occur partly as *first syllables* of such compounds, and partly quite *separately* in the language. But for the most part the *monosyllabic stems* must be looked for in their *reduplicated* forms.

From this character of the disyllables, which at first sight seem simple, but are yet reducible to monosyllabic terms, there arises in the language a tendency to the *polysyllabic*, which – as may be seen from the frequency of reduplication – is in part also *phonetic* and not merely intellectual. But the conjoining syllables also become more of a *single word* than they do in Burmese, in that the *accent* binds them together. In Burmese, every monosyllabic word carries its own accent with it, and imports this into the compound. That the whole word now resulting should possess a single accent, holding its syllables together, is not only not stated, but is impossible in a pronunciation that audibly separates the syllables. In Tagalic the polysyllable does always have an accent that stresses the penultimate syllable, or lets it drop. *Letter-change*, however, is not associated with compounding.

I have directed my inquiries on this subject primarily to Tagalic and the language of New Zealand. The former, in my view, displays the Malayan language-structure in its greatest extent and purest consistency. It was important to include the South Sea languages in the inquiry, since their structure seems to be still more primeval, or at least to contain an even larger number of such elements. In the following examples drawn from Tagalic, I have confined myself almost exclusively to those cases in which the *monosyllabic stem*, at least in *reduplication*, also belongs as such to the language. Much larger, of course, is the number of such disyllables, whose monosyllabic stems appear only in *compoundings*, but are recognizable there by their always similar meaning. These cases, however, are not so convincing, in that normally other words are then present, in which this similarity seems to be less, or totally absent, although such seeming exceptions may quite well be due to the fact that a more remote connection of ideas is not discerned. It will be obvious why I have sought throughout to authenticate *both syllables*, since the opposite procedure could indicate the nature of these word-formations only in a doubtful fashion. Attention must naturally be paid also to words whose original stem is located, not in the language in question, but in another one, as is the case in Tagalic with some that have migrated from Sanscrit, or from the South Sea languages as well.

Examples from the Tagalic Language

bag-sàc, to throw something forcefully to earth, or crush against something; *bag-bàg*, to run ashore, to till a cornfield (used, therefore, of forceful thrusting or throwing); *sac-sàc*, to insert something firmly, to press in, to stop up, to throw into something (*apretar embutiendo algo, atestar, hincar*). *lab-sàc*, to throw something in the mire, privy – from the word just cited and *lab-làb*, cesspool, manure-heap, privy. From this word and the term *as-às*, which is to appear shortly, comes the compound *lab-às, semen suis ipsius manibus elicere*. Probably belonging here also we have *sac-àl*, to press someone's neck, hand or foot, although the meaning of the second element *al-àl*, to file down the teeth with a pebble, has little aptness here, and likewise *sac-yòr*, to catch grasshoppers, though I do not know how to explain the second element. We cannot, however, reckon *sacsì*, witness, to testify, in this group, since the word is undoubtedly the Sanscrit साक्षिन् *sâkshin*, and as a legal term may have entered the language along with Indian culture. The same word also occurs, with the same meaning, in Malayan proper.

bac-às, footsteps, tracks of men and animals, the left-over sign of a physical impression, of tears, beating, etc; *bac-bàc*, to remove the rind, or to lose; *ás-as*, to be rubbed away, used of clothing and other things.

bac-làs, a wound, and particularly one that comes of scratching; from the above-cited *bac-bàc* and *las-làs*, to remove leaves or roof-tiles, also used of the destruction of branches and roofs by the wind. The word is also rendered *bac-lìs*, from *lis-lìs*, to weed, pull up grass (see below).

ás-al, an introduced usage, adopted custom, from the afore-mentioned *ás-as* and *al-àl*, i.e. from combining the concepts of using up and filing down.

it-ìt, to suck in, and *im-ìm*, to close up, used of the mouth. These two are presumably the source of *it-ìm*, black (Malayan *ētam*), since this colour may very well be compared with something sucked in and closed up.

tac-lìs, to whet, sharpen – especially one knife with another; *tac* means emptying the body, the relief of natural needs; the reduplicated *tac-tàc* means a large spade, a hoe (*azadon*), and when turned into a verb, to work with this implement, to hollow out. From this it becomes clear that this latter concept is actually the basic meaning of the simple root as well. *lis-lìs* will occur again below, but combines within itself the concepts of destruction and the small, of diminishing. Both are very well suited to the abrasion of whetting.

lis-pìs, with the prefix *pa*, to clean the corn for sowing, is derived from the oft-mentioned *lis-lìs*, and from *pis-pìs*, to sweep or clean off, used especially of breadcrumbs with a brush.

lá-bay, a bundle of silk, yarn or cotton (*madeja*), and hence, as a verb, to reel; *lá-la*, to weave rugs; *bay-baỳ*, to go, especially to the seashore, hence in a definite direction, which fits well with the motion of reeling.

tú-lis, a point, to sharpen, used in fact of large wooden nails (*estacas*), and applied in Javanese and Malayan to the concept of writing.[5] *lis-lìs*, to destroy bad, useless growths, to pull out, has already appeared above. The concept is actually *to diminish*, and therefore appropriate to shaving-off in order to produce a point; *lisà* are the nits of the louse, and from the concept of smallness, of dust, we also get the application of the word to cleaning or sweeping out, as in *ua-lìs*, the general word for this work. The first element of *tú-lis* I find neither alone nor reduplicated in Tagalic, though it certainly occurs in the South Sea languages, in the Tongan *tu* (written *too* by Mariner), to cut, to get up, to stand upright; in the New Zealand tongue it has this latter meaning, besides that of *to strike*.

---

[5] See my letter to M. Jacquet, *Nouveau Journal Asiatique*, IX, 496. The Tahitian word for *to write* is *papai* (*Acts of the Apostles*, 15.20), and on the Sandwich Islands, *palapala* (*Mark*. 10.4). In the New Zealand language, *tui:* means to write, sew or designate. As I know from written communications, Jacquet has conceived the happy idea that among these peoples the concepts of writing and tattooing are closely connected. The New Zealand language confirms this. For instead of *tuinga*, the act of writing, one may also say *tiwinga*; and *tiwana* is that part of the signs etched by tattooing, which stretches from the eye to the side of the head.

tó-bo, to come forth, to sprout, of plants (*nacer*), *bo-bò*, to empty something out; *tó-to* in Tagalic has only metaphorical meanings: to form a friendship, to agree with, to fulfil one's intention in speaking or acting. But in New Zealand *to* is life, animation, and thence *toto*, flood. In Tongan *tubu* (Mariner: *tooboo*) has the same meaning of sprouting as the Tagalic *tóbo*, but also means *to leap up. bu* occurs in Tongan as *bubula*, to swell; *tu* is to cut, separate and stand. The Tongan *tubu* is matched by New Zealand *tupu*, both in meaning and derivation. For *tu* is *to stand* or *get up*, and *pu* contains the concept of a body grown round by swelling, since it means a pregnant woman. The meanings cylinder, flint and tube, which Lee puts first, are merely derivative. That *pu* also contains already the concept of bursting through swelling, is shown by the compound *pu-ao*, daybreak.

Examples from the New Zealand Language

The Tagalic dictionary of de los Santos, like most missionary works of this kind, especially the older ones, is intended simply as a guide to writing and preaching in the language. It therefore always gives the most concrete meanings of the words, at which they have arrived through linguistic usage, and seldom goes back to the original general significance. Hence even quite simple sounds, that are actually among the roots of the language, very often bear the meanings of particular objects; *pay-pày*, for example, means shoulderblade, fan and sunshade, which all contain the notion of spreading out. We see this from *sam-pày*, to hang out washing or gear to dry on a line, pole and so forth (*tender*), *cá-pay*, to paddle with the arms in the absence of oars, to wave one's hands in calling, and from other compounds. Things are very different in the New Zealand dictionary very perceptively compiled by Professor Lee of Cambridge from material assembled on the spot by Thomas Kendall, who was assisted by two natives. The simplest sounds have exceedingly general meanings of motion, space, etc, as may be ascertained by comparison of the articles on the vowel-sounds.[6] We thereby run into perplexity at times as to the special application, and are even tempted to wonder whether this conceptual breadth is actually present in the spoken language, or has perhaps been only annexed to it. Yet Lee has certainly produced it from the information given by the native

---

[6] Thus the article on *a*, for example, begins as follows: 'A, signifies universal existence, animation, action, power, light, possession etc., also the present existence, animation, power, light, etc. of a being, or thing.'

speakers; and there is no denying the significant aid it provides in the derivation of New Zealand words.

ora, health, increase or restoration of this; *o*, motion, and also quite specifically, refreshment; *ra*, strength, health, and thereafter the sun; *ka-ha*, strength, a rising flame, to burn, animation as the act of this and as vigorous efficacy; *ha*, exhalation.

mara, a place exposed to the sun's warmth, then a person confronting the speaker, doubtless from the facial glow, hence used as a form of address; *ma*, clear, like the colour white; *ra*, the above-mentioned word for sun; *marama* is *light* and the *moon*.

pono, true, truth, *po*, night, the region of darkness, *noa*, free, unbound. If this derivation is really correct, the compounding of the concepts is a remarkably pregnant one.

mutu, the end, to terminate; *mu*, used as a particle, the last, finally; *tu*, to stand.

Examples from Tongan

fachi, to break, dislocate; *fa*, capable of being or doing something; *chi*, small, the New Zealand *iti*.

loto means the centre, mid-point, the internally enclosed, and unquestionably yields, by metaphor, mood, attitude, temperament, thought, opinion. The word is the same as New Zealand *roto*, which has only the physical meaning, though, not the figurative one, and so signifies merely *the inner*, and as a preposition, *in*. I think both words are correctly derivable from both languages. The first element I take to be the New Zealand *roro*, brain. The simple *ro* is translated in Lee's dictionary merely by the ambiguous *matter*, which here, however, must doubtless be taken as pus, ulcerous matter, and perhaps has the more general meaning of any enclosed viscous substance. The second element, *to*, has already been discussed, as a New Zealand word, under *tóbo*, and I merely note further here that it is also used of pregnancy, that is, of something living enclosed within. In Tongan it is known to me at present only as the name of a tree, whose berries have a sticky flesh that is used for gluing various things together. Hence this meaning also contains the notion of attachment to something else. But in Tongan the term for brain falls only partly into this word-group. For the brain is called *uto* (Mariner: *ooto*). The last part of the word I consider to be the *to* just referred to, since the stickiness applies very aptly to the brain-mass. The first syllable is no less expressive in describing the brain, since *u* is a bundle or package. I believe I also find this word again in Tagalic *ótac* and Malayan *ūtak*, whose roots I do not therefore look for in these languages themselves. As in other Malayan words, the final *k* may very well not be radical in nature. Both words have the double meaning of *marrow* and *brain*, obviously from the likeness of the material, and hence are often, indeed normally, distinguished by the addition of *head* or *bone*. In Madecassian, according to Flacourt, the same word, as marrow, is *oteche*, and as brain *otechendoha*, head-marrow, in that by a quite normal metathesis he writes the word *loha*, head, as *doha*, and attaches it to the other word by a nasal. A different-sounding term for brain, in Challan, is *tso ondola*, and likewise for marrow *tsoc*, *tsoco*. Whether *ondola* must necessarily belong to *tso* is hard to decide. But probably the distinction-sign has merely been omitted; for in the Madecassian-French part the word *ondola*, which I cannot as yet explain, is found alone for brain. In the manuscript word-list issued by Jacquet, brain is given as *tsokou loha*, and he remarks there that he finds no corresponding word in the other dialects.[7] But I consider *tsokou* and the variants in Challan to be merely a distortion of the Malayan *ūtak*, by omission of the initial vowel and with a hissing pronunciation of the *t*, and hence equivalent to Flacourt's *oteche*, which is still more reminiscent of the Tagalic *ótac*. Chapelier's manuscript dictionary, which I owe to the kindness of M. Lesson, has *tsoudoa* for brain, where again the final *doa*, head, stands for *loa*. I much regret that I do not know the word in the form given it nowadays by the English missionaries. But the brain is mentioned by the Latin Vulgate Bible only in two passages from the Book of Judges, and the English Bible, which the missionaries translate from, renders it as *skull*.

The disyllabic form of the Semitic stems (leaving aside here the small number that have fewer or more syllables) is of quite a different kind from that so far considered, since it is more inseparably *embedded* in the lexical grammatical *structure*. It forms an essential part of the *character* of these languages, and wherever allusion is made to their origin, evolution and influence, it cannot be left out of account. Yet it may be taken for a fact that even this multisyllabic system is based on an originally monosyllabic one, of which clear traces are still discernible in the present-day language. This has been acknowledged by several Semitic scholars, notably Michaelis, though even before him, and has been worked out and delimited more closely by Gesenius and Ewald.[8] There are, says Gesenius, whole sequences of

---

[7] *Nouveau Journal Asiatique*, xi, p. 108, No. 13, and p. 126, No. 13.

[8] F. H. W. Gesenius, *Hebräisch-Deutsches Handwörterbuch*, i, p. 132; ii, Preface, p. xiv; the same author's *Geschichte der hebräischen Sprache und Schrift*, p. 125, but more especially its detailed conspectus of the Hebrew Language, p. 183 *et seq*. H. von Ewald's *Kritische Grammatik der hebräischen Sprache*, pp. 166, 167.

stem-verbs having only the *first two stem-consonants* in common, though
the third is quite different, and which yet agree in meaning, at least
in the major concept. He calls it a mere exaggeration for Caspar
Neumann, who died in Breslau at the beginning of last century, to
have wished to reduce all disyllabic roots to monosyllables. In the
cases referred to, the present-day disyllabic stem-words are based on
monosyllabic roots consisting of two consonants that enclose a vowel,
to which a third consonant has been added when the language was
later rewritten with a second vowel. Klaproth has likewise observed
this, and in a paper of his own has listed a number of those sequences
pointed out by Gesenius.[9] He also shows there, in a remarkable and
intelligent way, how the monosyllabic roots, once freed of their third
consonant, are very often in total or preponderant agreement, in
sound and meaning, with those of Sanscrit. Ewald remarks that such
a carefully instituted comparison of stems would lead to many new
results, but adds that by such etymology we transcend the epoch of
truly Semitic language and form. I fully concur with him on the latter
point, since it is precisely my own conviction that with every
essentially new form attained, in course of time, by the idiom even
of the population in question, a new language in fact begins.

In considering the *scope* of this origin of *disyllabic* from *monosyllabic
roots*, it would first have to be precisely established in fact, how far
etymological analysis can actually go in this respect. Now if, as can
hardly be doubted, some irreducible cases were left over, the blame
for this could still lie on a want of terms that would show the
sequences to be complete. Yet even on general grounds it strikes me
as actually necessary to assume that the system of extending all roots
to two syllables was directly preceded, not by a *thoroughly monosyllabic*
system, but by a mixture of *mono-* and *disyllabic* word-stems. One
should never suppose the changes in languages to be so forcible, and
at least so theoretical, that a new principle of formation, for which
previous examples were lacking, could be thrust upon the people (for
that means upon the language too). There would need to be cases
already on hand, and in fair numbers, if certain sound-characteristics
are to be made general by grammatical law-making, which in
general is certainly more powerful in eradicating existing forms than

---

[9] *Observations sur les racines des langues Sémitiques*. This monograph constitutes a
supplement to A. A. von Merian's *Principes de l'étude comparative des langues*, which
appeared immediately after his death (he died on 25 April 1828). Through an
unlucky chance, the work of Merian vanished from the bookshops soon after its
appearance. So Klaproth's piece has likewise come into the hands of few readers,
and is in need of reprinting.

in introducing new ones. For the mere sake of the general principle that a root must always be monosyllabic, I would by no means wish to deny the presence of originally disyllabic roots as well. I have declared myself plainly on this point in what has gone before. But if I thereupon myself attribute the disyllabic character to compounding, so that two syllables are also the combined presentation of two impressions, the compounding may already reside in the mind of him who pronounces the word for the first time. This is all the more possible here, in that we are talking of a people endowed with a sense of inflection. In the case of the Semitic languages, a second important circumstance is in fact added to this. Though even the abolition of the law of disyllabic formation projects us into a period that transcends the present linguistic structure, there are still two other characteristic marks remaining there, namely that the root-syllable we are led to by analysis of the current stems was always one *closed by a consonant*, and that the vowel was regarded as of no moment for conceptual significance. For if the median vowels had really possessed conceptual significance, it would have been impossible to again take it away from them. As to the relation of the vowels to the consonants in these monosyllabic roots, I have already stated my opinion above.[10] But on the other hand, even the earlier formation of the language could have been led already into the expression of a *two-fold feeling* in two connected syllables. The *sense of inflection* permits one to regard the word as a whole that includes difference within itself; and the tendency to embed the grammatical indication in the bosom of the word itself was bound to result in lending it more scope. The reasons here elaborated which seem to me in no way forced, could indeed be used to defend the hypothesis of roots that were originally in large part *disyllabic*. The uniform meaning of the first syllable in many of them would merely prove the likeness of the main impression given by various objects. But it appears to me more natural to assume the existence of *monosyllabic* roots, though without on that account excluding *disyllabic* ones alongside them. It is regrettable that the inquiries known to me do not seek to examine the *meaning* of the *third* consonant added to the two that precede it. Only this admittedly most difficult labour would shed the fullest light on this material. But if we also consider all disyllabic Semitic word-stems as *compounds*, we then see at first glance that such compounding is of quite a different sort from that in the languages already dealt with here. In those, *every member* of the compound consists of an *individual word*. Even though, in Burmese and Malayan at least, there are actually many cases

---

[10] Compare generally, with this passage, pp. 220–3 of the present work.

where words no longer make any appearance by themselves, but only in such compounds, this is still no more than a consequence of linguistic use. There is nothing intrinsically in them that contradicts their independence; they have certainly, indeed, been true words earlier on, and have only fallen out of use as such, because their meaning was exceptionally suitable for designating modifications in compounds. But the *second syllable* added in this fashion to the Semitic word-stems could not exist alone and *for itself*, since with preceding vowel and following consonant it simply does not harbour the legitimate form of the nouns and verbs. We see clearly from thence that such a formation of disyllabic word-stems is based on a mental practice in the people entirely different from that in Chinese and those languages that are akin to it in this part of their structure. It is not *two words that are compounded*, but *one that is formed by enlargement*, with an unmistakable view to word-unity. In this respect also, the Semitic language-group preserves its nobler form, more in keeping with the demands of the linguistic sense, and more surely and freely conducive to the progress of thought.

The few *polysyllabic roots* of Sanscrit can be traced back to *monosyllabic* ones, and from these, according to the theory of the Indian grammarians, all other words in the language arise. So Sanscrit, on this view, knows no other *polysyllabic character* save that engendered by grammatical attachment or overt compounding. But it has already been mentioned above (p. 97–8) that in this the grammarians perhaps go too far, so that among the words of uncertain origin, which cannot be naturally derived from the roots, there are also disyllables whose origin remains doubtful, inasmuch as neither derivation nor compounding is visible in them. But they probably still harbour the latter, albeit that not only has the original meaning of the particular elements become lost in popular memory, but even their sound has gradually undergone an erosion making them similar to mere suffixes. Even the principle of thoroughgoing derivation, that was by degrees established by the grammarians, was bound to lead to both consequences.

In some, however, *compounding* is genuinely recognizable. Thus Bopp, already, has perceived शरद् *śarad*, autumn, the rainy season, to be a composite from शार *śara*, water, and द *da*, giving, and other *unâdi*-words to be similar compounds.[11] The *meaning* of the words transformed into a *unâdi*-word may likewise have become so changed in application, once this form was introduced, that the original can

---

[11] *Lehrgebaüde der Sanskrita-Sprache*, para. 646, p. 296.

no longer be perceived there. The generally prevailing tendency in the language, towards formation by *affixes*, could have led to a similar treatment of these forms. In some cases *unâdi*-suffixes assume throughout the aspect of *substantives* existing *independently* in the language as well. Of this kind are अण्ड *anda*, and अङ्ग *anga*. Now *substantives*, indeed, by the laws of the language, would not admit of combination with a *root*, as end-terms of a compound, and to that extent the nature of this formation continues to present a puzzle. Yet on closer enumeration of every single case, the matter should certainly be fully disposed of. Where the word can be assigned neither to the given root, nor to another, by natural derivation, the difficulty is automatically resolved, since in that case no root is present in the word. In other cases it can be presumed that the root has first been transformed into a noun by means of the *krit*-suffix *a*. But lastly there seem to be a number of *unâdi*-suffixes that would more properly be reckoned among the *krit*-suffixes. The difference between the two categories is actually hard to determine; and I could cite no other but this, which admittedly often remains vacillating in particular application, that the *krit*-suffixes are applicable to whole *categories* of words by means of a general concept that is plainly declared in them, whereas the *unâdi*-suffixes engender only *single words*, and without this formation admitting of explanation from *concepts*. At bottom, the *unâdi* words are nothing else but those that were attemptedly reduced to roots in an anomalous fashion, since they did not permit application of the normal suffixes of the language. Wherever this reduction occurs naturally, and the frequency of the appearing suffix occasions it, there seems to me scarcely any reason for not adding them to the *krit*-suffixes. Hence Bopp, too, in his Latin grammar, and also in the abridged German one, has followed the method of arranging the commonest *unâdi*-suffixes, and those that most frequently function as such, in alphabetical order along with the *krit*-suffixes.

अण्ड *anda*, egg, itself a *unâdi* word, from the root अण् *an*, to breathe, and the suffix ड *da*, was doubtless, in origin at least, one and the same word as the *unâdi*-suffix of like sound. The concepts of nourishment or round shape, derived from that of the egg, are more or less apt to the words formed with this suffix, even where there may be no thought of the egg itself. In वरण्ड *waranda*, meaning an open portico, the same concept is perhaps implicit in some part of the shape or decoration of these structures. The concepts of roundness and covering, given by the two elements of the word, are most clearly apparent in the meaning, which it also has, of a skin-disease consisting of pimples in the face. Into the other meanings, of the multitude, and of an arcade covered on top and open at the sides, they have entered partly in isolation and partly conjoined.[12] From the examples I know of, the *unâdi*-suffix अण्ड *aṇḍa*, combines merely with roots whose final sound is the vocalic *r*, and then always undergoes *guna*. We might therefore regard the first syllable (*war*) as a noun formed from the root. Now this explanation, indeed, is contradicted by the fact that its final *a* does not conjoin with the initial *a* of *aṇḍa* into a long *a*. Yet it seems natural, since though this may originally have been true, such a formation is nonetheless treated in the later language, not as a compound, but as a derivation; and it is anyway difficult to suppose that the homophonic words for egg and this *unâdi*-suffix should have been utterly different, and far easier to understand how in meaning and grammatical treatment a suffix might have gradually been made out of the substantive.

Of the *unâdi*-suffix अङ्ग *anga*, much the same may be said as of *aṇḍa*, and perhaps with even greater justice, since the substantive अङ्ग *anga*, as body, going, moving, etc, has a still broader meaning that is better suited to the formation of a suffix. Such a suffix could not improperly be compared with our German *thum*, *heit* etc. Bopp, however, has dissected this suffix in a manner so ingenious and so neatly applicable to all such words that I know of, by making the first syllable into an accusative ending of the main word, and deriving the second from गा *gâ*, that I would not care to contradict him by insisting on its restoration. Yet *anga* is employed in the Kawi language, and also in some contemporary Malayan languages, in a manner so strikingly similar to its usage, on the common account, in Sanscrit, that I do not think I can avoid mention of it here. In the *Brata Yuddha*, the

---

[12] Cf. F. Carey's *Sanskrit Grammar*, p. 613, no. 168, and C. Wilkins' *Sanskrit Grammar*, p. 487, no. 863. A. W. von Schlegel (*Berliner Kalender* for 1831, p. 65) calls *waranda* a Portuguese name for the open porches customary in India, which the English adopted into their language. And Marsden, too, in his dictionary, assigns a Portuguese origin to the equivalent Malayan word *barāndah*. But can this really be correct? There is no denying that *waranda* is a genuine Sanscrit word. It already occurs in the *Amara Kôsha* (Ch. 6, sec. 2 p. 381). The word has several meanings, and so there could have been doubt about whether that of a colonnade were truly Sanscritic. H. H. Wilson and H. T. Colebrooke, the latter in his notes to the *Amara Kôsha*, have taken it to be so. And again it would have been too strange for so long a word to have become current in different meanings, with complete likeness of sound, in both Portugal and India. Hence the word seems to me to have come from India to Portugal, and to have passed into the language. In Hindustani, according to Gilchrist (*Hindoostanee Philology*, Vol. I, s.v. Balcony, Gallery, Portico), it is rendered *burandu* and *buramudu*. The English could, indeed, have borrowed the name of these structures from the Portuguese. But Johnson's *Dictionary* (Ed. Todd) calls it 'a word adopted from the East'.

Kawi poem to be dealt with in detail in the sequel to this work, there are Sanscrit substantives of the first declension with the additional endings *anga* and *angana*: along with *sura* (1, *a*), hero (शूर *śûra*), also *suranga* (97, *a.*); in addition to *rana* (82, *d.*), battle (रण *raṇa*), also *rananga* (83, *d.*) and *ranangana* (86, *b.*). These appendages seem to have no influence at all on the meaning, since the manuscript paraphrase explains both simple and lengthened words by the same term in modern Javanese. As a poetic language, Kawi should certainly permit both abbreviations and also the addition of quite meaningless syllables. But the agreement of these additions with the Sanscrit substantives अङ्ग *anga* and अङ्गन *angana*, of which the latter also has a very general meaning, is too striking, in a language quite definitely given to creating from Sanscrit, for us not to be obliged to think of the latter here. The substantives, and the similar-sounding *unâdi-*suffix, were able to produce such endings, congenial to the sound of the syllables. I would be unable to point to them in the common speech of Java today. Yet *anga* is found there, with but little change, as a substantive, while in the languages of New Zealand and Tonga it occurs quite unaltered as both substantive and ending, in a manner that may well provoke the surmise that here, too, we should be thinking of a Sanscrit origin. The Javanese word is *hanggê*: the mode and manner in which anything happens; and the fact that this word belongs to upper-class speech itself points to India as its source of derivation. In Tongan *anga* means frame of mind, custom, usage, the place where anything occurs; in New Zealand the word also has this latter meaning, as may be seen from compounds, but its primary sense is that of doing, especially of communal work. These meanings admittedly coincide only with the general idea of motion in the Sanscrit word; yet this, too, has the meaning of *soul* and *temperament*. But the true resemblance seems to me to lie in the breadth of the concept, which could then be regarded in a variety of ways. In the New Zealand language, the use of *anga* as the final term of a compound is so frequent, that it virtually becomes, in consequence, the grammatical ending for abstract substantives: *udi*, to turn around, revolve, also used of the year, *udinga*, a revolution; *rongo*, to hear, *rongonga*, the act or time of hearing; *tono*, to order, *tononga*, a command; *tao*, a long spear, *taonga*, possessions won by the spear; *toa*, a stout, courageous fellow, *toanga*, enforcement, conquest; *tui*, to sew, designate or write, *tuinga*, writing, the tablet one writes on; *tu*, to stand, *tunga*, the place where one stands, the anchorage of a ship; *toi*, to dive into the water, *toinga*, diving in; *tupu*, a shoot, to sprout, *tupunga*, forebears, the place where anything has grown; *ngaki*, to till a field, *ngakinga*, a farmstead. One might think from these examples that *nga*, and not *anga*, was the ending. But the initial *a* has merely been dropped because of the preceding vowel. For as Lee expressly tells us, it is also usual to say *udi anga*, rather than *udinga*, and Tongan retains the *a* even after vowels, as is shown by such words as *maanga*, a bite, from *ma*, to chew; *taanga*, tree-felling, but also (no doubt figuratively, from the beating sound of the rhythm), song, verse, poetry, from *ta*, to beat (resembling the Chinese word in sound and meaning); and *nofoanga*, dwelling, from *nofo*, to dwell. To what extent the Madecassian *manghe*, to do, is connected with these words, would need further special investigation. But it might well point to kinship, since the initial *m* in this word, itself used as an auxiliary and prefix, may very easily be a verb-prefix to be separated therefrom. Froberville[13] derives *magne* (as he writes it) from *maha aigne* or *maha angam*, and cites numerous sound-changes of this word. Since these forms also include *manganou*, the Javanese *mangun*, to build, bring about, may well belong here too.[14]

So if we raise the question whether, after removing all affixes, there are *simple words* in Sanscrit having two or more syllables, we must necessarily say yes, since such words do occur, in which the final term cannot with certainty be regarded as a suffix attached to a root. However, the simplicity of these words is assuredly only apparent. They are undeniably *compounds*, in which the meaning of the one element has been lost.

Aside from the *visible occurrence of polysyllables*, we may ask whether, in Sanscrit, another *concealed* form of it is not also present. For it may appear doubtful whether the roots beginning with doubled consonants, and especially those terminating in consonants, have not become *monosyllables* from *originally disyllabic words*, the former by contraction, and the latter by dropping the final vowel. I have voiced this opinion in an earlier work,[15] *à propos* of Burmese. The simple syllabic structure with *final vowel*, to which numerous East Asian languages have still remained largely faithful, seems to be actually the most natural one; and hence the roots that now seem monosyllabic to us could easily have been actual disyllables of an earlier language underlying the one we are now acquainted with, or of a more primitive state of the latter. The final *end-consonant* would then have been the *initial consonant* of a new syllable, or a *new word*. For this last

---

[13] He is the author of the collections on the Madecassian language mentioned by Jacquet (*Nouveau Journal Asiatique*, XI, 102 n.), which are now lodged in London, in the hands of the brother of the late Governor Farquhar.

[14] J. F. C. Gericke's Javanese dictionary (Batavia 1831). In J. Crawfurd's manuscript dictionary, it is translated *to adjust, to put right*.

[15] *Nouveau Journal Asiatique*, IX, pp. 500–6.

element of the present-day roots would then, according to the varying genius of the languages, have been either a more definite patterning of the *main concept* through a closer *modification*, or a true *compounding* of two independent words. In Burmese, for example, a visible compound would thus arise on the basis of one that is now no longer recognized. This would most readily come about from roots having the same initial and final consonants, with a simple vowel lying between them. In Sanscrit, if we except such as दद् *dad*, which may well be of quite a different character, these roots have a meaning appropriate to expression by reduplication, in that, like कक् जज् शश् (*kak, jaj, śaś*) they designate violent motion, or like लल् *lal*, express wish or desire, or like मस् *sas*, to sleep, refer to a uniformly prolonged condition. Such forms as ककक् खकख् यगय् (*kakk, khakkh, ghaggh*), which imitate the sound of laughter, can hardly be thought of, originally, save with repetition of the full syllable. But I would doubt whether we could get much further by analysis on these lines; and such a terminal consonant could also very easily have been really just terminal in origin. Even in Chinese, which in the Mandarin and literary language knows nothing of any true consonants in final position, the provincial dialects very frequently add them to words that end in a vowel.

In another connection, and probably also in another sense, the *disyllabic character* of all Sanscrit *roots ending in consonants* has quite recently been upheld by Lepsius.[16] In the logical and ingenious system set forth in his work, the necessity of this is derived from the fact that in Sanscrit generally a syllabic division alone prevails, and that in elaboration of the root, the indivisible syllable cannot engender a single letter, but only a further indivisible syllable. The author insists, that is, on the necessity of regarding the inflectional sounds, not as quasi-arbitrary insertions or additions of letters, but simply as organic developments of the root; and it then becomes a question of whether, for example, the *â* in बोधामि *bôdhâmi*, should be regarded as the final vowel of बुध *budha*, or as a vowel appended merely externally in conjugating, to the root बुध् *budh*. For our present topic, it is primarily a question of the meaning of the seeming or genuine final consonants. But since the author, in this first part of his work, enlarges merely on the vowel aspect, he there has nothing at all to say on this point. So I simply remark that even if one does not employ what seems a merely picturesque way of talking about a self-elaboration of the root, but speaks of addition and insertion instead, then on a correct view of the matter, anything and everything

---

[16] *Paläographie*, pp. 61–74, §47–52; pp. 91–3, nos. 25–30, and especially p. 83, n.1.

arbitrary still remains excluded, since even addition or insertion always occur according to, and by virtue of, merely organic laws.

We have already seen in the foregoing that the *concrete concept* is at times supplemented, in languages, by its *generic* counterpart; and since this is one of the chief ways in which *disyllabic words* can arise in *monosyllabic languages*, I must again return to the subject here. With regard to *natural objects*, such as plants, animals etc., which very obviously fall into distinct classes, there are numerous examples of this to be found in all languages. But in some we encounter this combination of two concepts in a manner that is strange to us: and it is this that I intend to allude to here. For what is combined is not always the true *species-concept* of the concrete object, but rather the term for something that falls under it in respect of some *general similarity*, as when the concept of an extended length is conveyed by such terms as knife, sword, lance, bread, line, rope, etc., so that the most diverse objects are put into the same classes, merely insofar as they have some property in common with one another. If these word-combinations testify, therefore, on the one hand, to a sense of logical arrangement, they still more frequently bespeak the activity of a lively *imagination*; such is the case in Burmese, when the *hand* serves as a generic concept for all kinds of implements, the firearm no less than the chisel. On the whole, this type of expression consists in a delineation of objects, sometimes to aid understanding, sometimes to add colour. In certain cases, however, it may be based on a real necessity for *clarification*, even though this is no longer discernible to ourselves. We are everywhere far removed from the *basic meanings* of words. Those things which in all languages are called air, fire, water, man, etc., are for us, with few exceptions, mere conventional sounds. What these words are based on, the primal conception that peoples have of objects, in accordance with those properties that determine the verbal sign, remains alien to us. But this is precisely where the need may lie, for a clarification by addition of a *generic concept*. Suppose, for example, the Chinese *ji*, sun and day, to have meant originally that which warms and gives light; it would then be necessary to supplement it with *tseoû*, as the name for a material, spherical object, in order to make clear that the reference is not to the warmth or brightness diffused in the air, but to the heavenly body that warms and gives light. For a similar reason, the day could then, through the addition of *tseù*, be called, by another metaphor, the *son of warmth and light*. It is very notable that the foregoing expressions belong only to the newer and not the old style of Chinese, since, on this type of explanation, the mode of representation contained in them seems, rather, to be the more ancient one. This favours the opinion that such terms have been formed with a view to obviating misunderstandings that could have arisen from use of the same word for several concepts or ideograms. But should the language still have been metaphorically imitative in this fashion, even at a later time? And should it not rather, to achieve a mere aim of the understanding, have also employed similar means, and therefore distinguished *day* by something other than a notion of kinship?

I cannot, in this connection, suppress a doubt that I have already harboured on many occasions when comparing the *old* and the *new* *styles*. We know the *old* entirely from *writings*, and largely from philosophical writings alone. Of the *spoken language* of that period we know nothing. Now might not much, and perhaps a large amount, of what we now attribute to the newer style, have already been current in the old, as a spoken language? There is one fact that really seems to confirm this. The older style of *koù wên* contains, if we set aside the conjoint forms of several, a moderate number of *particles*; the newer style of *kouân hoá* has a much larger number, especially of those that give closer definition to grammatical relations. The *historical* style, *wên tchang*, must be regarded, in effect, as a third form, differing essentially from the other two; and this makes a very sparing use of particles, indeed abstains from them almost altogether. Yet the historical style begins, later indeed than the old style, but still already some two hundred years before our time-reckoning. On the normal course of development in languages, this divergent treatment of a part of speech so doubly important as the particles are in Chinese, is impossible to explain. But if we suppose the *three styles* to be merely three *renderings of the same spoken language* for different purposes, it becomes intelligible. The greater frequency of particles would naturally belong to the spoken language, which is always anxious to make itself more understandable by new additions, and in this respect does not even reject what really seems of no use. The older style, already presupposing effort by the material it dealt with, disdained the use of particles for purposes of clarification, but did find in them, by differentiation of concepts and clauses, an excellent method of giving to the lecture a symmetrical placing of terms, corresponding to the inner logical arrangement of the thoughts. The historical style has the same reason as the latter for rejecting the multiplicity of particles, but not the same motive for recalling them into its sphere for another purpose. It was written for serious readers, but in a simpler narrative concerning matters that were easy to understand. It may stem from this difference, that historical writings even dispense with the use of the normal terminating particle (*yè*) on passing from one topic to another. The newer style, of the stage, the novel, and the lighter forms of poetry, since it depicted society and all its doings, and presented people speaking, was also obliged to adopt the whole compass of their language, and hence their whole stock of particles.[17]

After this discussion, I return to those seemingly *disyllabic words*, in *monosyllabic languages*, which arise through the attachment of a *generic term*. Insofar as we mean thereby terms for *simple concepts*, in whose designation the individual syllables participate, not as such, but only in combination, they may originate in one of two ways, either *relatively*, for subsequent understanding, or in truly *absolute* fashion, in and for themselves. The origin of the generic term may vanish from the nation's memory, and the term itself become, in consequence, a *meaningless* appendage. In that case the concept of the whole word does really rest upon *both* syllables; but it is *relative* only to ourselves, that it can no longer be constructed from the meanings of each component. But the appendage itself can also, despite *known meaning* and frequency of application, attach, because of thoughtless usage, as it were, to objects it is quite unrelated to, so that in *combination* it again becomes *meaningless*. In that case the concept of the whole word does really lie in the union of *both syllables*, but it is an *absolute* property thereof, that the meaning does not proceed from the union of the senses of each. It is self-evident that both kinds of disyllabicity can easily arise through the passage of words from one language into another. A special class of such constructions, sometimes more explicable and sometimes not, is imposed upon speech by the usage of certain languages, when *numbers* are combined with *concrete objects*. I know of four languages in which this law obtains to a notable extent: Chinese, Burmese, Siamese and Mexican. But there are certainly quite a few of them, and particular examples can probably be found in all, including even our own German. Two causes, as I see it, combine in this usage: firstly the general appending of a generic concept, to which I have just referred, but then also the special nature of certain objects subjected to numbering, where, if an actual measure is not stated, the individuals to be counted must first be artificially created, as when we say *four head of cabbage* for *one bale of hay*, etc., or where we seek, as it were, by the general number, to

[17] I am happy to be able to add here, that Professor Klaproth, to whom I owe the data contained in the foregoing, concurs with the doubt I have expressed, concerning the relationship of the different Chinese styles. From his extensive reading in Chinese, particularly in historical writings, he must have collected a rich store of observations on the language, of which it is to be hoped that a major portion will overflow into the new Chinese dictionary that he plans to publish. But in that case it would be very desirable, also, to have a summary of his general observations on the Chinese language-structure in a special introduction.

abolish the differences among the objects counted, as when cows and steers are included in the term *four head of cattle*. Now of the four languages mentioned, none has extended this usage so far as Burmese. Apart from a large number of genuinely established terms for particular classes, the speaker may always go on to use for this purpose any word in the language that indicates a similarity covering a number of objects; and lastly, there is also a general word (*hku*) that can be applied to all objects of whatever kind. The compound, moreover, is so formed that, regardless of how many distinctions are attached, the concrete word constitutes the first member, the number the middle one, and the generic term the last. If the concrete object is bound to be known in some way to the hearer, the generic term is used by itself. Given this extension, such compounds must occur very frequently, especially in conversation, since they are already evoked by the mere use of unity, as an indefinite article.[18] In that many of the generic concepts are expressed by words in which no relation at all can be conjectured to the concrete object, or which may well have become quite meaningless apart from this usage, these numerical words have also come to be called particles in the grammars. Originally, however, they are all of them substantives.

From the considerations here set forth it emerges, both for the indication of *grammatical relationships* by *special* sounds, and for the *syllabic range* of the *words*, that if we consider Chinese and Sanscrit as the two *extremes*, there prevails in the *intervening languages*, whether they *keep the syllables apart from one another*, or *attempt imperfectly to combine them, a gradually* increasing *tendency* towards more visible *grammatical indication*, and *freer syllabic scope*. Without at present drawing conclusions from this about any *historical progression*, I am content to have here exhibited this *situation* as a *whole*, and to have displayed some individual *varieties* of the same.

[18] Cf. on this whole topic, Burnouf, *Nouveau Journal Asiatique*, IV, 221; Low's *Siamese Grammar*, pp. 21, 66–70; Carey's *Burmese Grammar*, pp. 120–141, §10–56; Rémusat's *Chinese Grammar*, p. 50, nos. 113–15, p. 116, nos. 309–10; *Asiatick Researches*, x, 245. If Rémusat treats these number-words under the old style, he has doubtless placed them there only for other reasons. For they actually belong to the newer one.

Index

Abel Rémusat, J.P., xi, lxi, lxiv, 5, 199, 231, 254, 261–3, 287
Accent, 98, 111, 125–7, 199, 237, 241, 245, 252–3, 265, 270
Accretion, 103–4, 106, 113 (*see* Inflection)
Achaguas, 197
Adelung, J.C., 197
Adjectives, 95, 119, 192, 239–44, 251, 254–8, 260, 264
Adverbs, 248–9, 254–5
Aeolian, 159
Aeschylus, 4
Aesthetics (*see* Art)
Affixes, xxiv, 94, 104, 134, 165, 184, 196–8, 200, 224, 236, 242–3, 245–6, 263–4, 270, 279
Agglutination, xxiv–v, xxviii, xxxi, 27, 100, 107–8, 145, 187, 200, 216, 225, 259, 267
Alaman, Mr, 131
Alcibiades, 180
Alexander the Great, 176
Algebra, 30–1
Alphabet, 52, 67, 215, 222, 232, 237–9
Amara Kôsha, 280
American-Indian languages, x, xii, xxiv–vi, xlii, lxi–iv, 5, 33, 137, 154, 186, 194, 199–200, 227, 233, 236, 269
    North, xi, 9, 134, 229
    South, 9, 129, 193–7, 229
Ampère, J.J., 263
Analogy, verbal, 74, 77, 91, 105–6, 113, 187 8, 203, 212, 235, 266, 268
Analysis, lxv, 96, 145, 155, 206, 213, 276
Andaman islands, 14
Anderson, R., 237
Animal cries, xxi, 65–6, 68
Annamese, 252–3
Anthropology, xi, xlvi, xlix
Antiquity, classical, 24, 29, 39–40, 155
Aorist, 192, 199
Arabic, lxi, 17, 19, 67, 74–7, 88, 165, 217, 220
Arabs, 182
Aracan, 238
Arcadius, 126
Architecture, 161
Aristophanes, 126, 172
Aristotle, 174, 176
Art, xvii, xx, xxii, xxix, xxxix, li–ii, lvii–xi,

lxv, 29–30, 34–5, 42, 89, 91, 161–3, 172, 182
Articulation, xx–xxii, xxvi–vii, 57–8, 65–9, 73, 75–9, 84, 106–9, 112–13, 121, 133, 145, 214–15
Asiatic languages, 9, 67, 237, 262, 282
Aspirates, 67, 108, 221, 237, 265
Association, 156
Attributive, 192–3, 195, 198
Augment, 121–3, 130, 188
Auxiliary verbs, 193, 198, 206, 249–50
Aveyron, Boy of, xlvii

Basile, 269
Basque, ix–x, xii, xli, xliii, xlv, xlviii, lxiii, 134, 136, 146, 179, 207
Battas, 20
Baudelaire, C., lii, lvi
'to be', 88, 185, 188, 196–8, 236, 238, 246, 249–50, 261
Beauty, xvii, lviii–ix, 91, 112, 126, 162, 166, 170, 228
Bees, xxii–iii
Being and becoming, 189
Berghaus, H., 237
Berlin, viii–ix, xiii, xlvi
Bernhardi, G., 171, 192
Betoi, 199
Bible, the, 251, 275
Böckh, A., 5, 161
Bohlen, P. von, 4
Bopp, F., xi, xv, 3–4, 79, 82, 96–7, 106, 111, 116–18, 120, 123, 188, 190, 279–80
Borneo, 11, 13
Brata Yuddha, 3, 280
Breton, xli
Buddhism, 16
Buenaventura, G. de S., 195
Bugis, 14, 17, 222
Bunsen, C.K.J., 194
Burmese, 8–9, 11, 33, 225, 227, 233, 236–61, 269–70, 273–8, 282–7
Burnouf, E., 4, 250, 254, 287
Buschmann, E., 3, 5, 126, 129, 131
Byzantine authors, 176
    empire, 211

Cahita, 131
Camaño, Fr., 129

Cambridge Platonism, xxxiv
Capellen, Baron van der, 5
Carey, F., 237–41, 243, 245–51, 260, 280, 287
Carey, W., 237
Carthage, 182
Casanare (river), 194, 199
Case, 136, 205, 208–9, 224–5, 231, 245, 247–8, 250, 256, 266
Cassirer, E., xxxiii–vi, xxxix, xlii, lx
Castorena, Mr, 131
Categories, xx, xxv, xxviii, 93, 100–2, 105–7, 140–1, 167, 184, 189, 197, 235, 243–4, 254, 279
Causal verbs, 190
Celebes, 11, 13–14, 17
Ceylon (Lankâ), 16
Challan, 275
Chamisso, A. von, 5
Champollion, J.F., xi, 5
Chapelier, J., 275
Character, linguistic, 31, 148–63, 172, 177, 203, 205, 207, 210, 260, 262, 275
national, 85–6, 126, 149, 152–5, 158, 163–8, 172, 176–7, 182, 203, 207, 213, 217, 229, 231
Children, language-learning in, 57–9, 93
Chinese, x, xiv, xxi, xxiv–vi, xxviii, xxxi, lxi, lxiii, 9, 20, 22, 32, 40, 69, 72, 78, 96, 106, 128–9, 132–3, 145–6, 185, 191, 199–200, 206, 216–18, 230–4, 237, 239, 248, 252–69, 278, 282–7
Chiquitin, 129
Chouillet, J., xxxix–xl, lv
Cicero, 125
Civilization, lxiii, 25, 30, 32–6, 42
Clauses, 200–2, 250–2, 257, 285
Climate, xxi
Colebrooke, H.T., 280
Comedy, 162, 172
Communication, xxii–iii
Compensation, law of, 123
Compounding, xxiv, xlix, 101–4, 106–7, 110, 114, 136, 138, 165–6, 188, 225–9, 238–44, 246–8, 251, 253, 257–8, 260, 262, 264–71, 273–4, 277–8, 280–3, 287
Concept, xix–xx, xxiii, xxvii, xxx, xxxvii, 33–4, 52, 54, 69–71, 73–5, 79, 83–7, 90–7, 100–2, 106–7, 109–11, 117, 138–9, 151–2, 154–7, 165–8, 173–4, 183–4, 186, 189–90, 219–20, 222, 224–5, 227–8, 232, 235–42, 254–5, 258–9, 262–9, 272–4, 279, 281, 283–7
Condillac, E.B. de, xxxiii–xl, xlii–iv, xlvii, xlix, liii–v, lx, lxiv–v
Conjugation, 114, 120, 134–5, 150, 186, 190, 194, 196, 199, 205, 207, 226, 246, 249, 283

Conjunctions, 138–9, 185, 200–1, 257
Connectives, 250, 260
Consonants, xxvii, 67, 69, 79, 97, 111–12, 114–15, 124, 221–4, 237–8, 253, 276–8, 282–3
Contrariety, 268–9
Cooper, J.F., 135
Copula, 193 (*see* 'to be')
Cora, 129, 131
Court de Gébelin, lxiv
Crawfurd, J., xiv, 3–4, 15, 282
Culture, xiv, xxxii, xli, xlvi–vii, lviii, lxii, 32–6, 42, 163, 171, 182, 217–18, 230

Daco-Rumanian, 210
Dance, 159, 161
Deaf-mutes, xxxiv, xliii, lii–iii, lv, lix, 65–6
Declension, 114, 136–7, 150, 205, 231, 245–8
Definition, 167–8
Degérando, M.-J., xxxii, xlv–ix, lx, lxiv–v
Delaware Indians, 227
    language, 33, 134–5, 146, 226–9, 236
Demetrius, 201
Denominative, 190
Des Brosses, lxiv
Desiderative, 189–90
Designation and classification, 100–2, 230, 265, 284, 286–7
Destutt de Tracy, xxxviii, lxi, lxiv
Dialects, xli, 161–2, 164, 166, 208, 253, 259–60, 275, 283
Diderot, D., xxix, xxxii, xxxiv, xxxvi, xxxviii–xl, xliv, xlvii, xlix–lii, lv–x, lxv
Diefenbach, L., 208
Dionysius of Halicarnassus, 173
Disyllabism, 79, 113, 145, 222, 240, 270–1, 275–8, 282–4, 286
Dorian, 159, 164
Drama, 172, 180
Dual, 79
Duponceau, P.S., xi, lxi–v, 4, 135, 226

Easter Island, 11
Edwards, J., 135
Egyptian art, 29
Elephants, xxii, 156
Eliot, J., 135
Enclitic, 125, 127
Endeh (Flores), 14
Energy, liv–v, lxv
Engel, J.J., 1
English, x, liii, lv, lvii, 9, 80, 126, 199, 206–7, 280
Ergon and *energeia*, xvii–xx, xxviii, xxx–i, xxxiv, xxxvi, xxxix, lvii, 49
Euphony, 34, 69, 72, 75, 80, 88, 104, 110, 112, 115–16, 121–4, 126, 165, 188–9, 205, 226, 266–7

Europe, 182, 229
Europo-centrism, x, lxiii
Ewald, H. von, 79, 223, 275–6
Expression, xix, xxii
Eysinga, R. van, 5

Family, 153
    linguistic, 182–3
Fichte, J.G., 175
Flacourt, E. de, 275
Folk-tales, 179
Form, grammatical, 51, 82–3, 86, 107, 114,
        140–2, 149, 190, 194, 206–7, 230, 246,
        248, 252, 259
    linguistic, xvi, xix–xxi, 48–54, 66, 70, 77,
        79, 81–7, 89, 145–6, 148–9, 157,
        165–6, 171, 183, 185, 191, 208, 210,
        215–18, 233–5, 260–1, 276
Forneri, Fr, 194–5
Forster, H.P., 124
Freedom, xxi, xxxvii, 64, 144–6, 156, 162,
        169, 176, 214, 220, 229
Freeman, Mr, 5
French, xl–xli, liii–iv, lvii, 9, 129, 212
Froberville, E., 282
Future, 78, 188, 190, 199–200, 246–7, 250

Garat, J.D., xxxii, xl, xliii–v, xlvii, xlix, liii,
        lv, lx, lxv
Gender, 79, 101, 114, 119, 154, 198, 245
Genitive, 137, 245, 249, 254–5
Genius, xxix, xxxiv, xxxvi, lii, lv, lvii–x,
        lxii, 30, 32, 42, 89, 151, 172–3
Geography, xxi
Gericke, J.F.C., 5, 282
German, x, xli, 85, 121, 129, 165–6, 182,
        189, 201, 206–7, 280, 286
    people, 162, 172
Gerund, 195–6, 243, 247
Gesenius, F.H.W., 4, 275–6
Gesture, xxxviii
Gilchrist, J.B., 280
Gilij, F.S., 129
God, 226
Goethe, J.W. von, viii, xlviii, l–lii, 172
Grammar, xiv, xxiv, 71–2, 139–40, 154,
        165–6, 184–6, 207, 221–2, 224, 231,
        256, 263, 287
    universal, xix–xx, xxv–viii, xxxii,
        xxxiv–v, xlii, liii–iv, lx, lxii–iii, lxv
Grammarians, 150
    American, 135
    Greek, 125, 127, 192, 201
    Indian, 71–2, 94, 97–8, 118, 190, 278
    Latin, 125
    Malayan, 191
    Pali, 245, 260
    Spanish, 129–30

Greek, x, xxv, xxix, xlv, lv–vii, lxi–iii, 24,
        29, 39, 82, 85–6, 114, 120–1, 125, 130,
        138–9, 141–2, 149, 151, 155, 165–6,
        176, 182, 189, 192, 196, 203, 210–12,
        217, 222, 228
    people, 139, 159–63, 170–3, 176–8, 180,
        210
Grégoire, H., xli
Grimm, J., 121, 222
Grimm, M., l, lviii
Guna and *vriddhi*, 116–22, 187, 280

Hamann, J.G., xxxiii–iv, xlii, l
Haraforas, 13
Harris, J., xxxiv, 192
Haughton, Sir G.C., 188–9
Haym, R., xxxiii
Hearing, 55, 58–9
Hebrew, 76, 136, 138, 220
    people, 170–1
Heckewelder, J.G.E., 227
Hellenism, 161
Herder, J.G., xxxiii–iv, xxxvi, xxxviii,
        xlii–iv, xlvii, l–li
Hermann, G., 4
Hermann und Dorothea (Goethe), xv, li
Hervas, Sr, 194–5
Hieroglyphs, l, liii, lvi–viii, lx
Hinduism, 16–18
Hindustani, 189, 280
History, xlvi–viii
Hitôpadêśa, 177
Homer, lvii–viii, 24, 39, 127, 142, 160, 176,
        178, 203
Hough, G.H., 238–9, 241–2, 244–7, 249,
        261
Huasteca, 195
Humboldt, A. von, vii–ix, xiii, xv, xxi, xlvi,
        175
Humboldt, W. von, life, vii–ix
    studies, ix–xv, 3–6
    writing habits, xv–xvii
    views, xvii–lxv

I and thou, 95
Iambic, 123–4
Ideal, 82–3, 161–2, 169
Idéologues, xxxviii, xl–xli, xliii, xlv
Imagination, xx, xxii, xxvi, xxxiv, xlvii–viii,
        lii, liv, lvi, lviii–lx, lxv
Imitation, verbal, 73, 75
Imperative, 247–8, 250
Imperfect, 194–5
Incorporation, xxiv–v, xxviii, xxxi, 130–4,
        136–8, 141, 145, 216, 227, 229, 232
India, xii, 12, 15–20, 22, 29, 32–3, 35, 38,
        40, 85, 163, 172, 177, 180, 260, 280
Indicative, 244, 247–8

Individuality, xx, xxii, xxxviii, lviii–ix, 21, 23–6, 30–1, 35–7, 41–2, 44, 47, 50, 52, 59, 63, 82, 85–6, 95, 151–2, 155, 157–68, 170–1, 173, 175–6, 178, 183, 204, 211, 213–15, 235, 263, 265
Indo-Chinese languages, 252–3
Infinitive, 82–3, 187, 190
Inflection, xxv, xlix, liv–v, lx, 27, 78, 84, 91–2, 100–9, 113–14, 117, 128, 134, 136, 138, 140–1, 145–6, 164–5, 184, 186–8, 190, 193, 200, 202–3, 205–7, 209–10, 216–17, 220–5, 230, 232–3, 243, 246, 259, 265, 267, 277
Inner linguistic sense, 107, 110, 113, 115, 132, 135, 141–4, 203, 206–9, 214–15, 220, 223, 225, 228, 233–4, 245, 255–6, 259–60, 278
Instrumental, 244–5
Intensive, 189, 195
Intention, 105, 115
Interrogative, 250
Intuition, 84, 140–1, 161–3, 169, 234
Inuit, xxiv
Inversion, xliv–v, liii–v, lx, lxv
Ionian, 164
Isolation, xxiv, 100, 206
Italian, xli, lvii, 129, 210–11

Jacquet, E., xii, 5, 238, 272, 275, 282
Java, 11, 14, 16, 18, 32, 35
Javanese, xii, xv, 4–5, 7–8, 17, 19, 119, 192, 281–2
Jesuits, 194
Johnson, S., 280
Johnston, Sir A., 5
Judson, A., 11, 237–8, 241–3, 247–9

Kant, I., xvi, xlii, l, lix–x, 175
Kawi, x, xii, xiv–v, xxix, xxxv, 3–4, 20, 53, 280–1
  Introduction (KI), vii, x–xi, xiii–vii, xl
Kendall, T., 273
Keynes, J.M., xliii
Klaproth, H.J. von, 5, 13–14, 239, 269, 276, 286
Körner, xv
Kosegarten, 5
kridanta words, 114, 119
krit suffixes, 115, 279

La Curne de Ste Palaye, xli
Language, as organism, xix, xxiv, xxxi, xxxv, lix, lxiv, 21, 27, 31, 34, 42, 44, 48–9, 51–2, 58, 61–2, 69–70, 77, 80, 90, 93, 100, 108–9, 129, 140, 152, 202–3, 207, 213, 220–1, 264–6
  imperfections of, xxv–vi, xxviii, xxxi–ii,

lxi–xii, 32–4, 78–9, 82–3, 89, 107, 136, 140, 144–6, 184, 187, 190–1, 200–1, 206, 213, 216–20, 223–5, 227–31, 234–7, 257, 260, 267–8
  origin and development of, xix–xx, 24, 26–8, 32, 34, 40, 42–3, 46–50, 60, 77, 81, 133, 143–4, 146, 148–50, 153, 156–7, 164–6, 190, 204–6, 209–13, 218, 232–4, 276
  philosophy of, xxxiii–v, xxxix–xl, xlii, xlvii
  social nature of, xxii–iii, xxxvii, 56–7, 59–60, 62, 151–3, 156, 206
  and Nature, 61, 85, 155, 183, 214, 285
  and thought, xiv, xviii–ix, xxviii, xxx, xxxii, xxxv–vii, xliv, xlix, lv–vi, lxv, 54–7, 62–3, 77–8, 80–92, 100, 103, 105, 109–12, 137–8, 140, 144–6, 148–70, 172–5, 183, 185, 203–6, 210, 213–15, 217–20, 223, 228, 231, 233, 259, 278
Languages, identity and affinity of, 52–3, 76–7, 149–51, 155–6, 182, 207–12, 261
  uniformity and diversity of, xxi, xxiv, 215, 234–5
  dead, 93, 143, 157
  foreign, 93, 207, 216
  classification of, 235–6
Lassen, C., 4, 250
Latin, x, xxv, xxix, xliii–iv, liii–vii, lxi, lxiii, 5, 29, 43, 149, 151, 155, 165–6, 177, 182, 189, 192, 207–12, 275
Laws, linguistic, 81–2, 88, 90, 113–16, 215, 255, 284
Lee, S., 273–4, 282
Leibniz, G.W. von, xxxv
Lenni Lenape, 135, 227
Lepsius, R., 4, 116, 222, 238, 283
Lessing, G.E., 1
Lesson, M., 5, 275
Letter-change, 111–16, 123, 182, 237, 247, 258, 270
Leyden, J., 237–8, 252, 254
Lingua franca, 156
Linguistics, comparative, 21, 27, 44, 147, 155
Literature, xlviii, 17, 19, 63, 85, 87, 89, 150, 154–5, 162, 165–6, 171, 176–7, 203–4, 208, 210, 230, 285–6
Lithuanian, 204
Locke, J., liii–iv
London, ix, xiii–iv
Low, J., 253–4, 287
Lyric, 162, 170

'm-one', xxii–iii, xxvii–viii, xxxi, xxxiv, xxxvii, xxxix, lv, lx, lxiii, lxv

Madagascar, 11, 17, 20
Madecassian, 3, 5, 9, 18, 76, 275, 282
Madrid, xl
Maipure, 197
Malacca, 11, 14, 192
Malayan languages, x, xii, xiv, 3–5, 8,
    17–19, 53, 75–7, 80, 121, 124, 134,
    145–6, 190–2, 200, 225, 233, 236,
    270–1, 274–5, 277–8, 280
  peoples, 11–20
Manchu, 227, 236
Mandarin, 283
Marianas, 12
Mariner, W., 179, 272–4
Marsden, W., 5, 8, 13–15, 280
Massachusetts language, 134–5
Materialism, lii
Maupertuis, P.L. de, lxiv
May, G., lii
Mayan, 185–7, 199
Meaning, 72–6, 92, 104, 152, 156, 166–7,
    221, 223–5, 230, 237, 239, 241–5, 248,
    262, 265–6, 273–4, 278–81, 284, 286
Meinicke, Dr, 5, 15
Meister, J.H., l–li
Mental powers, human, xxii, lxi, 21–3,
    25–30, 32, 37–8, 41, 44, 46, 48, 50, 54,
    63, 81, 85, 89, 91–2, 143–4, 152, 155,
    162, 168–76, 203–4, 214, 217–19,
    229–30
Merian, A.A. von, 276
Metaphor, 33, 87, 154, 168, 265, 268,
    284–5
Mexican, xxv, 5, 32–3, 129–34, 136–7,
    192–3, 196, 202, 232, 236, 286
Mexico, 129
Meyen, Prof., 5
Michaelis, D., 275
Mindanao, 13
Minto, Earl of, 5
Mixteca, 193
Mohican, 135
Moluccas, 13
Mongolian, 227, 236
Monogenesis and polygenesis, xx–xxi
Monosyllabism, 252–3, 262–87
Montaigne, M. de, li
Mood, 82–3, 186, 188, 191, 196, 200, 236,
    240, 245–7, 257
Morrison, R., 261
Müller-Vollmer, K., lii
Music, xxxviii, 24, 30, 60–1, 65, 91, 159,
    161–2, 170–2, 174, 178, 204–5, 253

Naigeon, li
Nation and individual, xxi, xxiii, 21, 24,

32, 41–7, 53, 63, 85–6, 150–3, 158–9,
    213 (*see* Character)
Nature, 61, 85, 159, 163, 172
Negritos, 12–15, 17, 19
Neumann, C., 4, 276
New Britain, 13
New Caledonia, 14
New England, 134
New Guinea, 11–14, 19
New Hebrides, 13–14
New Holland, 13–14
New Ireland, 13
New South Wales, 13
New Spain (Mexico), 5, 9, 129, 193, 195
New Zealand, 11
  language, 3, 12, 270, 272–4, 281
Nominative and accusative, 106, 136, 244,
    248, 252, 255
Nouns, 95, 119, 130, 132, 134, 137–8,
    184–8, 191–4, 196, 198–202, 209, 224,
    227, 231, 235, 237, 239–45, 247–9,
    251–2, 254–7, 264, 278–9, 281, 287
Number, 286–7

Objectivity, 85, 96, 100–1, 105, 157, 168,
    173, 176
Oral tradition, 178–9
Oratory, 180–1, 218, 269
Orinoco, 194, 197, 199

Painting, lii–iii, lvi
Pali, xii, 33, 245, 250, 252, 260
Papuan, 19
Paris, viii–xi, xiii, xl, xlvi, xlviii–ix, li
Parthey, G., 5
Participles, 138, 192, 225, 228, 236, 243,
    246–51, 256
Particles, 194–6, 200, 208, 227, 230, 232–3,
    235, 238–9, 242, 244–8, 250–1, 254,
    256–61, 285–7
Passive, 189–91, 258
Pause, 75, 111
Pericles, 180
Persian, 80
Person, 84, 95, 105, 134–8, 141, 190,
    194–200, 209, 224–5, 236, 245, 250
Peru, 201, 229
Peruvian, 32
Philippines, 11–14, 33
Philology, 155
Philosophy, xxx, xxxvi, xlviii ix, lvii, lx,
    lxv, 29, 40, 42, 85–7, 167, 174–5, 181,
    204, 218, 269, 285
Physiology, 90
Pickering, J., xi, xv, lxi–iv, 4, 135
Pindar, xl, 161–2
Plato, l, 174

Plural, 107–8, 134, 197, 245–6, 258, 261
Poetry, xxiii, xxxii, xxxvi, xxxix, l, lii–iii,
	lvi–vii, lx, lxv, 12, 29, 42, 87, 150, 156,
	158–62, 165, 168–81, 205, 207, 211,
	218, 220–1
Polynesian, x, xii (*see* Malayan)
Polysyllabism, xxxi, 262–87
Portuguese, 280
	people, 229
Positing (synthesis), 184–5, 192, 200–2,
	204, 209, 236, 256
Possessive, 137–8, 195, 198–9
Potential mood, 82, 190
Pott, A.F., 4, 72, 97
Prefixes, 121, 134–5, 146, 192, 195, 197–8,
	225, 240, 242, 282
Prémare, J.H. de, 263, 269
Prepositions, 95, 206, 208–9, 224, 246
Preterite, 107–8, 120, 122–4, 188, 246
Privacy, xxii, xxxv, xxviii–ix, lx
Progress, xxi, 25, 27–8, 30–2, 37, 90
Pronouns, 84, 95, 103, 105–6, 130–1,
	133–8, 141, 187–8, 191–202, 209, 224,
	226–7, 236, 238, 245, 261, 266
	demonstrative, 197–8, 202, 248
	relative, 185, 197, 201–2, 209
Pronunciation, 115, 126, 129–31, 208, 223,
	231, 238–9, 247, 252–3, 258, 263, 265,
	270
Prose, xxiii, xxx, xxxii, xxxvi, xxxviii–ix, l,
	lvii, lx, lxv, 168–81

Quichua, 201–2

Racism, x, lxiii
Raffles, Sir T.S., xii, xiv, 5, 14
Rectification, xxii–iii, xxxviii
Reduplication, 75, 121–4, 188, 195, 237,
	264, 270–2, 283
Reflection, xlii–iii, xlvii–viii
Reitz, F.W., 192
Relations, xx, 74, 76, 83–4, 91, 104, 187,
	189, 201–2, 208, 221, 223–5, 227–8,
	230, 232–3, 235, 244–6, 254, 258–9,
	287
Religion, 226, 229, 260
Reyes, A. de los, 193
Rhaeto-Romansh, 210
Ricken, U., liii
Rio Negro, 197
Rivarol, A. de, xliii–iv
Rodriguez, D., 195
Romance languages, xxix, 29, 182, 206–13
Romans, 29, 39, 162–3, 177–8, 182
Rome, ix, xvii, xl, xlviii
Roots, xx, xxiii, 51, 69–72, 79, 83, 94,
	96–8, 100, 103, 105, 118–24, 184,

	186–7, 197–200, 222–3, 239–44, 246–9,
	263, 265, 267, 270, 272–80, 282–3
Rosen, 4
Rukhéng, 238

's-two', xxii–iii, xxvii–viii, xxx, xxxiv,
	xxxvii–ix, lx, lxiii, lxv
Sacy, S. de, xi, xlv, xlvii, 4
Saint Julien, 268
Sandwich islands, 12
	language, 5, 12, 131, 272
Sanscrit, x, xii, xiv, xxi, xxv–ix, xxxi–ii,
	xxxv, lx–xiii, lxv, 4, 7–9, 13, 17–19,
	32, 48, 53, 67–8, 71–3, 75, 80, 82–8,
	94, 96–8, 104–6, 111–24, 128–9,
	132–4, 137–9, 141–2, 145, 149, 151,
	165–7, 177, 182–3, 186–92, 204,
	206–7, 212, 216–17, 221–2, 224, 228,
	230–3, 239–40, 242–3, 245, 250,
	259–60, 266, 269, 271, 276, 278–83,
	287
Santos, D. de los, 273
Schelling, F.W.J., 175
Schiller, F., viii, xv, xlviii, l–li, lviii, 6
Schlegel, A.W. von, 4, 180, 280
Schlegel, F. von, 118
Schlözer, von, 129
Schulz, F.E., 5
Schwa, 221, 223
Science, xxx, xxxvi, xxxix, lvii, lx, lxv, 30,
	34–5, 42, 87, 156, 167, 173–6, 182,
	203–4, 210, 218, 220, 230, 232, 260
Semang, 14
Semitic languages, xxvii, 20, 22, 48, 77, 79,
	87, 108, 113, 118, 138, 145–6, 165,
	220–5, 231–2, 275–8
Sentence-structure, xxx–i, liv, 86, 109–11,
	128–39, 141, 145–6, 164, 168, 173,
	184, 194, 200–3, 216, 219–20, 227–9,
	245–6, 249–59
Shaftesbury, 3rd Earl of, xxxiv, l
Shakespeare, W., lii, 172
Siamese, 236, 252–4, 286
Singular, 134, 197–8
Sophocles, 125
Sound, 52, 54–5, 59–61, 65–76, 78–81, 84,
	90–2, 94, 98–9, 103–4, 107, 110–13,
	152–3, 157, 164, 183–4, 188–9,
	214–15, 217, 220–1, 225, 228, 230–2,
	252, 260, 262–7, 276, 287
	change, 18–19, 69–72, 74, 78, 98–9, 105,
	108, 111–21, 164–5, 188–9, 205, 221,
	232, 238, 245, 250, 282
	form, xix–xx, xxvi, vii, lx, 54, 72, 76–9,
	83–5, 88, 90, 140, 142–5, 164–5, 190,
	223

system, 68, 72, 74, 80, 124
South Sea Islands, 12, 14, 17, 19
  languages, 3, 5, 9, 15, 18, 20, 76, 227,
    236, 264, 270–2
Spanish, 9, 129–31, 179, 211
  people, 229
Spatial relation, 84, 95
Species, 101, 257–8, 284
Speech, 49, 54, 56–8, 62–3, 65–6, 68, 70–1,
  82, 86, 100, 109–12, 141, 143, 148,
  154, 168, 170, 177, 180, 183, 203, 223,
  228, 242, 244, 251–2, 254, 256, 269,
  285
  parts of, 140–1, 185, 198–9, 201, 209,
    248, 256
Spinoza, B. de, l
Stael, Mme de, ix, xlv, li
Stenzler, 4
Style, 164, 170, 174–5, 177, 180, 201,
  268–9, 285–6
Subject and object, lix, 250, 254–6
  and predicate, 185, 236
Subjectivity, 85, 96, 101, 105, 157, 168,
  173, 176
Subjunctive, 78, 82, 194–5, 236, 248, 250
Substantive (*see* Nouns)
Suffixes, 97–8, 103–6, 108, 113–15, 135–6,
  184, 187, 189, 194–5, 199–200, 242,
  252, 258–9, 270, 278–82
Sumatra, 11, 17, 20
Syllables, 67, 70, 75, 77–9, 86, 98, 104–6,
  113, 116–21, 123–7, 186–7, 190, 194,
  196–7, 199, 206, 221–2, 226, 231, 233,
  235, 237–40, 242, 252–3, 258–9,
  262–8, 270–1, 277–8, 280–3, 286–7
Symbolism, verbal, 73, 104–5, 108, 110,
  112, 119, 145, 189, 191, 199–200, 202,
  215, 243, 268
Synonyms, 167
Syntax, laws of, xlvii, 83, 86, 137
Synthesis, xix–xx, xxiv–vii, xxix–xxxi,
  xxxiv, lvi, lx, lxv, 88–9, 183–6, 191,
  200–4, 206, 209

Tableau, xxix, l, liii–iv, lvi–viii, lx–xi, lxv
Tacitus, 178
taddhita-suffixes, 113, 115, 119
Tagalic, 3, 9, 17–18, 20, 77, 80, 190, 192,
  226, 261, 270–5
Tahitian, 3, 12, 131, 272
Tamil, 237–8
Tanna, 14
Tapia Zenteno, C. de, 130–1, 195
Technique, linguistic, 79–80, 94, 164, 166,
  235–6

Telingic, 112
Tense, 79, 82, 88, 134, 186–9, 191–6,
  198–9, 225, 236, 245–8, 250
Themistocles, 180
Thiersch, 4
Thought, 54–7, 61–2, 65–6, 74, 76–8, 81,
  88, 90, 109–12, 126, 128, 137, 148,
  153, 163, 166–8, 170, 217, 223, 228,
  252
Threlkeld, Mr, 13
Time, 82, 95, 192
Timor, 14
Tonga, 179
  language, 3, 12, 272–4, 281–2
Tragedy, 162
Transitive and intransitive, 196, 198, 224
Translation, xxxix
Trochee, 123–4
Truth, 57, 173, 179–80
Turajas, 13

unâdi-words, 97–8, 239, 278–81
Understanding, xxii, xxxviii, 57–8, 62–3,
  152, 159, 206, 228, 249, 251, 269, 285

Vandeul, Mme A., li
Van Diemen's Land, 13
Vater, J.S., 197
Verb, 75, 77, 82–3, 97, 103, 105, 115,
  118–20, 122–3, 129–30, 132–8, 146,
  185–202, 209, 224–7, 235–7, 239–40,
  242–52, 254–8, 260, 278
Vernet, J.-F., xxxviii
Vetancourt, A. de, 192–3
Virgil, lvii
Vocabulary, 33, 93–4
Vowels, xxvii, 67, 69, 75, 78–9, 108,
  111–12, 116–21, 123–4, 164–5, 187,
  189, 221–5, 253, 273, 276–8, 282–3

Welcker, F.G., xiii–iv
Werther (Goethe), 172
Wilken, 5
Wilkins, C., 118, 280
Wilson, A.M., lii
Wilson, H.H., 280
Wolf, F.A., 178, 192
Word, 33, 51, 57–60, 70–2, 78–9, 84, 91–3,
  96–7, 100–2, 110–11, 113, 128, 133,
  137, 151–2, 154, 156, 160, 166, 183–4,
  226–7, 232, 254, 262, 264, 267, 269,
  277–9, 281–2, 287
  unity, xxxi, lx, 98, 103–4, 107, 109–16,
    119, 121–8, 134, 136–7, 139, 145, 187,

203, 220, 223, 228, 233, 236, 239, 243, 258–9, 263, 267, 270, 277–8
Wordsworth, W., xxii–iii, xxviii, xxxii, xxxvi, xxxix
World-view, xxx, xxxvii–viii, 60, 140, 154, 157, 166, 216
Writing, 12, 17, 49, 62–3, 65–7, 178–80,

232, 238–9, 251, 253, 258, 266, 269, 272, 285

Yarura, 194–5
Yucatan, 195

Zeisberger, D., 226
Zend, 47, 182

Humboldt's idealization of India would differ radically from the British tendency to see the Indians as wogs. So in the sliding scale of racism, wouldn't Humbolt occupy a relatively enlightened spot?